NOLAN RYAN

THE MAKING OF A PITCHER

NOLAN RYAN

THE MAKING OF A PITCHER

Rob Goldman

Library of Congress Cataloging-in-Publication Data
Goldman, Rob.
Nolan Ryan : the making of a pitcher / Rob Goldman.
pages cm.
ISBN 978-1-60078-922-9 (hardback)
1. Ryan, Nolan, 1947– 2. Baseball players—United States—Biography. 3. Pitchers (Baseball)—United States—Biography. I. Title.
GV865.R9G65 2014
796.357092—dc23
[B] 2013045697

This book is available in quantity at special discounts for your group or organization. For further information, contact:
Triumph Books LLC
814 North Franklin Street
Chicago, Illinois 60610
(312) 337-0747
www.triumphbooks.com

Printed in U.S.A.
ISBN: 978-1-60078-922-9
Design by Sue Knopf

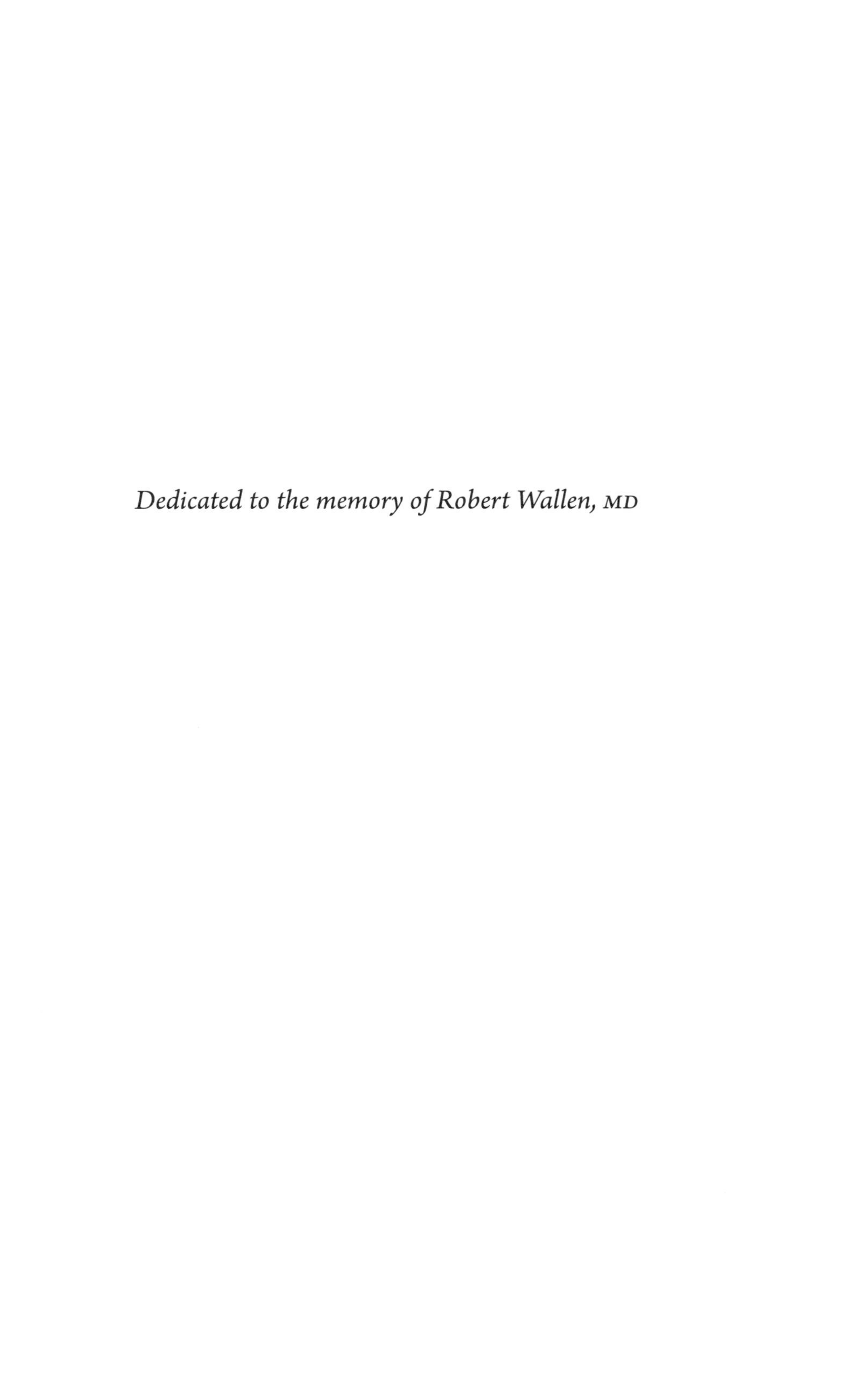

Dedicated to the memory of Robert Wallen, MD

Contents

PART V: BUILDING THE PERFECT BEAST: THE HOUSTON ASTROS: 1980–88

PART VI: THE PERFECT STORM: THE TEXAS RANGERS: 1989–93

PART VII: THE VIEW FROM THE TOP: 1994–

I think you have a large task to get Nolan Ryan in a book, because it's bigger than a book. It's more like an encyclopedia. 'Cause there's the baseball Ryan, there's the business Ryan, there's the cowboy Ryan, and there's the family Ryan, but they all integrate, they all work with each other. It's pretty cool.

Nolan is more than the sum of his parts—call it what you want, he's a legend plus. What you're writing about is the plus. And I don't think the plus has ever been written about.

—Tom House

Foreword

It is a special pleasure to introduce this book about my father.

Rob Goldman is a close family friend who knew Dad back in their days with the Angels, when Rob was a batboy for the team. His biography covers territory and issues not explored by other Nolan Ryan books.

For one, it weaves together my father's personality with his achievements in a way never presented before. It shows how Dad's work ethic, his no-nonsense Texas character, his openness to new ideas about training, and, most significantly, his relationship with my mother, all worked together to enable him to achieve what most thought was impossible—pitching for 27 seasons at the top of his game, throwing seven no-hitters, amassing 5,714 strikeouts, and achieving 324 victories.

The way Rob went about researching *The Making of a Pitcher* gives the book a depth that makes it a classic. He spent five years interviewing those who coached, trained, and played with and against Nolan. In this book are eyewitness accounts of key moments as viewed from the field, the press box, and the stands.

Rob's personal stories about time shared in the dugout and at home on the ranch reveal so much about how my parents feel about each other, and about their concept of friendship and loyalty. They also shine a very welcome light on the character of my parents.

I am glad to see Dad's story told so fully, and to see my mother given her rightful place beside him. This is a treasure for our family, as I expect it will be for Nolan Ryan fans and for anyone who wants to better understand the game and how my dad helped to change it during his long career.

The Making of a Pitcher is also a story told by Dad's peers.

More than 80 former teammates and adversaries contributed; all the greats of his era are represented. From Reggie Jackson, we learn of Nolan's love of competition and challenge. Pete Rose testifies to his aggressiveness and their mutual respect. Don Baylor, Randy Johnson, and Rod Carew talk about the uniqueness they witnessed firsthand.

Stretch Suba, his bullpen catcher at Houston, talks about Dad's sense of humor. Jeff Russell and Mike Stanley, who caught Dad's sixth and seventh no-hitters, respectively, provide insight about his focus and desire.

There has been a lot written about Dad's 27 seasons; most is about what he did but not how he did it. This is where *The Making of a Pitcher* really shines. My dad's career wasn't pure happenstance—there was always a plan of attack and focus. He was born with unique gifts, but it was up to him to maximize them.

Thankfully, he had help along the way.

From the Angels' Jeff Torborg, we learn of how he harnessed his wildness; from Dr. Gene Coleman, Nolan's conditioning coach in Houston, how he used research and experimentation to slow the aging process; from Tom House, Dad's pitching coach in Texas, how they maximized his talent through constant refinement in the weight room and cutting-edge fitness routines.

Finally, *The Making of a Pitcher* is about Texas and Texans. The Ryan clan has been in America since the late 18th century. They have been farmers, church builders, and soldiers. My dad took a little something from each generation, and in so doing, kept their Lone Star traditions and values alive.

So this is much more than a baseball book. It weaves together a great sports story with American and Texas history. It's also a primer on values and perseverance, and a love story.

Other books about Nolan Ryan tell the story of no-hitters and strikeouts, but none so thoroughly present the back story and themes that give us rare insight into the times and the man who put his indelible imprint on them and baseball history.

—Reid Ryan

Reid Ryan, the eldest son of Nolan Ryan, was a minor league pitcher and co-founder of Ryan-Sanders Baseball. He is currently the president of the Houston Astros.

Preface

I was in Creedmoor, Texas, headed for Nolan Ryan's 60th birthday bash. I had just exited Hwy 35 and passed the sign for the TDS Ranch. It was unfamiliar territory. As I rolled along the Texas-style private drive I glanced down at the invitation, a simple card emblazoned with a pair of caricature cowboy boots and a horseshoe. Nolan's message was equally simple: *Rob—Glad to be able to invite you to my 60th. Dress Western casual.*

Since this wasn't one of Nolan's ranches, I checked the map for reassurance that I was going the right way. When I looked up I got the surprise of my life. I had expected the familiar sight of grazing cattle, but instead all of a sudden there were gazelles racing around and a herd of water buffalo gazing at me. I glanced again at the card. It said nothing about creatures from the Serengeti.

Man, I was a long way from home and the crowded freeways of Los Angeles. I took a deep breath and smiled. This was going to be one amazing Texas hoedown, Nolan Ryan–style.

Weaving the car past a pair of zebras, I arrived at the main ranch house. Entering the foyer I was relieved to see the host wearing his familiar Stetson, not a safari hat. The only animals inside were the stuffed heads of zebras and gazelles hanging from the ceiling. I guess they hadn't been as swift as the ones outside.

Nolan and his wife, Ruth, greeted each guest warmly and made everyone feel welcome.

The setting was informal. There were no nameplates on the tables, and the crowd of ranchers, bankers, ex-ballplayers, and friends mingled freely as we feasted not on fried gazelle or water buffalo steaks but on Nolan Ryan's Natural Beef.

After dinner it was time for entertainment. Gospel singers started things off, followed by a clever puppeteer who brought down the house. Charming and hokey, she set the stage for longtime Ryan friend Charley Pride, the country music legend, whose set included his classic hits "Kiss an Angel Good Mornin'" and "Is Anybody Goin' to San Antone."

Most of the guests were cattlemen, and the room was peppered with Stetsons. Luminaries in the crowd included former Dallas Cowboy Lee Roy Jordan and ex–Houston Oilers coach Bum Phillips. The only former California Angels present were Ron Jackson, then the hitting coach with the Round Rock Express, team physician Jules Rasinski—and me, a former Angels batboy.

No former Mets were there, but some ex-Astros and Rangers were, including former pitching coach Tom House and infielders Jeff Huson and Steve Buechele.

The diversity and character of the crowd impressed the perceptive House, who, as Ryan's cutting-edge coach and confidant in Texas, had helped add four years to the fireballer's career. "No matter what occupation they were in," House later recalled about that night, "from bankers to secretaries to ranch workers to owners to cattle people—they were all real. I dined with a bunch of cattlemen and I could just as easily have been sitting with a group of ballplayers, because they all had one thing in common: all were authentic individuals who didn't have any hidden agendas. What you saw is what you got. They all wore the hat and they all rode the horse."

Country rocker Neal McCoy kicked a box of CDs onto the stage for the guests to help themselves to, and then kicked the party into overdrive with some foot-stompin' music that had couples up and dancing.

The show was reflective of our host—simple, fun, energetic, and unpretentious. Sitting stage right, Rasinski and I, former Angels in a land of cowboy hat–clad Texans, felt right at home.

Ron Jackson returned to our table. "Get your poster yet?" he asked, displaying a giveaway lithograph of Ryan looking fierce in Rangers garb. "Better hurry. They're going fast!"

I got to the lobby just in time to grab two off the rapidly shrinking stack. The print was by Cajun artist George Rodrigue, whose trademark blue dog was imprinted directly under the pitcher's mound.

Back at the table I handed one to Rasinski. Doc and Ryan go way back. Rasinski took care of Ryan's ailments in Anaheim and is a historical footnote to one of his greatest games. On September 27, 1973, it was Doc who, in the late innings at Anaheim Stadium, massaged Ryan's strained calves in the tunnel leading to the dugout. This allowed Nolan to stay in the game and get his 383rd strikeout—still the single-season strikeout record.

Thinking back to that game opened the floodgates, and memories of being with and around Nolan came freely. Funny enough, during the years I was a batboy for the Angels he rarely spoke to me about his no-hitters or record-breaking games. Our talks generally focused on *my* concerns. Usually when I brought up a particular play or player, he'd just mutter something or get quiet.

It was the same way when he returned to Anaheim 15 years later as a Texas Ranger. I'd often drive him back to the hotel after games, and he never talked about baseball. It didn't matter if there'd been 42,000 fans in the stands that night and he'd thrown a three-hitter. It was always, "How's school going, Robby? Still playing ball? Done any acting?" If I brought up baseball, he'd just keep on talking about my activities or sit there silently.

I always had the feeling that Nolan was happiest when he wasn't the center of the universe. He was interested in other people's concerns as much as or even more than his own. I later figured out that his humility and empathy were keys to his success, both on and off the field. They kept him open to new ideas that led to personal growth and self-improvement.

"Did you ask him yet, Robby?"

Jolted out of my reverie, I looked up and saw Reid Ryan, Nolan's eldest son, standing over me. Like his folks, Reid is unfailingly optimistic and supportive. He had reacted positively when I mentioned the idea of doing a book with Nolan, and now he wanted to know if I'd followed up with his dad.

I told Reid that I was waiting for the right time, and after chatting a bit he returned to the dance floor with his lovely wife, Nicole. Also out there were Reid's younger brother, Reese, and his pretty wife, Allison.

The obvious devotion of Ryan's sons to their spouses made me think about what I considered the book's key question—what exactly were the attributes Nolan possessed that made him rise so far above the competition and made him so successful on and off the field, and for such a long period of time?

Looking around the room filled with Nolan's friends and admirers, it occurred to me that the general public only knew one side of the story—the no-hitters, the strikeouts, the Hall of Fame career. But those of us who'd been with him a while knew it wasn't all success and glory.

There was a steady struggle from the day Ryan's high school coach in Alvin noticed his powerful right arm, all the way to the last pitch of his 27-year career. It was a constant battle between the gift he'd been given and the fight to control and maintain it—an inner battle the public never saw that made Ryan want to throw in the towel on baseball at least twice.

Looking over at Nolan's table, I couldn't help but notice the elegant lady with the Scandinavian smile seated next to him. She was the integral factor in Ryan's life that kept him on track.

As Neal McCoy launched into another raucous number, memories of Ruth and Nolan poured over me like a soft Texas rain. Simple things mostly, like driving around in a pickup at their ranch in Alvin. The countless meals we'd shared. Just hanging out with them. I saw their heartfelt embrace after his fourth no-hitter, and strolling together down the Anaheim Stadium tunnel after games. She was always the mainstay, the quiet, resolute cheerleader who kept the home fires burning. The cities had changed, their ranch properties grew bigger, and their hours more crowded, but the one constant for Nolan was Ruth.

After McCoy's set, Nashville singer-songwriter Steve Wariner sang a song he'd written just for the occasion that emphasized "the things that last." It was a song about values and permanent things, and it fit the guest of honor like the proverbial glove. Nolan has had the same wife, phone number, friends, values, and accent all his life.

But his apparent conservatism is deceiving. He doesn't ever seem to change, yet he does, easily sliding from one occupation to the next—from player to banker to rancher to entrepreneur; from parent to grandparent; from minor league owner to major league franchise president.

The one constant through it all is Ruth. At the height of Ryanmania she sometimes seemed lost in the shadows, but never to Nolan. Steady, strong, and resilient, she's been his closest friend and his most valuable counselor. They've been inseparable from the day they first lit the spark at an Alvin High School lawn party a half-century ago.

As Steve Wariner crooned, couples embraced and the room seemed smaller. When Ruth and Nolan took to the dance floor, all heads turned their way. They smiled as they looked into each other's eyes, and Nolan engulfed her like a giant bear.

It was as obvious as the vast Texas sky to me and everybody else watching—at the core of Nolan Ryan's success in baseball and in life was a love story.

Under the staring zebra heads, the music played on. Nolan and Ruth maneuvered around the other dancers, oblivious to everything but one another. After a while their grandkids joined them on the floor. Caught up in the magic of the moment, the Ryans glided effortlessly between the dancers like 12-to-6 curveballs bounding for the plate.

PART I

Alvin, Ruthie, and Raw Talent: 1963–64

1

Daylight on Dezso Drive

Across the murky waters of Mustang Bayou in Alvin, Texas, the morning sun danced across the window of the modest stucco home on Dezso Drive. Inside, a boy not quite 16 years old crammed his book and baseball glove into a duffle bag. For other guys his age the day was just starting, but he had already accomplished what most teenagers would consider a full day's work before dawn when he wrapped, stacked, and delivered 1,500 *Houston Post* newspapers.

Later, after a long day of papers, pencils, and pitches, he was happy to brush the dirt from his baseball pants and accept a ride on a teammate's motorbike from the practice field to the parking lot. Little did he know then it would turn out to be the most momentous ride of his life.

At the nearby tennis courts, Ruthie Holdorff concentrated on keeping her swing flat and smooth. She was waiting for Aubrey Horner, the varsity tennis coach, to come by and give her a few pointers, and she wanted to be ready. Horner admired Ruthie's spunk and backhand, and knowing she couldn't afford private lessons, he always made sure to help her a little while working with the varsity girls.

As Ruthie pounded balls off the wall, she heard the whir of the motorbike. Its driver, a boy she knew, gave her a friendly wave. His passenger stared at her intently as they passed and then asked his friend, "Who's that?"

"That's Ruthie, Lynn Holdorff's little sister," answered the driver.

The passenger took a second look. Living in a small town, he'd crossed paths with Ruthie several times without really noticing her. But now he took a long, serious look.

And no wonder...

Ruthie was no longer Lynn's tag-along little sister who came with her to his Little League games, but a blossoming beauty.

Ruthie was still a freshman, so the boy waited a year before making a move.

"Would it be all right with your mom if I took you to the show?" he asked her between classes one day.

"I think so," she answered shyly, "but I'll have to check first."

Her mom said okay, and no doubt Ruthie was excited. After all, Nolan Ryan was a sophisticated junior and had been voted "Best Looking" in his grade, just as she had been in hers. And, unlike most boys in Alvin, Nolan had a car he used for his paper route.

The date was set for the following Saturday. Lynn lent Ruthie a dress their mother had sewn, along with some perfume. She was still getting ready when Nolan pulled up in his 1956 Chevy.

The Holdorff and Ryan families knew each other, so double dating wasn't required. Nolan and Ruthie knew about the 11:00 PM curfew, and the movie had been approved by their folks.

Nolan led Ruthie to the Chevy and opened her door. As he made his way to the other side, she discreetly scooted to the middle of the seat.

The Alvin Theater, near the corner of Gordon and Sealy, was very familiar territory for Nolan. It was where he and his dad wrapped stacks of the *Houston Post* newspaper every morning.

But driving up to the theater that night, newspapers were the last thing on his mind.

Rome Adventure was the movie on the theater marquee, but neither teenager really cared what was showing. Nolan threw a buck down for tickets and headed straight for the concessions. Moments later, a tub of popcorn between them, the theater went dark. As the scenes flew by, Ruthie did her best to concentrate on sunny Italy. It was a romantic moment when Suzanne Pleshette kissed Troy Donahue midway through the second act of the movie. But because this was Nolan and Ruth's first date, there were no thoughts of kisses between these two.

After the show they headed up Gordon to Dairy Land and topped the night off with sodas. Several friends joined them, and after a bit of friendly banter Nolan took Ruthie home. Lynn was waiting to hear all about her sister's date.

As for Nolan, after going home for a quick nap, he got up at 2:00 AM and headed right back to the corner of Gordon and Sealy with his dad to pick up the fresh stacks of *Posts* that awaited morning delivery. The father-son combo had been following this routine for three years, and the work came as natural to the boy as pelting turtles with rocks in Mustang Bayou.

As Nolan worked he saw an occasional drunk stumbling out from one of the nearby bars, or a skunk scurrying from a storm drain in search of popcorn discarded by the night's moviegoers.

But his mind wasn't on drunks, skunks, or popcorn.

Normally he folded and wrapped 1,500 papers at breakneck speed. But now his mind was cloudy and all he could think of was Ruthie's long hair, pretty smile, and the easy way about her that made him open up.

By 5:00 AM Nolan was back in the Chevy, the stack of newspapers neatly folded beside him. Weaving his way through Alvin's sleepy rural side streets, his mind was tired but his heart was beating to the drum of the wonderful soaring energy that new love brings.

2

Hand Holders

> I first noticed Nolan when he was in the sixth grade with my sister. I thought he was cute, but the reason I liked him later on in high school was that he was confident and quiet. He wasn't the bragging type, but was kind and courteous.
>
> —RUTH RYAN

Except for sports, Nolan and Ruthie had totally different interests. Though she grew up in a small town, Ruthie was a city type who liked ballet, theater, and music. Nolan was more outdoorsy, and on dates he took her practice shooting and to feed the baby calves he kept in a pen at a relative's house.

Nolan's quiet, reserved nature might have been due in part to difficulties caused by dyslexia and a lisp. He had trouble reading, and it set him back in some of his classes. In junior high, an impatient teacher called him stupid and threatened to hold him back a grade. A torrid tongue-lashing by Nolan's mom put an end to that, but Nolan still got Ds and Fs in English, and that thoughtless teacher's remarks left an indelible scar.

Sports brought him out of himself, and it was on the basketball court where the 6'2" natural athlete excelled.

By the time he and Ruthie started dating, Nolan had already made a name for himself on the court as a star forward. But he also loved baseball and was just beginning to feel some of the raw power in his right arm.

Nolan wasn't the only one making waves. Ruthie's countless hours of tennis practice had paid off, and her backhand was quickly moving her up the ranks as one the state's best doubles players.

"Her father got her started in tennis in the fifth or sixth grade," recalls Coach Horner. "She won a big tournament in Houston as a freshman at one of the country clubs, and surprised a lot of Houston people when she won the singles championship. Many pro coaches who worked with the Houston kids were shocked that a little country gal could go to the big town and shut everyone down.

"She was a great athlete and could have played anything. She just chose tennis. I used to hear stories that she played football with the boys, and I assume it was true. But that didn't have anything to do with her ladylike attitude."

Loyal, sensitive, and smart, Ruthie cut through Nolan's shyness, and they became, in Horner's words, "hand holders," inseparable as any couple walking the hallways at Alvin High. And when she wasn't playing tennis, you could usually find her down at the ballfield or the basketball court with Nolan.

In a glimpse of what their life would become, Nolan took her to Colt Stadium in Houston to see Sandy Koufax pitch against the Colt .45s. Even at an early age, Ryan felt a kinship with the Dodgers lefty who threw as hard as anyone on the planet. Within 10 years, Ryan would break nearly every one of his hero's strikeout records, but on this summer night, young Nolan was there only to watch and learn.

Watching from their box seats behind the Dodgers dugout, Ruthie had never seen Nolan so serious. When he told her they were there to see Sandy Koufax pitch, she didn't think much about it. She'd been to lots of Nolan's ballgames, and in her mind one pitcher wasn't all that much different from the next.

"Who's Sandy Koufax?" Ruthie asked innocently as they watched him warm up.

"The fastest pitcher in the game," Nolan told her. "If there was someone I'd like to model myself after, it would be him."

Koufax didn't disappoint that day, as he beat the Colts 4–3. What impressed Nolan the most wasn't his blazing fastball but his curveball. It was a giant wake-up call, because for the first time Ryan saw that it took more than just speed to be an effective pitcher.

Back home that night, Nolan removed the crumpled ticket stub from his pocket and tossed it into a drawer as a reminder of what he wanted to shoot for. Ruthie kept her ticket stub too, but for altogether different reasons.

3

Two Reds

I didn't know what I had—no one did.
Only Red Murff.

—NOLAN RYAN

Jim Watson was Alvin High's varsity baseball coach in the spring and the football coach in the fall. The gridiron was his true passion, so he approached baseball with a football bent and tried to make up for his lack of baseball knowledge with discipline. But the tough coach had a soft side, too. He wasn't married, had no children, and treated his athletes as if they were his own kids. "Tough love," he liked to call it, and his athletes soaked it up and revered him.

One fall day in 1963, Watson was out on the track observing a softball toss when something out of the ordinary caught his eye. The memory of it still makes him shake his head a half-century later.

"Some sophomore kid threw a softball the entire length of the football field," Watson recalls.

"Who in the world is that?" he asked at the time.

Answered the track coach, "That's old Nolan."

"When nobody came within 40 yards of him," Watson remembers, "my mind began to work. I felt this boy could definitely help us when baseball rolled around. I heard he'd done some pitching in Little League, so I began to talk to some of the coaches. 'How was Nolan? Did he ever pitch for you? Was he effective? How was his control?' Stuff like that."

The following spring, Watson invited Nolan out to throw batting practice to the varsity team. Not entirely to his surprise, no one could hit him. Watson tried facing Ryan himself and couldn't touch him. Before he left the field that day, the coach knew he'd found something special and had already penciled Nolan in as the top varsity pitcher.

"Nolan was more worried about his control than anything else, because he was wild and hit a lot of kids," recalls the coach. "He didn't know where the ball was going and neither did the batter, which worked to his advantage, because the hitters didn't want to hang in there with him."

Ryan agrees.

"My ability to throw hard didn't happen until I was a sophomore," he said. "Prior to that, I wasn't a harder thrower than any of the other kids. I could always throw a ball farther, but I couldn't throw it harder. The other thing was, I could throw hard, but that didn't mean I could throw strikes and get people out. I didn't have the ability to do that yet."

With Nolan anchoring the varsity pitching staff, Alvin High began winning. In his sophomore season the team was regional champ. In Nolan's senior year it played in the state finals.

It was during his junior year that pro scouts, including local scout Red Gaskill, began taking serious notice of Nolan's fastball.

Gaskill was a "bird dog" scout; he'd go to small towns, watch the games, and, if he saw something interesting, report it to New York Mets district scout Red Murff, a former Milwaukee Braves pitcher.

There's long been a chicken-or-the egg debate about which Red saw Ryan first, Gaskill or Murff.

Until the day he died, Murff maintained he had discovered Ryan, and even went so far as to claim that a premonition made him stop on his way to Houston at the high school tournament in Clear Creek, where he first saw Ryan.

Gaskill has passed on too, and wherever old baseball scouts end up they are probably still arguing about who deserves the credit for discovering Nolan Ryan.

Jim Watson definitely remembers the day Murff first saw Ryan, whenever it may have been.

"We were playing in the final playoff game at Clear Creek. Nolan was pitching but it started raining around the fifth inning, and so we stopped the game. I went under the concession stand to get out of the weather when Murff, who I'd just met, walked over, pointed to Nolan, and said, 'Who is that? Where'd you get that boy?'

"I told him, and he said, 'That's the fastest ball I've ever seen from a pitcher's hand to the plate.'

"I just smiled and said, 'You oughta see him when he's on.'"

As soon as Murff got home that day he took out a white scouting card, put the name Lynn Nolan Ryan at the top, and underneath it he wrote:

> This skinny high school junior HAS THE BEST ARM I'VE EVER SEEN IN MY LIFE. This kid Ryan throws much harder than Jim Maloney of the Cincinnati Reds or Turk Farrell of the Houston Colt .45s (I saw them pitch Thursday night, 4-23-63).

On the back he scribbled, "Ryan has the potential to be a high-performance starting pitcher on a major league staff. A smiling, friendly-faced kid—wide shoulders, long arms, and strong hands. Good athlete."

He signed his name, and in the space for the time wrote "12:00, High Noon." He dated it April 26, 1963, and went to sleep.

From that day forward somebody named Red went to every game Ryan pitched. The varsity played twice a week. Murff attended the Tuesday games, when Nolan was fresh and gave the scout a truer read of his ability. Gaskill would go on Fridays.

A concern other scouts had was that at 145 pounds, Ryan was too small to have big league potential. But Murff wasn't bothered by that. He'd seen Nolan Ryan Sr. at some of the games and had been impressed by the man's quiet nature, as well as by the thick arms and wrists on his 245-pound frame. He figured the boy still had some growing to do.

"They didn't think I would hold up physically," says Ryan, "but Red, being an ex-pitcher, recognized my ability to throw and saw how big my dad was, and luckily that settled it for him."

But Murff was worried that the football-oriented Watson would overwork Nolan and ruin his arm. To make sure he'd get the proper coaching, Murff asked Watson to let him personally tutor Ryan on some of the basics.

"It was illegal for scouts to help kids," recalls Watson. "It was okay to go out there and watch, but you couldn't say anything to them. I'd already been warned by my superintendent to not let them do any coaching. But Murff wanted to coach Nolan so badly, I had to really get after him to not do it."

But Watson wasn't around all the time, and Murff managed to get Ryan alone for a few sessions, where they mostly concentrated on harnessing Nolan's fastball.

Nolan dominated every game he pitched with both his speed and lack of control. For every 10 strikeouts, there might be three hit batsmen and nine walks. He was breaking both bats and limbs, and it got to the point where nobody wanted to face him.

"I was as raw as you could get," recalls Ryan. "I didn't know anything about pitching and didn't get a lot of the things Red was trying to tell me. All I knew was winding up and throwing. I didn't understand anything about gripping balls or trying to put a spin on it or how important your delivery was. Red would bring a catcher and he'd teach me the curve and work with me on some part of my delivery. But I had a lot to learn."

With fresh interest brewing every time Nolan pitched, Watson found himself in the middle of a whirlwind. Ryan was drawing lots of attention, with scouts and college coaches constantly seeking updates on his progress.

"The *Houston Chronicle* and the *Post* were writing about Nolan, and it seemed every day there was another article on him," says Watson. "One night Red pulled me aside and said, 'I want to ask you a favor. I can get Nolan into the big leagues if you'll let me have him and do this thing. If he pitches an outstanding game or a no-hitter, don't call the newspapers. I want to keep him hidden out here as long as I can.'"

Watson wasn't nuts about calling in the score to the papers after a game anyway, so he went along with the plan. He also respected Murff and figured he had Ryan's best interests at heart.

Ruthie wasn't so sure. To her, Murff was cantankerous, married to baseball, and not easy to like. "Red kept saying things like 'Nolan, you have this talent that nobody else has.' After Nolan and I got engaged, he even had the nerve to tell me, 'Ruthie, you are going to have to share Nolan with the world.'

"I didn't like that. He made it sound like Nolan was going to be something big in baseball. But we didn't believe him. We thought he was just saying that to get Nolan to sign a contract."

Computers, radar guns, and the other sophisticated methods routinely employed today by big league scouts were the stuff of science fiction then. For all Ryan knew, he was not much different than all the other kids dreaming about playing big league baseball.

"He would watch major league games on TV on Saturday but he was very innocent," says Ruth. "He didn't even have people trying to get him to go to college. He wanted to go to Texas A&M and talked to the baseball coach there, but the coach wasn't interested. He told Nolan to go play at a junior college for a couple of years, and he'd see how he did and then maybe reconsider having him come to A&M."

During Nolan's senior year, Murff began lobbying Mets de facto general manager Bing Devine to pick Ryan in the 1965 draft. Murff was so convinced Ryan was the real deal that he demanded that Devine come to Texas and see for himself why Ryan was a can't-miss prospect.

It would have helped if Murff had told Coach Watson which day Devine was coming.

"Alvin was in the midst of a nine-game district tournament that would help determine the state championship," recalls Watson. "We had been favored to win the first three games, but lost the first two due to lack of hitting. Nolan had pitched a one-hitter and a two-hitter but we goofed around and lost both games.

"I was mad. We had two days before we played again, so at practice the next day I ordered them to run until they were puking. That night I went to a JV game in Texas City, and Murff was there. He asked how Nolan was doing, and I said the last time I saw him he was puking his guts out.

"It looked like Murff might start hurling right then himself. 'Good God,' he said, 'Bing Devine's coming tomorrow to watch y'all play Channel View!'

"'Why didn't you tell me!' I yelled at him. 'I can't pitch him tomorrow! The last time I saw him he was sick as a dog.'"

Murff tried to call Devine and head him off, but it was too late. Devine was in the stands the next day watching as Channel View smacked the great Nolan Ryan around like a piñata.

"I had never seen him pitch so badly," says Watson. "After three innings we were behind 6–0, and Nolan had no energy or life on the ball. He was so bad that Bing left in the third inning. The last thing I saw was Murff chasing after him in the parking lot screaming, 'He'll get back on it! I'll talk to the coach!'

"'I'll find a pitcher somewhere else!' Devine yelled as he got in the car and slammed the door."

"Nolan was devastated," recalls friend and teammate George Pugh. "It really bothered him. He was thinking. *I blew my big chance,* but Red knew he was sick and took him aside. 'Don't worry about it,' he told him. 'You got a lot of games left. Everybody has a bad day.'"

Murff was so convinced about Ryan's future that when the Mets came to Houston in late April, he persuaded Mets coach Yogi Berra, the former Yankee All-Star catcher and manager, to take a look at Nolan himself. He arranged for Ryan to throw to Mets catcher John Stephenson, with Berra calling the pitches.

On one pitch the signs got crossed and Nolan hit Stephenson on the chest so hard he injured the catcher's collarbone. Berra was impressed.

"The kid can bring it," he told Devine. "Just sign him."

All the talk about the upcoming draft upset Ruth. The first time Nolan told her he might get drafted, she thought he meant into the Army. The Vietnam War was in full swing then, and many of their friends were getting drafted, going overseas, and not coming back.

"I was 16, and I didn't know what the baseball draft was," says Ruth. "It hadn't been around that long. After Nolan explained it to me, I asked him, 'So, you're going off to play baseball?'

"He said, 'I think I am. It'll let me help out my mom and dad, too. And I'll go to college in the winter.'

"I didn't like that either. I was a little girl in love."

On June 8, 1965, the New York Mets chose Nolan Ryan in the 12th round, the 295th player chosen overall.

But despite what Ryan had told Ruthie, actually getting him to sign a contract was no slam dunk. For a small-town kid who'd never been out of Texas, the uncertainty of a career in professional baseball was scary.

"My original thought was to go to college like anybody else," Nolan remembers. "Until Red Murff put the idea in my head and kept after me,

I always played whatever sport was in season. It never entered my mind to play baseball as a career. I really wanted to go to college on a basketball scholarship. I didn't really think about being a professional baseball player until my senior year."

Besides, if he was as good as Murff said he was, how come 294 players had been chosen in the draft before him?

That wasn't the only troublesome figure. When the Mets sent his contract, Ryan showed it to Murff and said, "A $25,000 bonus is a far cry from the $50,000 you promised."

In fact, the offer was very respectable. In addition to a cash bonus of $19,000 (big money in 1965), Ryan would get $700 a month during his first year in the minors, four semesters of college at $1,000 per semester, and a $7,500 bonus after 90 days in the majors.

"Don't turn it down," his dad urged him. Nolan Sr. knew how hard it was to earn that kind of money.

With Nolan and his folks at the kitchen table that day were Red Murff and a local reporter. Murff had invited the latter on the condition he not disclose the terms of the contract. If he so much as opened his mouth at all in the Ryans' house, the scout warned, the reporter would be out of there before he even knew what hit him.

Nolan stared blankly at the contract until finally Murff spoke up.

"Nolan, it's your turn to get on the mound now. Your mom and dad are waiting for you to sign," he said.

Ryan didn't respond, and suddenly the reporter leapt from his chair and broke his vow of silence.

"What's the matter with you, boy?" he cried. "No one ever offered me that much money to do any kind of a job! You crazy? Sign!"

The reporter's unexpected outburst shook Nolan out of his trance, and rather than killing him, Murff probably wanted to kiss him after the young pitcher scrawled "Lynn Nolan Ryan" in his best penmanship on the dotted line.

PART II

The Minors: A Test of Faith: 1965–67

1

Marion's Mets

Robert Garnett looked down the street and sighed. The bus from Bristol would be arriving soon, and the new kid from Texas would probably be as scared as he was hungry. As president of the minor league Marion Mets in Virginia, Garnett always took it upon himself to be at the bus station to welcome new arrivals. His team was currently in Wytheville, and the plan was to pick up the new pitcher, feed him, then shuttle him to the game. Garnett had done it a hundred times before, a routine as familiar to him as the changing of the seasons.

But when the bus pulled in and the kid got off, something seemed a little off. Garnett couldn't believe that the skinny youngster shuffling toward the depot between two suitcases was really a ballplayer. He looked too frail to be an athlete, and the way he was struggling with his bags made Garnett think he might break in two. Garnett went over and grabbed the suitcases, and as he steered the kid to the car, he wondered, *I wonder how long this one will last. Judging from his physique, probably not long.*

Life with the Marion Mets, as with all rookie league teams, was all about survival. Former high school and college stars were shuttled in and out of town like cattle. Competition was fierce, players were routinely cut, and it wasn't unusual to a see a hot-shot prospect, his big league dreams shattered, crying as he left the clubhouse.

The goal at Marion was to survive long enough to get to the next level. For Nolan and some of the others who had been given signing bonuses, the process was less cruel, but they still had to prove themselves or end up in the dreaded revolving door.

Fortunately for Nolan, Marion manager Pete Pavlick was a thoughtful man who knew talent. And even though Ryan was raw, Pavlick saw through his deficiencies and concentrated on what worked—his fastball and steely demeanor.

Pavlick's progress reports on Ryan were generally favorable. The combination of his fastball and poor field lighting was a lethal combo, allowing Nolan to mow down Appalachian League hitters like they were Little Leaguers. His performance with Marion was the first clue to the outside world that Ryan had more going for him than the average rookie league pitcher.

That was exactly what Ruthie was afraid of. She had not handled Nolan's departure well; at Houston's Hobby Airport, she had sobbed with Ryan's parents as his plane left the tarmac, and then cried even harder when she got home. She slammed the door to her room and wouldn't come out. Her dad tried to help, but she was too devastated to respond. With Nolan gone, it felt like her whole world had collapsed.

Nolan had similar thoughts. Separated from Ruthie by a couple thousand miles, he began to understand how much she really meant to him.

His letters home detailed how scared he was when he arrived in Marion, and made it clear that life in rookie ball was far from glamorous. Thanks to a lack of uniforms, only 29 players on the 40-man roster could suit up for games. Nolan had to wait a week until he got one, and when he did, it was three sizes too big.

He told Ruthie that players had to stand in the aisles of the inadequate team bus for hundreds of miles at a time, and that the two shower heads in the overcrowded locker room ran only cold water.

Totally devoted to Ruth, Nolan never dated in Marion. When he wasn't playing ball or at practice, he played pool, went to movies, or hung out at the little house he and a few teammates rented from one of the locals.

His letters helped ease her pain, but Ruthie was so miserable without Nolan that in the late summer of 1965 her dad loaded her, her two brothers, and Nolan's best friend, George Pugh, into the family station wagon and headed east.

When they arrived in Marion two days later, the beauty of Virginia's Blue Ridge Mountains was almost as eye-popping as the new red Impala car Nolan had bought with some of his bonus money. But best of all to Ruthie was that her normally reserved boyfriend now seemed far less cautious when it came to expressing his true feelings to her.

When they went to the Marion ballpark, Ruthie saw that it wasn't much better than the kind of sandlot high school kids played on. The lighting Nolan mentioned in his letters was indeed awful, and the Brunswick bowling alley visible in straight-away center further hindered the batters. The most interesting thing was the enthusiastic group of patients from a nearby mental hospital who sat in one corner of the bleachers and screamed at every pitch like it was the seventh game of the World Series.

The week in Marion went far too quickly for Ruthie, and when she returned to Alvin, her longing for Nolan returned with a vengeance. Nobody else was like him. She spent most of her time on the tennis court, and stayed away from school dances and other social events.

2

Rings and Things

Nolan's return to Alvin in the fall gave him and Ruthie a small window of precious time together before orders came for him to report for the winter Instructional League in Fort Lauderdale, Florida.

There, two members of the Mets coaching staff who had seen Ryan's potential in Marion began working with him in earnest.

Eddie "The Brat" Stanky had been a scrappy second baseman for several teams in the 1940s and '50s before finding his true calling as a manager and instructor. He joined the Mets player development team in 1964 and was Ryan's manager in the Instructional League. A stern disciplinarian, the 5'8" Stanky stressed the mental part of the game.

"Nolan had a lot to learn," Stanky recalls, "but he wanted to learn, was willing to listen, and worked hard. I wasn't a pitcher, but I could see this kid could be one of the best. He had more ability than other kids his age. He just needed polishing."

Ryan credits Stanky as a major influence on his mind-set and career.

"Stanky taught me more about the game than any other person I was ever associated with," he said. "He took the Instructional League seriously and was the first to show me how important the mental side of the game was. He explained several key elements of pitching, including understanding the strengths and weaknesses of hitters and what pitch to make on certain counts and situations."

The other instructor who had a huge impact on him was Whitey Herzog, whose nickname was "The White Rat." One of the most astute baseball minds of the last half-century, Herzog saw Ryan as someone who could help turn the perennial doormat Mets into a championship-caliber club.

"I had some awful good arms in the Instructional League that fall," recalls Herzog. "We were stacked. We had Gary Gentry, Jerry Koosman; we already had Tom Seaver up there. There was Jim Bibby and Jon Matlack, and lesser guys like Steve Renko and Bill Denehy. Of the 14 pitchers I had in the Instructional League that year, 10 of them became pretty good big league pitchers. Five or six kids could throw about 100 miles per hour, and Nolan topped 'em out at about 105."

Thanks to Stanky and Herzog's special attention, the following spring Ryan graduated to the Greenville, South Carolina, team in the Single A Western Carolina League. While it was a step up professionally, Greenville's Meadowbrook Park, built in 1938, was so rundown it made Marion's little park feel like Yankee Stadium. The ramshackle clubhouse was so tiny that players had to get dressed in shifts. The showers were no better—that is, hotter—than the ones back in Marion.

But none of that kept Ryan from leading the league in wins and strikeouts that season. He also was top-of-the-pile when it came to walks and hit batsmen. One of his victims was a female season ticket holder who had the misfortune of standing too close to the backstop fence when an errant Ryan fastball ripped through the mesh and broke her arm.

Nolan called Ruthie frequently, and when the phone rang at dinnertime and she leapt up to get it, no one at the table raised an eyebrow. Even when Ruthie took the phone into the hallway closet for privacy, most of the Holdorffs gave it little thought. The exception was her younger brother, who often playfully locked the outside latch on her.

Ryan's calls were full of tales of life in the low minors, but the baseball stuff went right over Ruthie's head. She didn't have a clue what Rookie League or Single A meant; all that mattered was hearing Nolan's voice on the other end saying that he missed her.

That summer when Ruthie and her folks visited Greenville, he told her in person, for the first time, how much she meant to him. One afternoon not long before she went home, Nolan walked Ruthie downtown to Kingoff's Jewelers and made a down payment on her engagement and wedding rings.

As if in celebration, in his last start before she left, Nolan struck out 19 of the 21 batters he faced in a seven-inning game.

His strikeout total that season was a startling 272 in 183 innings, a number so outrageous it forced the brass in New York to take serious notice.

As soon as Greenville's season ended in September, Nolan was dispatched to Williamsport, Pennsylvania, of the Double A Eastern League, for some advanced seasoning.

By 1966, Whitey Herzog was the third-base coach of the New York Mets. A disciple of Casey Stengel, Herzog had heeded the "Old Perfessor's" advice after a so-so stint in the majors and turned his energies to player development.

Herzog had liked what he'd seen of Ryan in Fort Lauderdale the winter before, but he was still taken aback by the report he'd just received from Williamsport, and he immediately called over Mets pitching coach Harvey Haddix.

"It says here that Ryan kid struck out 21 at Williamsport last week," Herzog said. "Nineteen in regulation, two in extra innings—and they still lost the friggin' game to Pawtucket!"

Haddix gave a long whistle and said, "Twenty-one strikeouts—holy cow! How the hell can you strike out 21 batters and lose? Let me see that!"

According to the report, Pawtucket had tied the game in the ninth inning after a batter singled, stole second, took third on Ryan's errant pickoff throw, and then stole home. The next batter beat out a bunt, reached second on another Ryan throwing error, and, after moving to third on a passed ball, stole home for the winning run.

"This kid could win 30 games if he had his noggin on straight," said Haddix.

"Not on this horseshit club he wouldn't!" snapped Herzog, tossing the report down and reaching for his fungo bat. "Hell, he could strike out 27 and we'd still manage to screw it up."

"I say bring the kid up now," Haddix suggested as they went down the ramp. "We could use some pick-me-up around here."

"We need more than that," sighed Herzog. "A frigging enema couldn't clean up this mess."

3

Cup of Coffee

Ryan was actually throwing a no-hitter when Williamsport manager Bill Virdon approached him between innings.

"Nolan, the Mets want you to report for the game tonight," the skipper said. "I know you got a no-hitter going, but you'll miss your flight if you don't go now. What do you want to do?"

Ryan didn't hesitate for a millisecond. "If it's all right with you, Mr. Virdon, I'd just as soon move along to New York," he said.

Since their inaugural year in 1962, the Mets had been the laughingstock of baseball, and in 1966 the team's prospects weren't looking any better. For the most part the club consisted of cast-offs, over-the-hill vets hanging around for another paycheck, and not-so-promising youngsters.

When Nolan arrived in the clubhouse that September, the Mets were 23 games out of first place and stunk as badly as the cigar smoke that clouded his lungs and vision when he walked in. As his eyes adjusted, Ryan saw a group of veterans playing cards in their underwear. Nobody jumped up to pump his hand and welcome him to the big leagues. In fact, nobody took much notice of him at all.

Recalls Ryan, "I looked around the clubhouse in Shea Stadium through 19-year-old eyes and I saw people whose records I admired—Jack Hamilton, Roy McMillan, Chuck Hiller, and the rest. They were 30 to

35 years old and they had that kicked-around look. I thought to myself, *Gawd, I don't want to look like that in 10 or 12 years!*"

For a polite, small-town kid raised to respect his elders, their indifference, if not outright hostility, hurt Ryan. He wouldn't learn until later that nobody talked to him because they were all afraid he was there to take their jobs.

Spotting him, Mets manager Wes Westrum called Ryan into his office. He went, though the fact that Westrum was buck-naked at the time gave the young pitcher further pause.

"Nolan, you're up here just for us to take a look at you," Westrum told him. "Your major league future doesn't depend on how well you do. We want you to relax, and when I call on you to pitch just do the best you can."

Though Westrum meant to be reassuring, Nolan wondered what he had gotten himself into. A bunch of veterans smoking cigars in their underwear and a middle-aged manager in his birthday suit weren't what he had envisioned when he left Williamsport.

Only after he put on his uniform and walked down the tunnel into the dugout and then stepped out onto a major league field for the first time did the magnitude of what had happened really hit him.

The entire city of Alvin, Texas, had a population of 6,000 people. Shea Stadium held more than 50,000. Looking around, the butterflies in Ryan's gut furiously flapped their wings, and he asked himself, *Can I really do this?*

In his first week as a Met, Nolan did nothing but shag fly balls and warm up occasionally in the bullpen. Except for catcher John Stephenson and a couple of the coaches, nobody paid much heed to him at all. He hated it.

"I was alone, lonely, and scared to death that I'd blow my chance," Ryan recalls. "All of a sudden, I didn't even want to pitch."

But that's why he was there, and Ryan's big league debut came against the Atlanta Braves on September 11, 1966, in front of 19,764 fans at Shea Stadium.

"All I remember is that I was nervous," says Ryan. "And I was about to face a bunch of guys who a year earlier were in my baseball card collection."

The Mets were losing when Ryan got the call in the top the sixth inning. In the bullpen he was afraid he might toss his cookies. Fortunately, the first batter he faced was Braves pitcher Pat Jarvis, who became the first of Nolan's 5,714 career strikeout victims.

Next up was the always-dangerous Felipe Alou, who flied out to left.

That brought future Hall of Famer Eddie Mathews to the plate.

Mets catcher John Stephenson signaled for a fastball.

Mathews didn't see it, but he heard something whiz past him and exclaimed, "What the fuck was that?!"

All Stephenson knew was that he'd never caught anything that fast before.

Two more fastballs sent Matthews back to the dugout. He never got the bat off his shoulder. He and Ryan walked back to their respective benches in a daze.

The seventh inning proved more challenging, because the Atlanta hitters knew Ryan was throwing only heat and they were looking for it.

Henry Aaron led off with a hopper toward first. Ryan raced over to the bag to take the throw from the first baseman, and the future Strikeout King beat the future Home Run King by two feet.

Then All-Star catcher Joe Torre hit Ryan's second pitch high and deep over the right-field bullpen for a home run.

Flustered, Ryan walked Rico Carty.

Mack Jones smacked a liner to the left fielder for out number two.

Denis Menke went down on strikes to end the inning.

Ryan was prepared to go out for the eighth, but Westrum had seen enough.

In the clubhouse after the game, no one said anything as Ryan sat in front of his locker until veteran Jim Hickman passed by and grunted, "Torre hits 'em off everyone."

That was small comfort to the unhappy rookie. For the first time in his life, opposing hitters hadn't feared Ryan. Instead of dodging his fastball, they were waiting for it.

"Torre hit one of the best balls I threw all day," Ryan later recalled. "A fastball, up and in. I realized I might overpower minor leaguers with a good fastball, but not major leaguers. If they knew it was coming, they'd just wait for it and hit it."

Too bad Ryan couldn't hear what they were saying about him in the Braves clubhouse.

"He throws about as hard as I've seen it thrown," Aaron told the press.

"That kid can hum that thing," seconded Torre.

That kid didn't sleep much that night. Ryan knew there were a lot of hopes pinned on him, and he didn't want to let anyone down. But he wasn't sure he could stand the pressure, and between his self-doubt and the intense loneliness he felt without Ruth and his folks around, he wasn't at all sure he wanted to find out.

By dawn he had arrived at a decision. The next week the Mets would be in Houston. He'd give most of his luggage to his parents to take home for him, and when the season ended, he'd start classes at Alvin Community College.

The next day, Harvey Haddix called him over during batting practice.

"Hey, Nolan, how about a start in Houston next week? What do you say?" he asked.

It seemed like all of Alvin showed up at the Astrodome for Ryan's homecoming. Arriving late, they'd barely found parking spots when word spread that the hometown hero hadn't made it past the first inning. Ryan gave up four runs on four hits and two walks.

The far from glorious performance got Nolan even more down on himself and the idea of a future in baseball. When the season ended, he started business classes at Alvin Community College and pumped gas. His new plan was to try to last five seasons in the majors, qualify for his pension, and start a career as a veterinarian.

The Mets had a different idea. In Ryan's two years with the organization, he'd struck out 428 batters in 283 innings. They still saw him as a big key to their future.

In January 1967, a powerful third party weighed in. The Vietnam War was raging, and President Lyndon Johnson had requested an additional 205,000 American troops over the next year. Young men across America were receiving draft notices, including Nolan Ryan. He considered it the death knell for his baseball career, figuring that even if he survived a two-year hitch in the jungle of Southeast Asia, the time off from pitching would be the end of him as a big league hurler.

Sharing the same fear, the Mets exerted influence to get Nolan assigned to an Army Reserve unit in Texas. A lot of professional clubs did the same for their top prospects.

Ryan's enlistment in the Army Reserves would require him to spend a few months in basic training, and then one weekend a month in Houston for the next six years. Plus, every summer he'd have to report to Reserve camp for two or three weeks.

Being away from baseball every four weeks, plus up to three weeks each summer, made it impossible for Ryan to get into any kind of pitching groove. It put a big crimp in his development and was a major reason he didn't realize his full potential with the Mets.

But there was no arguing about one thing: a travel bag was a hell of a lot better than a body bag.

When Nolan's first Reserve stint was up in the spring of '67, the Mets sent him to Winter Haven, Florida (Class A), to get the kinks out, and then to Triple A Jacksonville.

In his first appearance in Jacksonville he struck out 18 of 21 hitters, sending shock waves from the Florida panhandle all the way to Flushing Meadows. The next time Nolan took the mound in Jacksonville, it was before a standing-room-only crowd. Kids sat on their parents' shoulders to see the man being hyped as the next Bob Feller. They were disappointed, for in the haste to fast-track Ryan the Mets overworked him and his arm popped during pregame warm-ups.

When Ryan told Jacksonville general manager Danny Menendez he couldn't pitch, the GM demanded that Nolan suck it up and get on the mound. He refused, whereupon the officious official instructed Ryan to apologize to the fans who had packed the stadium to see him.

Only when manager Bill Virdon sided with Ryan did Menendez back down.

Whitey Herzog was there that day. "When Ryan left the game, the stadium practically emptied," he recollects. "It was the first time I saw his potential drawing power."

Ryan waited two weeks before testing his arm again. The team was in Richmond, Virginia, playing the Braves. Mets vice president Johnny Murphy stopped by to see the game.

Nolan came in to relieve in the late innings with the bases loaded and put three fastballs by Richmond's Dave Nicholson. But up in the stands, Murphy, a former pitcher himself, could tell something was wrong. Ryan's ball had very little pop, and after each pitch he grimaced in pain. At the inning's end Murphy rushed to the dugout and ordered Ryan out of the game. Nolan was flown to New York to be examined by the Mets' physician.

There were two more sessions with the sawbones, and when the doc finally threw up his hands and proposed exploratory surgery to find the trouble, Nolan balked. He'd quit baseball before letting anybody cut into him.

His stubbornness persisted even after a torn forearm tendon was diagnosed and management pressed harder for him to have an operation. He knew his body best, he insisted, and the arm would heal itself over time.

Amazingly, Ryan won out, and for the rest of that season he only threw a little on the side and not at all in games.

No one can say, of course, whether surgery would have solved the problem; it can be argued that it might even have set him back more. In any case, Ryan was left not knowing when or even if he would pitch again. All he could do was rehab, wait, and hope.

And get married. There was no point in waiting anymore, and after Nolan's six-month Army Reserve commitment was fulfilled, he asked the Mets if he could have an additional day off before returning to the team.

The plan was for him and Ruth to tie the knot on the Monday after his Saturday Reserve meeting in Houston. The next day the newlyweds would fly to Jacksonville for the game that night. Permission granted.

"We got married on Monday night," says Ruth. "Our wedding dinner was at the local Sonic Drive-Thru, and our wedding night at a motel near the airport. We left on a flight to Florida the next morning, and a day later Nolan left on a 10-day road trip."

All by herself that night in a city far from home, Mrs. Nolan Ryan Jr. sat and thought, *I don't know one other person here.*

"We had a car, a '65 Impala stick-shift, but I hadn't driven it much," she says. "I had never been away from home before by myself. I called my parents on June 29 to wish my dad a happy birthday and just broke down in tears. 'I want to come home!' I told him."

Her parents convinced her to stay. What got her and Nolan through then (and in the years that followed in the minors) was pure faith and perseverance, and the ability to take each day as it came.

"We didn't know what to expect," says Ruth. "Nolan didn't know himself well enough to say, 'I am going to make it big in this job.' He didn't have high expectations, because we didn't want to be disappointed if something happened and it didn't work out."

One thing that did work out was her husband's decision to nix surgery on his ailing arm. It felt better when he rejoined the big club in the spring of 1968, and that wasn't the only thing that had improved—the Mets' team chemistry had drastically changed over the off-season. The stigma of losing had been replaced with a youthful vigor and optimism. Gone were the washed-up, stogie-sucking vets and their jaded attitudes. In their place was a crop of brash, talented rookies with unlimited potential.

After six years, the team mocked by the title of Jimmy Breslin's 1963 book about the Mets, *Can't Anybody Here Play This Game?*, was determined to abdicate its role as laughingstock of the National Pastime.

PART III

Lost in New York: The New York Mets: 1968–71

1

The Phantom: 1968

"Who is this guy 'Ryan'?"
"He's 'The Phantom.'"
"Is he as good as they say he is?"
"Not sure, never seen him."

Though likely apocryphal, that locker room conversation related by Mets teammate Ron Swoboda does underscore the fact that by the time spring training convened in Florida in 1968, Nolan Ryan was still an enigma in the clubhouse. Some of the players had heard of his harrowing fastball, but few had actually seen it, since he'd seen limited time in Double A ball and skipped Triple A entirely. It seemed that Ryan periodically popped into town, overwhelmed a few batters with 100-mph fastballs, then got hurt or disappeared into the Army, only to reappear again somewhere down the line.

"I never hung with him," says Swoboda. "He didn't go out or run around and drink beer like the rest of us. He wasn't into that. Nolan was Nolan. There wasn't a lot of artifice about him. When you were with him, you were around a completely authentic person."

When The Phantom arrived in camp in February, his arm had healed and there were lots of new faces. Under new manager Gil Hodges, the Mets camp had a completely different feel. A combination of scouting and luck had given the club some of the best young arms in the game. To make the squad, pitchers had to meet strict guidelines. If you couldn't throw a consistent 90-mph heater, you were cut.

This was a far cry from the old days, when if a player showed up with a glove and spikes, he'd probably make the team.

At 25, lefty Jerry Koosman was the oldest of the young guns. He credits Hodges for the team's new attitude.

"Gil would always pull a stick of Juicy Fruit out of his back pocket, unwrap it, casually look down, and say to you in a mellow voice, 'You know, I've kind of been watching you, and it looks to me like you're a bit out of shape.' Then he'd turn around and walk away.

"We took that as a challenge. He'd make us try harder for him, and we'd go out and run 10 extra wind sprints. He'd see that and appreciate it. He could get stuff out of you like that."

According to Koosman, with Hodges there were no stars on the ballclub; everybody was treated the same way. Over time, Ryan would form a far different opinion of his manager than Koosman.

As a Met, Ryan never delivered as much as his talent promised. There were definite moments of brilliance during his four seasons in New York, but for the most part it was a constant struggle.

For one thing, Ryan had the misfortune of being a high-ball pitcher in a low-ball league. In the 1960s, National League umpires wore their chest protectors underneath their jackets and crouched down low and inside, next to the catcher's face.

American League umpires wore bulky inflatable protection outside their jackets that made them unable to crouch, so they set up higher.

As a result, American League umpires called higher strikes, which is where most of Ryan's strikes were. And National League umpires called lower strikes, and thus were inclined to call more balls than strikes on Nolan.

Another hindrance was Ryan's quick elevation to the majors. Because he spent so little time in the minor leagues, his mechanics hadn't been fine-tuned by years of coaching. Had he been with a lesser team with fewer young arms than the Mets, he might have gotten the personalized training he desperately needed.

But it wasn't all gloom in New York, thanks to Ryan's relationship with Tom Seaver.

"He was the first close friend I had on the Mets," says Ryan. "Up to that point I hadn't looked at baseball as a career. I was not really committed nor had that burning desire to be the best player I could possibly be.

"But being around him, watching him go about his work and hearing him talk about what he wanted to achieve in baseball, that really got me thinking about what I should try to accomplish. He was the first person I was ever around with that kind of dedication who had some influence on me.

"He was open and articulate, I was wary and unpolished. I think Tom believed in me when a lot of people were unsure."

Seaver had what Ryan badly needed—poise and polish. At the Mets spring training camp in 1968, Seaver was already a success. He had come up to the big club after one year in the minors, won 16 games, and left no doubt about how good he was.

"If there's one person who helped change Nolan's attitude and showed him what hard work meant, it was Tom Seaver," says Whitey Herzog. "When Nolan went to spring training and saw how hard Seaver worked, it affected him, and he and Tom became very close.

"Nolan didn't realize that you had to get yourself in shape. I don't want to take anything away from [pitching coach] Rube Walker, but Rube wasn't the kind of guy to stand over you and make you run 20 times hard from foul line to foul line and do all the stuff that Seaver did.

"Nolan emulated Tom, and I think Seaver had a lot to do with Nolan eventually turning his career around. He started working like Tom worked, got strong-legged, and really built himself up. After that, he still had the great arm and also a great lower body. That's what made him last 27 years."

In his first full season in the majors, Ryan won six games and lost nine, with 133 strikeouts in 134 innings and a 3.09 ERA. He started out strong, striking out 44 batters in his first 35 innings, but in a 14-strikeout performance against Cincinnati on May 14, a painful blister developed on his pitching finger. The inflamed digit limited him to six or seven innings per game thereafter, even after Ryan followed the advice of Mets trainer Gus Mauch and soaked his finger in pickle brine to harden the skin. Mauch's remedy—borrowed from old prizefighters who thought pickle brine protected them from facial cuts—didn't help, though it did provide grist for *Life* magazine when it ran a spread on "The Next Sandy Koufax" in the May 31 issue.

In August, Mets GM Johnny Murphy, impatient with Ryan's progress, placed him on the 30-day disabled list.

"That Ryan always has some ache or pain," the unsympathetic Murphy grumbled to the press. "You guys call him a myth, and I believe he is one."

Ryan finished the season deep in the bullpen, and nobody was more frustrated with the situation than he was.

"I didn't pitch on a regular basis," he recalls of that time. "I was gone every other weekend [because of his Army Reserve obligation], and the way it worked was, if you missed your start, you had to wait five days for your next one. If I was doing Reserve duty that weekend and supposed to start on Sunday, I'd have to fly back by Sunday morning, which made it impossible to get into a pitching and practice rhythm. Then between starts, they'd put me in the bullpen, which made it even more troublesome."

Mets pitching coach Rube Walker was not much help.

"Walker was better suited for a veteran pitching staff," says Ryan. "He wasn't good for pitchers like me who still needed help on their mechanics. I should have been down in the minor leagues pitching and getting help with the basics. But they didn't even have minor league pitching coaches in those days. I suffered badly for it."

As for manager Gil Hodges, he knew Ryan was chock-full of talent, but with the luxury of several other strong arms at his disposal, he stuck with whoever was hot at the time. He didn't spend much time worrying or even thinking about Ryan; as a result, coming to the ballpark every day became about as much fun as going to the dentist.

Ryan wasn't the only one who felt that way.

"None of us had a friendly relationship with Gil," says Jerry Koosman. "We weren't allowed to go to the hotel bar or bring our golf clubs on the plane like [players] do today. We weren't allowed to go swimming on the day we pitched. If you got sunburned, they'd stop your paycheck.

"In Gil's eyes, there were no stars. It didn't matter who was late—the bus was leaving. You didn't want to be called into his office, 'cause if you did you were pretty much gonna get your ass chewed."

Koosman recalls the time Ryan was stretching in the outfield during batting practice and Hodges hit a line drive from his fungo bat that missed him by inches. There was no apology from the manager—in fact, he'd actually been aiming at Ryan.

"Gil believed that during BP you were supposed to be out there shagging and working," says Koosman, "and in his eyes Nolan was slacking. Gil did that to a lot of us. He hit one at me one time that just missed me.

"But we worshipped him. He made everyone toe the line."

Things weren't any better for the Ryans on the home front. Nolan and Ruth lived in a tiny apartment in Elmhurst, Queens, in what she describes as "a pretty scary neighborhood." The Welcome Wagon must've thought so too, because it never showed up. Their very first visitor, who lived in the apartment beneath them, set the tone.

This is nice, thought Ruth as she answered the knock on the door. *A neighbor is coming to welcome me to the neighborhood.* "In Texas," says Ruth, "if somebody moves in next door you bring them a cake and come say hello. So I open the door and she points her finger at me and snarls, 'Why are you making so much noise at night?' We'd come home at night after the game around 11:30 PM, have a bite to eat, and go to bed. We didn't have parties or make any noise.

"But she didn't look like the type to argue with, so I said 'Sorry, lady!' and closed the door. I was stunned. We were totally two fish out of water. It was a total culture shock.

"Then, there was the alternate street parking on different days of the week. On certain days you could park right in front of your building, but other days it wasn't allowed. We had an old beat-up Chevrolet, and after some night games I would drive around and around until we found a place to park, then we'd have to walk forever to get back to the apartment."

As simple a task as buying groceries turned out to be not so simple, because there was no one-stop shopping in the Big Apple. "You had a little meat market, a little fruit market, and a little place to buy bread," says Ruth. "You'd buy something at each place and then have to carry it all back with you.

"'It can't be that bad,' scoffed Nolan one day. 'I'll go with you to get groceries.' It was the middle of summer, and after we bought all the stuff he wanted at all these separate markets, we had to walk back to our place, and it was all uphill.

"When we got to our building, the elevator wasn't working. So we charged upstairs, and just when we got to the apartment door, the grocery sack broke. Nolan flung everything inside and said, 'I'm not doing that again!'"

According to Ryan's sister, Mary Lou Williams, the upside to all that misery was that it strengthened the bond between her brother and Ruth.

"Their closeness increased when they went to New York, because they really had to depend on one another," says Mary Lou, who visited them that summer. "Here were these two kids, just 19 or 20 years old, coming from such a different situation. They were really out of their element.

"They were on the 14th floor of this apartment building. You parked your car, and then if you moved it, you'd probably never find another parking place in the same zip code again, so you usually took the subway. Nolan was totally miserable until Ruth got there and made things better just by being herself."

Nolan himself has always called marrying Ruth the best decision he ever made. Thanks to her, the dreadfulness of the big city was tolerable. And he returned her love and commitment 100 percent. On road trips, when teammates went on the prowl for female companionship and fun, he stayed in his hotel room and read cattle magazines.

The suits in the Mets front office couldn't have cared less about Ryan's personal life. Professional ballplayers didn't get paid to act like Boy Scouts, and during that off-season there was plenty of hand-wringing about Ryan's prospects in 1969. The fact was that nobody was more disappointed with the way things had gone than Ryan himself, and as he pondered his future in baseball, no one was more confounded, either.

How could someone with so much natural talent languish the way he had?

Now, as the Mets prepared to take the field for what would go down as one of the most miraculous seasons in the history of the game, the more pressing question was, which Ryan would be there—The Phantom or The Phenom?

2

Miraculous: 1969

Believe It!

—SHEA STADIUM SIGNAGE AND SLOGAN

In their first eight years in the National League, the New York Mets had never finished above ninth place or won more than 73 games.

When the 1969 season started, the perennial doormats were considered 100-to-1 long shots to win the World Series.

That would have been a pretty smart—and very lucrative—bet. The 1969 Mets would be celebrated as the "Miracle Mets," winners of 100 of their 162 regular season games that year.

It would be nice to say that the season saw a miraculous turnaround by Nolan Ryan as well, but the fact is that in '69 he started only 10 games—eight fewer than he had the year before. Between his military commitments, the wildness that continued to plague him, and the team's abundance of available arms, manager Gil Hodges used Ryan very sparingly. Relegated mostly to long relief, Ryan was the proverbial odd man out.

What makes the performance of the '69 Mets so impressive is that, on paper, the team was by no means a powerhouse.

With the exception of Tom Seaver, there were no standouts. Nobody looked at Tommie Agee, Cleon Jones, Ron Swoboda, Donn Clendenon, Ed

Charles, and Bud Harrelson and was reminded of the 1927 Yankees. What did it for the Mets was consistent pitching, defense, and team chemistry.

Seaver was the lynchpin. After two straight 16-win seasons, he was the team's unquestioned leader, and to him the Mets' reputation for mediocrity was simply unacceptable. Leading by example, he challenged his teammates to play above expectations and to think like winners.

To Seaver, there was nothing cute or funny about losing. He, along with Gil Hodges, changed the way the players thought.

It didn't happen overnight. In mid-May, the Mets were struggling near .500. Seaver declared publicly that they were much better than that and set out to prove it. He and Jerry Koosman (17–9, 2.28 ERA) combined to win 18 of their last 19 decisions.

Seaver's 25–7 performance that season earned him the Cy Young and *Sports Illustrated* "Sportsman of the Year" awards.

Credit for the Mets' amazing 180-degree turnaround also belonged to former "Boy of Summer" Gil Hodges, says Koosman.

"When Gil came to the Mets in '68, we'd heard how strict he was. But in truth, it was just the opposite. He was laughing, having a great time, and was never stern. But then in '69 everything changed, and we later figured out why. In '68, he observed. Then he made some trades over the winter, and in '69 he knew the talent he had and put it to use. He bore down and became fairly strict and we won. He told us, 'Mind your own business, do your own job, and don't worry about the next guy.'"

The Chicago Cubs presented the greatest challenge to the Mets in the regular season. With future Hall of Famers Billy Williams, Ron Santo, Ernie Banks, and Fergie Jenkins, the Cubs seemed to have the Mets outmanned and outgunned, and after leading the division for most of the season, they looked like a shoo-in for the playoffs. On August 13, they led the Mets by 10 games.

But then, with Seaver and Koosman throwing flames, the Mets won 38 of their last 49 games.

"We got through the dog days of summer and started to feel that touch of cool air out of the north," recalls Koosman. "Toward the first of September, our pitchers got a second wind and came alive. It was like getting strong again, and it gave us new life."

Ryan's biggest contribution to the stretch run came in the second game of a September 10 doubleheader against Montreal. His 7–1 complete-game victory gave the Mets a one-game lead over the Cubs. The Mets never looked back and won the Eastern Division by eight games.

In the inaugural NLCS, the Mets played the Western Division champion Atlanta Braves in a five-game playoff for the right to play in the World Series. With stalwarts Hank Aaron, Orlando Cepeda, and Phil Niekro, the Braves were favored going into the series most experts figured would be decided by pitching. Instead it turned into a slugfest, and when the New Yorkers outhit their hosts to win the first two games, the fact that the once-lowly Mets were only one game away from the National League pennant seemed bizarre beyond belief.

A two-run homer by Hank Aaron in the first inning off Mets starter Gary Gentry put Atlanta up right out of the gate in Game 3 in New York. In the third inning, the Braves had runners on second and third with no outs, and when the count against right-handed, .340-hitting Rico Carty was 1-2, Hodges pulled the plug on Gentry.

The manager's decision to bring in Nolan Ryan out of the bullpen, instead of Cal Koonce or Tug McGraw, sent the Mets dugout into an emotional tailspin.

"We thought Gil was giving up," recalls Jerry Koosman. "We had all seen Ryan pitch before and knew he was capable of walking the ballpark. Nolan wasn't conveniently wild—he was just plain wild, and when Gil brought him in it blew all the air out of our lungs."

"Keep it down," Hodges ordered the nervous Texan as he handed him the ball. "Just keep it down."

With 54,195 screaming fans and a national TV audience looking on, Ryan—who'd been flinging balls all over the bullpen during his warm-up—took a deep breath, glanced over at Tony Gonzalez dancing off third base, and went into his windup.

Ryan wheeled, grunted, and threw. When umpire Ed Sudol cried "Strike three!" the Mets dugout erupted.

The elation didn't last long; next up was Orlando Cepeda.

Hodges' instructed Ryan to issue the former batting champion an intentional walk to load the bases, which meant that another walk or a wild pitch would score a run.

With laser-like focus that belied his nervousness, Ryan got Clete Boyer on strikes. Then Bob Didier lifted a fly ball to left to end the inning, and Gil Hodges looked like the greatest baseball genius since Connie Mack.

"It made Gil look that much better, because so many times that year he had done things we didn't understand that worked out," says Koosman. "It turned out he knew us a lot better than we knew ourselves."

From that point on, Ryan's only mistake came in the fifth, when he gave up a two-run home run to Cepeda to give the Braves a 4–3 lead. But, as they'd done all year, the Mets fought back, scoring three of their own in the bottom of the inning to go ahead 7–4. Ryan himself started the rally with a single.

They won it when Ryan got Tony Gonzalez to ground out for the final out. The Nowhere Man had nailed down the NL pennant.

"We were elated, absolutely overjoyed," remembers Koosman. "We were so happy and proud of Nolie. We just couldn't believe it."

Nolan still has trouble believing it himself.

"I was surprised Gil brought me in in that position, because I wasn't known for my control," he says. "I think he was hoping I might get a strike on Carty because of my ability to strike people out. He was just trying to get out of the inning without any further damage. Seeing I was effective, he then decided to give me the opportunity to pitch, with the hope I'd be able to get us later into the game so he didn't have to deplete his bullpen."

It was a memorable night for both Ryans.

At the postgame celebration in the Diamond Club at Shea Stadium, Ruth—who'd never had a single beer or drop of alcohol in her life—decided the occasion warranted a touch of the bubbly... or three or four.

"That was the first and last time in my life I was drunk," she says. "I don't know how much I drank, but the next day I couldn't even get out of bed without being dizzy. I was sick and very, very upset with myself."

Unlike his game-saving appearance on the mound, this time her husband wasn't much good in relief. When her hangover stretched into its third day, Nolan magnanimously offered to get her some Alka-Seltzer. "He made it pretty clear that I was on my own," says Ruth. "He didn't feel sorry for me. He was like, 'Lady, you made your bed—now lie in it!'

"To this day, I can't drink three or four sips. It cured me forever."

3

Amazin': 1969

Bring on Rod Gaspar!

—BALTIMORE'S FRANK ROBINSON, MOCKING THE METS BEFORE THE 1969 WORLD SERIES.

The 1969 World Series captivated the nation. With the Vietnam War raging and America reeling from civil unrest and violence at home, people craved diversion. And the 1969 "David vs. Goliath" World Series provided it in spades. The experts thought the Mets would be lucky to win one game against the mighty Baltimore Orioles, whose potent offense featured Boog Powell, Paul Blair, Don Buford, and Frank and Brooks Robinson. Hurlers Jim Palmer, Dave McNally, and Mike Cuellar were stellar for the Birds.

But the upstart Mets were either too young or too tough to be intimidated.

"We were charged up a lot more going into the Series than we were in the playoffs," recalls Koosman. "We were told they had a good team, but none of us knew them. Personally, I went in there with everything I had. I didn't want to be embarrassed, and neither did the rest of us.

"In the meeting before the first game, our scouts kept saying, 'Don't throw this, don't throw that!' for each guy in their lineup. Finally I said, 'Well, what the hell do we throw these guys?' We never did get an answer."

Even after Baltimore took the opener 4–1 at home, the Mets viewed their obituaries as premature.

"After the game, somebody—I think it was Donn Clendenon—yelled out, 'Dammit, we can beat these guys!'" recalls Tom Seaver, who'd lost for the first time in 13 games. "And we believed it. A team knows if it's been badly beaten or outplayed. And we felt we hadn't been. We hadn't been more than a hit or two from turning it around. It hit us like a ton of bricks."

In Game 2, Clendenon put the Mets on the board in the fourth with a solo home run, and Koosman pitched six innings of no-hit ball. But an inning later, a Brooks Robinson single brought in a run to tie the game, and with the momentum seeming to shift in the Orioles' favor, the Mets needed a jolt of inspiration. It came from an unexpected quarter.

Sitting in the bullpen in the top of the eighth, Ryan heard a commotion in the right-field stands. Looking up, he recalls, "I saw what looked like four young women parading around the grandstand with a large banner. I was curious what the fuss was all about, and on closer inspection I noticed their banner read LET'S GO METS! And one of the girls looked a lot like my wife. I grabbed the binoculars, and, sure enough, there she was. The fans were throwing hot dogs and popcorn and even pouring beer on the gals. I had a fit. I don't remember all I said to Ruth later, but I let her know how I felt."

"We wanted to do something to show our support and to make it seem a little like Shea Stadium," recalls Lynn Dyer, wife of Mets third-string catcher Duffy Dyer. "It was so quiet for Game 1 of the World Series, and there were so few fans cheering for the Mets. I stole a bed sheet from our hotel and got some black shoe polish and made up the sign. We didn't go out with it earlier because Jerry Koosman had a no-hitter going and we didn't want to jinx him."

Hosting the banner with Lynn were Nancy Seaver, Michelle Pfeil, and Ruth Ryan. Their effort was rewarded in the ninth inning when the Mets pushed across the go-ahead run on consecutive singles by Ed Charles, Jerry Grote, and Al Weis. After Koosman walked Frank Robinson and Boog Powell with two outs in the bottom of the inning, Mets reliever Ron Taylor came in and got Brooks Robinson on a grounder to third, sending the teams to New York tied at a game apiece.

In the sold-out crowd for the first World Series ever played game at Shea Stadium were Casey Stengel, the first Mets manager, and former First Lady Jackie Kennedy Onassis.

On the hill for the Mets was 23-year-old Gary Gentry. Sixteen-game winner Jim Palmer pitched for the Birds.

The Mets got on the board in the first inning on Tommie Agee's leadoff homer. They added two more in the second on Gentry's double. Grote doubled home a run in the sixth, and when Ed Kranepool hit a solo homer in the eighth, the Mets led 5–0.

Gentry tossed shutout ball before trouble found him in the seventh. After retiring Elrod Hendricks and Davey Johnson on fly balls, he gave up walks to Mark Belanger, pinch hitter Dave May, and Don Buford. That brought Gil Hodges to the mound in a hurry. Gentry was done, and in came the unlikely savior in the Mets' NLCS clincher.

This time there was no uproar in the dugout when Nolan Ryan took the mound. While he warmed up, Mets center fielder Tommie Agee assessed the situation. A pillar of defense all season, Agee had chased down a long drive by Hendricks in the fourth inning, saving at least two runs. Now, with the bases loaded, Agee knew Ryan couldn't risk walking anybody and would go right after Paul Blair with the heater.

The first two pitches were strikes. But then Ryan committed the cardinal sin of challenging a good hitter when up 0-2 in the count.

"Blair was digging in, and I guess I should have brushed him back or wasted a pitch," Ryan recalls. "But I was anxious to get out of the inning."

Ryan knew it was a mistake the moment the pitch left his hand. The high fastball was right in Blair's wheelhouse, and he smacked it into deep right-center. Everyone in the park, including Ryan, assumed it would go for extra bases.

But Agee knew the wind currents at Shea better than anybody, and he knew that balls hit to center would generally hang. Racing to the warning track, he fell to his knees with his glove extended and made the catch just inches from the ground.

Ryan made quick work of the Birds in the eighth, but in the ninth a two-out walk to Mark Belanger, a pinch-hit single by Clay Dalrymple, and another walk to Don Buford loaded the bases. With Blair due up and New York ahead 5–0, Hodges decided to stick with Ryan. The pitcher fired two quick strikes to Blair, and then fooled the All-Star with a curveball for the final out.

"We certainly had more confidence in Nolan when they brought him into the Series," recalls Koosman. "He didn't have the same luck he had against the Braves, but he did a good job. Of course, there was some great defense out there, too, that helped out."

In a long season of personal struggle, Ryan had again come through when his team needed him most. The win was especially emotional for him because his dad was in the stands. Nolan Sr. was desperately ill with lung cancer, and it was the last time he ever saw his son pitch.

As the teams warmed up before Game 4, Baltimore pitcher Jim Hardin went up to Jerry Koosman on the field. "What are you guys doing here?" he sneered. "You don't belong on the same field with us!"

Koosman just shook his head. What games had Hardin been watching? The Mets were up 2–1 in the series, and their ace, Tom Seaver, was about to take the mound, though it was not exactly a serene time for the pitcher. Vietnam War protesters had been passing out fliers at Shea that featured an unauthorized photo of Seaver. When he objected to the use of his picture, the anti-war movement accused Seaver of being a tool of the Nixon Administration. Then New York mayor John Lindsay, a loud critic of American foreign policy in Southeast Asia, got into the act by ordering that the flag at Shea be flown at half-mast for Game 4 in honor of American soldiers killed in Vietnam. Baseball commissioner Bowie Kuhn, a staunch conservative, countermanded Lindsay's order, lest the 200 wounded soldiers at the stadium be offended.

The political kerfuffle notwithstanding, Seaver held the Orioles to one run in nine innings. But Baltimore hurler Mike Cuellar was equally sharp, and the game went into extra innings tied 1–1.

It ended abruptly in the 10th when Baltimore reliever Pete Richert fielded a bunt by pinch hitter J.C. Martin and his throw to first hit Martin in the back. The Birds accused Martin of running inside the baseline, and replays showed they had a legitimate gripe. But the first-base umpire missed the call, and after Rod Gaspar scored from second on the play, the Mets were just one win away from the most improbable world championship in the history of professional sports.

In Game 5, Baltimore tagged Jerry Koosman for three runs in the third on homers by pitcher Dave McNally and right fielder Frank Robinson. McNally was sharp on the mound, holding the Mets scoreless for five innings before controversy again reared its head. With nobody out in the sixth, McNally appeared to bounce a pitch off the foot of leadoff hitter Cleon Jones. While Baltimore manager Earl Weaver argued to the home-plate umpire that the ball had hit the ground, not Jones, the ball itself rolled into the Mets dugout and ended up under Koosman's seat.

"I picked up the ball," recalls Koosman, "and Gil [Hodges] says, 'Rub it on your shoe!' I did as instructed, and then handed the ball to Gil, and he took it out to the umpire, showed him the shoe polish, and the umpire gave Cleon first base."

The rattled McNally promptly gave up a two-run home run to Clendenon, and in the seventh a homer by unheralded Mets second baseman Al Weis tied it up. They went ahead in the eighth when Ron Swoboda doubled in Jones, and added another run when Swoboda scored on a miscue by Baltimore first baseman Boog Powell.

Koosman sealed it by pitching a scoreless ninth.

The New York Mets were the world champions of baseball. The story sent shock waves through the sports universe. There was a ticker-tape parade up Broadway, and the offers flooded in for TV appearances and other perks for the champs.

Orioles great Frank Robinson's memories of the Series are succinct.

"The Mets deserved to win, they did what they had to do," he recalls. "I still watch it on classic sports, and I still don't believe we lost.

"They got contributions from everybody, including the little guys, as we used to call them, and they also had some great pitching.

"That's all I got to say about '69."

In spite of his postseason contributions to the Mets' success, Nolan Ryan wanted no part of it. He reluctantly agreed to join his teammates to sing the old baseball chestnut, "You Gotta Have Heart," on *The Ed Sullivan Show*, but then put his foot down.

"They wanted him to join the others on this all-expense-paid cruise to the Caribbean," recalls Ruth. "I was all for it, but he said, 'Nope, I'm not giving up my off-season to go on a cruise with a bunch of people I don't know. I don't want to travel. I don't want to go anywhere. I just want to stay home in Texas.'"

With his share of the World Series money—not all that much, according to Ruth—Nolan bought 200 acres of land. "This is something I have always wanted," he told Ruth. "This is my chance."

4

Flustered in Flushing: 1970–71

> Nolan and I were from out in the country. We just weren't ready for the culture shock of New York.
>
> —JERRY KOOSMAN

> Nolan could throw the ball through a brick wall—provided he could hit the wall.
>
> —GIL HODGES

The last trip this author and his father took together was to Houston for the 1968 All-Star Game. He was 55, I was 12. Less than a year later, he lost a long battle with cancer. Texas was my last great memory of him.

We stayed at the Shamrock Hilton, same as the players. For three days I sat in the lobby as Willie Mays, Willie McCovey, and Pete Rose came by and posed for my dad's Honeywell Pentax and signed my postcards and baseballs. When I got home, baseball was as ingrained in me as Henry Aaron's signature on a Louisville Slugger. It owned my every waking hour.

A year later, I asked my mom if she and I could go back. God love her, she agreed, and the following August I was back at the Shamrock, where the defending world champion New York Mets were staying.

My goal was to cover a baseball with autographs from the team's key players. By the third day, the only signatures I didn't have were those of manager Gil Hodges and the hard-throwing hero of the 1969 postseason, Nolan Ryan.

I snagged Hodges that morning in the hotel drugstore. Actually, Mom did. She told him her son was a big fan and ran off to fetch me. I remember how my hand disappeared into his when I shook it, and that his eyes shined like the lights at Ebbets Field when he smiled.

"How are you doing, young man?" he boomed as he inscribed his name on the sweet spot of the ball.

"Fine, sir."

One more to go.

For three days I patrolled the hotel lobby, sat by the team bus, and waited by the Mets dugout at the ballpark. Not a sign of Ryan.

On the final day, I got up enough nerve to ask a player, "Where's Ryan?"

"Nolan doesn't stay at the hotel because he lives around here," he told me. "But he should be around today. It's getaway day."

"Do you have a room number for Nolan Ryan?" I asked the hotel concierge. "He's ... umm ... my cousin."

Just before entering the elevator, I decided that one more autograph would destroy my prize baseball's symmetry, and grabbed a notepad from a nearby desk.

When the door opened to my timid knock, the kindest face beamed at me as if Mrs. Nolan Ryan had been waiting for me to show up. She stepped aside, and all these years later I can still see Nolan sitting on a chair in a suit, all smiles himself.

"Come on in," he said in a thick Texas drawl, like he was welcoming an old pal.

He signed the notepad, I thanked him, and then floated back to the lobby.

Forty years after that first encounter with Nolan and Ruth Ryan, I am still awed by the basic human kindness they showed to a boy intruding on their precious time and space.

And I remember, too, how with baseball filling my days, the void left by my dad's death suddenly didn't seem quite as huge and bleak.

• • •

Based on Ryan's 1969 postseason performance, Gil Hodges figured that Nolan would really come into his own as the new season began. But while there were glimpses of greatness from Ryan in 1970—including a 15-strikeout one-hitter in his first appearance and two 13-strikeout games later—it ended up another disappointing season for him.

What hurt most, though, had nothing to do with baseball.

That summer, Nolan Ryan Sr. succumbed to lung cancer.

The impact his father had on Nolan Jr.'s life and career cannot be minimized.

"When he died, it put a very big void in my life," says Ryan. "I missed him a lot. There were times I wished I could pick up the phone and talk to him about things. He was a very big influence on me. As a kid I never wanted to disappoint my dad, and the way he lived and the influence he had on me I've tried to pass on to my kids, and hopefully they will pass it on to theirs."

Recalls George Pugh, "Mr. Ryan was a big guy, and because of his stature he demanded your respect. I worked the oilfields in the summer during college, and Mr. Ryan was my immediate supervisor. Whatever Mr. Ryan said, you said, 'Yes, sir,' and you did it. The thing he imparted to Nolan and his five siblings was you've got to work hard to get anything out of life. Nolan learned at an early age life is full of hard work, and that is probably a big reason he became a success."

Jeff Torborg, later Ryan's battery mate with the Angels, recalls a time in 1974 when he saw the effect Nolan Sr. had had on his son. Torborg had just been released by St. Louis. At the time, Yankee Stadium was being renovated, and the Yankees shared Shea Stadium with the Mets. Torborg lived on the East Coast and was in town to throw batting practice for the Angels. Ryan asked if he could warm him up in the bullpen and go over his mechanics. Torborg recalls that Ryan almost broke his hand with a few fastballs, but what happened later left an even more indelible memory.

"Nolan's dad had been very sick for a long time," recalls Torborg. "I think he was in a coma for an extended period of time. That day at Shea Stadium, we were in the shower when I mentioned to him that my dad was with me and was sitting out by my locker. When I said he had been diagnosed with lung cancer, Nolan just walked away from me.

"I thought, *God, what did I say?* Well, Nolan collected himself and came back a while later and said, 'Did you know that's what took my dad?" I said no, and he said, 'You have no idea what you're in for.'

"I still remember that comment. I knew how difficult it was for him, because he wanted to go home and see his dad, because they didn't know how long he was going to live.

"His family was one of the driving forces with Nolan. All of us have different experiences in our backgrounds that cause us to react in different ways. This is just my own opinion, but I got a feeling that Nolan's drive to succeed was driven in part by his love for his mom and dad and the difficult times they had working and supporting a family."

On the plane after the funeral, a dejected Nolan told Ruth he was thinking about throwing in the towel on his baseball career.

"I was so frustrated I wanted to quit," says Ryan. "I was disappointed when I didn't get to pitch, and then when I did, I was so wild that I wasn't effective. I had that military obligation and I didn't particularly care about living in New York, so out of frustration I thought I should be doing something else."

The death of his dad seemed like the final straw. But Ruth urged Nolan not to make any rash decisions. "If you quit now," she told him, "you'll always wonder what might have been. Let's try giving it a bit longer."

• • •

Joe Durso, the Mets beat reporter for *The New York Times*, recalls Ryan as "a shy, humble kid who didn't know how to handle the press. There were a lot of writers and broadcasters coming at him all the time. He was nice to them, but awed by them. On the mound he could throw hard, but he was unsure of himself. When he'd walk a guy, he'd sort of walk around with his head down. You hardly got the impression he was in charge out there."

Cincinnati's Pete Rose saw some similarities between Ryan and Sandy Koufax, and a couple big differences. "Their speed was the same, but Koufax threw strikes and he had confidence," says Rose. "But Nolan couldn't throw the friggin' ball over the plate. At the time he was just a big old country boy who threw hard.

"The Mets had Seaver, Koosman, Gentry, Selma, Matlack, and McAndrew. Nolan was in the bullpen, and if you're a set-up man in the late '60s in a bullpen with Tug McGraw, you're not making any money or glamour. You're just on the pitching staff—and that was Nolan Ryan."

"We had a young staff," said Jerry Koosman. "I was the oldest at 25. A lot of pitchers are wild when they're young, and in order to get to the big leagues you need to harness that. But Nolie had so much talent they brought him up early.

"Back then you were allowed to protect one guy on the roster, and [the Mets] didn't want to risk losing him, so he never got sent to the minors for the proper training."

Ryan pitched in just 27 games in 1970, going 7–11 with a 3.43 ERA and 125 strikeouts.

The struggles continued in 1971. Shuttling back and forth between military bases in Texas and New York City took a heavy toll on Ryan. He might strike out 16 batters in one game, but then be gone for a week because of his military commitment. When he pitched again, he'd get shelled. Gil Hodges wasn't especially interested in accommodating Ryan, and Nolan finished 10–14 that year, completing only three of his 26 starts.

Returning to New York from a road trip in September, Ryan accepted a ride home from GM Bob Scheffing and vented his frustration.

"I'm not happy with the way I'm pitching," Ryan said, "and under the circumstances maybe it would be best for all of us that you trade me if the opportunity arises. It would give me a new start, and maybe you can get something you need."

Nolan had already talked to Ruth about it. She was pregnant, and they both wanted out of New York City.

"He was frustrated, and he told me, 'I know that I am not coming back here. I know that the Mets are going to trade me. They have enough young pitchers. They don't like me, they don't need me, and I know in my heart that I won't be back. This may be the end of our baseball.'

"I knew if he didn't get traded he would probably quit. It was so bad that the night the season ended we threw our stuff in the car and left right after the game instead of waiting until the next morning."

Two months later, just before Nolan left for classes at Alvin Community College, he told Ruth, "Today is the last day of interleague trading. If I am going to be traded to the other league, it will happen today."

The call came that morning. "They said he was traded to California," recalls Ruth, "and Nolan said, 'Oh, the Dodgers?'

"And they said, 'No, the Angels.'"

Nobody was more surprised than Whitey Herzog, then director of player personnel for the Mets.

"I'll never forget it," says Herzog. "Bob Scheffing called me and asked me to call Leroy Stanton and tell him that we'd traded him to the Angels for [Jim] Fregosi. I thought that was the deal, not realizing that we were giving them Nolan Ryan, Francisco Estrada, and Don Rose along with Stanton. I said, 'Shit! I wouldn't trade Stanton for Fregosi. I like Stanton!'

"When I picked up the paper the next morning and discovered Nolan Ryan was in there too, I about threw up. From the day Nolan signed a contract he was the talk of the Mets organization. That second year, he had 272 strikeouts in less than 200 innings, and then he had 22 strikeouts this one game in Double A. I just couldn't believe we traded Nolan Ryan!

"I really think Dee Fondy, who worked in the front office, recommended the trade because Dee and Fregosi were very tight. I think Scheffing, Gil, and Rube felt Nolan wasn't going to do it in New York. I really felt that's how they thought about it. It's the only reason I could see for getting rid of him."

"That was the worst trade in the history of baseball," echoes Pete Rose.

Koosman blames the New York writers.

"The press was so on the Mets management about getting a long-ball-hitting third baseman that they traded Nolan Ryan for Fregosi, who was supposed to be that guy," he says. "That's why Nolan got traded—because Dick Young, Jack Lang, Maury Allen, and the rest of the press box boys were on the Mets so hard.

"I was sad and disappointed. You talk about potential! Certainly Nolan had that potential. When our rookie card came out, he and I were on the same one. We were both a little perturbed that we weren't good enough to have our own card. Who would have known that the guys on that card would win over 500 ballgames?"

Fact is, though, Ryan's stellar career path would likely not have occurred had he stayed in Flushing. His stats with the Mets tell a story of regression, not progress. When he was finally traded, Durso's report in *The New York Times* summed it up thusly: "The Mets finally gave up on Nolan Ryan's wandering fastball today."

Ryan himself says his erratic schedule was responsible for his problems in New York, not the venue itself.

"The New York media suggested that I didn't like being in New York and the pressures. It's true—I didn't like living in New York—but that wasn't a detrimental factor in my life and success there. The biggest problem was my military commitments. I was in and out all the time and not pitching on a regular basis. That all worked against me and is why I had so many control problems and didn't pitch a lot of innings.

"It's hard to say if things might've changed had I stayed there, because in 1972 I would have been without any kind of military obligation and so my schedule wouldn't have been interrupted every other weekend.

"The other thing is, I might not have had pitching coaches that had positive influences on me, like Tom Morgan did in Anaheim. Hodges and Walker were just different personalities and in different situations. Tom realized what I had to do to be consistent and he helped me get there. I'm not sure Rube and Gil would have ever been able to do that."

One other thing that is worth mentioning of Ryan's New York experience: Tom House, his future pitching coach in Texas, believed part of Nolan's longevity was the result of his light workload during his early days with the Mets, a light workload about which Ryan himself complained.

PART IV

The Altar of Speed: The California Angels: 1972–79

1

Breakout: 1972

Highway 10 can make you believe
You're leaving behind everything you don't need.

—SINGER-SONGWRITER AMILIA K. SPICER

The ordeal of the three-month voyage took its toll on Daniel Ryan. Huge swales had incessantly battered the ship, and he had found it hard to find his sea legs. Only when the tall vessel finally disengaged itself from the gray Atlantic into the calmer waters of the Savannah River did Daniel and his small congregation get relief from the relentless pounding.

Exhausted as he was, Daniel figured that whatever lay ahead could be no worse than what they had left behind. In Ireland, the "Great Frost" that devastated the countryside had made it impossible to farm. With no alternative way to make a living, Daniel and the others had to make a choice. The broadsides with which shipping companies blanketed Ireland raved about unlimited opportunities in the New World across the great sea. Eager to start new lives, the congregation pooled their meager savings and went for it.

If Daniel had one advantage over the rest, it was that he was stronger than two men. His thick bones and stout legs were perfect for the physical challenges ahead. His strongest characteristic wasn't his physicality, though, nor was it his industrious nature. His belief in divine providence guided him. His faith was so strong that when the town of Savannah finally came into view and the ship tied up to the dock that drizzly November day, Daniel Ryan felt no fear.

The America he reached in 1758 was bustling with rebellion. What the broadsides extolling the "Land of Liberty" neglected to point out was that the oppressive acts imposed on Ireland by the British Crown were in place there, too. The air was thick with revolution. Daniel was well aware that a place so filled with unrest was not for the meek. But he also knew that amid the turmoil lay boundless opportunity.

Within two years, he married Marguerite Butler of Georgia and secured land grants for 100 acres of prime farmland in St. John's Parish. Their first son, Isaac Milton—Nolan Ryan's great-great-great-grandfather—was born shortly thereafter.

Over the next 13 years the Ryans would have four more children. To support his burgeoning family, Daniel petitioned the Crown for several hundred additional acres. By 1775 he was wealthy and respected enough to represent St. Mary's District at Savannah's first provincial congress.

Daniel remained in Georgia until he died in 1780. His children, inheritors of their father's independent spirit, became pioneers in the new American territories of Mississippi and Louisiana. And like their father, they became farmers and planters.

• • •

For Nolan Ryan, 1972 marked the first time in his baseball career that he would not be going to Florida for spring training. The calm waterways of St. Petersburg and fishing with Tom Seaver and the boys were a thing of the past. Now, all roads pointed west.

As he and Ruth packed their 1968 red Chevy station wagon for the long trip, the early morning light imbued them with optimism about what lay ahead. Never again would he have to deal with the stoic indifference of Gil Hodges and Mets pitching coach Rube Walker, or the craziness of daily life in New York City.

The Ryans—including new baby Reid—headed west from Houston on Interstate 10 not to Palm Springs, California, as they'd first thought, but instead to someplace called Holtville, not far from the Mexican border.

It took Ruth a while to find it on the map, and when she did she told Nolan it was "just a tiny dot on the map, and there is nothing near it but desert."

The three-day trek took them through country that defined the word *monotonous*; Holtville itself wasn't much better. Cruising the main drag in search of the ballpark, the Ryans saw a sign featuring a large caricature of a rabbit and the message, WELCOME TO HOLTVILLE, CARROT CAPITAL OF THE WORLD!

Unless you were Bugs Bunny, Holtville had all of the amenities of a glorified truck stop. The biggest draw for the players was the neighboring border town of Mexicali, its all-night cantinas and friendly señoritas a magnet for one-night stands marinated in cheap tequila.

The Angels used Holtville as a three-week training base before heading north to begin the exhibition season in Palm Springs.

Turning down 5th Street, the Ryans found the baseball complex. A configuration of four diamonds with an observation tower looming over them, it looked more like a Soviet gulag than a big league training camp.

Next door, a refurbished barn called "Autry's Corral" was where the 100 or so players dressed and showered daily.

Ruth glanced at her husband and knew exactly what he was thinking: *What have I gotten us into?*

The next day, Nolan got another shock when general manager Harry Dalton told him that wives and children were not welcome at camp.

Determined to keep his family together, Nolan turned to the only person in the Golden State he could count on for help.

"I'm not leaving Ruth and Reid behind," he told his older sister Mary Lou. "I don't care what management says."

Seven years his senior, Mary Lou knew better than anyone her brother's strong family values. Being in such a remote outpost without Ruth and their baby was unthinkable.

An hour later, Mary Lou called back with a solution. She and her husband owned a small travel trailer. "It doesn't have any air-conditioning or heat, but it's yours if you want it," she told Nolan.

The next day, the trailer was delivered to the Holtville KOA Campground. Mary Lou's husband, Jackie, connected the water, and Mary Lou attached a small awning to provide a bit of life-saving shade.

The last thing Mary Lou heard as they drove away was four-month-old Reid screaming like a banshee. She could only wonder what was in store for the Ryans in such a God-forsaken place.

That spring the temperature in Holtville got up to 100 degrees during the day and dropped into the low 40s at night.

"It got so cold that after Nolan went to work out in the mornings I would just sit there and not go outside," says Ruth. "I didn't have a car or anything, so I would just lie around and take care of the baby all day until Nolan got back and tried fixing us some dinner. It was a crazy time, but we always had faith that we'd come out of it okay."

On top of the breakfast nook in the trailer was a roster with the names and phone numbers of Ryan's new teammates. Crunching his morning cereal that first day, Nolan surveyed the list: Sandy Alomar, Ken Berry, Leo Cardenas, Billy Cowan, Vada Pinson, Mickey Rivers, Lee Stanton, John Stephenson, Jeff Torborg...

Only the names of Alomar, Stanton, and Stephenson had more than passing familiarity to him. Ryan had played with Alomar briefly in Jacksonville. Stanton, of course, had been traded with him from the Mets. Stephenson was the catcher at Ryan's tryout in front of Yogi Berra back in high school, whose collarbone Nolan had injured with a wild fastball. As for the others, he'd faced Pinson and Cardenas when they were with Cincinnati, but the rest were American Leaguers he didn't know.

Breakfast done, Nolan looked in on his sleeping family, and his resolve to succeed intensified. He had requested a trade, a second chance in baseball, and he'd gotten it. With no college education or job experience, he had to make good or risk spending the rest of his life in a trailer just like the one he was in.

At the practice field a mile away, Nolan introduced himself to some new teammates and started to stretch when an elderly man in uniform, carrying an odd-looking ancient bat with a sawed-off barrel, intruded.

"Hey, kid, let me hit you a few."

Figuring the old codger was a coach and not wanting to ruffle any feathers on his first day, Ryan agreed and positioned himself in the infield for what he imagined would be a bit of lazy exercise.

But the old guy started whacking balls toward him faster than expected, sending another one his way before Ryan had even gloved the previous one and tossed it back.

Crack!

Crack!

"A couple more to your left now," warned the old-timer.

Crack!

"Bet you a Coke you don't get this one!"

Crack!

"Double or nothing…"

After 20 minutes, Ryan's sweat and competitive juices were flowing, and he decided that if the old guy wasn't going to stop, neither would he. It was a contest he had no chance of winning, though, because when it came to fungo hitting, no one outlasted Jimmie Reese.

Crack! Crack! Crack!

After 45 minutes, Nolan had the same queasy feeling he got after eating too many soft-serve cones at Alvin's Dairy Land. Then someone yelled, "Nolan Ryan! Get your butt over here! Let's hope you're a better pitcher than a second baseman!"

"That Reese giving you the treatment?" asked pitching coach Tom Morgan when Ryan joined him, trying not to appear as out of breath as he felt. "Next time, when you've had enough just tell him. Sometimes he gets carried away."

Jimmie Reese, whose birth handle was James Herman Solomon, was a virtual walking baseball museum. Now 70, he had played, coached, scouted, or managed for over six decades. A star in the Pacific Coast League in the 1920s, he later played for the Yankees and roomed with Babe Ruth. Along the line he had perfected the art of fungo hitting.

His real skill, though, was communicating. Reese didn't have a mean bone in his body, and Nolan, like everyone else, was quickly won over by the old man's charm and kindness.

Tom Morgan was slow and gruff. Using knowledge gained as a pitcher with several teams in the 1950s and '60s, the loud "Plowboy" was the perfect mentor for the low-key Ryan. Arms crossed and face stern, Morgan would become a fixture on the sideline whenever Nolan pitched.

Just hours after putting his California Angels jersey on for the first time, Nolan had met the two men who would transform him from a frustrated, undisciplined fireballer into one of baseball's best.

"Your ball's sailing up and in!" Morgan would critique during a typical bullpen session. "Try slowing it down!"

"You need to be more efficient and compact your delivery."

"Your head's moving too much toward first after you release."

"You're opening up too soon. Keep your body straight."

"Better... now do it again!"

"Again!"

"Again!"

And again and again and again.

Meanwhile, Ruth fought off the heat and bugs and desert dust back at the trailer as best as she could. Worst of all was the monotony. With no car, she was stuck in the trailer park all day. Since it was hotter inside than out, she and Reid sat in a lawn chair most of the time and every few minutes moved it to stay in the awning's shadow. For excitement, she watched scorpions and other desert creatures crawl around on the hot gravel and wondered what Nolan would bring home for supper.

After practice the next day, Nolan and three other pitchers ran from foul pole to foul pole in the outfield to improve their endurance. The mercury had topped 100 degrees, and after two guys dropped out, Clyde Wright quit too and invited Ryan to join the rest of the guys at the local watering hole for some cold liquid refreshment.

Tempting as that sounded, Nolan declined.

"Come on down to Texas, Clyde, you'll see what hot is really like," he said with a friendly wave before resuming his sprinting.

With Wright's departure, the field was entirely his. Even fungo machine Jimmie Reese was gone. Running his umpteenth lap, Ryan finally noticed someone watching from the bleachers and then recalled his appointment with reporter Ross Newhan of the *Los Angeles Times*. He stopped running and joined Newhan in the stands, and then for more than an hour poured out all his frustrations.

"I've been here only two days and Tom Morgan has already talked with me almost as much as Walker and Hodges did all last year," Ryan told Newhan. "The Angels brought me here to be a starting pitcher, and I know I'm going to have to prove to them I can do the job."

He talked about pickle brine, and how his military commitments made it hard to find any kind of rhythm. Newhan was struck by the young man's honesty and humility.

"For someone coming out of the New York environment, I found him to be a down-to-earth guy without a lot of attitude." Newhan recalls. "As a Met, he felt there had been opportunities for him to step up on a full-time basis, but it never really happened. And after three or four years of being on the fringe, he was ready for a fresh start."

Newhan had already talked to Tom Morgan. "I've given Nolan some of my ideas and he has given me some of his," said the pitching coach. "We think we've already detected a little thing in his motion that may have contributed to his wildness."

Verbalizing his thoughts to Newhan was liberating and invigorating, and after the interview Ryan started a new series of sprints and plowed ahead until dusk. After showering, he picked up groceries and arrived back at the trailer in time to put Reid to bed, already looking forward to starting the process anew in the morning. Each day was another chance to improve, another opportunity to show his stuff, and, more important than anything, deliver himself and his family out of the wilderness.

For all that, Ryan's first performance as an Angel on March 5 was hardly Koufaxesque. He threw three innings in an intrasquad game and allowed three runs on as many hits.

Morgan recruited veteran catcher Jeff Torborg to solve the mystery, and in their first workout together Torborg noticed immediately the immense effort Ryan made while throwing. His face contorted into a grimace before each pitch—a sure sign he was trying too hard and overthrowing. It was a problem similar to the one Koufax had in his early years with the Dodgers.

"You don't have to work so hard to get the ball to the plate," Torborg advised Ryan.

"I thought that's what accounts for my speed," Nolan responded somewhat sarcastically.

"No. You're rushing your motion and overthrowing. Try taking something off."

Not throwing so hard seemed unthinkable, but Torborg seemed so sure that Ryan relaxed his grip on the ball and took something off his pitch. The result was stunning—not only was it a strike, but the ball's movement was significantly more pronounced.

What other tricks does this Torborg have up his sleeve? wondered Ryan.

A lot more, as it turned out. As a rookie with the Dodgers in the mid-1960s, Torborg was schooled in the art of pitching by both Koufax and Don Drysdale. He snatched up their pearls of wisdom, giving the Dartmouth grad insights into pitching no catcher his age could match.

"Where do you want me to sit?" he'd asked Koufax.

"Sit in the middle of the plate," was the pitcher's response. "When I start hitting your glove, then we can start moving to the corners."

Torborg discovered other flaws in Ryan's delivery, including his habit of opening up his body too soon before releasing, which forced the ball in on right-handed hitters.

"Jeff could see my body flying open, but he really didn't know how to correct it," Nolan remembers. "I knew I had to stay on line, but I didn't have the knowledge of how to do it consistently. We'd keep talking about it and keep trying to correct it, and that's how we eventually fixed it."

On March 10, 1972, Nolan took his big league hopes 200 miles north to Palm Springs and the start of the Angels' exhibition season. Although the desert oasis was a big step up from Holtville, his control problems didn't improve overnight, and with three other pitchers vying for the remaining starting slots, the stress was taking a toll on him.

To make it even tougher, the ban on wives and families remained in effect, and Ruth and Reid headed to Anaheim to stay in the house they'd rented for the season.

In his exhibition debut against the Cubs on March 13, Nolan pitched three innings and allowed five runs on four hits, with five walks. Against Oakland five days later, he gave up four runs, walked six, hit a batter, and threw two wild pitches.

There was a glimmer of things to come on March 26, when in six innings against Cleveland he struck out six, walked three, and allowed only one run. But then he took a giant step back in his last outing of the spring against San Francisco, giving up four runs and igniting a major brawl by beaning two batters.

Afterward, he wondered if the struggle was really worth it. If he couldn't crack the starting staff on a rebuilding club like the Angels, what chance would he have anywhere else?

There'd be no extra running with Jimmie Reese that day—Ryan just wanted to get out of there. He dressed, slipped out the back door, and headed for his car. Almost instantly a horde of young autograph hounds surrounded him and thrust their pens and scraps of paper at him. He signed until reaching the safety of his car, an ancient VW bug with a cracked windshield, a loaner from a friend of Mary Lou's.

The drive to Anaheim was 90 miles. "I always admired him for doing the commute," says Ruth. "He didn't have to, but the Angels wouldn't allow players' wives and children at the team's hotel. He felt that spring training would be the only time he could see his son at night."

Near Banning on Interstate 10, Ryan flipped on KLAC, Los Angeles' only country music station. But static garbled the reception. Somewhere near Beaumont, the signal improved and the lush baritone of Merle Haggard's "Carolyn" flowed through the Bug's little speaker. Cramming his big legs against the wheel, Ryan felt like a sardine. To keep his mind fresh, he reviewed the day's game and the pitches he threw—the curveball to McCovey, the fastball to Mays.

Why can't I pitch two good games in a row? Why does everything go smooth when I work in the bullpen, but when I get into the actual games it all falls apart?

Nearing Riverside, he reviewed his mechanics yet again—his motion and leg kick, his release and follow-through.

Passing Corona, Donna Fargo started singing "I'm the Happiest Girl in the Whole USA." Tammy Wynette followed with a soothing "Bedtime Story." But it didn't help.

The sign ahead said YORBA LINDA, and the increased traffic flow told him he was close to home. Within the hour he'd be back to Ruth and Reid and a few precious hours of domestic bliss. Then in the morning, back to the grind.

Though he was discouraged, changes were occurring in his delivery that looked promising. Despite the inconsistencies, Morgan was able to get him into a rhythm he'd never felt before.

Nolan recognized the changes in his approach and liked them, and in his mind it was only a matter of time before he put it all together. But how much time did he have, especially since looming on the horizon like a menacing storm was baseball's first players strike?

Deciding to test the owners' resolve on the reserve clause, Major League Baseball Players Association representative Marvin Miller had just announced that the players would go on strike on March 31 if a settlement wasn't reached.

For Nolan, the move couldn't have come at a worse time. A day before the team was scheduled to break camp, manager Del Rice penciled in Clyde Wright and Andy Messersmith as his top two starters. The other two starting spots were a toss-up between Rudy May, Tom Murphy, Alan Foster, Rickey Clark, and Ryan.

"Stick with him a little longer," Morgan urged the skipper over dinner. "He's close."

"I don't know, Tom, he hasn't shown me much."

"Stay with him, Del," said Morgan firmly. "I think he's on the cusp of something big."

Rice knew his old battery mate from the 1961 original Angels didn't mince words. He was also aware that GM Harry Dalton expected big things from Ryan.

Later that night, after countless Chesterfields, Rice penciled Ryan in as the fourth starter and then reached for the Maalox.

The next day, the team voted 34–0 in support of a walkout.

Despite the most bitter split between players and owners in the game's 102-year history, the mood at the 15th annual Baseball Awards Dinner in Los Angeles on April 7 was congenial.

"Nolan has to be delighted," quipped Dalton. "This is the first strike he's been involved with all spring."

Ryan laughed through gritted teeth. How long the strike would last was anyone's guess, and the Ryans couldn't hang on indefinitely in their financial state. With the season in limbo, Nolan returned to Anaheim to hunker down with Ruth and Reid in their modest rental and await the outcome.

Once the strike was official, the big league facilities at Anaheim Stadium were closed to the players. To stay in shape, Nolan and some teammates who lived around Anaheim decided to find a place to work out.

Boysen Park was typical of the city parks that dotted Anaheim's middle-class landscape in 1972, with one exception: next to the swing set, cement airplane, and tennis courts was a regulation baseball diamond used by local high schools.

With pitcher Clyde Wright's nearby garage serving as a dressing room, players used the park for batting practice and intrasquad games. Since coaches were banned, it was the players' responsibility to run the workouts.

For lucky local fans, the park became a field of dreams. Sitting on blankets just a few yards from the players, they could watch their team practice and play in an informal setting.

The trouble for Ryan was that without Morgan looking over his shoulder, he was in danger of falling back into his old habits.

Luckily, catcher Jeff Torborg was more than willing to carry the conditioning torch, and on a nondescript pitcher's mound in a public park, Ryan started finding his groove.

Practicing as much as possible, the pair stayed long after the other players had left, refining and re-tooling Ryan's mechanics as Morgan had preached. One of Ryan's biggest problems was a tendency to take his left leg back past the rubber, which made him open up his front leg too much and overthrow.

"When Nolie overthrew, he was wild up and in on right-handers, which would generally send them flying with their heads going one direction and their helmets another," Torborg recalls. "All we were trying to do was to get him to stop opening up too soon, get behind the ball, and drive it down and away from right-handed hitters."

The surface around home plate was uneven, which made balls thrown into the hard dirt ricochet unpredictably. With a fireballer like Ryan shooting wild bullets his way, Torborg always had to be on his toes.

"When you have the lip of the plate sticking up and the mound isn't the greatest, a simple bounce off the dirt can be dangerous, and he almost killed me more than once," says Torborg.

His sacrifice meant a lot to Ryan.

"Those two weeks were very important to me," Nolan remembers. "That park is where I really started to figure things out. Jeff could see my problems clearer, because he was a catcher and could point things out to me from a different point of view."

What wasn't improving as the strike wore on was Ryan's bank account.

One afternoon when Ruth drove to the park to get some fresh air and pick him up, Nolan hit her with a bombshell.

"If the strike doesn't end soon, we'll have to go back home so I can get a job somewhere."

"Okay," she said after a short pause. "I think you have the talent to do this, but you have to be your own cheerleader and not listen to your critics. You've got something special, you've got an opportunity here, and you've got a few people finally believing in you. Maybe we could borrow some money and give this a little more time."

Ryan didn't speak again until they pulled into the driveway. "A couple more days," he said. "And that's it."

"We were going to give ourselves maybe another week," recalls Ruth. "Then, through a banker friend in Alvin, Nolan borrowed $600 against his tax return. Two days later the strike ended. Nolan stuck it out, and we were awfully glad he did."

• • •

Seated in front of his Anaheim Stadium locker, Ryan was anxious. It had been 24 days since his last spring training start, and even though he worked out regularly with Torborg during the strike, nothing was more nerve-wracking than getting ready to pitch your first game for a new team.

For his Angels debut he drew the Minnesota Twins, champions of the Western Division in 1969 and 1970. Checking their lineup card he spotted the name of Rod Carew, a past and future American League batting champion and one of the most dangerous hitters in the major leagues.

"Hey, Art," Nolan asked starting catcher Art Kusnyer, "how do you pitch Carew?"

"Just throw something around the plate and pray he doesn't hit a double," Kusnyer replied. "The SOB hits everything. He can't always get around on the high heat, but anything else—forget it!"

With temperatures hovering in the low 60s, Ryan started stretching to get loose. On chilly nights a pitcher has a distinct advantage over the guys he faces; hitters don't relish being jammed by fastballs when it's cold. Midway through his routine, Tom Morgan put a new ball in the pocket of Ryan's Wilson A2000 glove, and a minute later they headed to the bullpen to finish warming up. Nolan glanced at the stands behind home plate. Ruth was there somewhere.

The bullpen session went well. After several days of rest, his fastball was popping and his rhythm and timing were in synch. The first Twins batter, Cesar Tovar, couldn't get around on a heater and managed a weak pop-up to Jim Spencer at first.

After Danny Thompson struck out, the feared Carew came to the plate.

Ryan's first pitch started slow, and then a few feet from the plate it exploded like a rocket up into the strike zone. Carew didn't even flinch. Two similar pitches later he walked back to the dugout, shaking his head as though he'd seen an apparition.

The first inning was a template for the whole game. The Twins hitters were overmatched, and by the ninth inning the remaining 5,000 or so fans sensed they had witnessed the start of something special. When the last pitch was thrown, Ryan had shut out the Twins, allowing only four hits, striking out 10, and walking five.

"I was probably more nervous prior to this start than any in several years," a relieved Ryan told reporters afterward. "I knew how important it was both for my confidence and the club's confidence in me."

In the Twins clubhouse, Rod Carew brooded about his three strikeouts. He'd faced hard throwers before, guys like Sam McDowell, Jim Palmer, and Mickey Lolich—but nothing like this. He just couldn't get around on Ryan's high heat.

How can you hit what you can't see?

In time, he would reconfigure his batting stance to accommodate Ryan's fastball. But for now all he could do was shake his head.

That's what Ryan did after his next outing, in Texas on April 23. He was rocked for five runs before exiting the game in the third inning.

At Baltimore the following week he was again yanked in the third, and watched from the bench as the Birds humiliated the Angels 12–2.

It was time for another Maalox moment for Del Rice.

"I'm going to have to put you in the bullpen, Nolan," Rice told Ryan. "Maybe you'll come around there. I just can't go with you as starter. I can't afford it the way the team is going."

Ryan didn't argue with him, but Tom Morgan did. He got Rice to agree to keep Nolan as a starter on the promise they would move heaven and earth to solve Ryan's problems.

From April 29 to May 5, the sharp echoes of Ryan's fastball popping leather was heard before games in stadiums around the league. Even during a May 3 rain delay in New York, Ryan and Morgan worked for 20 minutes beneath the stands.

"You're still pulling off, Nolie," Morgan said. "Keep your body straight and your follow-through down." To help him get the message, Morgan stood in front of and just a bit to Ryan's side, forcing him to keep his body straight after a pitch.

"It was exhausting, mechanical work, even boring at times," Ryan recalls. "But those days turned my career around. To accomplish anything in life you need faith and you sometimes need help. I got the faith from the help they gave me, and it finally started to pay off."

In front of a May 5 "Bat Night" crowd of 20,061 against Milwaukee, Ryan shut out the Brewers on three hits and stuck out 14. In his next start facing Boston five days later, he retired the first 13 batters before a groin strain forced him out of the game.

"All I can do is hope it doesn't take me out of the rotation, that it doesn't cost me my rhythm," he told reporters afterward.

He was back on the mound May 15, against the Oakland A's. But his injury flared up and he exited early again. Ryan didn't toe the mark again until May 22, in Oakland. He lost, but his fastball made a lasting impression on one A's hitter.

"He's faster than instant coffee," Reggie Jackson told reporters after the game. "I've never been afraid at the plate, but Mr. Ryan makes me uncomfortable. He's the only pitcher who's ever made me consider wearing a helmet with ear-flaps. When he finally becomes a complete pitcher and learns to hit spots consistently, there will be no way to hit him."

But that time was still a ways off. On May 26 against Kansas City, Ryan threw 130 pitches over 5⅔ innings, walking nine but giving up no runs. The Angels still won, but after that the team fell into a prolonged slump. Not even the arrival of power-hitting first baseman Bob Oliver from Kansas City could ignite the sputtering Angels offense. The starting pitchers didn't fare much better, especially after ace Andy Messersmith went on the disabled list.

Through it all, Rice assured Ryan that he'd stick with him, giving the pitcher the confidence to plow ahead. Nolan's quest to succeed and desire to find new ways to improve would take him to some strange places; had management known what he was thinking and doing, they might have changed their minds and shipped him off permanently.

• • •

Clad in running shorts and sneakers, Nolan peered out of the training room door into the tunnel behind the Angels clubhouse. Seeing no one, he slipped out and headed toward the visiting clubhouse. After a few steps he veered left and made his way down a dark, narrow passageway with just the dim light from a distant laundry room window to guide him. Stopping at a door that could be easily missed if one didn't know it was there, he glanced around to make sure he wasn't being followed before turning the large doorknob and letting himself in.

He flipped on the light in the concrete cave that was empty except for a steely apparatus in its center and, next to the contraption, a bench and stool whose bright-red plastic coverings seemed out of place in such a drab environment.

Ever since a Muscle Beach enthusiast invented the four-station Universal Gym in 1957, it had been a staple of conditioning for athletes worldwide except for baseball players, who shunned it due to the widely held belief that lifting weights caused bound-up muscles and tightness.

Ryan didn't believe that. Defying conventional wisdom and experimenting on the sly, he incorporated the Universal Gym into his training routine, doing three sets of 10 reps on the bench press, military press, lateral press, and the curling bar.

Most of his time was devoted to the leg press apparatus, having discovered that it was his legs that powered his irrepressible right arm.

"I just happened to stumble into it," Ryan recalls. "I had some time on my hands and was checking out some of the rooms in that tunnel and found it. So I asked trainer Freddie Frederico about it."

Frederico told him the Universal Gym belonged to the local Continental football team, which had left it behind when the team moved.

Ryan didn't tell Frederico that he had started using the contraption himself, but Freddie noticed him once heading for the room and asked what he was up to. When Ryan confessed that he had been "piddling with that machine," the trainer looked at him oddly and said, "Well, don't let anybody know you're doing it."

Nolan didn't. And suddenly he was pitching longer into games and, unlike most pitchers, he got stronger the more innings he pitched.

"The weights gave me stamina," Ryan says. "I was bouncing back from starts quicker and able to complete a lot of games. It all came from the amount of time I spent lifting weights and taking fungos with Jimmie Reese. The weights made a huge contribution to my game and career."

Ryan's curiosity and willingness to venture out on his own brought conditioning for baseball players—especially pitchers—into the 20th century. In time, every major league clubhouse would have a weight room.

Acknowledgement of his pioneering efforts would come years later. For now, the weight room remained Ryan and Frederico's little secret.

His transformation into the quintessential Nolan Ryan began in Anaheim on May 30, when he shut out the White Sox 6–0, allowing seven hits and collecting 10 strikeouts.

In June he went 4–1, with two three-hitters and a two-hitter, and never gave up more than seven hits in any of his eight starts.

He began July by manhandling the A's with a career-high 16 Ks. In Anaheim on July 5 he shut out Milwaukee 1–0 for his fourth consecutive win.

"Ryan is half a plate away from becoming a superstar," quipped Angels coach and former Dodgers catcher John Roseboro. "I've only seen him from the sidelines, so I can't compare his fastball to Sandy [Koufax]'s, but he scares batters in a manner Sandy didn't, simply because Koufax never threw close to a batter."

Roseboro also noticed that Ryan's personas on and off the field were polar opposites. In street clothes, he was a gentleman. When his work clothes went on, it was a different story.

"Off the field he's a very easy-going guy," said Roseboro. "Very quiet, likes to hunt and fish. He's mean, though. Baby-faced, but mean. Guys on other teams have been known to yell at him from the bench, 'Get that garbage over!' and so on. But if Nolan really gets mad, he'll deck somebody. They've got to be pretty stupid, ridiculing a guy who can throw 120 miles per hour."

Ryan's reputation as a fastball pitcher who wasn't afraid to use the inside part of the plate quickly became the talk of the league.

"It was 1972, my first full year, and we were facing this guy named Nolan Ryan who only a few of us knew much about," recalls Bobby Grich of the Orioles. "We had heard stories about his velocity, but as far as we knew he was just this hard-throwing pitcher the Angels got in a trade with the Mets for Jim Fregosi.

"So we're facing him for the first time, and I'm batting second. One of the things I could do pretty well was hit the ball to right field. So when he threw a fastball on the outside corner, I leaned out and hit the ball down the right-field line right at the foul pole. I'm running down to first base, yelling 'Stay fair! Stay fair!' But at the last second the ball sliced foul.

"By the time I made the turn and was trotting back to home, Nolan had already gotten, another ball from the umpire and had walked halfway from the mound to first base. He had his glove under his right arm and was rubbing the ball with both hands and just staring at me like he was thinking, *Ah-ha!*

"I didn't get it. I'd just hit a foul ball down the right-field line—so what? So I get back in the box and the next pitch he throws is a 98-mph fastball right at my head! I went down quick.

"That really woke me up. I was like, *My god, this guy is serious!*

"So now I'm really mad. Veins are popping out of my neck, and sometimes when I get tense I try to swing harder and actually swing slower. And that's what I did. I was trying to hit the ball 500 feet, and when the next pitch was a bit up and in, I jammed myself and hit a weak pop-up to the shortstop.

"It was the only time in my life I didn't run out a ball. I just turned and walked back to the dugout. I was so mad [manager Earl] Weaver didn't even say a word to me.

"*I'm going to get that son of a bitch next time!* I told myself. But my next two times up he threw fastballs right by me. Ryan struck me out twice and there was nothing I could do about it. I was as intense, energized, and as focused as I could possibly be, but I couldn't hit him. He just blew me away."

Ryan does not apologize for his aggressiveness on the mound.

"I grew up in an era where you established that you would pitch inside and protected your teammates," he explains. "A hitter had to decide what part of the plate was his, the inside or the outside. But he didn't get both sides."

The outside corner was where Ryan would make his living and do the most damage. He did this by establishing that he would throw inside, which got the hitter thinking twice about reaching for a ball outside.

On July 9, *Los Angeles Times* columnist Jim Murray wrote a column titled, "Nolan Ryan: Coiled to Strike…Thanks to Snake Oil." It was replete with Murray's Pulitzer Prize–winning humor:

> "His most reliable pitch was ball four, and in a pinch he could always throw it."
>
> "Nolan Ryan could walk the Empire State Building."
>
> "He had a wide assortment of pitches. Ball one, ball two, ball three, wild, and ouch!"

Murray's widely read column announced to the world that Nolan Ryan had finally arrived, and that same night at the Big A, Ryan made Murray look like a savant by tossing his finest game to date.

Following a first-inning walk to Tommy Harper and a base hit by Carl Yastrzemski, he retired the final 26 Red Sox batters in a row. He struck out eight straight Boston hitters in the first three innings, three of them on nine consecutive pitches, an American League record.

"I had more confidence today than I ever had," Ryan told reporters after the game. "I have a feeling now that I can throw to spots, and today I got 80 percent of my pitches where I wanted them."

"Sending a batter against Nolan Ryan in the twilight is the same as capital punishment," quipped Red Sox manager Eddie Kasko. "I may appeal to the Supreme Court."

Nolan had now pitched five complete games in a row, allowing just five runs, striking out 57, and walking only 17. His record was 11–5 and his ERA 2.30, a whole run and a half better than the previous year. He also led the league in strikeouts.

Los Angeles Times beat reporter Ross Newhan—the only reporter who wanted to talk to Ryan back in spring training—now had trouble getting to see him alone. He finally caught up with the pitcher on July 13.

The interview resulted in a column titled "Leg Man," in which Newhan wrote about conditioning and how different pitchers developed their speed. "A man whose arm may put him in the Hall of Fame says his legs are the primary source of his celebrated speed," Newhan wrote.

What Ryan didn't tell him was that it was more than running that kept his legs in top working order.

At the All-Star break, Ryan was 11–8 with a 3.14 ERA, and led the league in strikeouts. Baltimore manager Earl Weaver acknowledged his outstanding work by naming Ryan to the AL's All-Star Game roster.

For the first time in his career, Ryan felt 20 wins were within his grasp. That would quiet the remaining critics and prove he could be consistent and wasn't just a one-pitch wonder.

The biggest remaining doubter was Nolan himself. In his own mind he still didn't have full control of his pitches, and it seemed there were two walks and a wild pitch for every strikeout or shutout.

Three losses on the road surrounding the All-Star break shook his confidence further. In those three starts, he allowed 18 runs and 19 hits in 18⅓ innings. Ryan didn't get back on track until July 27, when he flirted with a no-hitter for 7⅔ innings in a 5–0 win over Texas, his sixth shutout of the year.

In his next outing, against Kansas City, Nolan kept the opposition hitless until the eighth, when leadoff batter Steve Hovley whacked a clean base hit to center. The Royals' lone run came in bizarre fashion when Amos Otis, after taking third base on a wild pickoff attempt in the fourth inning, stole home. It was all they needed against the hapless Angels offense, and Ryan lost the game 1–0.

In a "Talk of the Town" piece the next day in the *Times,* John Hall wrote what many were feeling:

> A routine home stand closeout against Kansas City Monday night found a surprising healthy 10,344 in the seats… Club officials felt that at least 5,000 extra showed up because Nolan Ryan was on the mound… It's not exactly Sandy Koufax stuff yet, but it may be coming… As with Sandy in his dazzle days at Dodger Stadium, you get the feeling quiet Nolan Ryan is about to set a strikeout record or pitch a no-hitter every time he picks up his lunch pail and goes to work.

• • •

As a teenager, this author's goal was to attend as many baseball games as possible. Now it seems strange that my mom let me travel by bus or go with a friend to Anaheim and Dodger Stadium after school, but that's what I wanted, and Mom, doing her best to fill in for Dad, indulged me.

For my 15th birthday I got a new MacGregor Willie Mays model glove to use in winter league at Palisades High School. It had open webbing and presoftened leather, and it was made in the USA.

By the fall of 1972 it was obvious Nolan Ryan was going to be the Angels' first legitimate superstar. I'd already gotten his autograph several times, but one afternoon before a game I worked my way through the band of autograph seekers, thrust my MacGregor glove at him, and said, "Please sign the thumb." He smiled and carefully penned his name on the fresh leather. I remember staring hopefully at the glove at practice the next day, as if the signature might elevate my performance.

A week later I was back at Anaheim Stadium, waiting alone for autographs, when Ryan's familiar red station wagon approached the Gate 5 parking area. I was startled when he honked his horn and waved in my direction.

Why would Nolan Ryan notice *me*?

I thought about chasing him down for another autograph, but suddenly that didn't seem so important anymore.

The rest of the afternoon I wondered why Ryan had honked at me and why I didn't chase him down. I came to the conclusion that his greeting was far more satisfying than his signature. A name scribbled on a ball or glove only led to a need for more. A honk and a wave—that was in a whole different league!

I realized players had become a target for material gain and hero worship. At age 15, Ryan's kind gesture helped me to understand that by putting players on pedestals, I diminished both them and myself. For the rest of the game I wondered if the feeling was momentary or had legs. As the months passed and Ryan's name faded from my glove, I didn't seem to mind.

Amazing, what a honk and a wave can do…

• • •

Ryan's streak of 33 consecutive scoreless innings ended in Oakland on September 4. With a month to go, two milestones awaited: 300 strikeouts and 20 wins.

"The next two weeks are the critical period," said Ryan as he stood at 16 wins. "If you have 18 or 19 wins by then, you have a good shot at it. But if you lose a game, you lose eight days. But things have turned around here lately. The team's getting me more runs."

Ryan spoke too soon. The offense reverted to form in his next three games, scoring only one run. He lost them all.

A squeaker in Kansas City on the September 21 broke the losing streak, putting Ryan three wins away from his goal.

Number 18 came four days later when Ryan three-hit the Rangers in a 2–1 game. He finished with 12 strikeouts, putting him over the 300 mark.

Ryan needed to win his last two starts for the magical 20. Number 19 came on September 30 when he stopped Minnesota 3–2, with a personal-high 17 strikeouts.

But in his 39th and last start of the season, against Oakland at home on October 5, the Angels offense took the night off again and he finished at 19–16.

However, his 10 strikeouts gave him a whopping 329 for the season, the fourth-highest total in modern baseball history.

"Until this year, I never really had a whole lot of confidence in myself," Nolan told reporters after the game. "What happened this year should mean a great deal to my future. I think I can go right on."

It was an incredible year for Ryan. Not only did he lead the league in strikeouts and shutouts (nine), but his 284 innings pitched were sixth best, his 2.28 ERA was seventh best, and his 5.26 hits per nine innings was the lowest rate in baseball. He also led in walks (157) and wild pitches (18).

Thanks to his diligent workouts with Reese and Morgan, plus his subterranean weight training, he actually gained strength and endurance in August and September, when most pitchers wear down.

Of his 39 starts in 1972, 20 were complete games, and nine of those were shutouts. All told, he threw about 5,000 pitches.

"There were two reasons I threw as many pitches as I did then," Ryan says. "The first was my control, and the second was that because I was a fastball pitcher who pitched up in the strike zone quite a bit, I got a lot of balls fouled off.

"I would have good games, but then I might start overthrowing again and end up walking a lot of people.

"Another reason I was successful that season was I finally got into a rotation where I could pitch on a regular basis and feel like I had a chance to turn things around and have a productive career."

To think he'd actually considered packing it in before the season even started.

Says Ryan's pal Whitey Herzog, "The best thing that ever happened to Nolan Ryan was when they traded him to Anaheim. Nolan was a laid-back Texas kid, a wonderful young man, married to that wonderful wife. But a lot of young people can't play in New York, and it just didn't pan out for him there.

"But when he went to Anaheim—and at that time pitching in Anaheim was like pitching in a graveyard with lights—he became something to talk about. It was just the perfect place to get his career to take off."

2

Countdown: 1973

> One of the beautiful things about baseball is that once in a while you come into a situation where you want to—and have to—reach down and prove something.
>
> —NOLAN RYAN

Perseverance is rooted in the belief that discipline, hard work, patience, faith, and time will overcome all obstacles. It exemplifies Nolan Ryan to a tee.

His work ethic is a product of his perseverance, and the major credit for it goes to his Depression-era parents, who instilled in him the belief that work was a privilege.

Perseverance is also the result of a lifetime of good habits. For Ryan, those habits began at an early age in downtown Alvin, near the old Sinclair Station at the corner of Gordon and Sealy.

From ages eight to 18, Nolan and his dad wrapped newspapers from 3:00 AM to 6:00 AM, seven mornings a week. After going home for a brief nap, Nolan went to school, where he lettered in two sports. For most kids, that kind of workload would have been impossible. But for Ryan, it laid the foundation for his impeccable work habits.

There were additional lessons learned on the corner of Sealy and Gordon. Extra newspapers needed to be thrown away, but the nearest dumpster was in an alley where drunks lingered. Preferring not to be hassled by a wino, Ryan tossed the surplus papers onto the gas station roof instead. After it rained steadily for a week, the weight of the waterlogged papers caused the roof to cave in. Nolan had to work a long time to pay for that mistake, but he learned the valuable lesson of not cutting corners.

• • •

Manager Del Rice didn't survive 1972. Lackluster leadership and a fifth-place finish didn't cut it with Angels GM Harry Dalton, and Rice was replaced by third-base coach Bobby Winkles.

In truth, Dalton had been grooming Winkles for the job for a year. As Arizona State's head baseball coach, Winkles had built a mini-dynasty that paved the way for Sal Bando, Rick Monday, Reggie Jackson, Gary Gentry, and a slew of others into the majors.

Dalton hoped the three-time collegiate champion would infuse the Angels with his rah-rah spirit.

Winkles had some interesting concepts, including shortening the games by having players run everywhere, a concept that didn't get much traction. A few younger players went along, but Winkles' theories and incessant cheerleading irked the vets—especially Frank Robinson, who the Angels had acquired in a trade with the Dodgers. The former two-time MVP at Baltimore believed he was more qualified to manage a professional team than Winkles, who had never played a day in the majors. In time, Robinson's resentment came full boil and caused dissension. But for now he just bided his time and only ran when he felt like it.

To Winkles' credit, many of his innovations stuck. Every time a pitcher runs to and from the bullpen or back to the bench, it's thanks to him. Credit him, too, for helping to bring stretching into the major league mainstream.

As for Nolan Ryan, as the 1973 campaign got underway many felt that he was ready to stake a claim to true greatness, and more and more he was compared with Sandy Koufax, who in 1965 had set the single-season strikeout record with 382.

The specter of Koufax shadowed Ryan all that spring, as fans and the media wondered if Ryan would make a run at the Dodger great's strikeout record.

Ryan wondered about that himself. In a March interview with the *Los Angeles Times,* he mused that if anybody had a chance of breaking the record, it would be someone on the West Coast.

"You couldn't do it on the East Coast," he said. "It's too hot. But if you happen to hit your games just right, not on hot days, it might make a difference. If you look at a lot of my games when the weather's hot, you'll see I have a lot of strikeouts early in the game."

A new factor at play was the designated hitter rule just instituted in the American League, which meant that pitchers wouldn't have to bat. Since pitchers were notoriously bad hitters, it stood to reason there would be fewer strikeouts—up to 60 fewer over 20 games, according to Ryan.

But rather than openly talk about going after Koufax's record, Ryan made it a point to say his main goal was consistency and winning 20 games.

On April 6, an opening night crowd that included President Richard Nixon saw Ryan notch his first victory and Frank Robinson hit a dramatic home run in his first at-bat as an Angel.

Ryan struck out 12, and his raw power so impressed Dick Miller of the *Los Angeles Herald-Examiner* that in his report of the game he called him the "Ryan Express," a play on the popular movie *Von Ryan's Express,* starring Frank Sinatra.

The nickname stuck.

The question was, did the Ryan Express have what it took to catch up to the immortal Koufax?

To do so he would need to avoid injury, extend himself beyond his limits, and remain open to new methods of improvement.

• • •

In 1973, Golden West College assistant football coach Don Rowe moonlighted as an Angels batting practice pitcher. Rowe was a popular figure in the clubhouse and, with his collegiate background, a particular favorite of Winkles'. One afternoon in April, Rowe informed the skipper that he had a "hippie" kid working with his football players whose specialty was flexibility and stretching exercises.

"His name's Bob Anderson," Rowe told Winkles, "and he's over at Long Beach State working on his PhD. He lives at the beach and is a bit scraggly, but he knows his business."

Winkles was already aware of the benefits of stretching, including added dexterity and fewer injuries, and was intrigued enough to bring the matter up with his coaches and the two players he trusted most—Ryan and Clyde Wright. He told them it couldn't hurt to bring Anderson out and see what he had to offer.

"A few days later," recalls Winkles, "I brought out a young man with a big beard and long hair, put him down the right-field line, and had him give a demonstration. The players liked it so much we invited him to come back anytime he wanted. At first there were only 12 or 15 guys, but pretty soon the whole team was out there."

The message expounded by Anderson and his compatriots, Jean Pursell and Herman Clayburn, was "The Power of Positive Stretching." They were idealistic and willing to work for free with anyone who'd listen. Their one-on-one sessions on the Anaheim Stadium grass were voluntary, the exercises simple.

"The doctors and trainers didn't like us much," recalls Anderson. "They wanted to know who the weirdos were. At the time, baseball had many taboos. Lifting weights was at the top of the list, and stretching wasn't even on the radar."

Ryan found the stretches very helpful. The added flexibility gave his leg kick more extension, resulting in extra thrust on the mound. Combined with his weights and running, his endurance again improved, and he found himself going deeper into games.

Meeting Anderson was a major turning point in his career.

"He was extremely important, because he introduced me to a whole new concept," Ryan said years later. "Up until 1973, I never stretched, but because I was already flexible Bob's stretches came easy to me. His routines were what I based my program on for the rest of my career."

"He was ahead of his time basically," says Anderson of Ryan. "Nolan knew his body and how to exercise without hurting himself. He was really into self-development and serious about getting better."

Noting Ryan's increased durability and success, players from other teams started to emulate his training regimen. Within a few years almost every player in the majors was doing some sort of stretching and weight lifting.

Ryan's 54 strikeouts in April put him well on pace to eclipse Koufax's 382. He was 3–1 for the month, but following a victory over Detroit in extra innings on May 2, he dropped his next two starts. It wasn't until May 11, in a rare relief appearance against Chicago, that he got back on track. When the Angels trooped into Kansas City's brand-new Royals Stadium for a two-game set on May 14, he was feeling good. Not scheduled to start until the following day, Ryan hunkered down in his hotel room with a pile of cattle magazines and rested.

By holing up in his room, he unknowingly dodged a bullet. The day before the game, center fielder Ken Berry, who lived in the Kansas City area, invited his teammates out to his farm for an afternoon of fishing in a private stock pond. The pond was infested with chiggers, a miniscule insect whose bite resulted in a breakout of hives. Several Angels were bitten, some bad enough to require medical attention and miss the opening game of the series the next day.

Before Ryan's start, his bullpen throwing session was especially strong, recalls Jeff Torborg. "Nolan was really crisp, throwing hard right from the beginning. His fastball was working well, and like in Sandy Koufax's perfect game, he had a big rolling curveball."

Ryan's teammates staked him to an early 2–0 lead, and the Royals, overwhelmed by fastballs and knee-buckling curves, got nowhere through the first six innings.

Recalls Angels shortstop Rudy Meoli, "I remember thinking to myself, *You know what, they haven't even gotten a hit yet.* So I started looking at who was coming up and made sure I put myself in the proper position."

Meoli's extra effort paid off in the eighth, when journeyman lefty Gail Hopkins thumped an inside fastball that appeared likely to soar over Meoli's head.

"I turned around and started running," says Meoli. "When I looked up again, I figured I could catch the ball. It was almost like a Willie Mays–type catch. On a 1-to-10 degree of difficulty, I figure it was about a nine."

Meoli's fantastic catch turned out to be the play of the game.

"I didn't realize the magnitude of it," Meoli recalls, "because at the time I was just so into the whole thing of winning the game and that he's got a no-hitter going and thinking, *This is cool, this is good.*"

Squinting at the game on the tiny TV in the Ryans' living room in Anaheim, Ruth's excitement built until finally she grabbed Reid and went next door to their neighbors' house to watch on their larger set. Soon another family joined them and everyone huddled silently around the tube as Ryan got through the seventh and eighth innings unscathed.

The Halos were held scoreless in their half of the ninth. When Ryan marched out to the mound in the bottom of the frame, he was still ahead 3–0 and hadn't allowed a hit.

He glanced at the scoreboard. Due up were Freddie Patek, Steve Hovly, and Amos Otis. Ryan made quick work of Patek and Hovly, and now all that remained between him and his first no-hitter was Otis, a former teammate from the Mets and a perennial .300 hitter.

Swinging from his heels, Otis missed badly on Ryan's first offering. When the next fastball came down the pike, Otis was ready, and his bat met the ball with a resounding crack.

"Oh, no! Not now, not now!" yelled Torborg from behind the dish.

The ball sailed toward deep right-center field. Both Ryan and Torborg thought it had enough on it to reach the fence and maybe go over it. But two innings before, Bobby Winkles had put Gold Glover Ken Berry—who'd somehow avoided the chiggers infestation the day before—into right field in place of Bob Oliver.

Berry had started running back the moment Otis made contact with the ball. Just a few feet from the wall he turned, brought up his glove, and made the catch.

"I didn't really give the no-hitter any thought until the eighth inning," Ryan told the press afterward. "But after Meoli made that catch, in my own mind I decided I was going to throw a no-hitter, and if they did hit me, it was going to be off my best stuff. I only threw two curves in the last inning."

"Oh, god, it was beautiful, absolutely beautiful," exalted Torborg, who'd now caught no-hitters by both Ryan and Koufax. "Nolie had good stuff early, and when I saw nothing up there on the board in the fourth I started counting the outs myself."

So, who threw harder—Koufax or Ryan? No one would know better than the man who caught them both.

"It's very difficult to say," says Torborg. "Both threw over the top and had explosive fastballs. Sandy eventually achieved a much more rhythmic delivery, but I've never seen anybody throw as hard down in the strike zone as Nolan did. He could drive the ball at knee-high level...unbelievable!

"When Sandy got two strikes he would be throwing the ball right by you, letter-high. But when Nolan had two strikes, I had to be careful. If we were trying to get a ball down and away, I really was very careful to protect down, which is what you do with a curveball. But then there were times he just shocked you with a fastball up, and would blow it right by the batter—and me if I wasn't careful. It was one of those things where a ball would come out of nowhere and just explode.

"Nolan had another thing: he could throw a ball that years ago they would call a dry spitter. He would choke the ball so tightly in his palm and throw it so hard that he overpowered the ball, and it would come in and dive like a spitball. Invariably it would be with two strikes on the hitter and when you least expected it, and the bottom would fall out of the darn thing. So whenever he had two strikes I'd look for anything.

"Both Koufax and Ryan were very sincere. There was no phoniness about them. You really knew where you stood with both these guys."

Royals manager Jack McKeon insisted that Ryan had cheated during the early innings of his no-hitter and filed a protest. "He was breaking contact with the rubber and pitching two inches in front of it, which is illegal," McKeon barked until a few of his own players who knew better told him to withdraw his protest.

"If they had a higher league than the majors, Ryan would be in it," outfielder Hal McRae told reporters. "As a matter of fact, he could be it."

"Is this his first [no-hitter]?" asked Royals shortstop Freddie Patek. "Well, I don't believe it will be his last."

When Ruth answered her phone later that night, she couldn't contain her excitement.

"We all watched the game at the Smiths' because their TV is bigger!" she shouted before Nolan even said hello. "We were all screaming for you. Do I sound hoarse?"

There was a pause as she fought to calm herself down.

"You pitched a great game, Nolan," she resumed, almost in a whisper.

"Yeah, I guess I pitched a pretty good game," Nolan responded as matter-of-factly as if he'd started an intersquad game at Holtville. "I'm just glad it's over."

The next day, Ryan's hotel phone rang off the hook. The calls were mostly from family and friends, but there was also one from Cooperstown, New York. The Baseball Hall of Fame wanted the cap he'd worn the night before.

• • •

Asked to identify the best pitcher in baseball, Angels broadcaster Don Drysdale replied, "Nolan Ryan has the capabilities, but he's still a thrower. It's that way with all young pitchers. It was that way for Sandy Koufax and with me. You start out as a thrower, and then one day a light bulb just pops in your head and you become a pitcher. When that light pops for Nolan, he'll be twice as good as he is now."

The light flickered off and on over the next few weeks, but it didn't pop.

Between May 19 and July 11, Ryan went 5–8, with 121 strikeouts in 107 innings. He also gave myriad interviews, made numerous covert trips to the weight room, learned how to stretch his leg over the back of his neck, caught thousands of fungos off the bat of Jimmie Reese, and threatened Johnny Vander Meer's record for consecutive no-hitters.

A loss to the A's on July 3 put Ryan below .500 for the first time all season. He bested Cleveland 3–1 four days later, but his fastball was soggier than Lake Erie and he was pounded for 11 hits.

"That's what happens when you don't have [expletive]," a discouraged Ryan told reporters.

Despite striking out 11 over six innings in his next start, Ryan's six walks kept him in trouble, and he was slammed 7–1, his eighth loss in 12 decisions. The Angels were in third place, 4.5 games behind Oakland, and with a big weekend series coming up in Detroit, Ryan knew he had to rediscover his groove now if he was going to help the team and overtake Koufax's record.

A few hours before the game at Tiger Stadium on July 15, Ryan found out that Jeff Torborg had a broken finger and would be replaced behind the plate by his former roommate, Art "Caveman" Kusnyer. The two hadn't worked together in weeks, so Ryan took Kusnyer aside and went over the signs.

"Fingers in the front of the hat for a curve and on the back for a fastball," Ryan told him. "You can flash whatever you want, but those are the signs we'll follow."

Ryan's pregame bullpen session was impressive. His fastball was smoking, and at one point Ryan turned to Tom Morgan and said with a big grin, "With the kind of stuff I have, if I ever get another chance to throw a no-hitter, it will be today."

About 3,000 miles to the west, Ruth Ryan was having the exact same thought. She was at the Smiths' house again, and watching Nolan she had a feeling he had "something special going."

Art Kusnyer joined that club after Ryan's first pitch to Jim Northrup dropped a foot, ricocheted off Kusnyer's shin guard, and struck umpire Ron Luciano on the right knee.

"Ball!" cried Luciano.

"How can it be a ball if it hit you on the knee!" Ryan barked. "It came square over the middle of the plate!"

He's gonna pitch a no-hitter, Kusnyer thought. *I could hardly see that pitch!*

After Northrup flew out to right, Ryan got Mickey Stanley looking, then walked Gates Brown. After Norm Cash struck out to end the inning, Tigers catcher Duke Sims asked his teammate how Ryan was throwing.

"Don't go up there," Cash muttered.

In the dugout before the second inning, Ryan told Kusnyer that some guy in the upper deck was stealing his signs and relaying them to the Tigers bench. "He's rolling up his pants leg for a fastball and letting it down for a curve," Ryan said.

The catcher looked at his battery mate incredulously. "How the hell can you see that?" he asked. "There are 45,000 people out there. What's this guy wearing, an orange suit or something?"

Ryan changed the signs anyway. The next inning, he forgot the sequence, and his third pitch crossed up Kusnyer. The ball hit Luciano, this time on his left knee.

Kusnyer called time and went to the mound. "You need to get these signs straight or I'm going to end up with this friggin' mask twisted around my head!" the catcher said. "From now on I'm calling the signs and you can shake me off, okay?"

Five of the six ensuing Tiger batters went down on strikes.

Taking it upon himself to fluster Ryan, Detroit manager Billy Martin planted himself on the front step of the dugout and hurled insults toward the mound. Ryan was impervious, striking out the first Tiger to start the third inning. At that point, Martin had seen enough.

"Martin had the clubhouse guy go upstairs, get 27 numbers, and put them in a hat," recalls reliever Ed Farmer, who was in the Detroit bullpen at the time. "He then ordered everybody on the bench to put in $5 and pick out a number predicting how many strikeouts Ryan was going to get.

"This is in the *third inning*. The guys in the bullpen started pulling numbers in the fourth. The bullpen was down the left-field line, but I had to come down to the bench and pull a number."

In the third inning, Vada Pinson's sacrifice fly gave the Angels a 1–0 lead.

Ryan fanned the side again in the fourth, added two more Ks in the fifth, and then fanned the side again in the seventh.

With two innings left, he had a total of 16 Ks, and the Tigers were still hitless.

At the time, Tom Seaver and Steve Carlton shared the major league record with 19 Ks, and Bob Feller held the AL mark with 18.

In the eighth inning the Angels scored five runs. Their long at-bat forced Ryan to sit on the bench longer than he preferred, and by the time he returned to the mound in the bottom of the inning, his right arm had stiffened up.

"I knew with the layoff I was going to lose some movement on the ball," he said later. "Pitching in the bottom of the eighth, I didn't have the same stuff."

With some of the edge gone from his fastball, Detroit hitters started timing his pitches. Ryan mixed in an occasional curveball to keep them off-balance. He got through the eighth unscathed, but with no strikeouts.

In the ninth, Ryan got two strikes on leadoff hitter Mickey Stanley, who then grounded out to Meoli.

The next batter, Gates Brown, lined a screamer toward the 5-6 hole that seemed a sure hit, but out of nowhere Meoli, who'd been shading Brown to his right, threw up his glove and snagged the ball for the putout.

"Brown's line drive had base hit written all over it," recalls Meoli, "but Nolan was throwing so hard that I had positioned myself a little bit to the opposite field, and the line drive came to me. I jumped as high as I could to catch it. It turned out to be a big play in the game."

Detroit first baseman Norm Cash was, like Ryan, an avid outdoorsman. In a game against the Tigers a year before, Ryan got a base hit, and as he stood on first base Cash started chatting him up about cattle and hunting. Totally distracted, Ryan was easily picked off.

The next time they faced each other, Ryan threw a pitch that hit Cash so hard the big first baseman thought his arm was broken. ("Don't worry about it, kid," Cash told Ryan later. "It's nothing a little ice and bourbon won't heal.")

In a subsequent game in Detroit, Cash got a hit off Ryan with a man on second. Backing up a possible play at the plate, Ryan noticed that Cash's bat, lying in the grass, had a ring on top of it. He asked the umpire to check to see if it was corked. The ump did, it was, and the bat was thrown out of the game.

Now the last man standing between Ryan and his second no-hitter, Cash was already plenty irked. When he'd come up to bat in the sixth, Ryan urged umpire Ron Luciano to check Cash's bat. It was clean, and Cash grounded out. Heading back to the dugout, he fumed, "That friggin' Ryan's throwing that hard, and Luciano's checking my bat! Why the hell bother? I can't hit the SOB anyway!"

As Cash arrived at the plate in the ninth, he asked Luciano, "Want to check my bat now?"

It was a strange-looking one, all right.

"We had this table in the clubhouse that had candy and the pass list on it," said Farmer. "Before the inning started, Cash had ripped one of its legs off, and instead of a bat, that's what he carried out there."

By now even Luciano was laughing. "Get that thing outta here!" he ordered Cash. "You can't use it!"

"Why not?" said Cash. "I can't hit with my bat. What do I have to lose?"

Using a regulation bat, Cash hit a weak pop-up in no man's land behind shortstop and third. Once again, it was Rudy Meoli to the rescue.

"I got a good jump on it," recalls Meoli, "but back then Detroit's infield was higher than the outfield, and when you left the dirt you actually ran down a two-foot slope. There was always a chance that you would fall down because of the elevation change, but I was able to make the catch."

Ryan had his second no-hitter. This one excited him even more than the first one.

"I had better stuff today than in Kansas City," Ryan told reporters. "I had a better fastball and a better curve. In fact, the curve was probably the best it's ever been."

The proof was as plain as Caveman Kusnyer's swollen glove hand.

"He's parading around the clubhouse showing his hand to everybody," Ryan told Ruth in his call home. "It's so swollen his fingers are bent."

"I've never seen anybody throw that hard," lamented three-time strikeout victim Dick McAuliffe in the losers' clubhouse. "He's the best I've ever seen, bar none."

Duke Sims, who'd also whiffed three times, said, "That's the hardest I've ever seen anybody throw. It was no contest. He just had me overmatched."

"Super stuff," muttered Gates Brown. "Super stuff…"

Ryan always maintained that his second no-hitter in Detroit was his most overpowering performance. Anybody present that day would probably agree.

Unfortunately, Ryan's feat was not enough to put him on the American League's All-Star Game roster. Citing his 11–12 record, Oakland manager Dick Williams shunned the Angels ace and thereby ignited a national furor that was quelled only when baseball commissioner Bowie Kuhn issued a special proclamation putting Ryan on the AL team and the retiring Willie Mays of the Mets on the National League squad.

"Leftover is better than left out," quipped Ryan upon getting word he was headed to Kansas City for the game after all.

But first, all eyes turned to the Big A on July 19, when for the second time in two months Ryan would attempt to equal Johnny Vander Meer's feat of throwing back-to-back no-hitters, accomplished in 1938.

It almost happened. Ryan held the Orioles hitless for seven frames before Mark Belanger muscled an inside fastball just past the charging glove of Ken Berry for a hit. The game went 11 innings before the Birds pulled ahead for the win.

"It was the only game I ever watched that I cried," says Ruth. "It wasn't that he didn't get the no-hitter, but that he pitched so well and lost. The game had so much riding on it. It was just such a heartbreak."

At the All-Star break, Ryan had 233 strikeouts and the Angels were in fourth place in the AL West, seven games behind Oakland. The baseball world was wondering if Nolan could beat Sandy Koufax's strikeout record, and Ross Newhan of the *Los Angeles Times* decided to put the question directly to the record-holder himself.

Nestled at the northern end of the Appalachians, East Holden, Maine, was perfectly suited for a man distancing himself from the trappings of celebrity. As a rule, Sandy Koufax didn't indulge writers; but since Newhan had been the beat writer with the *Times* during his glory days, this time he made an exception.

Staring at the birches through the picture window of his old farmhouse, Koufax lit a cigarette and started talking.

"I don't believe I've seen him pitch since 1970, and that was in a situation where he wasn't very effective," Koufax said. "But to have pitched two no-hitters and struck out as many as he has, he has to have great stuff.

"With the DH rule, Ryan has the chance to go nine innings every game, which improves his chances for more strikeouts. If he's pitching well but losing a close game, say 2–1 or 3–2, he has the opportunity to stay in the game. I'd be surprised if he doesn't break the record because of the rule. The more innings, the more strikeouts. That's not to take anything away from Ryan's talent. But every pitcher encounters games where he has good stuff but has to come out for a pinch hitter...

"For a long time I tried not to let anybody hit me. The result was that I'd beat myself by walking people. I finally realized that I'd have to take a chance and that I'd have to put the ball around the plate. The confidence that came from that success allowed me to begin pitching to spots. I became, in fact, a pitcher rather than a thrower. When I was given the chance to pitch regularly, my control began to improve. But I found it was more of a matter of attitude. The changes I made were more mental than physical."

In 1962, a rare blood ailment called Reynaud's Phenomenon, affecting the circulation in Koufax's pitching hand, put him on the disabled list for much of the second half of the season.

"I was pitching better that year than I did in 1965," Koufax told Newhan. "I had over 200 strikeouts by the All-Star break. If it hadn't been for that injury, there's no telling what the record might be."

Was he worried or bothered by the prospect of Ryan breaking the record?

"My records were fine when I was playing and an important indication of how well I had pitched over the course of a season," said Koufax, "but I'm long past the stage where I lose sleep over it. If he breaks it, he breaks it...

"I wish him all the luck in the world."

Ryan began August defeating Texas 3–2, and striking out 11. Five days later in Milwaukee, he fanned eight straight Brewers, tying his AL record. The 6–5 victory made him 13–13 for the season.

After a 2–1 defeat in Boston in his next start, Ryan spoke frankly.

"Breaking Koufax's record won't mean a lot if I'm 15–18 or something like that," he said. "It's getting depressing losing these types of games. It seems every time I get around .500, and have a chance at becoming a winning pitcher, I lose one like this."

An anemic offense plagued Ryan almost his entire time in Anaheim. The argument has been made that had he been with a better team he would have had a better won-lost record. But on another team, he may not have reached his full potential. He wouldn't have had the benefit of a hands-on pitching coach like Tom Morgan, or a Jimmie Reese. Nor would he have found the type of laid-back atmosphere that allowed him to hook up with new-age stretching gurus and sneak off by himself into an abandoned weight room. Ryan was allowed to find himself in Anaheim. The downside was that in order to win games, he practically had to throw a shutout every time he pitched.

"Throwing for the Angels in the mid-1970s made me a better pitcher," says Ryan. "It forced me to take nothing for granted and to concentrate on every pitch and bear down harder than I normally would have."

On August 17 the Angels got Ryan 10 runs against Detroit for his 14th victory. His 13 strikeouts gave him 288 for the year.

With 19 complete games under his belt, Ryan was on pace to throw well over 300 innings. Ross Newhan computed that Ryan would need to average 9.4 strikeouts per game in his remaining 10 starts to catch Koufax.

In Anaheim on August 25, Ryan collared Boston's Carlton Fisk in the second inning for strikeout 300. Later, Fisk would help ignite a major brawl in a game the Angels were losing 3–0 in the top of the ninth. Then Ryan knocked Fisk down with a fastball under his chin. His next pitch hit Fisk flush on the shoulder.

"I have no idea if he was throwing at me," Fisk told reporters after the game. "But nothing he does surprises me."

"The pitches simply got away," Ryan said with a shrug.

"Conveniently wild," said Tom Morgan.

Four days later, Thurman Munson's flare in the first inning was the only Yankee hit of the night off Ryan. Ten more Ks brought his total to 314.

"If I'm within a couple games of Koufax's record, I'm going to go for it," acknowledged Ryan afterward. "I may never be this close again."

As good as he was in August, Ryan was even better in September. Pitching like a man possessed, he threw more than 1,000 pitches in six complete games, starting with a three-hitter against Oakland on August 3. The 12 Ks he notched gave him 326, and the win evened his record at 16–16.

In front of a big hometown crowd on September 11, Ryan threw a 3–1 complete game against the White Sox. Twelve strikeouts left him 44 shy of Koufax.

But would he get enough starts in the time remaining to get the job done? Newhan figured that if Ryan was just a few strikeouts within the record after his four remaining scheduled starts, he might pitch the final game of the season on just two days' rest. That sounded feasible to Ryan.

"If I'm no more than 10 or 12 strikeouts from the record, I'll probably make that extra start," Ryan said. "But I still think it's going to be a tough struggle that is probably out of reach."

September 15 was "Nolan Ryan Night" at the Big A, and the honoree struck out 10 Royals to tie Bob Feller's AL record of 348 Ks.

Ryan's next start against Texas would be crucial. "To have any chance at the record, I will need at least 12 Ks," Ryan told the press. "I intend to pump it up the rest of the way."

Ryan tossed seven strikeouts that game, eclipsing Waddell's 1904 mark of 349. With two scheduled starts remaining, he had 355. On September 23, he allowed 15 hits but still beat the hosting Twins 15–7 for his 20th win. Twelve strikeouts brought his total to 367.

Sixteen shy of Koufax.

• • •

"Don't take any chances tonight," Ruth said as Nolan backed their red Chevy station wagon out of the driveway on September 27. "You have your whole career ahead of you, and the strikeout record isn't worth risking your arm. You'll have other chances."

"We'll see what happens," he said.

Ruth's anxiety was lessened having George Pugh, Nolan's boyhood friend, staying with them. Today was Pugh's birthday, and she had bought a big cake hoping for a double celebration after the game.

In the Angels clubhouse, Jeff Torborg peeled off his street clothes and picked up his catcher's glove. "We were in Fenway and there was a runner at third base," he recalls. "Ryan threw a rocket that took off over my head. I stabbed at it and thought I had it, but Nolie threw it right through the webbing. The ball ended up going to the backstop and a run scored. When I got back home the shoemaker re-did the glove, and when he finished there was a new white leather patch in the pocket much bigger than the old one. Nolan told me, 'I like that patch because it's a good target.'"

Nearby, Bobby Winkles sketched out the night's lineup, writing Ryan's name at the bottom. It had been a tough season for Winkles. Most of the innovations he had instituted to ramp up the players' enthusiasm and energy had fallen by the wayside of another losing season. The last thing he needed now was for the club's franchise player to blow his arm out in his last start. If Ryan were seriously injured tonight, Harry Dalton would have Winkles' job in a heartbeat.

In a small office off the trainer's room, Dr. Jules Rasinski went over player charts in preparation for his pregame meeting with trainer Freddie Frederico. The team physician for the Angels and the Los Angeles Rams,

Rasinski had a reputation for helping players stay on the field. Coming to Ryan's chart, Doc recalled Nolan's recent complaint about tightening in his right hamstring and made a mental note.

At the Grand Hotel near Disneyland, the Minnesota Twins boarded their team bus for the two-mile trip to the stadium. The atmosphere on the usually animated bus was subdued that night. Everyone knew that with the strikeout record in reach, Ryan would be particularly tough. Near the stadium parking lot, the marquee's message couldn't have looked more ominous: RYAN VS MINNESOTA: 7:30.

Glancing at the sign, utility man Rich Reese sighed. In front of him was two-time batting champ Rod Carew. Sitting next to him was Harmon Killebrew, owner of 500-plus career home runs. Behind them sat a three-time batting champion, Tony Oliva. Elsewhere were George Mitterwald, Steve Brye, and Eric Soderholm. Reese would've bet that they were all thinking the same thing: *I sure as hell don't want to be the one Ryan rings up for number 383.*

In the clubhouse, Ryan got a styptic pencil from the trainer's table and began scraping at a callous on his right index finger. He had sliced the finger open on a tin can as a youngster, and whenever he pitched it blistered over, impairing his release. In a pregame ritual he had started in New York, he softened the callous with the pencil and filed the finger smooth.

Outside, ushers unwound the big steel gates, and the first of the 9,100 fans who would attend the game trickled into the park.

Five miles to the south, Ruth Ryan welcomed the babysitter and then hugged Reid good-bye. As she and George Pugh got into her car to go to the stadium, she thought of all the TV crews that had camped out in their driveway after Nolan threw his second no-hitter, and wondered if they would be besieged like that—or even worse—this time.

Ryan threw decently in the pregame bullpen session, but by game time he was so pumped he started overthrowing. The echoes of the national anthem had barely died away when Minnesota posted three runs, bringing a very concerned Bobby Winkles to the mound.

"You all right, Nolie?"

"Yeah. I'm just not loose yet."

"All right then, get loose! You've got a lot of pitching to do."

Ryan struck out the side.

In their half of the first, the Angels got three runs off Twins starter Dave Goltz to even the score.

If he can just get through the first couple frames, he'll likely be okay, Torborg thought as Ryan took his warm-ups. The catcher knew it was typical for power pitchers to struggle early, and Ryan always got tougher as the game went along.

Two more Twins went down on strikes in the second.

In the third he struck out another. In the bottom of the inning, the Angels pushed a run across to take a 4–3 lead.

After Ryan struck out the side in the fourth, the atmosphere in the Big A resembled the type of environment that surrounds an in-progress no-hitter. Even Ryan's teammates gave him a wide berth on the bench.

Ryan fanned two more in the fifth. He was just four away from Koufax.

Minnesota tied the game in the sixth, and Ryan failed to get any strikeouts.

In the seventh, he gave up a walk and a base hit, but struck out the side.

With two innings left, Ryan was a single strikeout away from tying Koufax.

Looking in Ryan's eyes on the bench, trainer Freddie Frederico thought he detected signs of fatigue. The trainer duly informed Winkles, but they both valued their own lives too much to try to take Ryan out of the game.

Neither organist Shay Torrent's peppy rendition of "Take Me Out to the Ball Game" nor the requests of several youngsters for her autograph distracted Ruth Ryan from her jitters. She had sat through a dozen flirtations with no-hitters, but they were nothing like this. In those contests, Nolan's adversaries wore the other team's uniform; tonight it was him against his own stamina and will.

Twins reliever Bill Hands made quick work of the Halos in the seventh, and the score remained tied.

As Ryan headed out for the eighth, the crowd rose in a heartfelt ovation. He walked Soderholm, who went to second when Nolan threw a wild pitch to Mike Adams. His next pitch sent Adams sprawling. Then Adams grounded to second, moving Soderholm to third. Soderholm tried to score on Jerry Terrell's subsequent grounder, but second baseman Billy Parker threw him out at the plate.

With two outs, Ryan snuck three fastballs by Steve Brye to join Sandy Koufax at the top of the mountain.

Everyone in the dugout joined in the thunderous ovation, but Freddy Frederico stopped clapping when he saw the wince of pain on Ryan's face as he came off the mound.

Ryan told the trainer his calves were cramping up, and Frederico immediately stepped out and gestured upstairs.

"Freddie had a way of signaling me if a player needed attention," recalls Doc Rasinski. "On this night, he had me come down because he wasn't sure Ryan could continue."

As Rasinski rushed downstairs, Ryan went to the runway leading into the clubhouse, and Frederico, figuring the problem was dehydration, gave him several salt tablets. When Rasinski joined them, he found that Ryan's sore hamstring was flaring up.

"We put him on the dugout steps, and Freddie and I took turns messaging his legs," Rasinski recalls. "We were trying to stimulate the muscles by getting the circulation back and taking away the waste by-products that produced the cramping. We also loaded him up with fluids, but it was too late for them to have much of an effect on him."

Winkles came over and told Ryan he could pitch again on Sunday if he couldn't continue, but Nolan wasn't having it.

"I want to get it tonight," Ryan told him bluntly.

"I decided at that point," recalls Winkles, "that I was not going to take him out until he said 'I've had it.'"

Ninth inning. Rod Carew and Tony Oliva went out on an infield pop-up and a fly ball, respectively. After Harmon Killebrew worked the count to 1-1, the exhausted Ryan circled the mound, scraping at the dirt with his spikes and obviously stalling for time. Winkles sent Frederico out to check on him, but Ryan sent him away.

With the count 3-1, Killebrew slammed one into center for a base hit.

Twins manager Frank Quilici sent Rich Reese in to run for Killebrew. Then Jim Holt hit a lazy fly to Ken Berry in left for the third out.

With Ryan tired and in pain, Winkles faced a real dilemma.

"I knew GM Harry Dalton wanted Nolan to come back Sunday, because he thought he could get a better crowd," he recalls. "Personally, I didn't really care about what the crowd was going to be like Sunday. I wanted Nolie to get that 383, so I left him out there and let him pitch."

The dugout tunnel began looking like a prizefighter's corner between rounds of a championship fight, with Rasinski and Frederico working furiously on Ryan's legs. Angels fans began actively rooting against their own team; they knew that if his teammates scored a walk-off victory, Ryan wouldn't get the record.

Ryan's pal George Pugh recalls the late-game craziness.

"I thought, man, this was the weirdest thing I ever seen," he said. "By the ninth inning, every time one of the Twins would put the bat on the ball and an Angels player would make the play, the fans would boo. They just as soon wanted the guy to get a hit so Nolan could get another opportunity for a strikeout."

While the Angels batted in the ninth, Winkles approached Ryan again. "All he said to me was 'Give me one more inning,' and I left it at that," says Winkles.

Minnesota's Bill Campbell held the Angels scoreless. When the Halos took the field for the top of the 10th, the mound was empty. A nervous silence permeated the Big A.

The reason for the delay was that Rasinski and Frederico were massaging Ryan's legs up until the last possible moment. When Ryan finally emerged, the crowd erupted in a standing ovation and remained standing through his entire warm-up.

"This will likely be his last inning," Dick Enberg told his radio audience. "There is virtually no chance at all of him returning on Sunday if he doesn't get the job done now."

George Mitterwald started the inning with a single, but then was erased on Eric Soderholm's double-play. Leaving the field, both were savagely booed for not striking out.

Winkles sent Frederico out to the mound. Ryan told the trainer he was all right.

Mike Adams slammed a single and then stole second. Ryan's legs were so sore and rubbery that when Torborg threw back the ball after his first pitch to Jerry Terrell, Ryan dropped it. Terrell popped out to second for the final out, and was showered with boos for making contact with the ball at all.

"You're up to around 170 pitches," Winkles told Ryan in the dugout. "I don't want to ruin you. I know you have a rubber arm, but this is it."

Ryan didn't reply. He knew if he didn't get the record in the 11th inning, it wasn't going to happen. His body would never stand up to another start.

Campbell held the Angels scoreless in the 10th. To begin the 11th, Ryan got Steve Brye 1-2 before Brye grounded out to short. It was the third time Ryan had been one strike away from the record.

He just didn't seem able to muster the strength to get that one last strike.

"Ryan is now like the heavyweight fighter that has gone so many rounds that he has his opponent staggering and staggering, but doesn't have enough left to deliver that one blow that will knock him to the canvas and put him away," intoned Enberg in the press box.

Rod Carew had struck out three times against Ryan. Now he took one strike and then walked on five pitches. The Big A was bedlam. The only person seemingly unfazed was Ryan.

The dangerous Tony Oliva followed. After working the former two-time batting champ to a 1-1 count, Ryan glanced at Carew and then went into his motion. As soon as Ryan lifted his front leg, Carew sprinted for second. After Oliva flayed at the pitch for strike two, Torborg sprung from his crouch and fired a perfect strike to Billy Parker straddling second base. Too late.

"It was the best throw I made all year," recalls Torborg. "After letting it go, I thought *Oh, no!* Thank god, the ump called him safe, or there might have been a riot."

With two strikes, Oliva, determined not to go down in the record books, was now protecting. On the next pitch, another fastball, he stuck out his bat and hit a weak fly ball to Mickey Rivers in center. Ignoring cries of "Drop it!" from the stands, Rivers camped under it for out number two.

In the dugout, Jimmie Reese, his glasses halfway down his nose, recorded pitch number 180 in his ledger.

Rich Reese hadn't faced Ryan yet, having pinch-run for Killebrew earlier. As Reese took his stance, Torborg flashed Ryan a sequence of signs that were totally superfluous. Everyone in the park including the peanut vendor knew Ryan would bring the heat. Reese swung and missed the first pitch by half a foot.

After a cursory look toward Carew, Ryan went into his motion. Reese waved at the pitch for strike two.

It was now or never.

"I decided to throw the next pitch as hard as I could," recalls Ryan. "I wasn't going to waste one. With Reese down 0-2, I decided this is it."

Raising his front leg, he grunted and fired a two-seamer with everything he had at the white patch in Torborg's glove.

Reese's swing missed the ball by a country mile. Home-plate umpire Red Flaherty signaled strike three as the crowd exploded.

"The pitches he threw Reese, he couldn't hit if he started swinging now and Nolan threw 'em five minutes from now!" says Torborg. "God, he missed 'em by a long way. It was probably as far I've seen a batter miss pitches."

The standing ovation lasted a good seven minutes. When pinch hitter Richie Scheinblum knocked home Tommy McCraw with a double in the Angels' half of the 11th, Ryan was doubly relieved. Not only did he get the strikeout record, but he also notched his 21st victory.

But it wasn't the victory that was first and foremost on Torborg's mind; rather, it was Ryan's toughness.

"I don't know how he continued pitching," recalls the catcher. "When you've got your legs bothering you like that, it's a good way to really hurt an arm. But Nolie kept saying, 'I'm gonna try. I'm gonna try to get that extra strikeout.'

"And you can imagine how hard the team was pulling for him. He was beloved. Nolan Ryan was really appreciated by his teammates."

In the clubhouse, Doc Rasinski advised Ryan to pass up the champagne in favor of potassium-rich orange juice. Frank Tanana had Nolan's share of the bubbly, and ended up dumping his jersey into the trash can, thinking it was the laundry hamper.

Ryan spoke to the press for over an hour and didn't get home until 1:00 AM. After having some cake with Ruth and birthday boy George Pugh, he finally got to bed at 3:00 AM but didn't get much sleep.

Sure enough, when dawn broke the Ryans' driveway was a parking lot for numerous TV trucks.

"They left it up to me," Ryan told the assembled reporters. "I wanted to get it over with. I wanted the strikeout record, but I wanted most of all to prove I was a winning pitcher."

When Ryan arrived at the ballpark the following night, a telegram from East Holden, Maine, was sitting on his stool. Its contents remain private.

The *Los Angeles Times* of September 29 carried the only public pronouncement from Sandy Koufax concerning the great single-season strikeout handoff of 1973.

"I have no thoughts except congratulations," he said. "It doesn't really matter. Records are nice when you're playing because it means you've had a good year. My record was then. His is now."

On the ride back to Texas a few days later, recalls George Pugh, Ryan didn't say a whole lot about the record.

"He always just took those things in stride," says Pugh. "I'm sure deep inside he was really proud of his achievement, but he was pretty humble about everything. He grew up appreciating everything he had, and he didn't expect anyone to give him anything. He expected to work and earn it, and in 1973 he earned every bit of that record."

Two months later, Ryan was working with his hunting dogs at his ranch when Ruth told him that a writer had called to give him some interesting news.

Ryan finished what he was doing and called the writer back to find out that he was runner-up to Jim Palmer for the American League's Cy Young Award. It didn't surprise him—he knew the writers who voted were primarily from the East Coast, and had half-expected the result.

"I felt my statistics were strong enough to win and I was kind of disappointed that I didn't," Ryan later said. "At the same time, when a guy wins over 20 games, sets a strikeout record, and pitches two no-hitters and two one-hitters, you'd have to think he'd have a solid chance for the award. But lose sleep over it? No way."

3

Fastest Man Alive: 1974

Nolan Ryan was the standard for a guy that threw hard. He was the measuring stick. There are few guys that on a given day could throw like Nolan did. I remember how many names would come up for the hardest thrower in the history of baseball. I think the person that stands out amongst everybody is Nolan Ryan.

But Nolan, to me, was never mean on the mound. He was determined, he was focused. He was going to leave it all out there and you were going to get all he had. Was he mean to me? No. Did he want to kick my butt? Yes, as much as any person could.

So you admire his determination and focus. You admire his manhood and professionalism. You admire what he was about.

—REGGIE JACKSON

When the 1974 Halos lost 44 of their first 74 games, it was plain that Bobby Winkles' gung-ho college style wasn't the game-changer the Angels had been hoping for. Not only were they struggling to stay out of the AL cellar, but Winkles' relationship with Frank Robinson had deteriorated to the point that they were no longer even communicating.

The other players had divided into separate factions, and the dissention on the team was rampant.

According to Ryan, Winkles and Robinson were pure water and oil.

"I don't think it was a good match. Bobby Winkles came in with a new style of managing and was accustomed to college kids, so it was a different situation for him," he said. "Frank, on the other hand, was as intelligent and aggressive a hitter as there was in the game, but with the type of ballclub we had and the fact that we were in a rebuilding mode, at that point in Frank's career he would probably have been better someplace else where he was competing for a pennant."

On June 27, GM Harry Dalton let Winkles go and brought former Oakland A's skipper Dick Williams out of retirement to right the Angels' sinking ship.

Departing with Winkles was Tom Morgan. Luckily for new pitching coach Billy Muffett, by then Ryan had mastered his mechanics and no longer required vigilant oversight.

With managers coming and going, there was a void in leadership at the top that Ryan helped to fill.

"We had a lot of young guys on that team at that point," recalls Rudy Meoli, who played shortstop with Ryan for three seasons, "and we were all just pretty glad to be out there playing. Nolan was one of the guys. He led by example and his work ethic, and he didn't need to say anything. He was quiet, but he would say something when credit was due. But he was not in your face if something was off."

Despite the changes, the team's losing ways continued. One of the few bright spots was the emergence of pitcher Frank Tanana, who with Ryan comprised one of the best pitching tandems in baseball. The straight-laced Ryan and gregarious Tanana had little in common off the field, but on it they both mesmerized batters with speed and finesse. "Tanana and Ryan and two days of crying," became the rallying cry of the Angels faithful.

But tension between the two pitchers surfaced when Williams decided to go with a five-man rotation. Ryan had built his conditioning program around three days' rest and objected to the extra day. Tanana lobbied for four days, and the five-man rotation remained.

Nevertheless, Ryan continued to excel. As his confidence grew, so did his aggressiveness and willingness to use the inside of the plate.

"Some hitters show fear more than others, and when you know that you pitch everyone accordingly," he told the *Los Angeles Times* in 1974. "I don't mean I ever tried to hit anyone, but the inside fastball is part of the game. Certainly it's scary and it bothers me for a while whenever I hit anyone, but I have no choice but to block it out or I risk losing my aggressiveness and become a defensive pitcher."

Catcher Tom Egan says that when Ryan got in a groove he was nothing short of scary. "When Nolan harnessed his mechanics he was unbelievable and intimidating," says Egan. "When he was taking warm-up pitches before the game, he would walk around the mound to see if there were any soft spots. Then he would look into the visiting dugout as if to say, 'This is my mound. What are you going to do about it?' He could run the ball up under the right-handers' chins without any second thoughts."

As Ryan's mystique grew, some established hitters actually invented excuses to avoid facing him.

"Guys developed what we used to call 'Ryanitis,'" says Don Baylor, who played with and against Ryan. "They'd come in on the day he pitched with some injury, disease, or whatever, and then were mysteriously healed the next day when somebody else was pitching."

Cleveland's Oscar Gamble won immortality when he said, "A good day against Ryan is going 0-for-4 and not getting hit on the head."

"It's not fear that he throws hard," said Oakland's Sal Bando. "It's a fear he won't get it over. The reaction time is reduced considerably. Let's face it, having a reputation helps him."

"I didn't look forward to facing Nolan Ryan," recalls former Dodger Ron Roenicke. "I faced him because the starters didn't want to face him, and I had to do it. Lucky me."

"You fear for your life," said Rangers outfielder Elliott Maddox. "That's one of the keys to Ryan's success. You can try to put it out of your mind, but it's no use. With other pitchers you have time to get your shoulder out in front of your face when the ball's coming at you. But there isn't that time with Ryan. You see the ball all right, but you just don't have the time to react.

"It's not that you go up to the plate thinking you can't hit him, it's the fear that he can hit you."

To Ryan, it was just business.

"I had to become aggressive and determined, because baseball is not only a sport but also a profession," he says. "You can't have a laid-back attitude and go out there to have a good time. When I started to pitch inside and be aggressive, a lot of guys said I was mean, but that was something I had to do to be successful."

Ryan's approach was no different than those of other flamethrowers of his generation. Bob Gibson, Sam McDowell, and Don Drysdale all used intimidation effectively. Then, intimidation was as much a part of the game as the national anthem. In today's game, it means ejections, fines, and five-game suspensions.

Ryan recalls the time he met pitching legend Satchel Paige before a TV show.

"Hey, Nolan, you know what the best pitch in baseball is?" Paige asked.

"I always understood it to be the fastball," Ryan said.

"No," Paige said, "it's a bow tie."

"What's a 'bow tie'?"

"When you throw the ball right here," said Paige, pointing to his neck.

Ryan started calling his purposeful pitches "Texas bow ties."

"It helps if the hitters think you're a little crazy," he said. "One of my biggest assets is that batters are afraid of me. They go up there ready to get out of there in a hurry."

By 1974, intimidation had become a major weapon in Ryan's arsenal. But what happened when that weapon misfired?

Alvin pal George Pugh remembers one time when it did. They were teenagers playing a summer league game in Galveston. Nolan had gotten drafted that very day, and it was the buzz at the ballpark.

"Galveston had a shortstop by the name of Castro," Pugh recalls. "Nolan was really pumped up and lost control on one and hit the kid in the arm and broke it. You could hear the limb break. It was terrible. Maybe getting drafted affected his concentration, but whatever it was, he scared them to death that day. Everybody was ducking—the umpire, the batters—just everybody."

• • •

It was overcast and cool when Ryan took the mound against the Red Sox at Fenway Park on April 30, 1974. His teammates had already put him up 1–0, but as he made his final warm-ups tosses, he knew his rhythm was off.

Leadoff hitter Rick Miller lined Ryan's second pitch, a high fastball, for a single to right. The next batter, second baseman Doug Griffin, was hoping to get a similar fat pitch, but after a first-pitch ball, Boston manager Darrell Johnson flashed the bunt sign to third-base coach Don Zimmer. Griffin would have preferred to take another pitch, but he followed instructions.

Griffin waited until Ryan lifted his front foot before squaring.

He wouldn't remember much after that.

When Ryan delivered he inadvertently dropped his pitching elbow, causing his 98-mph heater to sail up and in. He knew the pitch was trouble the moment he let go of the ball, and screamed, "Look out!"

Too late.

There was a sickening thud when the ball smashed into Griffin's helmet beneath his right ear. By the time Ryan got to the plate, the second baseman's eyes had rolled back in his head.

"Nolan was scared," Angels second baseman Jerry Remy remembers. "He always told me, 'Someday, I feel I'm going to kill somebody.'"

After Griffin was carried off the field, the clearly rattled Ryan hit Carl Yastrzemski on the foot with a pitch. But then he settled down, and the Angels won the game 16–6.

"This is the first time I've knocked anybody out," Ryan said at a postgame press conference. "I don't try to pitch people up around the head. You don't go around jeopardizing people's lives and careers. He just squared around to bunt and froze."

Later that night, Ryan called Griffin's home.

"My mommy can't talk right now," Griffin's little girl told him. "She's at the hospital with my daddy."

Reid Ryan was about the same age as Griffin's daughter. If circumstances had been reversed, how would Reid respond to a call from the guy who'd nearly killed his father?

Ryan called the hospital the next morning and learned that Griffin was out of intensive care, conscious and in stable condition. He asked a doctor to tell Griffin's wife he wished Doug a quick recovery.

Nolan Ryan Sr. and Martha Ryan, circa 1934. (Mary Lou Williams)

The youngest of six children, Nolan Ryan (front, right) was born in 1947 and spent his childhood in Alvin, Texas. (Mary Lou Williams)

Drafted in 1965 by the New York Mets, Ryan was the second-youngest player in the major leagues when he made his debut the following season. (Getty Images)

Mets manager Gil Hodges (left) was blessed with a talented pitching staff, including (left to right) Jerry Koosman, Tom Seaver, and Ryan. (Getty Images)

Pitching out of New York's bullpen, Ryan recorded the final out of the 1969 NLCS against the Atlanta Braves, which sent the Miracle Mets to the World Series. (AP Images)

After winning the World Series, Mets such as (left to right) Jim McAndrew, Bobby Pfeil, Ryan, and Seaver were the toast of New York. Incredibly, Ryan would be traded just two years later to the California Angels in what many consider the worst trade in Mets history. (Getty Images)

After experiencing some initial culture shock, Nolan and his wife, Ruth, acclimated to life in California. Ruth's love and support, both in and away from the ballpark, played an instrumental part in her husband's success. (Los Angeles Angels)

Fungo machine and coach Jimmie Reese would become one of Ryan's closest confidants on the Angels. (Nolan can be seen stretching in the background.) (Los Angeles Angels)

Angels manager Bobby Winkles congratulates Ryan after Nolan's second no-hitter of the 1973 season. (AP Images)

Another milestone: Ryan peers up at the sign celebrating his 383rd strikeout of the 1973 season, a major league single-season record. He and Ruth relived the moment the following morning via the local newspapers. (AP Images/Los Angeles Angels)

Ryan and his teammates leave the field after Nolan's third career no-hitter, thrown against the Twins in 1974. One of the men congratulating Nolan is author and then–bat boy Rob Goldman, whose hand rests atop the pitcher's head. (AP Images)

With his career at an all-time high, Nolan and Ruth were happier than ever in California. Ryan believed there was a good chance he would retire as an Angel. (Los Angeles Angels)

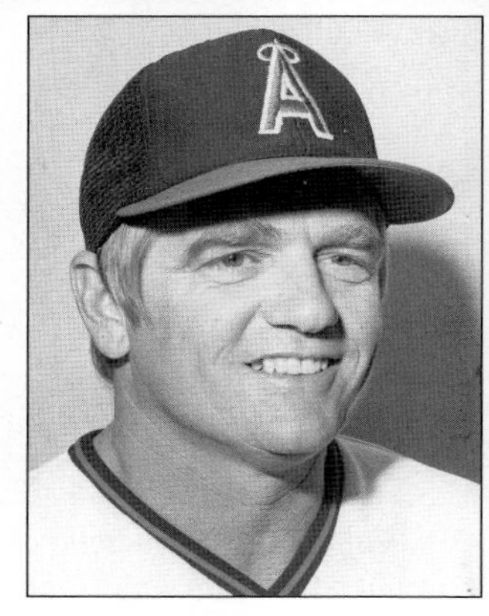

Some of the men who had the biggest impact on Ryan's career include (clockwise) Mets scout Red Murff, Angels owner Gene Autry, GM Buzzie Bavasi, pitching coach Tom Morgan, coach Whitey Herzog, and catcher Jeff Torborg. (Tyler Morning Telegraph/Los Angeles Angels)

The incident forced him to ask himself some serious questions.

How can I continue to compete if I'm pitching defensively?

If I stop using the inside of the plate, how can I be effective?

One reason Ryan suffered from inconsistency with the Mets was his hesitancy to use the inside of the plate. Hard throwers like Gibson and Drysdale had no problem throwing inside because they had pinpoint control. But Ryan lacked that, and always feared he might do serious damage.

By nature he was sensitive and kind. For him to achieve the necessary aggressive state when he pitched, he had to willfully put that aside and become a different animal.

"It took a lot of effort and preparation for me to become aggressive and as competitive as I was," Ryan recalled years later. "My preparation was key to getting me to that aggressive state. But after hitting Griffin, I lost some of that edge."

Ryan again hesitated to pitch inside for several starts after the incident. But in the end his desire to make a living won out.

Ryan came to terms with his speed and its inherent danger, and as the season progressed his fastball wreaked more havoc on Boston hitters. At the Big A on June 14, he fanned 19 Red Sox in 13 innings, including Cecil Cooper a record-breaking six times. The Angels won the game 4–3 in 15 innings, but Ryan, who threw more than 200 pitches that night, was not involved in the decision.

Unfortunately, the only official log that night was Jimmie Reese's game chart, which has long since vanished. The accounts of newspaper beat writers present that night vary from 229 to 259 pitches, but the exact number thrown by Ryan remains a mystery.

What is certain is that Ryan didn't suffer any ill effects from the marathon outing. At the Big A just four days later, he went six strong innings against New York, allowing just three hits and striking out seven for his eighth victory. Four days after that, he pitched a complete-game 7–4 victory against Texas, with 10 Ks. On June 27, he threw a 5–0 complete-game one-hitter against Texas.

"It just goes to show you what he could do if he really wanted to just bury people," recalls Whitey Herzog, the Angels' third-base coach and interim manager that season. "It was the damnedest performance period

I've ever seen for a pitcher. I was so worried after he threw that 13-inning game that he might overextend and hurt himself, but he got through that.

"He was 22–14 with the Angels in '74, and in 10 of his games, he gave up one or two runs. He could have been 30–3, for crying out loud. That's how good he pitched."

On August 12 the Red Sox were back in Anaheim, and this time Doug Griffin was with them for his first game against the Angels since getting off the DL. Ryan was on the mound, and Griffin smacked two hits off him.

"At that point, I realized I had to block out [hitting Griffin] in my mind," Ryan remembers. "I had no choice. If I didn't, I'd risk becoming a defensive pitcher instead of an aggressive one."

From then on, Ryan attacked the inside of the plate and struck out a record 19 Red Sox.

Never again would Ryan hesitate to throw inside fastballs and intimidate hitters.

"Nolan was a hell of a competitor, but he was never a guy who, just because he pitched 100 mph, was going to try to make somebody scared of him," says Herzog. "He wasn't mean or a head-hunter, but he knew what part of the plate was his and what wasn't. If he wanted to brush a hitter back, he could do it just by throwing the ball waist or belt high, up and in a little bit, and that got their attention."

• • •

The milestones continued to pile up. On August 30, Ryan became the first pitcher in modern baseball history to have three consecutive 300-strikeout seasons. On September 7, he broke the record for which he is perhaps most famous.

Rockwell-American International provided parts for the NASA space program and the U.S. Army. George Lederer, the director of communications for the Angels, had an idea about using the company's finely calibrated technology to measure the speed of Ryan's pitches. Rockwell-American was willing, and using a device more accurate even than today's hand-held radar gun, Ryan's fastball was unofficially clocked at 100.9 miles per hour in a game against Detroit. After further refinements were made to the equipment, the Rockwell-American instrument was brought to the Big A to take an official reading.

In the ninth inning, on a 3-1 count against Lee "Bee Bee" Richard, Ryan's fastball was measured at 100.8, easily surpassing Bob Feller's 1948 mark of 98.0.

Ever since, that pitch has been deemed by Guinness World Records as the fastest ever recorded.

But according to Angels catcher Tom Egan, it wasn't the fastest pitch Ryan ever threw.

"If that particular pitch was 100.8, then I would have to say he probably threw a few on other days that reached 105," he said. "I don't know whether they were strikes or not, but he could get it up there."

The Guinness pitch was belt high, says Egan, and balls Ryan threw from the belt up to the letters were always faster.

"I've thrown harder," Ryan himself said after that game. "The big build-up before the game got to me. I was a little tense and couldn't concentrate. I was worried I'd try to throw so hard, I'd blow the ballgame."

After the pitch to Richard, Ryanitis picked up a notch. Opposing hitters already had enough on their mind facing Ryan, and now they had to contend with the fact that every time they went to bat against him, they were facing the "Fastest Man Alive."

Heading into the last homestand the Angels were dead last in the AL West, 25 games behind Oakland.

Ryan's last scheduled start was on September 28, against Minnesota. With 352 strikeouts he was fast approaching his own record of 383. Williams gave him the option of another start against Oakland later in the week, but Ryan indicated little enthusiasm for that.

On the morning of the game, he was scheduled to attend autograph signings in Huntington Beach and Newport before heading to LAX to pick up his pal George Pugh. The plan was for Pugh to take in a couple games, then caravan back to Texas with Ryan and teammate Dave Chalk. Ruth and Reid had already left for Alvin.

Ryan was tired and not looking forward to pitching that night. He'd already won 20 games, and there wasn't anything riding on the contest.

But as he tossed in the bullpen before the game, he recalls, "I could feel the extra hop in my fastball. So I told Tom [Egan], 'I think I'll let it all hang out. What have I got to lose?'"

"When we started the game, I signaled down for a fastball that looked like it was going to be in the dirt, but when I went down to block it, it rose about two feet," recollects Egan. "The umpire called it a strike and told me I'd better sit still or he wouldn't be able to see the pitches. From then on I knew [Ryan] had a good day going."

As the game progressed and the Twins remained hitless, there was probably more pressure on Egan than Ryan, who had already been through this numerous times. This was Egan's first shot at a no-hitter, and he didn't want to call a bad pitch or make an errant throw that would give another Minnesota batter a chance to wreck it.

George Pugh remembers that it was lonely that night in the Big A.

"The Angels were [24] games out of first place and nobody was at the stadium," he said. "I was sitting behind home plate, and there were so few people in the stands that Nolan later told me he could see me sitting there."

Back in Alvin, Ruth—who'd missed her husband's first two no-hitters—kept track of the game by repeatedly calling the stadium switchboard operator for updates.

"I would ask the operator the score and how Nolan was doing, and she would just say 'He's doing okay,' because she was afraid she might jinx him. The third time I called, I said, 'Lizzy, how many hits has he given up?' She said, 'Uh ... none.'

"Well, that's when I was really aggravated I wasn't there. I was excited but I also felt left out, because Nolan's sister and all of his friends were there, and I was sitting at home in Texas."

In the ninth, Pugh had a nerve-wracking moment.

"The Twins had some really good players, including Harmon Killebrew. Since it was the last weekend of the season, they were resting him, but in the ninth they called on him to pinch-hit. I'm on the edge of my seat thinking, *Aw, god, Harmon Killebrew! They could have gotten the other guy out easily and now they pinch-hit Harmon Killebrew! Jeez.*"

But Killebrew walked, which brought Eric Soderholm to the plate. Ryan got two quick strikes past the big infielder. Once again, the pressure was on Egan.

"I called for a curveball," Egan recalls, "and said to myself, 'Tom, if you catch anything clean the rest of your career, you catch this one!' Well, Soderholm swung and missed, and the rest was history."

Soderholm's whiff sealed Ryan's third no-hitter. It was his 15th strikeout of the night, giving him 367 for the season. Just 16 more would break his own record, and again Dick Williams offered to let Nolan pitch the final game of the season.

"I'll settle for this," Ryan said. "I'm worn out. It was a struggle. Anytime you are as wild as I was, it's a struggle."

At the postgame birthday party at Ryan's house, Pugh told him, "Man, was I nervous when Harmon Killebrew came up."

"Why?" asked Ryan in genuine puzzlement.

"Nolan," said Pugh, "it's Harmon Killebrew!"

"He looked at me like I was crazy," recalls Pugh, "and said, 'So what?' It turned out I had put more pressure on myself than Nolan did on himself."

Overall, Ryan was 21–16 with a 2.89 ERA, had completed 26 games, and pitched a personal-high 332 innings. His 367 strikeouts were the most in either league, and his combined 750 Ks over the last two seasons was also a record.

But Ryan also became the first pitcher since Bob Feller to walk more than 200 batters. On April 5, against Chicago, he walked 10 batters but won 8–2.

Perhaps most striking was that he had won 22 games for a team that finished dead last and scored the fewest runs in the American League.

In a column titled "The Curse of Nolan Ryan: It's Pitching for the Angels," Jim Murray pointed out that Ryan was hardly alone when it came to pitching for underachieving clubs, citing Dizzy Dean, Grover Cleveland Alexander, and Walter Johnson as examples of other pitchers who'd been in the same boat.

"Nolan Ryan is in the great tradition when he pitched impeccable ballgames for highly peaceable ballclubs," wrote Murray. "But before Nolan Ryan breaks up any furniture or jumps the club, he should know that Walter Johnson was involved in 64 one-run games. But shucks! He won 38 of them."

According to Murray, Ryan just plain threw too many pitches. To become a complete pitcher, said the columnist, Ryan needed to narrow his strike zone.

"Of his 172 pitches in his record-breaking game against the Red Sox," Murray wrote, "114 were strikes and 58 were balls—which is an inefficient use of a million-dollar instrument."

In 1975, after three years of relatively good health, Ryan's million-dollar instrument would get the most severe test of his career. It would push his faith and fortitude to their limits.

4

Speed Bump: 1975

> Nolan's a little bit stubborn. I don't want to say hard-headed, but he has an opinion and he's one of those guys who likes to take control. He likes to be the guy driving the ship.
>
> —REESE RYAN

In a lot of ways, Nolan Ryan's 1975 season would prove his most challenging. Primarily because it was the first time he missed significant time due to injury.

It started in Minnesota on April 15. He won the 7–3 game, but his arm felt stiff and there was nothing special about his performance. The next morning he woke up to find his right elbow so swollen he couldn't straighten his arm. He immediately went to the ballpark, where it took 20 minutes of throwing at half-speed to loosen up the arm enough for him to extend it away from his body.

Two starts later against Texas, he gave up seven hits and four earned runs before leaving the game after pitching to one batter in the seventh inning.

When he told Dr. Joseph Triggs, the Angels team physician, about his arm, Triggs thought maybe Ryan had torn his triceps tendon. Instead,

X-rays showed what looked like a bone chip in the elbow. Believing it was related to an older injury, Triggs recommended rest.

So Ryan rested. The pain did not.

"The first 30 minutes of warming up, I would really have to suck it up to get to where I could really stand it," he recalls. "Once it got loose, I could pitch with it. But the velocity never was there. I was losing sleep over it, and it got to the point where I dreaded coming to the ballpark."

Even so, Ryan won eight of his first nine starts, and at the end of May he was 8–3, with 87 Ks.

"I kept winning because my control was good," says Ryan. "I was mixing my pitches and I was getting a lot of runs. But the longer I pitched, the worse it got."

As the pain continued, so too did Ryan's reluctance to address it. Scheduled to start on Sunday, June 1, the season-long pain in his elbow could no longer be ignored. This morning it was so bad he couldn't lift his arm to brush his teeth, and combing his hair required him to bend down.

He tried hiding the truth from Ruth, but that was always futile, and her own pained expression mirrored his.

If opposing hitters learned that Ryan was hurt, they'd dig in during every at-bat and eliminate his intimidation factor. If Angels management found out, they'd likely demand a thorough examination and perhaps surgery.

In the past, he had always played through elbow pain until it eventually subsided. But now he couldn't even put on his shirt or tie his shoes by himself. If it was this bad now, what could he expect in six hours when he took the mound against Baltimore?

The Orioles had some serious bats. Somehow he'd have to get through the first few innings and hope adrenalin kicked in.

"See you at the game," he told Ruth through gritted teeth.

At the ballpark, Nolan put on his game face. Passing the batboy in the towel room, he said, "How you doing, Robby?" as if nothing was wrong.

After leaving passes for Ruth and sister Mary Lou, Ryan went to his locker and got into his uniform. Picking up a stray rubber ball, he went up to starting catcher Ellie Rodriguez and started lightly bouncing it off his forehead. "I'll be throwing these today," Ryan joked, "so be ready."

Rodriguez had just come off the DL and was surprised to get the start. He had a cold and a headache, and joined Ryan in the trainer's room and downed a couple aspirins.

After filing down his blister, Nolan had the trainer apply eye black beneath his eyes. The afternoon sun would be bright. The black shade not only diminished glare but also gave him an intimidating look.

That was exactly what Bobby Grich was thinking too, over in the Baltimore clubhouse, as the Orioles second baseman applied his eye black. All the shadow in the world wouldn't slow down Ryan's fastball, but looking a little tougher couldn't hurt.

Ryan's bullpen session was shaky. It took him a long time to get loose, and when he finally did his fastball wasn't popping.

So instead he finessed the Orioles. By the fifth inning he had only four strikeouts, proof he was relying on his off-speed pitches and great location.

And he hadn't allowed a hit.

In the stands, Ruth, who was pregnant, was beginning to feel the stomach-fluttering "no-hit" sensation, and was grateful that Reid and Mary Lou were with her.

The guys in the visitors' dugout were dealing with their own angst.

"It was one of those days where, as the game wore on, you felt like you didn't have a chance," recalls Orioles right fielder Ken Singleton. "By the sixth, we were behind 1–0, but the way Nolan was throwing it seemed like 10–0. We were sitting on the bench, and I can recall Grich screaming to the mound, 'Hey, Nolan! Give us a chance!' But all Nolan did was kind of look over with that smile and shake his head."

Determined to break up Ryan's no-hitter, Birds skipper Earl Weaver sent Tommy Davis to bat for Don Baylor to start the seventh inning.

Playing for the Dodgers in the 1960s, Davis was one of the game's top hitters, winning batting titles in 1962 and '63. He might have added a third but for the broken ankle he suffered busting up a double play in 1965. He had slowed down in the years since, but the 36-year-old former All-Star could still hit, and as he approached the on-deck circle Ryan thought, *This is just the kind of guy who could wreck it. Need to be careful here.*

Davis hit his second pitch hard toward the middle. Getting a great jump on the ball, Jerry Remy made a spectacular backhanded stab, turned, and fired a perfect strike to Bruce Bochte at first. It was close, but umpire Hank Soar shot out a thumb, bringing the immediate wrath of Davis and Weaver.

"Jerry's play was the big one," Ryan later recalled. "When he made it, I said to myself, 'This might be our day.'"

Following a walk to Grich, Lee May hit a potential double-play ball that shortstop Billy Smith bobbled for an error. With the tying run on second, Ryan got Brooks Robinson on a grounder to third and then Elrod Hendricks on a pop up to end the inning. Ryan left the field to a standing ovation.

On the bench he called over the batboy with a request: "Robby, can you get the X balls?"

In the mid-1970s, American League baseballs were produced in Haiti, and the balls weren't uniform. Some were smaller with higher seams, others bigger with flatter seams. Ryan liked the smaller ones, and had stashed a dozen or so of them away for "special occasions."

The batboy charged up the runway, grabbed the box with the X on it, and brought it back to the bench. From that point on, every foul ball would be replaced by an X ball. By the time Ryan returned to the mound in the eighth, umpire Hank Morgenweck's pockets were full of them.

Going into the final inning the Halos were still ahead 1–0 and Ruth's stomach was in knots. That morning Nolan could hardly shave his face. Now he was just three outs away from his fourth no-hitter.

Glancing at the lineup card posted above the water cooler, Ryan saw the names Al Bumbry, Tommy Davis, and Bobby Grich. It was the meat of the Orioles batting order, and he knew each hitter had seen him three times already and was smart enough to be timing his pitches.

Ryan worked the speedy Bumbry with breaking balls before he hit a fly to Morris Nettles in left. Pitching carefully to Davis, Ryan wasted a couple breaking balls and then got him on a routine grounder to Remy.

Walking to the plate, Bobby Grich recollects, "The crowd was beside itself and I wanted to get a hit. I was really grinding and trying to focus but at that moment there was so much karma pulling against you. It's a very strange situation to be in, and I remember trying hard to get myself focused the other way."

Ryan threw two fastballs that Grich fouled straight back. Grich was obviously timing him, so with the count at 2-2, Ryan flashed his teeth at Rodriguez, signaling the changeup.

"I'm thinking he's gonna throw me a heater," Grich recalls, "and I'm going to rope him up the middle. As he began his windup, I started to stride, and I can't believe it. It's a changeup... I don't think he had thrown a handful the whole afternoon. I'm timing myself for a fastball but when I saw it was a change I held up and watched it go near the outside corner. It was an incredible pitch, and as the place went nuts all I could think was, *Oh, my god, I'm part of history!*"

As soon as Morgenweck signaled strike three, Ruth left her seat and bolted down the aisle for the rail. As his teammates mobbed her husband, the batboys brought the auxiliary staircase over so she could get onto the field.

"I got excited and just jumped out on the field and began hugging him," Ruth recalls. "I had never done that before, but I couldn't wait to see him."

It was her first no-hitter in person, after all.

"It was one of those deals when I warmed up just hoping I could get through the game," Ryan told a mob of reporters in the locker room. "The last thing that went through my mind while I warmed up was a game like that. All my pitches were effective today. For my second no-hitter I threw 80 percent fastballs. Today I threw 60 percent fastballs and 40 percent curveballs and changeups. I was giving the hitters more pitches to hit, which is the way I am trying to pitch now."

Asked about tying Koufax's record of four no-hitters, Ryan said, "He's been very supportive of me. That's just the type of person he is. He respects people's abilities and their work ethic. But I think all records are subject to being broken, and I think if they are going to be broken, you would like it to be broken by somebody that has the same value system as you."

A photographer asked the batboy for four baseballs and a marker. After putting a big zero on each ball, the photographer handed them to Ryan.

The next morning, pictures of Ryan, his face smeared with eye black and holding up the four balls, were featured in newsstands across the country.

Later that day a telegram was added to the growing stack on Ryan's chair. It conveyed congratulations from Sandy Koufax, now living on California's central coast. A couple days later, Koufax expressed his sentiments publicly to the *Los Angeles Times*.

"I have no sadness at all," he said. "There was no doubt [Ryan] was going to do it. The only question now is how many more he's going to pitch. It might be 10 or 12 with the kind of stuff he has."

Five days later, 29,513 fans at the Big A held their collective breath as Ryan no-hit the Milwaukee Brewers for five innings. With two outs in the sixth, 41-year-old Henry Aaron, baseball's all-time home run king, poked a hanging curve over second base for a clean single.

Afterward, Ryan (who pitched a two-hitter) joked to reporters that Aaron finally had a real career highlight to brag about. "He can say that he was the one who broke up Nolan Ryan's try for back-to-back no-hitters," he said.

The accolades for Ryan, now 10–3 with five shutouts, rolled in.

"The equivalent of a Whitey Ford or Catfish Hunter who used finesse and an assortment of pitches," complimented the *Times*.

Sports Illustrated put him on its cover. The story was titled "The Great Nolan Ryan." Newsweek put him on its cover the very same week; the headline read FASTEST ARM IN THE WEST.

Not so great was his elbow, which remained inflamed. After beating Milwaukee, Ryan lost three straight on the road.

When it rained, it poured. On June 18 in Kansas City, he lasted just two innings before coming out with a groin pull. After skipping his next start, Ryan took the mound against Oakland and strained a triceps. At the Big A on July 8, he lost to Baltimore, and this time suffered an inflamed shoulder.

Ryan finally went to team doctor Jules Rasinski and got a cortisone shot in the shoulder. For reasons he kept to himself, Ryan chose not to tell Rasinski that his elbow was a bigger problem than his shoulder. The shot, therefore, did little to ease his discomfort.

The pain continued to get worse. When Ryan's losing streak reached eight, newspaper writers started nosing around. Nolan blamed the groin pull for his troubles, but John Stellman of the *Long Beach Telegram* and

Dick Miller of the *Herald Examiner* found out about the cortisone shot and broke the story.

"I had been trying to keep my ailment a secret so hitters wouldn't know," Ryan says. "But some writers were speculating something that wasn't true, while others were saying I had lost interest and had given up on the season."

With his secret finally out, the speculation ran even more rampant. Angels broadcaster Don Drysdale told Miller that cortisone shots to the shoulder often spelled rotator cuff trouble. The next time Miller and Ryan crossed paths, Nolan yelled, "Never talk to me again!" He was so incensed he went out of his way to avoid the media, hiding out in the shower room when reporters were around and also venting his frustration by breaking bats and kicking water coolers.

"Everywhere I went, all over the country, everyone asked me about [the injury]," recalls Ryan. "I needed a release and that was it. I handled it wrong, but you never know these things until you go through them. I thought it was temporary, and sometimes these things get blown out of proportion. I didn't want attention attracted to me because of an arm problem."

Added Ryan, "I was the Angels players rep making $125,000 a season, and I figured there was already enough turmoil in the clubhouse with Dick Williams. So I clammed up."

Reporters accused Ryan of not talking to teammates, but Ryan had always kept to himself anyway, and the rumors of him being silent only made him more irate.

Frank Tanana became the team's new stopper, but bringing the team out of its tailspin was too much for just one player. Their offense was the worst in baseball, and the bullpen was so bad that Williams perversely nicknamed his relievers "The Arson Squad" for their ability to let potential saves go up in smoke.

Against Baltimore on July 22, Ryan was hit early and often, and came out of the game after a mere inning and a third. "He wasn't throwing hard," Elrod Hendricks told the *Times*. "I even dug in at the plate."

"I don't think he's throwing as consistently as he used to," said Cleveland's Frank Robinson.

Acting on his own, Ryan bypassed the Angels team doctors and called on respected orthopedic surgeon Dr. Frank Jobe. The doctor diagnosed calcium deposits in the elbow joint and recommended an immediate operation.

Obstinate as ever, when ordered by GM Harry Dalton to sit down with Dick Miller and talk about his medical problems, Ryan complied but kept mum about the elbow while blaming his shoulder for his pitching problems.

When rumors began circulating that the great (or once great) Nolan Ryan might be traded for a power hitter to boost the Angels offense, Dick Williams just shrugged and told reporters that Ryan was "no longer untouchable. When you're in last place, something has to be done. If the right trade comes along, one which would be beneficial to our overall position, we'd have to take it."

In just three months, Ryan had gone from franchise darling to trade bait.

Despite two respectable outings in mid-August, the pain and rumors persisted. On August 28, two days before his next scheduled start, Ryan asked Williams to pull him from the starting rotation.

At first, the Angels brass claimed that Ryan was missing his regular turn because the wet grounds at Tiger Stadium posed a risk. But nobody bought that reasoning, and finally team president Red Patterson issued a statement admitting, "There may be something wrong with Ryan's right elbow and surgery is being contemplated."

Two weeks later, Nolan went home. On September 23, the calcium deposits were successfully removed in Houston.

• • •

The elbow injury and Ryan's secretive and even duplicitous manner of dealing with it were a reminder that he was only human.

"It was very depressing, very frustrating, but to live in constant pain was miserable," he told the *Times* six months later. "It bothered me all the time, and when you live with something that long, it has to have some effect on you. I hope I never have to do it again."

Always stoic and self-reliant, Ryan himself had come to believe his arm invincible. His only previous scare was in 1967, and then he had rested his arm a year rather than risk a possible career-ending operation.

Until then he had always figured out his problems on his own. This time it fell on Ruth to calm him down and make sure he knew that even without baseball life would go on, and that in the long run his family was more important than the game.

"Ruth wanted to help and deserved the right," Ryan said. "I think our marriage became stronger because we grew closer when I did draw her into it."

Ruth believes her husband's stubbornness is rooted in the fiercely independent streak passed on by his mother, a distant relative of Founding Father John Hancock. (Nolan's mother's family also has historical ties to one of the earliest members of the Civil War–era Texas Rangers, a man named Jack Pullin.)

"If he wants to do something a certain way, he will stick with it," she says. "It's almost like, if you make a mistake, he wants it to be his mistake. He just has a lot of self-confidence, which is mixed into stubbornness.

"In baseball, people are always trying to pull you down. You get criticism from everybody, and at times you need to look out for yourself and be your own cheerleader. You hear and read things said about you, but you can't let that affect you. I think Nolan's stubbornness helped him in part to get through it."

But it also could drive her batty, like the time a couple months after the birth of their third child, Wendy, when Ruth suggested to Nolan that they get away from it all for a few days so she could recharge her batteries. An advertisement for the Virgin Islands she saw in a magazine sounded "heavenly," and they booked reservations.

"In order to get there we had to fly to Miami and then take another plane to the Virgin Islands," Ruth says. "We got to the airport in Houston plenty early, but without notifying us they had changed the schedule, and the plane we were supposed to take to Miami in time for our connecting flight to the Islands had just taken off."

She wanted to fly to Miami on the next available flight and spend the night there before proceeding to the Islands, but Nolan insisted that they return to the ranch so he could sleep in his own bed that night.

Recalls Ruth, "I said, 'Oh, no!' and we had a yelling argument right there at the airline counter. He won. We went home, and the next day we went through the same thing. We got to the airport plenty early, but there was fog and we almost didn't make that flight. When we finally got to the Virgin Islands, we had only two days there."

According to Ryan's sister Mary Lou, Nolan's stubbornness is offset by the extraordinary patience he inherited from their father. "My mom was very impatient," says Mary Lou. "She was quick to get over her temper but patience wasn't Mom's strong suit. My dad was very patient with us six kids. People used to come to Dad and talk to him about problems. Neighborhood people, the folks he'd work for, and people at church would search him out because he was easy-going and very patient.

"Nolan's demeanor is a lot like my dad's. He doesn't get excited. He just kind of takes things as they come."

Both his stubbornness and patience were put to the test in 1975, and everything Ryan looked forward to in the upcoming season was summed up by the title of the popular daytime soap opera on which he filmed a cameo appearance—as a doctor, no less—the day before his elbow surgery.

On the show's scheduled airdate, the whole clan gathered in Nolan's living room in Alvin to watch. But just minutes before it was supposed to start, the network broke in to report the attempted assassination of President Gerald Ford by Charles Manson disciple Lynette "Squeaky" Fromme.

Like Nolan's career, that episode of *Ryan's Hope* was put on hold.

5

Back in the Saddle: 1976

Nolan's orders were as straight as the Texas panhandle: "Whatever you do, Robby, don't let the gray out. She'll try to follow the brown horse. So make sure you shut that gate as soon as I'm out."

Having worked the stables at the Flaming Gorge Boys and Girls camp in Utah for three summers, I moved confidently into position.

While Nolan put the halter to the brown, I took his position at the gate. As predicted, when Nolan led his horse out, the gray followed close behind. As Nolan's horse cleared, I made my move. With both hands on the rail, I quickly pushed the gate toward the rapidly approaching gray.

Boom!

Before the gate closed, the gray's nose struck it so hard it almost knocked me over. Faster than I could say Secretariat, she'd stuck her head through. It's now 1,200 pounds vs. 165. Digging the heels of my new city-bought cowboy boots into the hard Texas soil, I threw all my weight against the gate but too late... the gate flew open and the gray gleefully made her escape.

"Dammit, Robby! I told you to shut that gate! Now you go get that horse!"

As a 17-year-old batboy for the California Angels, I had been invited to Nolan Ryan's ranch to help out with chores for a week. I had not gotten off to a great start.

As Nolan trudged toward the house in a black cloud, I rounded up a bucket and poured in some glistening seeds. What horse could resist oats? The gray stood a meager 20 yards away and was looking at me with Bride of Frankenstein eyes. I planned to recapture her within seconds and win back Nolan's trust.

"Here, Gray," I said, inching closer. "Nice Gray.

When I got within a few feet of the horse, I grabbed her mane. With one strong jerk of her head she broke free and pranced away, and for the next hour that comic scene repeated itself over and over.

My new boots took a beating in the rock-strewn pasture. I trampled over every inch. Yesterday's new cowboy boots were scuffed and muddied beyond recognition. Moisture was seeping in through the toes.

All the while I wondered what Nolan must have been thinking. I imagined he and the family sitting at dinner and Ruth asking, "Where's Robby?"

And Nolan shaking his head and saying, "He'll be in soon. He's just finishing up."

As the chase continued, I decided that Gray was not the right name for this monster.

"The Hellion" was much better.

A savvy and crafty veteran, The Hellion was not buying my oats-in-the-bucket deal. After an hour of chasing her, I sighed a conceding sigh…

This old horse had put me in quite a dilemma: if I crawled back to Nolan, asking for help, I'd look like a tenderfoot. If I didn't, I may be out there forever.

Stoically resolute, I stumbled forward.

"I will not return without The Hellion," I told myself. "The Hellion will not beat me."

Again and again I shook the oats in the bucket. Each time The Hellion showed interest before dancing off.

Then, as the sun began to descend, she made her last move. Either she made a tactical mistake or she was setting up a grand finish for her glorious game.

After she pranced away from me for the hundredth time, she went to the farthest corner of the property. She could bolt around me or run through me, but I got the feeling she was spent and, having enjoyed her freedom, was ready for some oats and rest.

Her halter still hidden behind my back, I placed the bucket in front of her. She didn't move. I clasped her mane, tossed the halter around her neck, and slipped the tip around her nose.

The Hellion was mine!

Leading her back, I was tired but pleased. The twilight was beautiful. My mistake was corrected.

By the time I got to the house, the sky was battleship gray with just a bit of fading purple. Removing my muddied and torn boots, I put on my best game face, opened the sliding glass door, and made my entrance.

"How'd it go?" Nolan asked, as if I had just returned from buying groceries.

"Good," I replied.

Ruth smiled.

"We saved a little plate for you," she said. "Go ahead and help yourself to something to drink."

"Thanks."

My dinner was wrapped in foil, on the kitchen table. I went to the fridge for some ice tea and dined alone.

The lesson learned, Nolan never mentioned The Hellion or her adventurous romp through his rocky pasture to me again.

Not one to live in the past, Nolan, I discovered, forgives, forgets, and moves on.

• • •

The nasally, stripped-down sound of Willie Nelson oozed from the new record player in the middle of the Angels clubhouse. To the Southern California crowd, unaccustomed to the new progressive country sound out of Austin, it seemed foreign and out of place.

Don't cross him
Don't boss him.
He's wild in his sorrow.
He's ridin an' hiding his pain.
Don't fight him. Don't spite him.
Just wait for tomorrow.
Maybe he'll ride on again.

But to one Texan in the room, Nelson's song was both a reminder of home sweet home and perhaps an omen.

Like Nelson's Red Headed Stranger, Nolan Ryan was waiting for tomorrow riding, hiding his pain.

As the 1976 season kicked into gear, Ryan found there was a world of difference between playing catch with his wife and bearing down on an American League hitter in the batter's box. There was muscle tightness in the arm, and to compensate for it, he tweaked his delivery. That put stress on other parts of his body, so he tweaked something else, and then yet another thing would hurt.

"It was like I was playing Russian Roulette with my arm," Ryan told the *Times*. "It's just a matter of time. A year from now, if I'm still throwing the way I am, there's a darn good chance I could re-injure my arm."

In early June he again went to see Dr. Frank Jobe. Jobe discovered additional calcium deposits in Ryan's elbow and injected the joint with cortisone, but the tightness continued to frustrate Ryan like his own personal Hellion. Every time a full recovery seemed tantalizingly close, it would suddenly dance away.

Finally, a desperate GM Harry Dalton set up an appointment for Nolan to see a hypnotist in Beverly Hills. Ryan went, willing at that point to try anything, and he actually found the sessions relaxing and helpful, and they helped him channel his frustration and to consider his problems from a different perspective.

By the All-Star break, Ryan was 7–10 with a 3.54 ERA. But he had 166 strikeouts, and was on track for 300.

Meanwhile, the rest of the Angels played as if they were in a deep trance. The off-season acquisitions of slugger Bobby Bonds from the Yankees and Bill Melton from the White Sox didn't pull the team out of its spiral. A hand injury to Bonds in April put a huge damper on the offense. The loss of their best hitter made it particularly tough on Ryan and the pitching staff to gain any traction.

In retaliation for their anemic play, manager Dick Williams took to humiliating his own players. After a dare by Billy Martin in Boston, he actually forced the team to take batting practice with Wiffle balls in the hotel lobby, assuring the worried management that nothing would be broken, because nobody could hit the ball that hard. Another time, Williams berated rookie Dave Collins so badly he made him cry.

On July 22, the Angels were 39–57, in last place and some 20 games behind Oakland. They had just returned home from another dismal road trip, and as the noisy team bus approached the Big A parking lot, Williams read his players the riot act.

Several outraged players responded with epithets, and Bill Melton took it even further by standing up, ripping a bus seat from its moorings, and screaming at Williams. Melton's beef with his manager actually went back to when Williams had left Melton, then in Chicago, off the All-Star team.

"You're suspended!" Williams shouted at Melton.

"This is the happiest day of my life!" Melton yelled back.

Williams proposed that they take it up in the parking lot, but cooler heads prevented it. Nevertheless, Harry Dalton had seen enough and gave Williams his walking papers.

The managerial reins were handed to coach Norm Sherry, a former Dodgers catcher who'd helped Sandy Koufax with his throwing mechanics. But Sherry was not effective as a manager and lasted less than a year. He was succeeded by Dave Garcia, whose reputation as another highly regarded baseball man was called into question as the Angels' nosedive continued.

Through all the turbulence, Ryan grinded out start after start, and by year's end he had piled up some pretty impressive numbers. In addition to four three-hitters and a respectable 3.36 ERA, he led the majors with 327 strikeouts, seven shutouts, 6.1 hits per nine innings, 10.4 strikeouts per nine innings, and 183 walks. His 21 complete games and 284⅓ innings pitched were also among the leaders.

But some observers, not bothering to look past his 17–18 record and the fact that he led the league in losses, concluded that he was no better than a .500 pitcher.

Ryan would be the first to admit the previous two seasons had been particularly challenging, but he also knew much of the discrepancies in his won-lost record was due to his team's offensive woes.

The Angels had never had a winning season since Ryan joined California in 1972, and he knew a change in philosophy was needed if the team was to ever become competitive.

"We were in the rebuilding process," Ryan recalls. "We were trying to be competitive and it wasn't working, because we didn't have enough talent. I don't know if they could have done anything differently, because the farm system was depleted."

There was one way out of the wilderness: make a splash in free agency. And that off-season, Angels owner Gene Autry told Harry Dalton to go shopping and stay out of the bargain basement.

Ryan was elated. With a powerful new offense behind him, he expected to finally get the support that had evaded him in Anaheim.

6

Respect: 1977

I don't worry about critics,
because that is just what they are—
critics.

—NOLAN RYAN

The phone rang. I was expecting it to be a friend I played ball with. Instead, it was Nolan Ryan, calling from Palm Springs

"Robby, my truck's back in Alvin. How 'bout I fly you down and then you drive it back to Anaheim? One hundred bucks sound all right?"

Three days later, I was in Alvin. Ruth packed me a dozen sandwiches and Cokes, along with Nolan's credit card in case of an emergency.

When I discovered the tapes on the seat, I smiled. Nolan and I had driven many miles together listening to country tunes. I had been hearing a lot about Waylon and Willie and the new *Wanted! The Outlaws* and *Dreaming My Dreams* records, and there they were.

By the time I hit El Paso, I'd listened to both tapes 20 times each.

It was musical nirvana. It was some of the best stuff I'd ever heard—authentic, poetic, and gritty, kind of like Nolan.

Combined with the rumbling of the truck's tires, I was lulled into a world of mystery women, bars, wine, and guitars.

Silver coins that jingle jangle
Fancy boots that step in time
Oh the secret of those dark eyes
She did play a gypsy rhyme

Waylon and Willie are a lot like Nolan. They didn't get the respect they deserved when they were in Nashville, so they moved to Austin. Kind of like when Nolan played in New York but didn't get much respect until he got to Anaheim. So it's no accident that Nolan liked these tapes. They spoke to his outlaw sensibilities.

Not that you'd think of Nolan as an outlaw. At first glance, he seems conservative and gentlemanly, but that's only one side of him. He's an outlaw in the way he thinks and pitched. How he controlled hitters with intimidation, and how he snuck into weight rooms and did stretches before anyone else gave it serious thought.

I streaked across the desert like a Saturn Five rocket. Six cylinders of American steel and rubber, gobbling up the miles like a kid gobbles up ice cream. Outside: the harshness of the American Southwest. The Great Empty, The Llano, the flattest, hottest part of Texas. Inside: bliss, music, and air-conditioning. The 8-track stereo played the tape over and over, automatically restarting after the last track. I hear Waylon's "Dreaming My Dreams" again.

I hope that I won't be that wrong anymore
I hope that I've learned this time
I hope that I find what I'm reaching for
The way that it is in my mind

Five hours later I was in New Mexico, speakers still blasting. Just me, Waylon, and Nolan's truck tooling through the Great Empty. I drove straight through, stopping only at rest stops and gas towns. My diet consisted of Ruth's sandwiches, candy bars, and fruit.

He does a little Shakespeare and he sings
He plays the mandolin and other things
He looks for love, beauty, and IQ
That's what makes the cowboy sing the blues

I was feeling good. This wasn't high school, watching TV, or working for the man. This was Nolan Ryan's blue truck, the one Gene Autry gave him for filling seats and being a good guy.

Blam!

The grinding, halting sound of metal against metal jolted me from my idyllic trance.

Blam! Blam!

I envisioned the worst. Not enough oil, my fault. Not enough water, my fault. Not enough anything, my fault.

Blam!

I slowed to the shoulder as the music played on. Willie and Waylon were oblivious to my plight.

Through teardrops and laughter
He does the best that he can
A good-hearted woman
Loving a good-timing man

I hugged the slow lane and searched for a gas station. The petrol gods were with me—within minutes I spotted a Chevron sign peeking over the horizon. I coasted into the filling station, where a young attendant popped the hood.

"The fan blade is loose," he said.

"How bad?"

"Pretty bad. If it had popped off, it might have torn a hole in the hood."

"Is it fixable?"

"Yeah, but I got to call in for the part."

Surrounded by nothing but desert, sky, and garage, I imagined calling Ruth: "Ruth, this is Robby. Nolan's car blew up. I'm in the middle of nowhere. Send sandwiches."

Somehow, the kid tracked down the part. Ordered it from somewhere from someone, and for the next several hours I explored every inch of the Chevron station. By the time the part arrived five hours later, I'd memorized every tire, torque wrench, oil can, and sexy calendar in the place.

The new blade was on in 10 minutes. I handed the kid Nolan's credit card. He gave it a disbelieving look.

"Yeah, it's his truck. I'm taking it to California for him."

I affixed a facsimile Nolan Ryan signature to the receipt. The attendant laughed.

Moments later I was back on Hwy 10 with a renewed faith in the human race, mechanics, and car parts. Two days later in Palm Springs, I handed Nolan the keys and the receipt for the new fan blade. He gave me a check for $100.

I didn't cash the check when I got home. I just left it in my dresser, as though I was protecting the memory.

• • •

In 1975, the long-standing renewal clause that tied players to one team was overturned by an arbitrator and later upheld in federal court, ending the stranglehold owners had had on players since the game's inception. The ruling led to a negotiated agreement between both parties that allowed players to become free agents after six seasons.

Worried that the ruling would hike salaries into the stratosphere and drastically change the game, Angels owner Gene Autry was reluctant to go along. But GM Harry Dalton warned him that if the Angels didn't jump into the free agency pool with both feet, they would be perennial league doormats.

Deciding that he had a responsibility to the fans and his sponsors to field the best team possible, Autry took $4.1 million out of his saddlebags and told Dalton to go hunting.

Among the players on his wish list was Oakland star left fielder Joe Rudi. Dalton acquired him for $2.1 million, and by year's end, free agents Bobby Grich and Don Baylor were also in the fold.

On paper and to long-suffering Angels fans, the new hitters looked like an instant fix to the team's problems. No one realized it at the time, but there would be a price to pay down the road. By turning to free agency, the Angels changed the focus from building from within to trying to buy a championship. Over the ensuing years, the Angels would pursue big-name free agents at the cost of their farm system. Under Autry's reign, the Angels would win three divisions but they were never consistent contenders.

Ryan began the season with a new three-year contract. He left for spring training in February without Ruth, who was back in Alvin expecting their third child. Nolan flew back home March 20 and was present two days later for the birth of their daughter, Wendy.

A couple weeks later Nolan went house hunting in Anaheim. He ended up buying a home in upscale Villa Park, right next door to teammate Rod Carew and his wife, Michelle. Ryan even picked out the furniture himself, which amazed Ruth to no end.

By the time she got to Anaheim in June with Wendy and the two boys, Ryan was already 8–4 with a major league–leading 113 strikeouts. He was in Minnesota on June 15 when he was embroiled in an ugly feud involving his old teammate and friend, Tom Seaver, and Dick Young, the legendary columnist for the *New York Daily News.*

In February, Seaver had complained to Mets team president M. Donald Grant about the club's unwillingness to sign any of the available free agents. Seaver also told Grant that in view of the escalating salaries free agents were getting, he wanted to renegotiate his own contract.

A tight-fisted Wall Street authoritarian, Grant told Seaver he was out of line and was publicly backed by Young, who had made a habit of bashing Seaver in his columns of late.

Jack Lang, another *Daily News* columnist, took Seaver's side and recommended that he take his concerns directly to Lorinda de Roulet, daughter of owner Joan Payson and Grant's boss.

He did so, and on June 13 de Roulet and GM Joe McDonald agreed to a contract extension giving Seaver $300,000 in 1978 and $400,000 in '79.

Satisfied that the matter was behind him, Seaver got the shock of his life the next morning when he picked up the paper and read Dick Young's column.

"In a way, Tom Seaver is like Walter O'Malley," Young wrote. "Both are very good at what they do. Both are very deceptive in what they say. Both are very greedy."

Two paragraphs later, Young exploded a bombshell that had Seaver's blood boiling:

"Nolan Ryan is getting more [money] now than Seaver, and that galls Tom because Nancy Seaver and Ruth Ryan are very friendly and Tom Seaver long has treated Nolan Ryan like a little brother."

It was true that Ryan was making $300,000 to Seaver's $225,000, but Seaver had never told anyone he was jealous of Ryan. As one of the game's premier pitchers, Seaver only wanted to stay in step with current salaries in the new free agent era.

Seaver immediately called Mets PR man Arthur Richman and screamed, "Get me out of here, do you hear me? Get me out of here!"

Seaver then informed de Roulet that the contract agreement reached the night before was null and void. Seaver skipped the Mets-Braves game and flew home. The following day, McDonald traded him to the Cincinnati Reds.

Back in Minnesota, Ryan didn't know what to think. Tom and Nancy Seaver were among the Ryans' closest friends. He assumed that Young had dragged him and Ruth into the story to stir up controversy.

It was a solid assumption. Ever since Young's son-in-law, Thornton Geary, had joined the Mets front office, Young had morphed from one of the most respected reporters in the country into a company hack who did Grant's bidding.

Young invented "facts" to make Seaver look bad. To this day, New Yorkers blame him for costing the Mets their ace.

Said Seaver later, "Bringing your family into it, with no truth whatsoever to what he wrote—I could not abide that. I had to go."

• • •

By the All-Star break, Ryan was 13–8 and still leading the majors in strikeouts.

Keeping apace with him was teammate Frank Tanana, who'd blossomed into one of the best arms in the game. Although the two often had personality clashes, Tanana was all business when he pitched. He ended up going 15–9 in 1977, with 205 strikeouts and a 2.54 ERA, plus a league-leading seven shutouts.

In July, Tanana was asked by Billy Martin to join the AL squad at Yankee Stadium for the All-Star Game. When he declined because of an injury, Martin turned to Ryan to replace him. But Ryan's pride had been wounded for not being selected in the first place, and he told Martin he was going to spend the break at the beach as planned. This got a fiery reaction from Martin and opposing NL manager Sparky Anderson, who both questioned Ryan's loyalty.

The drama between Ryan and Tanana continued later in the season when Tanana, concerned about being overworked, said the reason for his weariness was Ryan's insistence on pitching every four days. Ryan responded, somewhat tersely, "I'm tired of people using me as an excuse. I'm being made to feel like I'm the scapegoat for Frank's arm and I don't want it that way, and as far as I'm concerned he hasn't pushed himself since the All-Star break."

Ryan grew to respect Tanana for his eventual transformation from playboy to Christian fireballer to crafty veteran. After leaving the Angels in 1980, Tanana pitched 13 more seasons with the Red Sox, Rangers, Tigers, Mets, and Yankees, and ended up winning 240 games on a below-average fastball. Mixing his pitches, he kept hitters off-balance and became known on ESPN as "the guy who threw 90 in the '70s and 70 in the '90s."

"Frank Tanana is an interesting case, because he came to the Angels as one of the most talented left-handers and was extremely successful," says Ryan. "After his arm injury [in 1979], he completely changed his style of pitching and was very successful. It's not very often you find someone able to make the transition from power pitcher to finesse pitcher, but he did it. I think it tells you a lot about Frank as a competitor."

Much has been made of the supposed bad blood between Tanana and Ryan, but Tracy Ringolsby, longtime Ryan confidant and former Angels beat writer for the *Long Beach Telegram*, says it was overblown by the media.

"I thought it was two egos, two guys with a lot of pride," says Ringolsby. "Frankie was young and brash, Nolie was a little more quiet. But I saw them socialize together when they didn't have to, so I don't think there was as much bitterness as the press made out.

"Nolie was a little older, a little more stable. Frankie didn't want to pitch on a four-man, and Nolan did. I think we have a tendency to make things bigger than they are, but I never felt uncomfortable around both of them or felt like there was an edge."

The success of the Ryan-Tanana tandem notwithstanding, the big bang expected for Gene Autry's big bucks never materialized in 1977. Rudi and Grich were injured early, and Baylor never really got out of the gate. Winning just 74 games that season, the Angels ended up fifth in the AL West, 28 games behind Kansas City.

Thanks to another fifth-place finish, the revolving door on the Angels manager's office continued to twirl, as Dave Garcia replaced Norm Sherry, who had replaced Dick Williams the year before.

"When we would be in an extended losing streak and it was my turn to pitch, you felt pressure to try to turn it around," said Ryan. "It was like that in 1977 and for almost my entire stay in Anaheim."

Ryan went 19–16, with a 2.77 ERA and a league-leading 341 strikeouts and 22 complete games. Impressive figures, to be sure, but some observers pointed to his 204 walks—the most in the AL—and 21 hit batsmen, and clucked that they disqualified him from comparison with the greats of the past.

In a column entitled "The Anaheim Wild Man Is Almost Under Control," Jim Murray said that for all his success on the mound, Ryan wasn't making anybody forget about Walter Johnson or Christy Mathewson.

"With his natural ability, Ryan should be halfway to the Hall of Fame," Murray wrote. "But if Ryan's career ended today he'd be considered as a might-have-been, a player who would be considered darned good but not having really reached his potential."

And it was no use blaming the team's weak offense; Murray wrote, "After all, Walter Johnson lost 21 one-run games in his career and he went on to win 417 games."

"There's no secret to my problem," Ryan admitted. "It's been wildness. And 90 percent of my wildness has been on fastballs. But that wildness has subsided of late. When I was young I missed big, but lately I've been missing small."

Murray was unpersuaded. "A miss is a miss," he countered, "and until Ryan gets his control to where his misses are less, he will be considered among historians a sometimes-great and not an all-time great."

Hall of Famer George Brett of Kansas City says the case against Ryan made by his detractors is fatally flawed, because their opinions were formed at a typewriter or computer keyboard and not on the field of battle.

"They are full of BS!" says Brett. "I'd love to see one of those critics go up and face him and then walk away and say this guy is not worthy of all the accolades he's getting. They only said those things because they never faced him.

"If you're a power pitcher, you're gonna be a little wild. You're going to throw out of the strike zone when you throw that hard. And it was acceptable. Ryan might have walked a bunch of people, but it really doesn't matter how many people you walk—it's how many you strike out in situations when you need a strikeout. And in strikeout situations, nobody got any more out of them than he did. He had the ability to tune it up a little, and that's rare. His mantra was, 'Bring your game. I'm gonna throw it and if you hit it, congratulations. If you don't, sit the [bleep] down!'"

To Reggie Jackson, Ryan was "the most challenging pitcher" he ever faced.

"I don't look at the losses," says Reggie. "I look at the wins."

"The critics didn't hit off of him," says Pete Rose. "He was a .500 pitcher because of his teammates, and I know he won't say that. But check his ERA when he was a .500 pitcher, or his complete games when he was 16–16 or 19–17. Nolan didn't have much help. He was never on a dominant team."

Rod Carew maintains that people who said Ryan was a .500 pitcher don't know baseball very well. "Every time he took to the mound, you had a chance to win. He was a staff-saver. He didn't go out there and pitch two or three innings—he would pitch eight or nine. When he started the game he might be throwing 97 miles per hour, and at the end he'd be throwing 100. He usually kept our team in the game and gave us a chance to win."

Before Ryan came to the American League in 1972, Carew could handle most every pitcher he faced. But when he found himself flailing away at Ryan's 100-mph fastballs, Carew decided his stance at the plate needed an immediate overhaul.

"Nolan made me start looking at myself," he says. "When I came up to the big leagues, I would hold my hands straight up and hit anybody. But I couldn't hit Nolan, because he'd overpower me upstairs. So I started crouching and noticed I could see the difference in his fastball when I was down better than when I stood straight up. From then on, I was able to handle his fastball a little bit better."

Whitey Herzog says Ryan's lifetime won-lost record is deceptive.

"When he pitched for the Mets they couldn't score runs, and then he went to the Angels, who scored even less," Herzog said. "In Anaheim we had a bunch of little guys in our lineup, and he was 22–14 one year, and in 10 of his losses he gave up two runs or less. That will make anybody a .500 pitcher.

"If you're over .500 with the Mets and the Angels in the most productive years of your career, you're a great pitcher. So the reason for the discrepancy was the two teams he pitched on. If he'd pitched for a powerhouse—my god, I'd like to see some of the numbers he'd have put up!"

Jeff Torborg seconds that. "The Angels didn't have much of a bullpen, we didn't score much, and we weren't very good defensively," says the former catcher. "Other than that, we were a great team.

"Just ask the hitters he faced. Would they rather face Nolan on a given day, or somebody who had this enormous won-lost percentage? I know what everyone would say: 'I don't want to face Ryan—and certainly not in the twilight!'"

Longtime manager Jim Leyland first faced Ryan in the Instructional League in 1965. To Leyland, Ryan is one of the best he's seen in his 50-plus years in baseball.

"There are very few pitchers that make you wonder, *How'd that guy ever lose a game?*" says Leyland, whose Pirates faced Ryan several times in the late 1980s. "When you saw Ryan at times, you wondered how he ever lost a game. People say he's a .500 pitcher? He's not—he was 36 games over .500."

Today some still insist that Ryan doesn't belong among the greatest hurlers in the game. They point out that his won-lost record isn't as sparkling as 1970s contemporaries Steve Carlton, Don Sutton, and Jim Palmer. Sportswriter Jayson Stark went so far as to call Ryan "the most overrated right-handed pitcher in baseball history." Don Sutton groused, "If we both have as many wins [324], and I did it in three less years, why is he considered better?"

Respected baseball writer and commentator Rob Neyer claims Ryan doesn't belong in the same room with Walter Johnson or Tom Seaver. After fans voted Ryan one of the top nine pitchers of all time on the All-Century team in 1999, Neyer wrote that Ryan led his league in strikeouts 11 times, but in walks eight times. He pointed out that Johnson, Seaver, Christy Mathewson, and Roger Clemens all led their respective leagues in strikeouts numerous times, but never in walks.

"The truly great pitchers, the guys who belong on the all-time teams, were able to record great numbers of strikeouts and avoid issuing many walks," Neyer claims. "While Ryan's .204 batting average allowed is indeed the lowest in major league history, his .307 on-base percentage allowed isn't really close to being in the top 100. The other problem was Ryan didn't do any of the little things well, like fielding the ball and holding runners.

"People like to defend Ryan by pointing to the quality of the teams for which he pitched. In those 26 seasons, Ryan's teams won 2,104 games, and they lost 2,048 games. In those 26 seasons, Ryan's teams finished above .500 in 15 of them.

"But to suggest that Ryan is, say, one of baseball's nine greatest pitchers is, in a word, indefensible."

Pitcher Jim Deshaies, who played with Ryan in Houston, says that's revisionism at its worst.

"As time has gone by, certain perceptions have gotten out, and one of them is that Nolan was a .500 pitcher—that he walked all these guys, so now he's overrated. But I think he's underrated, because people take the negatives without really delving into the facts. When you look into the numbers and the way he pitched—the 3.19 lifetime ERA, the .204 batting average against him, the 9.5 strikeouts and 6.55 hits per game—it paints a different picture.

"Yes, he walked a lot of people, but all the low-run games he pitched trump that. He pitched for bad clubs. If you're a .500 pitcher on a team with a .300 or .400 winning percentage like the Angels were, that's pretty damn good."

None of which is to say that Ryan didn't have control problems. He is, after all, the all-time leader in walks, with 2,795. And he's the first to admit that he threw too many pitches out of the strike zone.

For instance, in a game against Boston in 1974, Ryan tied the single-game strikeout mark of 19. He threw a total of 172 pitches in the game, of which 114 were strikes. It took him 57 strikes to get his 19 strikeouts, which means he threw 115 extraneous pitches, far too many for all practical purposes.

Ruth Ryan thinks the critics only fed her husband's competitive nature and made him better in the long run.

"Nolan was always his own motivator, and if he believed in something or someone strong enough, no critic could deter him from it," she said. "If there were bad things written, he didn't want to read about it; he was already thinking about the next game and focusing on what he could do, and not on what people perceived him to be.

"He has always been the type of person that would give it 100 percent effort no matter what he was doing. He knew he had a God-given talent, and he also knew how to make the most of what he was given."

"A lot of the time the people critical of you really have no understanding of everything that comes into play," adds Nolan. "My attitude is, you can't worry about those things. You can't drive yourself into worrying about everything that people say about you."

In 1977, there was no better proof of the gulf between Ryan's judges in the Fourth Estate and his peers than the fact that in the balloting by the former for the American League's Cy Young Award, he came in third.

But based on a vote of the players themselves, Ryan was named AL "Pitcher of the Year" by the *Sporting News*.

7

Season of Discontent: 1978

It was a Saturday night, and the mean streets of Gary, Indiana, were about to get a whole lot meaner. Leonard Smith, laid-off steelworker, convicted felon, and jealous ex-husband, was in his Ford staked out in front of his ex-wife's sister's house. On the seat beside him was a loaded shotgun.

The house belonged to Joan Hawkins, sister of the stalker's ex-wife, Barbara Smith. Inside with them was Lyman Bostock, a friend of Hawkins' from childhood. Waiting outside was Bostock's uncle and chauffeur for the evening, Tom Turner.

Bostock had grown up in Gary and, though he now lived in Southern California and played baseball for the California Angels, he still considered it home.

At dinner earlier with Turner, Bostock had asked about Joan Hawkins, whom he hadn't seen in nine years. They ended up driving across town to her house, and had only been inside a few minutes when Hawkins asked Bostock if she and her sister could catch a ride to a nearby relative's house.

When they pulled away from the house, Leonard Smith followed.

Turner's Buick was stopped at a red light at the corner of 5th and Jackson when Smith rolled up alongside. Sitting with Barbara Smith in the back seat on the right-hand side, Bostock didn't notice the car. If he had, he might conceivably have seen Smith reach down and pick up the shotgun next to him, ram a shell into the chamber, and point the weapon at him.

But there was no earthly reason for him to notice. Bostock wasn't thinking of death that night. Life was too bright and full of promise.

Besides being a gifted ballplayer, he was one the most gregarious and friendly guys anyone would ever want to meet. His teammates revered him. Opposing pitchers may have dreaded the sight of him digging in at the plate, but otherwise even they loved him.

When the gun went off, Bostock took the full force of the explosion in the head. Before the light turned green, half of his face was gone.

"I saw Leonard look into our car," Barbara would testify at her ex-husband's trial. "He looked into the back seat and smirked."

Turner ran into the nearby Bi-Lo store and pleaded with someone to call 911. An ambulance took Bostock to St. Mary's hospital, but it was no use.

The funeral was held five days later in South Central, where Bostock had donated $36,000 to the parish for drug and alcohol recovery programs. Neighborhood kids Bostock had mentored pedaled their bikes to the church.

Inside were Bostock's young widow, his mother, and 25 heartbroken teammates and coaches. Too affected by the senseless tragedy to give the eulogy, Jim Fregosi asked players representative Ken Brett to stand in for him.

Brett was poignant: "We called him Jibber-Jabber, because he enlivened every clubhouse scene, chasing tension, drawing laughter in the darkest hour of defeat. When winning wasn't in the plan, Lyman knew the sun would come up the next morning… There's only one consolation: we're all better persons for having him touch our lives."

Why would God permit something like that to happen to such a special human being?

Thirty-five years later, the question still reverberates.

• • •

Of Nolan Ryan's eight seasons in Anaheim, 1978 was his most heartbreaking. Nothing puts the game of baseball into perspective like the death of a beloved teammate. Wins, losses, and strikeouts suddenly become irrelevant when one of your own is struck down in the prime of his life.

Ryan started strong, but the Angels offense couldn't muster much support, as usual; despite allowing just 19 hits in April, Ryan was 1–1 with a 1.98 ERA.

Overall, the team's play was much improved, and credit for that went to Buzzie Bavasi, the Angels' new general manager.

Architect of eight pennants and four world championships with the Dodgers, Bavasi replaced Harry Dalton after the 1977 season and had set about getting the team some needed firepower. His biggest coup was the acquisition of free agent Lyman Bostock from Minnesota. One of the game's rising stars, Bostock had hit .336 with 14 home runs in 1977, and Angels fans salivated at the prospect of him batting between Joe Rudi and Don Baylor.

Bavasi also dealt slugger Bobby Bonds to the White Sox, along with young outfielder Thad Bosley and pitching prospect Richard Dotson, in exchange for pitchers Chris Knapp and Dave Frost, and catcher Brian Downing.

By June 1, the rejuvenated Angels were only 1.5 games out. That's when Bavasi fired manager Dave Garcia and handed the reins to Jim Fregosi—whom the Angels had traded to the Mets in 1971 for Nolan Ryan.

Already linked by their involvement in one of the worst trades in baseball history, there was mutual respect between Fregosi and Ryan.

"I think everybody feels he's more like a permanent fixture in the organization," Ryan said of Fregosi when the move was announced. "More than that, he's a product of the organization. He was very successful. He's very popular in the community. He's the first homegrown player the organization ever had. He's not somebody else's reject."

Fregosi brought an air of authority the club didn't have with Garcia or his predecessors, and was still player-friendly. The Angels finally had a manager the players could respect.

"When I got here," Don Baylor said, "pitchers did what they wanted to do, regulars did what they wanted to do. There was no control in the organization. In doubleheaders, pitchers would leave the park once they were taken out of the game. The first time it happened, Ryan said, 'That's the way we do it. That's part of it.' Jimmy said, 'No, that's not part of it.' He stopped it right there."

Despite the club's winning makeover, Ryan's struggles continued. Battered by nagging injuries, he couldn't coordinate his conditioning program with Fregosi's new five-man rotation. Unable to find his rhythm, by mid-June Ryan was 3–6, with a 4.04 ERA.

On June 13, he told the *Times* that if the Angels had the opportunity to improve the club by dealing him to Texas, he would probably approve the trade.

"I don't think I've performed as well as I'm capable the last couple of years, and the change of scenery might do me good," he said. Texas Rangers owner Brad Corbett quickly indicated interest in acquiring Ryan and even announced his availability to fly to L.A. and personally make a deal.

Bavasi told him not to bother. "Corbett was crazy to say something like that," said the GM. "But nothing happened and nothing's going to happen."

That same month, Ryan let himself be talked into a foot race with catcher Terry Humphrey before batting practice one afternoon. Their teammates took bets on which runner was "the fastest of the slowest," and gathered on the outfield grass to find out. Ryan won the race, but in the process he tore a hamstring and for the first time as an Angel was put on the 21-day disabled list.

"It just seems like it has been that type of year for me," said the disgusted pitcher.

He returned on July 5, but in his next seven starts managed only one win. Hoping a change in appearance might bring about a change in his luck, Ryan grew a beard. When he beat Cleveland on July 19 for his first win in 57 days, Fregosi joked, "I don't mind you looking like Methuselah, but I hope we don't have to live that long before you get your next win."

His victory against the Tribe brought Ryan's record to 4–8 and the Angels within a half-game of first-place Kansas City. But after defeating Detroit in his next start, Ryan didn't win again until August 11, and there were reports in the press that he might be traded to Houston for Bob Watson.

New questions about Ryan's durability were raised, based on his output of about 7,000 pitches per year—almost double the average pitcher's total.

"Just how long can this go on?" wondered columnist Jim Murray. "How many pitches can one arm possess before running out of fastballs? Wouldn't it be wiser to hoard some of those pitches and pace yourself and conserve your body like Tom Seaver?"

Ryan waved off such concerns, saying that having pitched so infrequently when he was with New York made him "the equivalent of a 25-year-old rookie" when he joined the Angels. "The end result is that I am now able to throw 200-plus innings a year and not burn out," he said. "Tom Seaver wants to pitch until he's 40. Tom Seaver wants to win 300 games. Tom Seaver has goals, numbers. I don't have any numbers I want to set."

Even as late as 1978, Ryan didn't have much of a career plan. His goal was to earn a living by throwing as many pitches as he could and make up for all the time he had lost with the Mets. What Ryan's critics didn't take into account was that his conditioning, genetics, and mechanics would allow him to last much longer than anyone ever dreamed. Tom Seaver's vaunted arm would wear out; Ryan's seemingly never would.

Endurance wasn't his problem. Ryan was better prepared for a higher workload than most pitchers who did relatively little between starts to build their strength and stamina.

"He trained harder than any player I ever played with," recalls Don Baylor. "No human that ever pitched in the majors had the stamina Nolan had or could throw as many pitches as he would every night. His legs were strong, and he knew if his legs were strong, his arm was going to be strong and his endurance was going to be strong.

"He'd come out early with Jimmie Reese and chase fungos. And then you'd see him tossing the ball on the sideline while a lot of guys would be in the hot-cold tank. There's no way the other pitchers would be out there doing that."

Nevertheless, Ryan's difficulties continued into the dog days of summer that season. On August 16 he suffered a rib separation in a game in Boston, and for the second time in two months was placed on the 21-day DL.

He wasn't the only Angels pitcher with problems. Frank Tanana had struggled with a dead arm all season, and in an interview with the *Times* he blamed it on Ryan's insistence on a shorter rotation.

The bickering eventually took a back seat to more pertinent issues. Under the leadership of Fregosi—and with stellar pitching and the hot bats of Baylor, Downing, and Bostock—the Angels had turned into true contenders. When they rolled into Chicago on September 22 for a three-game set with the White Sox, they were in second place, 5.5 games back of Kansas City.

Then the unthinkable happened.

Don Baylor recalls Lyman Bostock's last game:

"Lyman went up to bat in the ninth inning with the winning run on base and two outs, and then grounded out to end the game. He was so pissed I'm not sure if he even took a shower. The last time I saw him was when he dashed by me wearing a sport coat. I asked him, 'Where you going?' But he didn't say a word. He just bolted by. That was the last time I ever saw him alive."

That evening, Baylor joined Ryan, Rudi, and Remy at Eli's nightclub for dinner and music. When they returned to the team's hotel, the phones were ringing off the hooks as the news about what had happened to Bostock spread.

"We asked Buzzie where Lyman was," recalls Baylor. "We wanted to go see him. But Buzzie said we couldn't go there because he had over a hundred [shotgun] pellets in his head and they didn't expect him to live.

"We were all stunned and sat out in the hallway just staring at the walls. Hotel guests walked around us, on us, and over us, but we didn't even notice. We just sat out in the hallway and cried. We couldn't believe it. It was the worst night I ever had in baseball.

"It was the end of the season and we were still in the race, but after that happened, the guys just wanted to get the season over with.

"Losing Lyman was a hard one. He was a great player. But losing a friend and a teammate, that was the worst of it. It was a brutal day, an absolutely brutal day."

Ryan was scheduled to pitch for the Angels the following day.

"We're all in too much of a state of shock to get any grip on our emotions," he told the press beforehand. "What can I say? I'm sure everyone on the club would rather not go out and play."

But Ryan ended up throwing seven strong innings, allowing five hits and three earned runs. The Angels were ahead 7–3 when Paul Hartzell relieved Ryan in the eighth inning. Hartzell closed it out with two perfect innings, and Ryan got his ninth win.

"We were devastated, because Lyman was so well liked," recalls Nolan.

And it wasn't just for his ability to hit a baseball. Ryan recalls that Bostock's season with the Angels actually got off to a slow start "because he was pressing so hard to do as well as he could."

Disappointed in himself and his .147 batting average, Bostock actually tried to give back his very first paycheck from the Angels. When owner Gene Autry wouldn't hear of it, Lyman donated the entire check to charity.

The Angels finished tied with Texas for second place in the AL West, five games behind Kansas City. Their 87–75 record was the best in franchise history.

Ryan finished a disappointing 10–13. He still led the league with 260 strikeouts, despite pitching 65 fewer innings than the previous year. He also led the league with 148 walks and 13 wild pitches. Ryan himself had to admit that at 31 years of age, his resilient body was showing signs of wear.

On top of everything else, he had a new contract to think about. Ryan figured he would ask for something in the $250,000 per year range for three years, and when that expired, he might retire.

He wanted to finish his career in Anaheim. In fact, he had just purchased a home in upscale Villa Park. His three children enjoyed the Southern California weather, and the thought of uprooting them had no appeal. But there were no guarantees, especially with Buzzie Bavasi making the decisions.

Bavasi's career was steeped in baseball history. As an advance man for the Dodgers, he had been instrumental in Jackie Robinson's entry into baseball. Bavasi had played hardball negotiating the contracts of Sandy Koufax and Don Drysdale.

In anticipation of a long, contentious contract negotiation, for the first time in his career Ryan decided to bring an agent on board.

It had been a painful season, physically and emotionally. Ryan returned to Alvin to rest and recuperate, and to contemplate what life might be like playing ball on a club other than the California Angels.

8

Buzzie's Folly: 1979

We can get two players to go 8–7
and we wouldn't miss Nolan Ryan.

—BUZZIE BAVASI

The sun peeking over the rugged San Jacintos made for a spectacular sight at Gene Autry Park in Palm Springs in March 1979. The shadows angled off the light standards and edged their way past the pitcher's mound, where Nolan Ryan was throwing batting practice. By the time he finished 15 minutes later, the shadows had lifted and the dry desert heat started to take over the diamond. As Ryan headed for the bench, trainer Rick Smith asked, "How do you feel, Tex?"

"Like I'm in need of an overhaul," drawled Ryan.

Since arriving in California in 1972, Ryan had thrown more than 56,000 pitches and basically re-written the record book for power pitchers. But for all that, the Angels had played just one season of .500 ball.

That was about to change. During the off-season, Buzzie Bavasi had acquired Minnesota infielder Rod Carew. With seven batting titles, the 12-time All-Star was a game-changer, and as he stepped into the batting cage and laid down a series of perfect bunts, Ryan couldn't help but feel relieved. Not only would he no longer have to face his old nemesis, but with Carew at the top of the order and Don Baylor, Bobby Grich, and

Brian Downing hitting behind him, the offensive drought that had plagued the Angels for so long should be over.

As Ryan admired Carew's swing, he was approached by Ross Newhan of the *Los Angeles Times*. Newhan was working on a feature piece about Ryan's conditioning regimen, and wanted to know how the slew of injuries Ryan had incurred in the last couple seasons had affected his workout routine.

At his age, Ryan said, he had to work harder to maintain his body. In the past he had used distance running to improve his cardiovascular ability and to keep his weight down, and though he liked the diversion distance running brought, he realized it was not really conducive to pitching.

While Ryan explained the benefits of sprinting over distance running, outfielder Joe Rudi took his turn in the cage. The former All-Star had struggled since injuring his hand two years ago, and Ryan frankly wondered how much the veteran had left. While Rudi took his hacks, Newhan brought up Jim Fregosi's five-man rotation and the adverse effect it had on Ryan's performance. With his recent tiff with Frank Tanana still on everybody's mind, Ryan chose his words carefully.

"The four days between starts felt like forever, and I often got lazy," he said. "I came up stiff the day after I pitched. From now on I'll try to do wind sprints to cover that extra day. Hopefully, the additional day of work on the off-day will help."

Rudi finished his round and Don Baylor stepped in. As the big man slammed ball after ball over the trees in left field, Newhan tiptoed into the touchy subject of Ryan's squabbles with GM Buzzie Bavasi over salary.

Ryan said he had told Bavasi in January he had no intention of becoming a free agent, and that he preferred to finish his career as an Angel. But he also put Bavasi on notice that if the Angels wanted to keep him long-term, negotiations needed be concluded before the start of the season.

When Newhan asked about specific demands, Ryan was straightforward: "Bavasi asked me to submit my proposal, and I informed him through my agent that I wanted four years at roughly $550,000 a year."

Baylor finished and Dan Ford stepped in. Acquired from the Twins for Ron Jackson, Ford was expected to take over Lyman Bostock's spot in right. As the bespectacled right-hander began his cuts, Fregosi looked on from behind the cage.

"Buzzie told us he would take the offer to Gene [Autry] and get back to us," Ryan told Newhan. "Gene thought it would be best to let me go ahead and play the year out, and if at that point the Angels were still interested, they could enter the bidding through the re-entry draft."

When Newhan suggested that in view of his disappointing 1978 season the front office might not be as enamored of him as before, Ryan studied the distant landscape before responding.

"If I had been healthy and had the type of year expected, I might have made the difference," he conceded. "I was frustrated and disappointed, but I didn't dwell on it. I expected them to react this way, because I was coming off a poor season. It will be a gamble on their part and mine to see the year through."

Brian Downing followed Ford into the batting cage. The way the catcher-outfielder had embraced the weights in the off-season was impressive.

"How come you're wearing a chest protector under your shirt?" Ryan called out as Downing roped ball after ball the opposite way.

Newhan wound up the interview with the million-dollar question:

"Since the Angels still haven't offered you a new contract and the current one is set to expire after the current season, what will happen if Buzzie fails to negotiate?"

Ryan looked off at the mountains again.

"I had my agent, Dick Moss, basically issue Buzzie Bavasi an ultimatum: have a new contract ready by opening day, or consider me a free agent after 1979."

With that, Ryan grabbed his cap and jogged out to the outfield, where Jimmie Reese was waiting with his fungo bat.

• • •

The acquisition of Carew made an immediate impact, as the Angels won 12 of their first 15 games. The strong start created a new energy at the Big A. Gone were the half-empty stands and lethargic fans; in their place was a ballpark filled with people, electricity, and hope.

Ryan got off to a fast start as well, and on May 2, when he faced off in a highly anticipated game against Yankees left-handed fireballer Ron Guidry, he was already 3–1 with 35 strikeouts in 29 innings.

An estimated 10,000 fans were turned away from the gates at game time. The exploding fan base at the Big A was unprecedented, and proved Angels fans would line up in droves for a winner.

Guidry—winner of the Cy Young Award the year before—recalls that as the game progressed, the crowd became engrossed in the contest between the two premier pitchers of that era.

"Nolan would go out and strike out one or two guys, then I'd go out and strike out one or two guys," said Guidry. "Next inning he'd strike out the side, and then I'd do the same. After a while the stadium just got quiet, the fans just left us to do what we could do, and when it was said and done, he won 1–0.

"After the game I was in the dugout and he happened to look over. I tipped my cap and he tipped his. That was a special moment."

It was for Angels fans, too, and the season ahead looked strewn with rose petals.

But for Ryan, there was a nasty thorn.

Ryan was on the bench at Fenway Park on May 9 when the visiting clubhouse man notified him there was a long-distance call from Ruth. As he ran upstairs, Ryan prepared himself for the worst. Ruth would never call during a game unless it was an emergency.

When he got on the line all he could hear was blubbering until a doctor took the phone from Ruth and told Ryan that his eldest son, Reid, had been struck by a car. The boy had a broken leg and possible internal injuries.

After composing herself, Ruth got back on the phone and said Reid had been showing off his new Little League uniform when two neighborhood bullies came by and threatened to rip it off his back. Reid started to run and they chased him. As he looked back to see how close they were, Reid stepped off the curb into the path of a neighbor's car as she turned into her driveway.

"I was with Marilyn Carew," Ruth said. "There was a screech. The driver didn't see him, because a tree blocked her view. Reid was screaming, 'My leg! Mama, they're gonna cut off my leg!'"

She broke down again. "Nolan, I need you," Ruth sobbed. "When can you get here?"

Ryan left immediately for the airport, where he discovered that the earliest flight to Orange County wasn't until the following morning. He spent the entire night in the terminal.

When he finally arrived at Children's Hospital, Ruth was asleep in a chair. When she opened her eyes, she saw Nolan, his face ravaged by worry and exhaustion, staring down at Reid. "What do the doctors say?" he asked her.

"They don't know. They're going to operate."

Surgeons found that Reid's floating rib had severed his spleen and part of a kidney. His urethra was also damaged, and urine was leaking into the abdominal cavity. In subsequent operations his spleen and part of the injured kidney were removed.

His injuries were so severe that Reid would be in a body cast for at least three months. For that entire period, which Ryan calls the lowest point of his career with the Angels, he didn't depart for road trips until the night before he pitched. When the team was home, he and Ruth took separate shifts at the hospital. She arrived at dawn and stayed until Nolan arrived at 11:00 AM. Ruth returned to the hospital at 4:00 PM so the pitcher could go to the ballpark.

When Reid slept, Ryan walked the halls of the hospital and was moved by the sight of kids much worse off than his son. Their parents often asked him to talk to their youngsters. Finding the right words was difficult, but Ryan always obliged and became friends with several children with fatal illnesses.

"Every day he would stop by and see me before he went to the ballpark," Reid recalls. "He would always bring me coloring books and jigsaw puzzles or little novelty batting helmets that he picked up on the road. He always spent time with the other sick kids too, and those visits meant a lot to them."

In his first start since Reid's accident, Ryan went six strong innings and struck out seven against Milwaukee on May 15 before leaving with a pull in his right calf. Don Baylor ended the game with a walk-off homer, and told reporters afterward, "I would rather Nolan got the win so he could go back to Reid and say, 'This one's for you.'"

Thousands of fans sent cards, flowers, and gifts to Reid in the hospital, and on June 9 Ryan acknowledged them in an ad in the *Los Angeles Times*:

"To all our friends and fans: Ruth and I would like to thank you for all your kind support during recent weeks following the accident of our son, Reid. It was truly comforting to know that your thoughts and prayers were with him."

Reminded again that there were more important things than baseball, Ryan pressed on, and entering July he was 9–5. Meanwhile, the absence of any word from Bavasi about a new contract also reminded him that baseball was a business, and, as promised, he declared he would become a free agent at the end of the season.

His statement coincided with a big weekend series at home against New York. Ryan was slated to face Luis Tiant on Friday, July 13, and to accommodate a national television audience the start time was moved to 5:15 PM. That meant Ryan would be pitching in twilight, which wouldn't make things any easier for the Yankees batters.

"You can tell Nolan that it won't matter what the light's like at 5:00," New York catcher Thurman Munson said before the game. "I can't hit him at 8:00 either."

The shadows helped Ryan keep the Yankees hitless for seven innings. With one out in the Yankees' eighth and darkness finally falling, Jim Spencer lined a shot to Rick Miller in shallow center. Miller was an excellent fielder, but he had just gotten off the DL with a hand injury. He slid to make the catch, but the ball caromed off his leg. It seemed like an obvious hit, but official scorer Dick Miller (no relation) called it an error on the Angels outfielder. The Yankees bench went ballistic. Players screamed obscenities, and Reggie Jackson grabbed a towel and waved it derisively in Miller's direction.

Some Angels weren't thrilled about the ruling, either. Buzzie Bavasi had promised a $25,000 bonus to any Angel who threw a no-hitter. "I'll give [Ryan] $25,000 for a one-hitter!" he screamed at Dick Miller. "You didn't have to do that. You embarrassed us!"

"The ball hit the top of his glove!" Miller barked back. "[Rick Miller] should have made the play!"

Incredibly, moments later Dick Miller was heard proclaiming in the press box, "If I can get him this no-hitter, we'll make a lot of money!"

"That's what Miller said after he made the call," recalls Tracy Ringolsby of the *Long Beach Telegram*. "I'm not gonna say that's why he made the call. He may have been trying to make light of it. I wasn't a confidant of Dick Miller's, so I couldn't tell you his thought process.

"One thing was certain: it would have been the record-setting fifth no-hitter, and I think Dick was sure he was going to write a book with Nolan or something. Dick was always looking for a way to make a buck. We used to always get four season tickets from the team. He would give his to a car dealer for a car, and then he'd call the Angels when he needed tickets for his family."

Ryan himself seemed unsettled by the controversy over Miller's call. The last thing he wanted was a tainted no-hitter. He got through the inning unscathed, and going into the ninth the Angels led 6–0.

To lock up his fifth no-hitter, Ryan needed to get through the heart of the Yankees lineup: Munson, Graig Nettles, and Reggie Jackson.

Munson hit a sharp grounder that shortstop Jim Anderson bobbled for an error. Then first-ball-swinging Nettles popped a foul ball behind the plate that was snagged by catcher Brian Downing for the first out.

When Jackson was announced, there was a crescendo of boos from the 41,805 fans. The self-described "straw that stirs the drink" was used to such a response, and in fact Jackson often seemed to feed off the negative reactions he received. Striding to the plate, he glared at Ryan like a boxer staring down his opponent before the opening bell of a heavyweight championship fight.

Throughout the 1970s there was no more riveting confrontation than Ryan vs. Jackson. Both were in their prime and considered the best at what they did.

"I loved the one-on-one confrontations," recalls Jackson. "It was one of the epitomes of my baseball career. Because when you are successful against Nolan Ryan and you hit his fastball, you can say, 'I hit the best fastball in history!'

"I never faced him when someone said, 'He isn't throwing good tonight.' He might have been a little wild, but he always had great stuff—always. I remember getting excited knowing he was going to be pitching. Some of my teammates were probably glad they were not playing, but I got excited playing against him. I got excited because I knew I was going to see one of the greats of the game. I had a ride on the 'Ryan Express,' and it was a special thing to do."

In his autobiography, Jackson recalled a game against the Angels in Oakland in 1974, when Ryan called catcher Ellie Rodriguez to the mound and instructed him to deliver a message to Reggie at the plate: "Expect nothing but heat."

"I didn't know whether to believe him," said Jackson. "They were behind 3–0, but Ryan delivered. He threw me all fastballs. I hit one. Sent it on a line drive to left. I thought it was going to drill a hole through the seats and wind up outside the ballpark, but I didn't get it high enough, and it was caught in front of the fence."

Ryan recollects it a little differently: "If you ask Reggie, he hit a vicious drive to left field. If you ask Nolan Ryan, he hit a lazy fly ball to left field."

Now, with millions glued to their TV sets and Ryan's no-hitter on the line, Jackson had only one thing in mind: "I wanted my team to *not* get no-hitted, and, more than anything else, I wanted to be the one to get the hit."

He swatted Ryan's first pitch just beyond the pitcher's outstretched glove for a clean single.

Ryan considers what happened next one of the most memorable events of his career. When Jackson got to first he gestured sarcastically toward Dick Miller in the press box. Then, as the crowd rose to give Ryan a standing ovation, Jackson started clapping with them and tipped his hat to Ryan.

"The moment moved me," Ryan wrote in his autobiography. "I realized I had lost the no-hitter, but also realized that it probably worked out for the best. I wouldn't have wanted to throw a no-hitter and have it constantly argued that it was a no-hitter only because of the official scorer."

Ryan promptly retired Lou Piniella and Chris Chambliss to notch his 12th win of the season.

A week later, *Sports Illustrated* again put Ryan on its cover. HOW CLOSE IT WAS, said the headline.

Buzzie Bavasi wasn't impressed. He and Ryan's agent, Dick Moss, bickered about a new contract until Bavasi threw up his hands and delegated the job of negotiating to his assistant, Mike Port.

Ryan's first-half stats—12–6, 2.54 ERA—earned him the start in the All-Star Game in Seattle. He was rocked for three runs on five hits, and the AL lost the game 7–6.

As the season resumed, Angels fans were pumped. During the Yankees series some had shouted, "Yes, We Can!" It became the rallying cry for the Angels faithful.

On July 25, Ryan strained his pitching elbow against the Yankees and had to go on the 14-day DL. When he returned, his rhythm was off, and in August he won only one of five starts. Bavasi didn't help their relationship by leaking to the media that Ryan was demanding $1 million per year, with incentives. Moss insisted that the figure represented a starting point for negotiations and was not set in stone, but it was another distraction that Ryan didn't need as the first-place Angels headed into the final month of the season.

Bavasi's posturing didn't alter Ryan's respect and affection for Gene Autry, and he was determined to do what he could to bring the old cowboy his first pennant.

On September 24, Ryan allowed just five hits in a 4–3 win against second-place Kansas City. The next day Frank Tanana sealed the deal with his own five-hitter, beating the Royals 4–1 to give the Angels their first division championship in the team's 19-year history.

An ecstatic Autry was waiting for his players at the clubhouse door. His warmest embrace was for Jim Fregosi. As the two original Angels hugged, delirious shortstop Jim Anderson doused Autry's special guest, former President Richard M. Nixon, with a can of Budweiser.

The best-of-five series against the Orioles to decide the American League pennant kicked off in Baltimore. As the senior arm on the staff, Ryan was given the honor of throwing the opener against Jim Palmer.

They were not on each other's Christmas card list.

In 1975, the two got into a verbal dust-up after the Baltimore ace said that Ryan got into too many long counts, which made his defense passive. "I always thought an out is an out," Ryan responded. "Isn't it the idea for the other team not to hit the ball?"

Over the next couple years the pitchers routinely exchanged barbs, and in 1977 Palmer turned it up a notch by criticizing Ryan for declining a last-minute invitation to play in the All-Star Game, because he'd already made plans for that date. Palmer said he "let down the league for selfish purposes," and AL manager Billy Martin, a longtime Ryan nemesis himself, echoed the charge.

Today Palmer has nothing but praise for his onetime rival.

"I recognize now that some of the things I said in the 1970s were frivolous and should never have been said," says Palmer. "I have nothing but respect for him."

According to Bobby Grich, who played with and against both Ryan and Palmer, the difference between them was one of style, not effectiveness.

"Palmer was confident he could get batters out by letting batters hit to his defense, and preferred batters swing earlier in the count than later," says Grich. "Ryan, on the other hand, knew his fastball was his bread and butter, and threw in a style that benefited him."

In the October 3 playoff opener, Palmer threw a professional nine innings on mediocre stuff, allowing three runs and striking out three. Ryan went seven strong innings, allowing just four hits and one earned run. Though Ryan had bested Palmer statistically, the Orioles won the game in the 10th inning on a three-run home run by pinch hitter John Lowenstein. Angels reliever John Montague, who had replaced Ryan in the seventh inning, took the loss.

"The one thing I don't do is compete with Nolan Ryan," a magnanimous Palmer told the press afterward. "I realize the strikeouts are glamorous, but they don't mean anything to me. If I had his ability, maybe I'd feel differently."

The next day, Baltimore scored nine times off Angels starter Dave Frost and reliever Mark Clear. The visitors battled back valiantly but lost 9–8, and the series shifted to California with the Angels down 2–0.

About 15 minutes before Game 3, the Angels were in the clubhouse, recalls Bobby Grich, "when suddenly there was this *kaboom!* I thought someone dropped a bomb on us. It turns out it was Nolan with a firecracker. I guess it was his idea of loosening us up. Nolan laughed, thinking it was funny, but we wanted to kill him."

The Angels took it out on the Orioles, instead. In one of the most memorable games in club history, the Halos came from behind in a thriller. Larry Harlow's double to center in the ninth drove in Brian Downing from second base for the winning run.

But the next day Baltimore southpaw Scotty McGregor shut down the Angels 8–0, and the Birds headed to the World Series.

"We were still learning," recalls Don Baylor. "After all those years of thinking about it, we were not ready to win at that particular time to get to the World Series. You can't just be lucky. You have to do well in every facet of the game. That was a learning process for us. The bottom line is we just weren't ready."

Ryan finished the season 16–14, with 223 strikeouts and a 3.60 ERA. He had pitched well enough down the stretch to get Autry his first division championship, but as he peeled off his jersey following the final loss to Baltimore, he knew there was a distinct possibility he would be wearing another team's logo when he suited up the following spring.

• • •

As Bavasi's director of player personnel, Mike Port acted as middleman between his boss and Dick Moss, and sometimes he felt like he was dealing with competing tidal waves. Not that the 34-year-old Port wasn't up to it—Bavasi had handpicked him for the job when the GM came over from San Diego in 1978. Bavasi had mentored him, even treated him like a son.

But now, staring at the phone on his desk, Port sighed wearily and wondered how he would ever get Bavasi and Moss on the same page concerning the Nolan Ryan matter.

Thus far, Ryan and team owner Gene Autry had stayed out of it. Ryan let Moss handle negotiations for him, while Autry, as was his custom, let his people do their jobs. In his heart he wanted Ryan to stay, but at the same time he was not going to mortgage the team's future for one player.

Baseball was in its first decade of agent representation. In the 1960s, Bavasi had negotiated contracts with the players themselves, when the Dodgers had Koufax and Drysdale, but now it was all done through agents like Moss. Bavasi was a guy for whom performance was the bottom line. To Buzzie, if a pitcher delivered 200-plus innings, a lot of strikeouts and excitement, but a .500 record, the last statistic was all that mattered.

Bavasi concerned himself with the statistics he thought important; Moss focused on intrinsic value and intangibles. In hindsight, Port thinks both points of view made sense.

"There will always be players about whom people are going to say, 'So-and-so is in town tonight, let's go see him!'" Port says. "They wanted to see Reggie Jackson play and Nolan Ryan pitch. Moss knew there weren't too many people who could measure up to that gold standard and put rear ends in the seats.

"Buzzie was a performance-based guy. But I think if he had said, 'Nolan, whatever it takes—five years, a million a year, six years, a million a year,' Mr. Autry would have been delighted.

"However, on the flip side, Mr. Autry was a businessman, and although it's speculation, in that day and age if a pitcher went and injured himself and there went his career, and Mr. Autry still owed him three-four-five million dollars, he may not have been too happy about it."

Negotiations had been stalled since January. It was now October, the game was in the proverbial ninth inning, and the future of the franchise hung in the balance.

After speaking with Autry, Bavasi offered four years at $550,000 per year, basically what Moss had asked for 10 months earlier.

Ryan's current salary, including bonuses, was around $350,000. To the GM, for a pitcher who'd gone 16–14 with a 3.60 ERA, $200,000 was a significant raise.

Port called Moss for the umpteenth time. In his heart he knew the agent wouldn't bite. The buzz was that Ryan could get more by testing the market, but as Buzzie's right-hand man, Port did his bidding.

When Moss demanded four years at a million per year, Bavasi could hardly see straight. He was so steamed he didn't even bother with a counter.

"I'm from the old school, where your record indicates how much you get," Bavasi later said. "For those first two years I was there [in 1978 and 1979] our ballclub was over .500, but Nolan's record during that time was under .500. He was 26–27 in those two years. I had fellas who were 11–8, 12–4. What am I going to do with them if I give Nolan all the money?"

Autry and Ryan, meanwhile, remained quietly on the sidelines. It would have been a good time for the two friends to meet privately, but that just wasn't their style.

That winter the Rangers, Astros, and Yankees made solid offers for Ryan's services, all significantly higher than the Angels' $550,000. Had Bavasi offered the sum in January, the Angels would have had themselves a bargain. Now, Bavasi's offer wasn't even in the ballpark.

When the smoke finally cleared, the Houston Astros' unprecedented four-year, $4 million contract offer was at the top of the pile and too good to turn down.

Ryan had revolutionized baseball again.

Don Sanders, a minority owner with Houston and Ryan's future business partner, recalls the tipping point when Ryan decided to become an Astro.

"When Houston owner John McMullen decided to sign Nolan in 1979, he came up with a brilliant idea," says Sanders. "Everybody that tried to sign him took him to the fanciest club in the city and wined and dined him. At the time, my wife and I and the kids lived in a nice home with a big backyard and a pool, so McMullen asked me to host a luncheon for Nolan and Ruth at my house, and I agreed.

"It was Nolan, my wife, John, and maybe one other couple, and I guess Nolan was impressed with the low-pressure family approach, because he signed with us right after that."

It was the first day of deer hunting season when George Pugh found out his pal Nolan was no longer a California Angel.

"We were down in Deer Lake, north of McAllen," recalls Pugh. "We got to talking, and Nolan said he wasn't going to be able to stay as long as we planned, that he'd have to go home early. When I asked why, Nolan kind of ducked his head and said, 'Well, I'm signing with the Astros tomorrow.'"

When Pugh asked how much Ryan would get, Ryan "kind of smiled and said, 'You're not gonna believe this. They're gonna give me a million dollars.'"

"You've got to be kidding me!" said Pugh.

"That's why I'm going home," Ryan said. "I don't want 'em changing their minds."

Reacting to Ryan's signing with Houston, Bavasi mentioned Ryan's 16–14 record to a reporter and snorted, "All I need to replace Ryan is hire two 8–7 pitchers."

Bavasi's handling of the Ryan situation marred his legacy in baseball for a whole generation of fans. Dodgers fans remember him as the chief architect of the club's successful runs in the 1950s and '60s, and for his role in ushering Jackie Robinson into the majors. But to Angels fans and some players, he'll always be the man who lost Nolan Ryan.

"I remember Bavasi saying we can get two players to go 8–7 and we wouldn't miss Nolan Ryan," says Don Baylor. "Well, we missed him. We missed him a lot. It took us a long time to get back to the playoffs. Every time he pitched there were 5,000 to 10,000 more people at the games, and that adds up. The people he drew when he pitched, that would have taken care of his salary right here in Anaheim."

"You just couldn't replace a Nolan Ryan," seconds Bobby Grich. "He was one of a kind. He put fear into the hearts of the other team. You always knew when we came into town, in one of those three games we'd be playing you'd probably be facing the strikeout leader of the league. He carried a presence with him that we couldn't replace. I think everybody, to a man, did not want to see him go. He was the anchor of our rotation, and we knew with him gone we would be weaker."

"He became the legend after the fact, but he always was an icon to the fans," adds Angels VP of communications Tim Mead. "He was what Angel fans could latch onto when Angel fans didn't have anything else to latch onto. When you watched Nolan Ryan, you were watching history, not just Nolan Ryan pitching a ballgame."

Port insists that Bavasi's "8–7" comment was never intended as a personal knock on Ryan, nor meant for public consumption.

"It was said in jest, and in Buzzie's Dodgers days it would have probably been passed over," says Port. "The game was different then. Whether there was less media scrutiny or the writers were coming from a little different direction, most of the Dodgers were close to Buzzie and would just have brushed that comment aside as an example of 'Buzzie being Buzzie.'

"I think the quote was said in the same spirit, but Nolan is a very proud and upstanding guy, and I think he was hurt by some of the comments that found their way into print.

"That particular comment was not meant maliciously. Certainly in subsequent years Buzzie made public comments very favorable in Nolan's regard.

"Buzzie was a good enough baseball man to know what Nolan Ryan was. We offered $550,000 and Dick wanted a million, and in those days that was a very wide spread. Baseball operator that Buzzie was, he looked at that extra $450,000 and thought about how many more people we'd have to draw at the gate, and what would happen if Nolan went down early through injury and couldn't perform.

"As the saying goes, I think time heals. Nolan was always first-class and above the whole thing. Buzzie was, I guess, a bit of a street fighter, and he and Dick probably got into it more so than Buzzie and Nolan."

Moss later stated that the $1 million was meant to be a starting point and he would have been willing to negotiate, but Bavasi never countered back.

Returning to the coast in January to put his home up for sale, Ryan held an impromptu press conference at a Mexican restaurant. He said he just couldn't take any more of Bavasi, who'd seemed to go out of his way to provoke him. Buzzie had, among other things, refused to send out his fan mail, and even deducted meal money when Ryan flew home from road trips early to visit his hospitalized son.

As far as baseball went, said Ryan, "I don't think trying to put the best possible club out there was [Bavasi's] number one concern."

The bottom line was that Ryan felt he couldn't remain with California as long as Bavasi was there.

Dick Moss accompanied Ryan to the restaurant and told reporters that Bavasi's hostility was predicated on a grudge he'd held against him going back to when he was working with the players association and Bavasi was general manager of the San Diego Padres. The disagreement, according to Moss, concerned a grievance of a mere $150. Bavasi had handled their entire negotiation personally, said Moss, not professionally.

Reached at his San Diego home, Bavasi responded indignantly: "I'm not going to comment on anything. Something this outrageous I wouldn't dignify with a comment. I'd like to do it in [Ryan's] face, though, not in the press, the way some people do things. He's got his money. What does he want?"

In eight seasons with the Halos, Ryan's winning percentage was .533, compared to the team's .481. In only two of those seasons did the Angels play over .500 ball. Ryan was 138–121 with the Angels, with an earned-run average of 3.07. The Angels averaged 1.95 runs in his losses—60 times scoring one run or fewer. Seven times Ryan led the league in strikeouts, with 300 or more in five of them. He pitched four no-hitters, five one-hitters, 13 two-hitters, and 19 three-hitters.

Why, then, didn't Gene Autry, with his vaunted business savvy, overrule his general manager and re-sign Ryan?

Not doing so, says Ross Newhan, was Autry's "biggest mistake."

"Gene had put a lot of faith in people he had working for him," says Newhan. "Should he have stepped in? Probably. But Buzzie was one of his favorites, and maybe he should have told him, 'Let's not lose him. Go to any length that is reasonable.' It was unfortunate. Up to that point [Ryan] was the biggest attraction in Angels history."

Several years later, on his way to the ballpark with his longtime confidant, John Moynihan, Autry made a comment his friend would never forget.

"I made a mistake with Nolan," he told Moynihan. "It was a bad business decision, and I should have gone into Buzzie's office and gave him the money. I should have gone in and given him whatever he needed."

Ruth Ryan says her husband's decision was a matter of principle. "He really wanted to be with the organization he felt appreciated him," she said. "It was unfortunate, but Buzzie was doing his job, and I don't know if we handled things the right way or wrong way. But once it happened, it happened. You just have to look ahead. You don't look back."

Ryan himself never has.

"I don't have any grudges or animosity toward anyone," he says. "I'm a believer that everything will work out for the best, and it did for me.

"My friendship with Gene Autry and the opportunity to play for somebody I looked up to as a child was a big thrill. I still think he was as good an owner that baseball ever had because of his love for the game.

"He tried to do everything within his power to give Southern California a winner with the Angels. It was an exciting time for me, because my career was developing, and I was establishing myself as a starting pitcher with some special things happening with strikeouts and no-hitters."

Nobody took Ryan's departure harder than the man who'd been instrumental in making him the pitcher he was.

Jimmie Reese's relationship with Ryan went back to the first day at Holtville, when he pulled the scared pitcher off the infield and began hitting him fungos. He charted every pitch Ryan threw as an Angel, and he and Tom Morgan were Nolan's staunchest supporters and most valued mentors. Mostly, Reese was Nolan's friend, and when he got word that Ryan was gone, the veteran coach broke down and cried.

PART V

Building the Perfect Beast: The Houston Astros: 1980–88

1

Home in the Dome: 1980

Here come the Astros, Burning with Desire!
Here come the Astros, Breathing Orange Fire!

—ASTROS FIGHT SONG, 1980

Houston Astros conditioning coach Dr. Gene Coleman was reviewing the training manual he was writing for NASA astronauts when the phone rang in his study. It was Astros GM Tal Smith.

"Gene, you may have heard we just signed Nolan Ryan," Smith said. "We're having a little party to introduce him to the media tonight. Could you swing by?"

Getting in the elevator to go up to the party, Coleman's interest was piqued by an elderly female co-passenger with vivacious eyes. The courtly doctor introduced himself: "Gene Coleman, ma'am. To whom do I owe the pleasure?"

"Martha Ryan. I'm Nolan's mom. Are you with the ballclub?"

Little did Mrs. Ryan realize that for the next several years, Coleman would see more of her son than she did.

At the party, Coleman was talking to pitcher Ken Forsch when Ryan himself came over. It was their first meeting, and Coleman didn't know what to expect.

"I was working hard to get to our goal of pitchers lifting weights once between starts, once every five days, and I was getting some resistance," recalls Coleman. "The guy giving me the most static was Kenny Forsch."

"Are you the strength coach?" asked Ryan, and when Coleman responded that he was, Ryan said, "Well, I think I'm going to have a problem with your weight lifting program."

Recalls Coleman, "I'm thinking, *This damn multimillion-dollar prima donna! First day on the job and he's already telling me what he's going to do!* Meanwhile, Forsch is smiling at me ear-to-ear.

"Then Nolan says, 'Yep, I can only lift twice between starts.'"

Forsch looked like he'd just swallowed something that didn't belong in the bean dip.

"It turned out that Nolan was already doing twice what I was trying to get the other pitchers to do," says Coleman. "I knew right then we had a keeper. With his reputation, there was no doubt in my mind that the other pitchers would follow his lead."

A full professor and chair of the fitness program and human performance at the University of Houston at Clear Lake, Coleman was among the first to research the physical, physiological, and performance profiles of professional baseball players.

Intelligent, personable, and driven, Coleman was well ahead of the curve when it came to conditioning. In Coleman, Ryan had found a kindred spirit.

"I gravitated to Gene because I realized he had a wealth of knowledge," recalls Ryan. "The Astros were the first organization I played for that incorporated weight training into their conditioning program that was specifically tailored for pitchers and position players. It was the first time I'd ever been exposed to specific exercises for what you do on the field."

By 1980 the Universal Gym had become passé, and a series of sleek, state-of-the-art machines called Nautilus had taken over the fitness scene. Nautilus enabled more flexibility and extension, and the Astros weight room was loaded with them. Coleman arranged for Ryan to come down to the clubhouse and try them out.

At each separate station, Coleman took the time to explain the apparatus and its purpose. "Power is a function of strength, and speed is directly related to your ability to apply force," he said at the parallel bench press.

"Your legs are your lifeblood," he said as he demonstrated the leg curls apparatus.

"You can't be weak and fast," Coleman noted at the lateral pull-down machine.

They stayed longest at the abdominal machines.

"A chain is only as strong as its weakest link," Coleman said, "and the weakest link is often the trunk. Forces originated in the legs are transferred through the trunk, where they are then applied to the baseball by the hand, arm, and shoulder."

When the Nautilus tour was done, Ryan was excited. To his mind, the Astros had designed a weight room expressly for pitchers.

Coleman led the way to the Astros clubhouse, where a jovial man with a pirate grin greeted Ryan. Equipment manager Dennis Liborio had the rare combination of gentleness and toughness Ryan appreciated, and over time they developed a lasting friendship. Since it was protocol for established veterans to get preferential lockers, Liborio led Ryan to two in the corner.

"We'll put you here next to Joe Niekro," Liborio told him. "Joe's a great guy, you'll get along fine."

"Dennis, I hope you don't mind me asking," said Nolan, "but I don't see a jersey in my locker. You trying to tell me something?"

"I still need to check with Jeff Leonard. He's got number 30. But I'm sure he will let you have it. He's a rookie."

Ryan checked out his new orange socks and ran his fingers through the stirrups before responding.

"No, a number's just a number. What else you got?"

"I have 34," said Liborio.

Ryan picked up his orange 7¼" hat with the blue star and white capital H. Adjusting the bill, he remembered being a rookie and how intimidating everything had been. The last thing he wanted now was to seem pretentious and make a new teammate uncomfortable.

"Isn't Earl Campbell 34?" he asked.

"Sure is," said Liborio.

"Well, if it's good enough for Earl, that's good enough for me."

• • •

In 1980, the Astros spring training complex in Cocoa Beach, Florida, was one of the worst in baseball. Forty chicken-wire lockers were crammed into the 700-square-foot clubhouse, the bathroom stalls had no doors, and the dirt parking lot was a perennial quagmire. Even the baseball diamonds themselves were unkempt and so rock-strewn they looked like practice lunar landing sites used by the folks next door at Cape Canaveral.

Each year after the Astros broke camp, the grounds went unused and untouched until the team came back the following spring. In February, Liborio and his assistant, Barry Waters, would open the doors, sweep out all the cobwebs, animal droppings, and insects, and give everything a good cleaning.

It was to this humble setting that Nolan Ryan arrived fit and early for his first spring training with the Astros. Gene Coleman believes Ryan's early arrival and excellent condition was intended as a statement to his new team.

"Nolan wanted to show appreciation for coming home," says Coleman. "From day one, he was in such good shape that by the time we got the other pitchers in shape, he was almost de-conditioned from all the work he'd done in the off-season and the stuff he was doing on his own."

Ryan joined a Houston squad that, for the most part, would remain intact the entire nine seasons he played there: shortstop Craig Reynolds; outfielders Jose Cruz and Terry Puhl; catcher Alan Ashby; and infielders Denny Walling, Enos Cabell, and Art Howe all had long and productive careers in Houston and made for a tightly knit group.

"There was great chemistry on our ballclub," recalls Puhl, who played with Ryan for nine seasons. "Throughout the 1980s, the Houston Astros had more wins than any other organization, and most of that was due to the fact that we knew each other really well and played well together."

They and manager Bill Virdon, Ryan's former minor league skipper at Williamsport, were determined to make up for the meltdown that cost them the division title in 1979, which was the main reason new Astros owner Dr. John McMullen went after Ryan to begin with.

The Astros starting staff was one of the best in baseball. At 6'8" and 222 pounds, J.R. Richard threw almost as hard as Ryan. The last few seasons Richard had dominated the National League, and Virdon's plan was to bookend the two right-handers around knuckleballer Joe Niekro.

Righty Ken Forsch would be the fourth starter. Dave Smith, Vern Ruhle, Joaquin Andujar, and Joe Sambito would supply relief from the pen.

McMullen had also picked up aging superstar Joe Morgan from the Cincinnati Reds. Morgan had begun his Hall of Fame career with Houston in 1963, was traded to Cincinnati in 1971, and helped lead the Big Red Machine to several titles. He and veteran Cesar Cedeno in center gave the relatively young Astros some genuine leadership.

Ryan made an immediate impression on his teammates.

"He fit right in," recalls Puhl, "Nolan wasn't afraid to use his influence if something needing fixing. Virdon had a club rule that starting pitchers weren't allowed to use a protective screen when they threw BP. He wanted his pitchers to really get after it, but most pitchers weren't quite ready yet. Well, Nolan walks out there his first day and goes, 'No screen, no Nolan Ryan.' The next day the screens were out and stayed out the rest of Bill's tenure with the club."

As spring unfolded, Gene Coleman found that Ryan was hungry to learn and easy to like.

"I would bet that except for the time he was standing on the mound or in the bullpen throwing, we were talking about something," recalls Coleman. "I was probably the closest thing to his age and our kids were approximately the same age, so it just worked out well."

Coleman called Ryan "Rook," because whenever they went out somewhere and Coleman called him "Nolan," heads inevitably turned and Ryan would end up signing autographs for 15 minutes.

Ryan's dry sense of humor fit right in, and during spring training he and noted prankster Joe Niekro targeted Coleman for his insistence that players run endless sprints from foul pole to foul pole.

"We were playing the Cardinals in Cocoa," recalls Coleman, "and since we had minimal facilities, starting pitchers had to do their running in the outfield while the game was going on.

"So the game's getting ready to start, and I'm down the left-field line with Nolan discussing what the pitchers were going to do. I was met with the usual complaining and bargaining: 'Do we have to do this?' 'Can't we talk about this?' Then Joe Niekro comes up, puts his arm around my shoulder, and says 'Let's talk about this.'

"The next thing I know, I'm on the ground on my belly, and a roll of tape comes out and my hands are taped behind my back and my feet are wrapped together. I look up for help, and Nolan's just kind of smiling.

"So I'm lying in the outfield and the pitchers take off and start running foul poles, going back and forth, and I'm saying, 'Hey, guys, how 'bout some help here!' But they just grinned and kept going. And when they finished, they all went in and just left me there.

"A few minutes later the game starts. Jose Cruz is playing left and I'm still out there floundering on the grass. My son—he's about seven or eight—is standing at the fence looking at me with tears in his eyes. I'm hollering at Cruz, 'Cheo! Hey, let me up!'

"'Man, I can't,' he says. 'I'm playing left field!'

"My son can't take it anymore. With all his determination he crawls over the fence and comes and unties me. How can they do this awful thing to my dad? He's never seen anything close to this.

"So we wait until the game is over and everybody goes home. I go in the trainer's room to get some tape, and we tape everything those pitchers have—their gloves, their bats, their shoes; we even tape Joe Sambito's hair dryer to something. My boy had a real good time, and he's feeling better about the whole thing.

"The next morning we start with a team meeting. Bill Virdon is an ex-Marine and tougher than nails. When the meeting starts the security guard comes to the door and calls for Bill. A moment later Bill comes back and says, 'Hey, Doc, it's for you.'

"So I go open the front door to the clubhouse and there stands Joe Niekro, and he's got my son. His hands and feet are taped together, and Niekro looks at me and says, 'It's over!'

"I un-taped my son and sent him on out to play. He thought that was the greatest thing that ever happened to him, because in his mind he'd been accepted.

"Now, in order for Niekro to do that, I know for a fact he had to get Nolan's blessing. It's that kind of thing, 'cause he was the new guy on the block with the big bucks. That was Nolan's way of being involved with something without being involved. It was like, 'Well, I was just going along with it,' but everyone knew he had to give his approval."

In mid-March, a brief mini-strike over a labor dispute didn't make getting in shape any easier, but Joe Morgan made sure the team stayed together and practiced on their own, so they'd be ready when the strike ended.

One day toward the end of the month, Ryan and Coleman were stretching in the outfield when coach Bob "Flea" Lillis walked over.

"Nolan, you think you're gonna make it?" asked Lillis.

Without cracking a smile, Ryan looked up and said, "Flea, its hard to believe a man would put himself through this for a million dollars a year."

• • •

The Houston Colt .45s née Astros had never won a championship. After entering the league in 1962, the closest they'd come was in 1979, when they ran neck-and-neck with Cincinnati in the NL West, only to lose the division by 1.5 games.

Their losing culture began to change when former Yankees partner Dr. John McMullen bought the club in 1979. McMullen immediately started investing his vast fortune, made as a shipping agent, into the cash-starved club.

The Astros played in the Astrodome, the world's first indoor baseball venue. Labeled "The Eighth Wonder of the World," its long fences and dead air made the Dome a pitcher's paradise, and general manager Tal Smith designed the team for speed and defense.

With the acquisition of Ryan, hopes were high among the players.

"He brought more credibility to the Astros," recalls catcher Alan Ashby. "He was already great, and with him and J.R. Richard, we had the two most feared pitchers in the game. We were primed and ready to be the team to beat, and just having a guy like Nolan around made you feel that you were the best in the league."

Before his first start, a representative of Pony athletic shoes approached Ryan about wearing Pony shoes in the nationally televised game. Ryan already had a shoe deal with Adidas, and told the Pony man he was happy with that brand.

"Well, I'm going to give you $10,000 to wear these shoes," said the Pony rep, as recollected by Gene Coleman.

"For the season?" asked Ryan incredulously.

"No," answered the shoe shill, "for the day."

"Let's try those shoes on," said Ryan.

He put them on, recalls Coleman, but after taking several exploratory steps in them, Ryan sat down, took off the shoes, and handed them back to the Pony representative with a polite "No, thank you."

"After the guy walked away," says Coleman, "Ryan turned to me and said, 'It sure is nice to be able to afford integrity. I'm making $1.1 million, and it's my first game with a new team. I'm not going out there for an extra $10,000, turn an ankle, and have a bad performance. If I don't do as well as I think, I could blame it on those shoes, but then I'm greedy, and I just couldn't live with myself."

Ryan wasn't paid to wear Adidas shoes, and when he subsequently found out that Bucky Dent, who had the same agent as Ryan, was getting $15,000 a year for wearing Adidas, he pounced on the company's rep next time they met.

When the embarrassed Adidas man stammered that the company would pay him too, Ryan told him he didn't want the money.

"I'm going to continue wearing your shoes," he said, "but I'm not going to wear them after this year. And if I make the All-Star team, I'm not wearing your shoes."

"He was true to his word," says Coleman. "In the All-Star Game, he wore Pony. Then he wore Adidas the rest of the year, and that was that for Adidas."

Ryan's season started with a literal bang. In the nationally televised game against the Dodgers, he slammed a three-run home run off Don Sutton in his second at-bat. It was the first of two homers in Ryan's entire career, and produced half of the six RBIs he would get the entire year.

"He got a lot of mileage out of that one," laughs Ruth Ryan. "He always took a lot of pride in his hitting, and we took it as an omen of good things to come. It was something we laughed about and celebrated for a long time."

But it took time to get adjusted to National League batters, and it didn't help when back spasms became a nagging problem. Ryan didn't really get going until May, when he tossed a four-hit shutout against the Phillies, a two-hitter against San Diego, and a combined one-hitter against

St. Louis. On July 4 at Riverfront Stadium in Cincinnati, Ryan recorded his 3,000th career strikeout, against Cesar Geronimo.

At the All-Star break the Astros were 45–33 and tied for the lead in the NL West. Much of their success was thanks to J.R. Richard's 10 wins, 115 strikeouts, and 1.96 ERA. But on July 30, when the Astros were at Philadelphia, Richard, who had complained of a tired arm and blurred vision, suffered a massive stroke back in Houston. An emergency operation was performed and a life-threatening blood clot in his neck was removed.

It was the end of Richard's career in the big leagues. After several unsuccessful comeback attempts, he retired from baseball.

Vern Ruhle came out of the pen to replace Richard in the rotation, and his six wins down the stretch kept the Astros in contention. Ryan gradually picked up steam, and after defeating San Francisco for his sixth victory on August 4, he remained undefeated the entire month.

National League umpires, Ryan discovered, didn't call high strikes as they did in the junior circuit, and for a pitcher with a rising fastball, this was no small concern.

"The strike zone shrunk for me by about 25 percent," Ryan says. "I also found I had to adjust to hitters who had different styles and personalities."

At the top of that list was San Diego's Dave Winfield.

At 6'6" and 220 pounds, Winfield's mere physical presence made most pitchers cringe. Winfield feared nobody and made it a point to dig in at the plate.

On August 9, Winfield led off the San Diego fourth against Ryan. San Diego was ahead 1–0, and Ryan's plan was to work the big man inside and not let him extend those long arms. Ryan had hit Ozzie Smith with a pitch in the third, and now he was throwing uncomfortably close to Winfield.

After Ryan's third pitch nearly dropped him, Winfield charged the mound.

"Luis Pujols, a big guy, was catching," recalls Alan Ashby, who was on the bench that day. "When Winfield started toward the mound, Luis tried to get between them, but Winfield took him out with a straight arm and then threw him aside like a rag doll. He was screaming at Nolan, 'Dammit! Don't you ever throw at me!'

"When he reached the mound he grabbed Ryan by the back of the neck and launched a haymaker at his head. I thought Nolan was dead meat, but he acquitted himself amazingly well. He must have had some boxing skills, because he ducked under the punch."

Players from both benches swallowed up the combatants, and when order was restored Winfield was tossed. Ryan stayed on the mound, but when the game resumed after an 11-minute delay he was so rattled he barely got through the rest of the inning. Relieved in the seventh, he was not involved in the decision, a 9–5 Astros victory.

"I thought there were too many pitches too close," said Winfield in the clubhouse. "It's not that a pitcher is trying to hit you, or a situation of establishing ground. You never know for sure, it's just a reaction."

Ryan was staunchly unapologetic. "I didn't hear anyone complaining when I walked four guys and threw a wild pitch," he said. "I don't know what's going on inside a guy's mind to cause a display like that. I was just trying to pitch inside and I was wild."

But on the way home that day with Ruth, he was much quieter than usual, and that night he didn't sleep well.

"Nolan vowed then that he would never again back away when somebody charged him," says Ruth. "'From now on,' he told me, 'if anyone comes to the mound looking for a fight, he'll get one!'"

As the season progressed, Puhl discovered the duality of Ryan's nature.

"On his off days he was always down in the dugout watching the game, and he didn't miss much," says Puhl, "but when he pitched I noticed he was different, and the level of play got much higher. There were a few guys who could do that. One was Roger Clemens. When those guys took the mound, everybody's level of play, concentration, and focus became much higher.

"He really did lead by example. I only saw him go crazy once when he was pitching. It was at Dodger Stadium, and our center fielder was out of position and butchered a play, and Nolan rightfully went off on him. The outfielder's focus came back real quick.

"Nolan knew what was going on with a lot of players and their lives. He just had a knack of knowing what was going on."

By the end of September the Astros needed just one win in their last series at Los Angeles to clinch the division. Joe Ferguson's clutch homer helped the Dodgers to a 3–2 win in the first game, and the pressure was on Ryan to get the job done in the following contest.

Before the game, some West Coast reporters asked Ryan about the recent decision of California Angels GM Buzzie Bavasi not to go shopping in the free agent market for a pitcher. Bavasi was quoted as saying, "Look at Nolan Ryan, a 9–9 pitcher and a million bucks!"

"Did my old friend Buzzie say that?" Ryan asked with a wide grin. "Well, he'll be going home in a couple days, and I'll be going to the playoffs."

"Did you hear Buzzie is looking for a pitcher who can work 230 innings next year?" asked another reporter.

"Good luck," said Ryan. "I know one he can't get."

"But you haven't heard his offer," smirked the reporter.

"If he offered me his house, he couldn't get me," said Ryan.

Ryan pitched well, but Houston lost 2–1, and then lost the final game of the series to the Dodgers. The two teams finished in a dead heat, and a one-game playoff would decide the Western Division title.

Joe Niekro was up to the task, scattering six hits in the 7–1 Astros victory.

Bullpen coach Stretch Suba delicately recalls the team's plane ride to Philadelphia to face the Eastern Division champion Phillies as "celebratory."

When they arrived at the hotel, several of the players were not so delicately soused, including the Million Dollar Man.

"Me, Nolie, and Danny Heep were in the upstairs hallway, and there happened to be a room service tray there," recalls Suba. "Danny picked up a Coke can and said to Nolie, 'Here, hit this!" and tossed the can at him.

"So Nolie grabbed a beer bottle. 'Oh yeah, Heeber,' he says, 'well, hit this!'

"And this beer bottle goes end-over-end and it hit the wall and shattered. Nolie looked at me and said, 'I think we better get out of here!'

"So we go walking down the hall at 2:00 in the morning, looking over our shoulders wondering when are the security guards gonna come looking for us."

• • •

Game 1 of the NLCS was a classic pitchers' duel, with Phillies ace Steve Carlton besting the Astros' Ken Forsch 3–1. A two-run homer by Greg Luzinski in the sixth provided the winning margin.

In a Game 2 extra-inning thriller, Ryan pitched 6⅓ strong innings, allowing just two runs. Houston won 7–4 thanks to a four-run 10th inning, capped by Dave Bergman's two-run triple.

Game 3 was another pitching duel that went into overtime, as Joe Niekro pitched 10 innings of shutout ball and Larry Christenson tossed six shutout frames for the Phils. In the 11th, Joe Morgan lined a triple to the wall. Tug McGraw intentionally walked the next two hitters to load the bases, and then Denny Walling hit a sacrifice fly to give the Astros the 1–0 win and a 2–1 series lead.

Game 4 was arguably one of the greatest playoff games ever played. It included a near triple play and more lead changes than a horse race. Starters Vern Ruhle and Steve Carlton were effective, tossing 5⅓ and seven innings, respectively. The Phillies finally broke through with three runs in the eighth for a 3–2 lead, but the Astros tied it up an inning later.

The game was decided in the 10th when pinch hitter Greg Luzinski hit a shot to the left-field corner that sent Pete Rose barreling past Houston catcher Bruce Bochy. Manny Trillo's RBI single added an insurance run, and the Phillies won 5–3.

With Ryan pitching at home in Game 5 against Phillies rookie Marty Bystrom, Houston seemed to have the advantage.

But when you went up against the uber-competitive Pete Rose, the warfare didn't wait for the umpire to call "Play ball!" Nothing got Charlie Hustle's juices flowing like playing one game for all the marbles—and what could be better than facing Nolan Ryan with the NL pennant on the line?

Before the game, Rose staked out the batting cage until Ryan showed up to take his mandatory swings, and then launched a preemptive strike.

"Hey, Ryan," he sneered. "I wish you could get that bullshit curveball over just once!"

"Why's that, Pete?" said Ryan.

"Because when you do, I'm gonna hit it right off your [bleeping] forehead!"

The Astros scratched together a few hits in the first inning to take an early 1–0 lead, but in the second the Phillies got two runs of their own.

In the sixth, with the Phillies still ahead 2–1, Rose came to the plate and proceeded to do exactly what he'd threatened if Ryan threw him a curve—on a 1-2 count he lined the ball right back at Ryan's (bleeping) forehead. All Nolan could do to save himself was throw up his hands and make the catch.

On his way back to the bench, Rose pointed at Ryan and barked, "Gotcha!"

"I knew it was going to be a battle," Rose said later. "But I hit everything up the middle, whether it was Ryan or anyone else, so it was no big deal."

The Astros tied the game in their half of the inning, and in the next frame jumped to a commanding 5–2 lead on a Walling RBI single, a wild pitch, and a Howe RBI triple.

"I thought the roof of the dome was going to come down," recalls Rose. "That was the loudest ovation I ever heard in a game."

Larry Bowa started off the Philly eighth with a single. Houston's Art Howe describes what happened next:

"Bob Boone got jammed and hit a one-hopper toward the middle. It was a sure double-play ball, and Craig Reynolds was coming over to catch it right at the bag and then throw it to first, but Nolan got a glove on the ball first and deflected it for an infield hit.

"Greg Gross, hitting in the pitcher's spot, dropped a bunt down toward third and loaded 'em up. With Pete Rose coming up then, I didn't feel very good about things."

"It started to unravel when Nolan failed to field a bunt and nobody went in to talk to him and tell him it didn't mean anything," says Joe Morgan. "If you get the next three guys it's over, but no one came to the mound to tell Nolan that. People don't realize that when you are the pitcher and standing on the mound with millions of people watching, that is the loneliest place in the world. Once in a while, you need a friend."

Rose worked the count full before fouling off several good pitches. He eventually got the walk, bringing Bowa in to make it 5–3. With the bases still juiced, Virdon took Ryan out and brought in Joe Sambito. The Phillies scored four more times, and going into the bottom of the eighth they led 7–5.

Houston clawed back for two to tie it up. Both teams went scoreless in the ninth, and in the 10th the Phils took the lead when Garry Maddox's sinking liner to center drove in Del Unser.

Maddox sealed the deal a half inning later when he snared the final out with a fine running catch.

"It was the first time I saw a group of men in tears," recalls Art Howe, describing the scene in the Astros clubhouse. "We felt we had the better team, and if we would have had J.R. Richard, it would have been a cakewalk."

No one was more downcast than Ryan. It was one of the few times in his career he had blown a game after the seventh inning.

"That was the first time Nolan sat in the clubhouse and cried over a game," says Ruth Ryan. "It was probably the toughest loss ever."

"You can't ask anything more from a pitcher than what he did," recalls center fielder Terry Puhl. "Nolan pitched his heart out, and that loss affected him more than any other loss I'm aware of.

"I remember earlier in the seventh inning when we took the lead, how the stadium was just going crazy. Frankly, we needed Nolan Ryan on the mound then anyway, because any other pitcher would have fallen apart under that kind of pressure."

"The whole thing collapsed for him in four or five pitches," adds Joe Morgan. "Nolan was a competitor, and I know he wanted to get that win more than anything in the world, but it just didn't happen. I think we would have won if Art Howe or myself had stayed in the game. I don't blame Nolan Ryan for the loss. I blame us—meaning we didn't give him enough support."

Pete Rose remembers it as the best series he ever played in: "Ryan was great, but we had Carlton and some other great pitchers. We needed everything to happen the way it did, and that's why we won it."

"We were all in tears wondering how come we're not going to the World Series," says Puhl. "In a lot of ways you can say we outplayed them. We just didn't get the job done."

Despite a bad back and tendinitis in both knees, Ryan went 11–10 in 1980, with 200 strikeouts and a 3.36 ERA. He threw 234 innings in 35 starts.

It was a better-than-average season, but because he came up one win short when it counted most, there were repercussions. Ryan had been hired to lead the Astros to the World Series. It shouldn't be realistically expected that one player could carry the whole team on his shoulders, but as the million-dollar face of the franchise and the highest-paid player in the game, Ryan took some of the heat for Houston's failure.

Dr. McMullen would never embrace and support his team as passionately again.

2

Changeup: 1981

When Nolan Ryan signed his hefty contract with the Astros in 1980, the first thing he did was start raising registered beef. All those cattle magazines he'd read made him knowledgeable in several aspects of the trade, but as longtime Astros bullpen coach Stretch Suba relates, the book learnin' only took Ryan so far.

"When we were in New Orleans playing an exhibition game, Nolan bought this bull for $25,000. He named it 'The Ryan Express' and took it back to Alvin. Trouble was, he already had two other bulls in an adjoining pasture—and bulls, as he was about to learn, are very territorial. His first morning back, Nolan looked out the window and saw the other bulls had broken through the fence and were beating the snot out of 'The Ryan Express.'

"Running out to break it up, he picked up a fencepost and hit one of the bulls across the back. The post broke like a toothpick, and all the bull did was stare at Nolan like, did you really want to do that?

"And Nolan, he's thinking, *Okay, I just signed for a million dollars, and I'm standing out here between 6,000 pounds of death and mutilation.*

"So he went back inside and called his vet, who came out and took care of it. I don't know how he got 'em separated, but in the process 'The Ryan Express' got knocked down and stepped on and got his pecker mangled. They ended up having to castrate him before Nolan could ever breed him.

But with bulls you can do artificial insemination, so they pulled a lot of stuff out of him, and that ol' bull was able to breed for several years after all. When he was 10 years old or so and got arthritis in his hips, that's when 'The Ryan Express' became bull burgers."

• • •

By the time Ryan returned to Cocoa Beach in the spring of 1981, Joe Morgan, Enos Cabell, and Ken Forsch were no longer Astros. To bolster the staff and replace Forsch, Houston signed former Dodgers ace Don Sutton to a four-year contract. Although he didn't possess the powerful arm of some of the other more established pitchers of his era, Sutton managed to carve out a nifty career using guile, control, and a myriad of pitches. He would go on to win more than 300 games in his Hall of Fame career.

It was Sutton off whom Ryan had hit his home run in his debut game with Houston the year before. Gene Coleman was charting pitches that day.

"I knew Nolan took pride in being able to throw the ball hard, so I decided to get a new radar gun and start measuring speeds," he says. "When Nolan came off the field in the first inning, the batboy came running over to me and said Nolan wanted to know how hard he was throwing. So I wrote down the velocities of each of his pitches and then scribbled on the back of the paper, 'Relax, Rook. You still got it!'

"The next inning the kid comes back and says, 'Nolan wants to know how hard Sutton is throwing!'

"The next year we end up signing Sutton. The first day he comes through the clubhouse and Nolan has a bat sitting in his locker. Sutton accidentally bumps the locker, the bat falls out, and Nolan looks up and says, 'Dang, Sutton! You walk by and my bat jumps out wanting to hit!'

"The next day Sutton had a T-shirt made that said IN CASE YOU HAVEN'T HEARD, NOLAN RYAN TOOK ME DEEP ON APRIL 12, 1980.

"They were good friends from that point on."

The 1981 Astros were eager to redeem themselves for the devastating loss to the Phillies in the 1980 NLCS. The team performed well in April, and despite lingering discomfort in his back, Ryan was 3–2 in May, with 39 strikeouts in 48 innings, and his 1.59 ERA was among the league's best. Unfortunately, the Astros couldn't get any traction and were nine games behind the Dodgers in the NL West.

In June, Ryan was 1–0 with a shutout when the specter of a players strike threatened to stop the '81 season dead in its tracks. Owners demanded compensation if they lost a free agent to another team, and players association head Marvin Miller said any form of compensation undermined the value of free agency. He gave owners until June 12 to ink an agreement.

Aside from the strike, the biggest story in baseball was Pete Rose's assault on Stan Musial's NL record of 3,630 career hits. Three days before the strike was to commence, Houston was scheduled to begin a three-game set in Philadelphia. The stat-savvy Rose had predicted three months earlier that he would break the record against Houston, with Ryan on the mound.

Rose was just two hits away from Musial when the game began in Philadelphia on June 10. With the strike scheduled to start the next day, it would conceivably be Rose's last chance at the record for the foreseeable future.

Looking in at the bundle of kinetic energy at the plate, Ryan toed the rubber and reminded himself, *Rose won't chase bad pitches, so don't expect any help.*

With a sellout crowd watching, Rose took Ryan's first pitch for a strike.

On the next pitch, he hit a fastball to center for a base hit, tying Stan Musial's record. Stan the Man himself was there.

Forced to wait at least three minutes as the crowd gave Rose a thunderous ovation, Ryan smoldered.

"I made up my mind that was all Pete Rose was going to get off me," he recalls. "I was determined I wouldn't be the one going into the record books with Pete Rose. That was one spot I definitely did not want."

Out in the bullpen, Stretch Suba put down his charts. "You could see a change in Nolan's body language after that," he says. "It was as if he was saying, *I don't care who you are, you are not going to hit the damn ball again.*"

Rose didn't touch Ryan the rest of the night.

In the third, it was three fastballs. In the fifth, it was a curveball, a fastball, and another curve. In the eighth, it was a fastball, a curveball, and a fastball.

Nine pitches. Three strikeouts.

"It was 'Morning, good afternoon, and see you [bleeping] later!'" recalls Rose. "He was just making bastard pitches, throwing 'em where I wasn't thinking. He picked himself up by his Texas bootstraps and said, 'You're not gonna get that friggin' hit! You're not gonna make history off me!'"

After the last strikeout, Rose hammered his bat on the turf, took a few strides toward the dugout, then turned and doffed his helmet in Ryan's direction.

"To see the two of them in that one-on-one battle was about as impressive as anything I've ever seen," says Suba. "Nolan basically said, 'Here it is, Pete. If you can hit it, hit it. But you're not going to!'"

The batter after Rose singled, and manager Bill Virdon pulled Ryan in favor of reliever Frank LaCorte.

"Ryan had like a one-hitter going in the eighth inning, and he got cramps in his calves and had to come out," recalls Suba. "We were up 4–0, and the next thing you know we lost 5–4. What made it worse was we were facing Steve Carlton and we hadn't beaten him in maybe 20 starts, and I know Nolan wanted that win."

Ryan wasn't the only one disappointed when the game ended. "What really hurt was after that night we went on strike for 50 days," says Rose. "Ryan made me wait for two months before I could break the hit record."

In time, Rose would come to realize that there were worse things than getting struck out by the great Nolan Ryan—like getting struck out by somebody not as great. "You don't get mad when a guy like Koufax, Drysdale, Gibson, or Seaver strike you out," he says, "because they struck a lot of people out. You get mad when guys like Randy Jones strike you out, or Oscar Zamora. Not Nolan Ryan."

Ryan likewise considered Rose one of his toughest opponents. In an ESPN clip aired before his Hall of Fame speech in 1999, Ryan said, "Pitching against him, I know the competitor he was. I know what he accomplished in the game, I know his dedication. My feeling is Pete should be in the Hall of Fame. I would have loved to have him as a teammate. I know he'd do anything to win."

The day after the Ryan-Rose showdown, the Astros waited at their Manhattan hotel to see if the players association would strike. Scheduled to play New York later that night, the Houston players were joined by members of the Cincinnati Reds, who had just finished up a series with the Mets and remained in New York to await Miller's decision.

In the hotel coffee shop, Ryan sat down in a booth with some Reds and their radio announcer, Joe Nuxhall. The conversation got around to Cincinnati's standout pitcher, Mario Soto, who was known for his exceptional changeup. Ryan asked Nuxhall, a former pitcher himself, how Soto gripped the ball when throwing the pitch. Nuxhall demonstrated by rolling up a napkin like a baseball and placing three fingers on the top and making a circle on the side with his thumb.

"He doesn't use his index finger to grip the ball," explained Nuxhall. "He lets his other three fingers do that. His thumb just sits there."

Ryan doesn't remember who paid the bill that morning, but says he scored the biggest tip of the day and his whole career.

When Ryan perfected his own circle changeup, says Pete Rose, he became a totally different and even more intimidating pitcher.

"That pitch gave him something to get left-handers out with," says Rose. "It was almost like a screwball. Imagine a guy throwing 97-98 mph, throwing a screwball? When he finally got enough confidence to use it regularly, believe me, everyone noticed. If Ryan had come up with that pitch earlier in his career, he would have struck out another six, seven hundred guys."

"Combined with his fastball, his circle changeup was unhittable," agrees Alan Ashby. "I remember a couple big hitters saying when they came up to bat, 'It was tough enough to hit him with the fastball and curveball. Now with this changeup, there's no sense of me even coming up here.'"

"When I executed it right, the pitch not only came off 15 mph slower than my fastball, but it had a reverse spin that acted like a screwball," says Ryan. "When I released the ball off my middle finger, the natural flow of the hand after releasing a pitch is to the right. It took me until 1985 to perfect it, and it became a big factor in my success."

The tangible cost of the baseball strike was substantial. An estimated $146 million was lost in player salaries, ticket sales, broadcast proceeds, and concessions. The players lost $4 million per week in salaries (including more than $100,000 by Ryan), and owners suffered a total loss of $72 million.

When the season resumed, commissioner Bowie Kuhn decided the best way to configure the season was to split it into two distinct pre-and-poststrike halves, with the winners of each half playing each other for the title. The two division winners would then go on to the NLCS.

The season reopened on August 9, with the All-Star Game in Cleveland. Ryan and teammate Bob Knepper joined a roster of NL stars that included Pete Rose, who was still seething over the way Ryan had shut him down in Philly two months earlier.

When Ryan entered the clubhouse for a workout the day before the game, Rose was there. "Hey, Pete!" called Mike Schmidt to Rose. "Look who's here!"

Rose turned slowly, lifted his arm, and flipped Ryan the bird.

Houston's 13–8 record in August put the team in contention for the second-half divisional crown. Despite pitching in pain, Ryan went 2–0 for the month with an impressive 1.38 ERA. They kept it up in September, and when the Dodgers pulled into Houston on September 25, the Astros were three games back of division-leading Los Angeles.

Ryan was slated to pitch the second game of the series. Since it was his last regular season start, Ruth invited the entire family and a contingent of friends to join her at the ballpark and then go out to dinner after the game.

"It was the one time everybody took time off to go to the game together," she recalls. Under the circumstances, "I wanted to wear something a little nicer than a pair of jeans, so I was a little bit dressed up for a ballgame with a dark green skirt."

A few rows behind Ruth, her parents, and Nolan's mom, scout Red Murff looked on with his traditional scorecard and stopwatch. Out in the center-field bleachers was Ryan's former high school coach, Jim Watson. Ryan's pal George Pugh somehow snagged a media pass and watched from the press box, as did Houston's managing partner Don Sanders and several guests from China.

Stretch Suba caught Ryan during warm-ups and hadn't noted anything spectacular. The fastball was working well enough, but Stretch knew warm-up sessions didn't mean much. There had been times in the bullpen when Nolan had great stuff and ended up giving up five runs.

Ryan's fastball was actually flat for the first two innings, bringing concerned pitching coach Mel Wright out to the mound. But the curve was very effective, and midway through the game Red Murff scribbled "Control of the curveball today" in his program.

By the sixth inning Houston was up 2–0, and third baseman Art Howe got the feeling "something special was brewing. You could feel it. The Dodgers were hitless and nobody on the Astros wanted to go near Ryan for fear of jinxing him."

His stamina in question because of recent injuries, Ryan felt he might have a legitimate shot at the no-hitter if he could get through the seventh inning.

Out in right field, Terry Puhl was watching Ryan like a hawk. Ryan was leaning on his curve, and Puhl knew that if the changeup was coming, Ryan would let his fielders know by coming down the mound toward the plate and brushing the dirt with his feet.

With two outs in the seventh, Puhl was locked on Ryan as he left a fastball up for Mike Scioscia. The big catcher lined the ball toward the gap in right-center, but Puhl, who was shading the gap, made a fine running catch. It would prove to be the play of the game.

"I got to that ball because we had our advance scouting positioned correctly," recalls Puhl. "We always played Scioscia the other way. I was probably five, six steps closer to center than I normally would play. He hit the ball just where we thought he would. I got a great jump and I caught it right by the warning track."

As Ryan breathed a sigh of relief, Red Murff started counting down the outs, and fans seated near Jim Watson started yelling "C'mon, Nolan! C'mon, Jim!"

In the press box, George Pugh, ignorant of standard protocol in such situations, caused all kinds of havoc.

"Nobody told me I wasn't supposed to be cheering," Pugh recalls. "So every time the Astros did something good, I'm clapping and hooraying. People kept looking at me like, *Who are you? Don't you understand you're not supposed to be doing that?* But I was so into it I didn't care."

Ryan made quick work of the Dodgers in the eighth, and the home team added three more runs in its half of the inning to make it 5–0.

Ryan had retired 16 straight batters and was looking stronger with every pitch.

In an effort to shake things up, Tommy Lasorda went to his bench.

"Grab a bat, Reggie!" the Dodgers manager yelled. "You're leading off the ninth!"

Reggie Smith shot Lasorda a look familiar to every daydreaming kid called on in class to solve an algebraic equation. Given his druthers, going in cold against a pitcher on the brink of a no-hitter and still throwing 97 mph was something the veteran outfielder would have preferred not to do.

"I was totally overmatched," Smith recalled later. "Three pitches later I was headed back to the bench, just thankful it was over."

When Kenny Landreaux followed with an easy ground ball to first baseman Denny Walling, the Astrodome crowd started whooping it up.

Heading to the plate, Dusty Baker yelled to his teammates in the dugout, "Don't worry about nothing, boys! I'll get a hit! Don't worry about nothing! I'm gonna bust up that mother!"

Ryan was more concerned about on-deck batter Steve Garvey. A contact hitter with a small strike zone, Garvey had enjoyed some success against Ryan in the past, and Nolan wasn't eager to face him now. Better to end it with Baker, whose weakness was breaking balls.

"I was prepared to go 3-0 to Baker before challenging him with a fastball, so I really wanted to get the curve over," Ryan recalls.

Thinking along the same lines was third baseman Art Howe. With Baker being a dead pull hitter and Ryan's curveball working, odds were that anything Baker hit would head his way.

Ryan stared in for the sign from Ashby, who flashed two fingers.

"The pitch was a curve, up in the hitting zone," says Howe. "Dusty had a big swing but got anxious, rolled his wrists, and hit a ground ball right at me. I said to myself, 'Get in front of it!' If I kicked it, I wanted an error."

He didn't kick it. Howe scooped up the ball, and his throw to Walling was on the money.

Ryan's teammates rushed the mound to celebrate his fifth no-hitter, and Ruth and Nolan's mother came down from the stands. Moments before TV and radio crews descended on the scene, Ruth and Nolan managed a brief embrace.

Jim Watson had made it over to the Astros dugout and was doing his best to make eye contact with Ryan. "They were having a little ceremony on the field and I was waving at Nolan," he said. "When he finally saw me he motioned for me to come down, but because of the crowd I only got as far as the railing. But that little wave was easily my biggest thrill of the day."

Six years after his last no-hitter, Ryan now stood alone as the only pitcher to throw five of them.

"It's hard to believe I got the no-hitter," he told the press. "It's the one thing I wanted. I've had a shot at it for a long time, but at my age I thought I wouldn't get it. I don't have the stamina I used to have. I didn't challenge guys in the later innings.

"I really didn't feel like I had good velocity today, but I got ahead on my curveballs. You can't win with one pitch. It doesn't matter how fast you can throw, but with a curve working as well as it was, they had to think about the breaking ball."

Don Sutton, who was to pitch the following day, added a touch of humor afterward: "I'm going to pitch tomorrow with an inferiority complex."

Terry Puhl, whose catch in the seventh inning saved the no-hitter, got the shock of his life in the midst of the postgame madness.

"About 10 minutes after the game, I'm sitting there and all of a sudden Nolan was right in front of my face," Puhl recalls. "He said he just wanted to thank me for the catch. I was surprised that with all the attention from the press he'd take the time to do that, and I was very touched."

A week later the Astros won the second-half Western Division title. Had the halves been combined, the Astros would have finished third behind Cincinnati and Los Angeles. Now, Houston would be host to their rivals from L.A. for a five-game mini-playoff for the right to go to the NLCS.

Ryan was stellar in Game 1, going the distance and allowing just two hits and one run. Alan Ashby's two-run walk-off homer in the bottom of the ninth was the deciding factor in the 3–1 victory.

An impressive performance by Joe Niekro the next day put the Astros ahead 2–0. Denny Walling's walk-off RBI single in the 11th was the game's only run.

The series shifted to California, where Burt Hooten and two relievers combined on a three-hit 6–1 gem to give the Dodgers new life. The day after that, rookie sensation Fernando Valenzuela threw a four-hitter and the Dodgers won 2–1, knotting the series up at two games apiece.

Ryan pitched well in the deciding game, allowing only four hits in six innings, but Houston's bats went cold and L.A. won 4–0 on a five-hitter by Jerry Reuss.

Despite playing much of the season in pain, Ryan led the majors with a 1.69 ERA and finished the abbreviated season at 11–5, with 140 strikeouts.

But with two consecutive playoff losses in as many years, his honeymoon with the Astros was officially over.

3

Humor: 1982

In the spring of 1982, a video production crew traveled to Cocoa Beach to capture on film what it was like to bat against Nolan Ryan. The plan was to film Ryan's delivery in slow-motion from a vantage point behind home plate, with a sheet of Plexiglas between the cameraman and the catcher.

Bullpen catcher Stretch Suba was behind the plate for the project.

"After Nolan got loose, the camera guy told me he couldn't get a good shot of him behind the Plexiglas, and would it be okay to remove it," recalls Suba. "I said, 'Okay by me, but you're going be standing behind the camera with no protection.'

"Nolan wasn't nuts about that idea himself. 'You guys are going to stand behind him and the camera while I'm throwing?' he asked.

"'It'll be all right,' the director told him. 'Your guy can catch, so don't worry about that.'

"Nolan just kind of shrugged like, *Okay, let's go to it,* and then turned one loose about 100 mph that sailed four feet over my glove and over the cameraman's head. The camera went one way and the cameraman went the other. I looked at Nolan and he had his glove up over his face and was dying laughing. He wasn't going to hurt the guy, but he sure made an impression.

"After that they put the Plexiglas back up, and it ended up being a very interesting film. You were able to see the strain on the arm and all the muscles and tendons and how much torque was behind each pitch. Nolan wasn't real comfortable with it, but he was a good sport and went along for three or four pitches."

• • •

Going into the 1982 season, Ryan had a number of concerns: Would fans, disgruntled about the players strike the previous season, still support baseball? Astros owner John McMullen was no longer actively promoting the team, and it was hurting player morale. Plus, Ryan was very concerned about his arthritic knees.

Since high school, Ryan's primary method of cardio training had been distance running. With the Angels he had run as much as five miles a day between starts. He eventually augmented his cardio routine with a stationary bike, but in the 1980s distance running began to lose its luster. The growing consensus among conditioning coaches was that since the only running during a baseball game was done in spurts, why not train that way?

In '82, Gene Coleman started having his pitchers do their running in short bursts, something Ryan and the rest of the pitching staff welcomed wholeheartedly.

"Nolan used to tell me he was so bowlegged he couldn't catch a hog in a ditch," recalls Coleman, "and to watch him run with his legs that bowed was really something to behold."

In fact, Ryan's bowleggedness presented a serious problem. After observing Ryan for two seasons, Coleman surmised the chronic difficulties Ryan was having with his knees and back were due to a pronated ankle that put pressure on his knees, hip, and back.

"Since muscles are the primary shock absorbers in the body, if the skeletal system gets out of alignment, then the muscles are working at less than optimal angles," says Coleman. "Nolan and I sat down one day and came to the conclusion that by the time he made his first pitch for the Astros he had already thrown over 100,000 pitches at over 90 mph. When you do something like that repetitively and do it all on three days' rest, that's going to put a lot of wear and tear on your back."

Coleman ended up constructing a special running track in the weight room above his office. Twenty-five-yards long and 10-yards wide, the wooden track was padded with Astroturf to absorb the pounding and make it easier on the runners' joints.

"The incline was pretty high," says Coleman. "But Nolan would run that thing forward, sideways, and backward up to 50 times a day.

"Beginning in 1982, distance running was no longer a major part of Nolan's routine. He never ran for more than 60 yards on the turf, something which paid off big-time for him down the road."

With less strain on his back and knees, Ryan spent less time on the DL, and for the first time since 1977, he threw 250 innings. He went 16–12 with a 3.16 ERA, and his 183 strikeouts were third in the NL behind Philadelphia's Steve Carlton and Cincinnati's Mario Soto. His 7.047 hits allowed per nine innings was the best mark in the league.

On the downside, 1982 marked the first time Houston failed to make the playoffs with Ryan. The team's fifth-place finish in the NL West resulted in the dismissal of manager Bill Virdon, who was replaced by third-base coach Bob Lillis. Pitching coach Les Moss remained, but by now Ryan could rectify most of his own problems. With Alan Ashby behind the plate practically every day, the two could make whatever adjustments were necessary if the pitcher's mechanics got out of whack.

Normally a pretty taciturn Texan, Ryan was comfortable enough on the Astros to put his dry sense of humor on display more than he had with the Angels. His on-field persona was so imposing that his lighter side came as a bit of a surprise to some.

When the team was going through an offensive slump, Ryan offered $100 for every RBI. "I'm not above trying to buy a win," he said. That very same night Jose Cruz hit a grand slam. When he opened his locker the next day, inside was a sack containing $400—in pennies.

Cruz was a very funny guy in his own right.

"Just before we went out for the national anthem it would be quiet, and all of a sudden all the boom boxes would come on," Terry Puhl recalls. "The music would be revved up and Cheo would start dancing and ripping his clothes off. Next thing you know it's game time and Cheo's sitting over there nude.

"He would do things like that to keep the team loose."

Puhl's locker was in the section of the Astros clubhouse that included the lockers of Cruz and a number of other Latin players.

"Cesar Cedeno was between us," says Puhl, "and Luis Pujols was on the other side next to Cheo. I called it 'The Latin Connection.' The row where Nolan and Joe Niekro were we called 'Wall Street.'"

Puhl remembers another Ryan prank that followed a bad at-bat the outfielder had in San Francisco.

"I shattered my bat really bad," Puhl said. "The ball went spinning down the line, and as I go down to first, Joe Morgan, who's playing for S.F., is standing at second laughing. We won the game, and when I came back to the clubhouse Nolan had taken that bat and strung it all back together with tape, and it was hanging above my locker on a hanger, and he's got the red stuff they would put on injuries that looked like blood all over my bat."

Stretch Suba recalls the time Ryan was rehabbing a hamstring injury and pitched a simulated game before his regular start.

"The team had a day off in Cincinnati and he wanted everyone to show up, including the position players," says Suba. "He said there was going to be a wienie roast afterward, because there was going to be a lot of firewood from all the broken bats. Well, everybody on the team showed up to hit and he threw a five-inning simulated game averaging about 95 mph. When the team went into the clubhouse, Nolan had gotten the clubby to set up these little hibachis with a bunch of bat handles burning in 'em, and there was a bunch of wienies on top of them."

Suba himself was a frequent victim of pranks by Ryan and the rest of the pitching staff. For one thing, Stretch was not a fan of underwear, and therefore often went without. After one game he was dressing in a hurry because it was a get-away day, and after getting into his pants he discovered he couldn't zip up the fly because it had been Super-Glued in the down position. Suba worked on it feverishly with a needle-nose pliers for a while but ended up hurrying to the bus with his shirt un-tucked to cover himself. The next day, Mike Scott handed him a hundred dollar bill in payment for the entertainment Suba provided him, Ryan, and Bob Knepper as they surreptitiously watched him try to un-stick his zipper.

Later that season, Ryan and Suba were in the outfield during batting practice when Suba asked the pitcher how he put up with things fans screamed at him on the field.

"You know, I look at it this way," Ryan said. "First of all, 30 percent of the people out there, no matter what you do, think you're really something special just because you're in uniform when you walk on the field.

"And 30 percent will think you're a hot dog just by the way you walk or the way your hat's on.

"The other 30 percent really won't have any thought about it at all."

After a moment, Suba said, "Wait a minute. That's only 90 percent. What about the other 10 percent?"

"They're the guys out getting a beer and a hot dog."

Ryan's compadre from Alvin, George Pugh, recalls the routine he and his college pals had whenever the Mets came to Houston and Nolan was pitching:

"The game plan was every time Nolan struck out somebody, we drank a beer. One time, about the third or fourth inning we had about eight beers and I was to the point where I hoped he doesn't strike anybody else out! I remember a couple games like that. At least we were all 21, so it was nothing illegal."

Ryan's displays of humor when he was actually on the mound were rare but memorable. Cincinnati reliever Brad Lesley was called "The Animal," because after each strikeout he'd throw his arms up and roar like a lion. In a mid-September game against Houston in 1984, Lesley went into his act after getting a strikeout in the eighth inning. A week later the Astros played Cincinnati again. Ryan pitched against Bob Shirley, a lefty whose hottest fastball clocked a mere 85 mph on the radar gun. Shirley got the Astros out in the bottom of the first, and when Ryan went out he threw the leadoff batter three straight balls before coming back with three strikes in a row. After the batter swung and missed the last pitch, Ryan threw his arms up and did a roaring imitation of Brad Lesley that had players on both sides holding their sides with laughter.

Ryan threw his fastball with so much intensity that fans could hear him grunt wherever they were sitting. When Bob Shirley came out to work the second inning, he issued a loud, exaggerated grunt as he threw a pitch that seemed to be traveling about 35 mph. Both teams erupted in laughter, and when Shirley looked over at Nolan, he was on the floor. When Ryan could breathe again, he tipped his hat to Shirley.

Sometimes, Ryan could get a little testy if the joke was on him. He wasn't amused, for example, when teammate Glenn Davis hid the homemade pies he'd brought in for the team, or when "Morganna the Kissing Bandit" planted one on him on the pitcher's mound with Ruth looking on from the stands.

Another time, Nolan got the surprise of his life when two of his teammates snuck into his condo during spring training.

"Craig Reynolds and I were rooming together the last week of spring training," recalls Terry Puhl. "The wives had all gone home, and one night after practice we told Nolan we were going to meet at the Kissimmee Steak House and asked if he'd like to come along. He said, 'Sure.'

"When it came time to go, Craig suggested we drive by his place and all go together. So we get there and his car's still in the driveway. We go to the front door, knock, but there's no answer. We go around and knock on the back door, with no answer. I try the knob and it's unlocked, so we walk in and hear the shower going.

"We figured as long as we're here, why don't we surprise him? The TV was on and we knew he'd turn it off before he left, so Craig and I hid behind the stairwell near the TV.

"A few minutes later the shower goes off. About then we started thinking, *Gosh, this might not be too smart,* because Nolan is very fond of guns. But we were committed, and when he came out and went to turn off the set, Craig and I jumped up and screamed, 'Don't turn the TV off!'

"Nolan just about jumped through the roof.

"The next road trip, we're in San Diego. Craig and I got our keys and bags and headed up to our room. First thing we did was take our clothes out of the bags and go hang 'em in the closet.

"When we opened up the closet, who do you think was standing in there with a big grin on his face? Somehow Nolan had beaten us to our room and gave us a dose of our own medicine."

• • •

What the 1982 season proved conclusively to Ryan and to his critics was that he had the stamina and will to do whatever it took to pitch effectively into his thirties. Credit also goes to Coleman, who by constantly coming up with new workout techniques helped Ryan overcome injuries and combat the aging process.

Ryan showed his appreciation that Christmas Eve when he dropped by Coleman's home.

"That was the year after he had pitched his fifth no-hitter and they did the famous LeRoy Neiman print," says Coleman. "He said to my wife, 'Would it be too forward of me to ask you to hang a picture of me in your house somewhere?' And he unrolled that LeRoy Neiman print. It was signed by him and Neiman, and he gave it to us for Christmas. By the time we got it framed we had been offered two or three thousand dollars for it.

"He also gave my son his 1982 road jersey for his graduation from college. Nolan signed it and we got it framed and we got it hanging up in the house. I've been offered seven or eight thousand dollars for that, but we'd never get rid of it."

Toward the end of the '82 season the buzz in baseball circles concerned the fact that Ryan, Philadelphia's Steve Carlton, and Seattle's Gaylord Perry were all closing in on Walter Johnson's all-time record for strikeouts—3,508, set in 1927. When the season ended, Ryan was just 14 away, Carlton 70 away, and Perry 56 away.

In the season ahead, old Walter Johnson's mark would be surpassed twice in three months.

4

Walter Johnson's Ghost: 1983

> I remember hearing Don Sutton say to Nolan, "You need to be aware of getting to 300 wins, and you'll get to the Hall of Fame."
>
> I believe that was a bit of an epiphany for Nolan. I'm not sure he had considered that at that time.
>
> —ALAN ASHBY

Nolan Ryan had never even heard of Walter Johnson until Tom Seaver mentioned him when Jim Bunning threw his 2,500th strikeout against the Mets in 1969. Seaver told Ryan the old Washington right-hander was baseball's all-time strikeout leader with 3,508 Ks (in later years, that total was adjusted to 3,509).

In the ensuing years Ryan didn't give the "Big Train" much thought, but now all the talk about him approaching Johnson's record piqued his interest.

Returning from a long road trip in April, Ryan took out a large book he'd purchased. He had never been a stat-monger; when a game ended, he generally forgot about it. Writers and fans knew more about his records than he did, and though he took pride in being known as the game's hardest thrower, that was about the extent of his interest in baseball history. Until now.

Opening the *Baseball Encyclopedia,* Ryan thought about something his former teammate Don Sutton (now with the Milwaukee Brewers) had told him: "The quickest way to the Hall of Fame for a pitcher is 300 wins. You need to be aware of getting to 300 and set goals along the way. You get your 300 wins, you get in the Hall of Fame."

Ryan was impressed by the way the veteran Sutton had carefully plotted his career path, and now for the first time he let himself think about the possibility of riding The Ryan Express all the way to Cooperstown.

Reading Walter Johnson's bio, Ryan had to admit the numbers were impressive: 21 years, 416 wins, 3,508 strikeouts, 110 shutouts, 1,363 walks, 5,923 innings, 2.1 runs per game...

Like Ryan, Johnson was a workhorse. In his 21-year career in Washington, the Big Train had averaged 31 starts per year.

Breaking Johnson's strikeout record would bring Ryan the respect he wanted and end once and for all the incessant carping about him being just a hard-throwing .500 pitcher unworthy of consideration among the all-time greats.

With my talent and drive, there's no reason I can't get the all-time strikeout record and then shoot for 300 wins, he thought.

In his first two starts, Ryan notched 10 strikeouts. Facing Montreal on April 27, he was five shy of breaking Johnson's record.

Sitting on his stool prior to the game, Montreal's Brad Mills couldn't help but grin as teammates pulled names from a hat in a lottery to predict who Ryan would nail for the record-breaking K. Mills figured it would be one of the starters, like Andre Dawson, Gary Carter, or Tim Raines. After all, they would face Ryan at least four times in the game. A utility guy, Mills didn't expect to even get an at-bat.

Ryan pitched well that afternoon, and through seven innings had yielded just four hits and was ahead 4–2, but he had only three strikeouts. When Mills found out in the eighth that he'd be pinch-hitting, that pregame business with the hat didn't seem so funny anymore.

"Ryan had only had a handful of Ks, and I knew he was getting close," recalls Mills. "He got the leadoff batter, Tim Blackwell, on strikes right before me, but we weren't sure if that had tied the record or broken it.

"I remember the count going to 0-2 when Ryan threw me a curveball outside. As a left-handed hitter, I was naturally looking into the Astros bench, and when the pitch came I saw everybody jump up because they thought it would be strike three, and I thought, *Oh shit! I'm it!*

"Now I knew anything close to the plate would probably go Ryan's way. I thought he was going to come back with another fastball, but he threw a back-door curve and struck me out looking. The consensus was the pitch was outside, but home-plate umpire Bob Engel gave Ryan the benefit of the doubt."

Mills, who would eventually go on to manage Houston (2010–12), has no regrets about being victim number 3,509.

"Ryan was gonna get somebody. I just happened to get my hand caught in the cookie jar," he said. "He made some good pitches, and if I would have had my choice I would have lined the ball to left field for a base hit and gone on down the road. But that's not how it worked out."

What impressed catcher Alan Ashby most was Ryan's demeanor following the historic K. "Nolan was modest and didn't like interacting with fans or the general public," recalls Ashby. "But after getting Mills he stepped to the end of the mound and almost painstakingly doffed his cap. It was like a revelation to his teammates to see him actually loosen up that far and say *Thank you* to the fans that were cheering. Up to that point I hadn't ever seen him do that."

The press conference afterward gave another clue to Ryan's mind-set.

"I think that this will draw some attention and respect to me that hasn't been there before," he said. "My critics, some of whom can't find too much positive to say about my career, will have to take notice of this. I think it will make people take notice after they study the record, they'll see that I did in 16 years what took Johnson 21 years, that I've been durable, pitched a lot of innings, and I have been consistent."

Now that he had the strikeout record, the question was how long would Ryan keep it. Steve Carlton had started the day just 24 Ks behind Johnson.

"I expect Carlton to get it," Ryan said. "I'm two years younger than he is, but he pitches more often than I do. He just signed a four-year contract, and I don't anticipate pitching for four or five more years."

Notably absent that historic day in Montreal were Astros owner John McMullen and commissioner Bowie Kuhn; present was Don Sanders. A 14 percent investor in the club, the affable Texan had earned Ryan's trust, and the two were at the beginning of a long association that would include several joint business ventures. Unlike the increasingly distant and silent McMullen, Sanders enjoyed the camaraderie of Ryan and his teammates. The only owner the players were in daily contact with, Sanders was readily welcomed in the Astros clubhouse.

McMullen's indifference became increasingly mean-spirited. He barred Sanders and the other limited partners from the clubhouse, and then even the players' children. Ryan was especially unhappy about the latter ruling; Reid and Reese had practically grown up in clubhouses, and McMullen's high-handedness would play a major part in Ryan's decision to leave the Astros several years down the road.

The immediate future held its own perils. At Shea Stadium on May 2, Ryan pitched seven strong innings when he came down hard on his landing foot after striking out Wally Backman.

"The way he went down, it looked like a sniper got him," recalls Gene Coleman. "It was so bad he could barely walk off the mound."

It was a popped hamstring, a serious injury. Team doctors handed the task of fixing Ryan to Coleman, who accepted the challenge with his usual zeal. Coleman consulted University of Texas track coach James Blackwood. Frustrated by seeing runners' knees and backs injured from the constant jarring on hard surfaces, Blackwood had started rehabbing them by having them run in a swimming pool.

"He put harnesses and floating devices on them in the deep end and had them do a running motion in the water," says Coleman. "There was absolutely no pounding involved. When I asked Blackwood if it would heal Ryan's hamstring, he said, 'It won't do any good, but it won't do any harm.'"

Coleman drove twice a week to Ryan's ranch in Alvin. He put Ryan in the deep end of his swimming pool, fastened a tether from the diving board, gave him a snorkel, and told him to sprint as hard as he could.

"With the resistance, he was running the equivalent of four miles of sprints a day," says Coleman. "Not only did the increased flow of blood help heal the hamstring, but he got his cardio in as well. The running also loosened his back muscles, alleviating some of the problems he was having with his discs."

Within a week, Ryan was running on the track again. Twenty-one days after his injury he threw a five-inning simulated game. Five days later he was throwing 95-mph fastballs against San Francisco at the Astrodome.

His recovery was unprecedented. Hamstring injuries as a general rule took the better part of a month to heal; Ryan did it in half that time. Eventually other pitchers including Rick Sutcliffe, Roger Clemens, and Andy Pettitte would rehab in the swimming pool, but Ryan was the first.

Even after his recovery, Ryan continued the swimming program. For the rest of the season, he ran in the pool for 10 minutes on nights after he pitched. The following morning he'd be back in the water for a 45-minute program. As the week progressed he shortened the pool workout each day. On the road, Coleman made sure Ryan had a pool lined up in every city they went.

"We were open-minded about the routines and whatever it was," says Ryan. "Whether it was a hamstring, quad, or strains, we'd go to the swimming pool to continue our conditioning and help speed up the healing process by pumping blood through the injured area without putting stress on the injured part."

Coleman remembered with a laugh one member of the Ryan family who wasn't so sure about his water therapy:

"We were running in the water one day. Ruth was fixing lunch and Nolan's mom came over, and Ruth re-introduced her to me. 'Oh, you're that guy who's trying to drown my son,' she said."

Ryan himself later joked that Coleman's pool sessions helped him accomplish two things he'd never before done: "One, I was home long enough to plant a garden, and two, I was in the pool long enough to get a suntan."

Ryan is the first to credit Coleman for his work in Houston, but Coleman himself is modest about his contributions.

"People always say, 'You really helped Nolan with his career,'" he said. "And my response is, 'Yeah, he only had about 4,000 Ks when I met him, so I really turned his career around!'"

But there's no question that Coleman helped Ryan immensely. Without his expertise, it's doubtful Ryan would have been able to manage the aging process and maintain his performance in Houston.

"The thing that caused Nolan and me to gravitate toward each other was that he had a very inquisitive mind," says Coleman. "I never said, 'Hey, Nolan, we need to do this or that.' I said, 'Hey, Nolan, let me tell you about this.' Or, 'What do you think about this?' And he'd start thinking and say, 'I want to try that!'"

• • •

Houston finished tied for third place in 1983, six games behind Los Angeles. Standouts included Dickie Thon, who led the league in assists at shortstop (533) and game-winning RBIs.

Ryan was 14–9, with a respectable 2.98 ERA and 183 strikeouts in 196 innings.

On June 12, against San Diego, Ryan went an entire game without allowing a single base on balls for the first time in his career. When both were with the Angels, Dick Williams—now managing the Padres—had told Ryan he'd buy him a new suit if he got through a whole game without walking a batter. Since they were now on opposing sides, the new suit was out, but when Ryan arrived at the park the next day a bottle of Dom Perignon on ice was waiting at his locker, compliments of Williams.

Ryan's 14 victories brought him to 219, 81 short of the magical number Sutton said was necessary for the Hall of Fame.

As for the strikeout record, Ryan and Steve Carlton traded it back and forth 14 times throughout the season. When the smoke cleared, Carlton had 3,709 Ks to Ryan's 3,677.

In 1984 Ryan would overtake Carlton for good, finishing that year with 3,874 strikeouts to Carlton's 3,872. He never looked back.

Overtaking Walter Johnson shined a bigger spotlight than ever on the indomitable Texan who, for all his 18 years in the major leagues, had remained something of a mystery to fans and players alike. The growing mystique of Nolan Ryan had its roots deep in his Lone Star heritage.

5

Texas Mystique: 1984

Throughout history, Texans have been cloaked in a mystique that sets them apart from other Americans. The roots of the mystique go back to the late 18th century, when settlers from the eastern states and abroad began populating the vast tracts of the Texas frontier. These forerunners, primarily of Irish-Scottish descent, brought with them Anglo-Celtic traits that included a fierce self-reliance and a belligerent fighting spirit. Frontier life infused in them an independent streak and identity all their own, far different from the settlers along the Oregon Trail or in California. They were called "Borderers" and resided primarily on the Trans-Mississippi plateaus. They were hunters mostly, followed closely in time by farmers, filibusterers, and entrepreneurs.

These frontier folk did not so much settle Texas as conquer it. But it came with a steep price. On their way to building an independent Republic, they stripped the topsoil, exterminated the Indians, subdued the Mexicans, and suppressed the Negroes. Where once Indians and buffalo roamed and tall grass grew and forests flourished, by the 1870s a rich cattle culture had emerged. By the time oil was discovered at Spindletop in 1901, Texas had become an imperialistic entity.

By establishing their own history, mores, and society, Texans created a country-within-a-country, one formed by struggle, rugged individuality, and a "moral superiority."

A third-generation Texan, Nolan Ryan inherited those traits. Crossing the white lines of a baseball field, all semblance of his innate, off-field humility vanished, and he became a rugged and belligerent Texan of the sort that chased Comanches with Captain McNelly of the Texas Rangers and fought Mexicans with Sam Houston.

David Crockett, William Travis, Jim Bowie, and many of the other heroes of the Alamo and San Jacinto were Anglo Celts; so was Audie Murphy of WWII fame. All had a belligerent streak that still exists in the British Isles. They are people not necessarily bound by blood as much as by culture. They tended to be grim borderers seeking new frontiers, and God help you if you got in their way.

A gentleman off the field, Ryan was pure Texas machismo once he tied on his spikes. The slow, deliberate circling of the mound, the blank gunfighter stare as he looked in for the sign, the guttural grunt as he released his fastball—all evoked the unmistakable Lone Star mystique. He approached hitters with a spirit like the one displayed by Audie Murphy fighting Nazis, and Bonnie and Clyde after walking into a bank. They all brought to their respective arenas a tenacious combative spirit and a will to be different.

"I believe in mound presence," Ryan told Gene Coleman. "When you go out there you need to look like you want to be there. I don't like hitters, and the reason I stare at 'em and make 'em feel uncomfortable is because I will do anything I can in my power to take their mind off hitting. I use intimidation and I use aggressiveness."

Ryan's teammate Enos Cabell remembers a game against Cincinnati in 1980 when a Reds pitcher plunked Cabell and two other Astros.

"I'll never forget it," says Cabell. "Nolan comes down the dugout with that slow walk of his toward me, Art Howe, Cesar Cedeno, and Joe Morgan. He asked us with that Texas drawl, 'Who do you want me to hit?'

"The others just looked at him kind of bewildered, but I said, 'Well, hit the catcher!'"

The catcher happened to be future Hall of Famer Johnny Bench. Ryan smoked him in the ribs with the first pitch.

"We were all laughing like heck," says Cabell, "and Nolie, all he did was turn and shake his head like he usually does. When I went up to bat next time, Bench asked me, 'Why did Nolie hit me?' I told him, 'Because you hit Cedeno and Morgan, and then you hit me. Somebody had to go, and Nolie asked us who. I told him you!' Bench just stared at me."

Off the field, Ryan had a kinder, gentler side.

Gene Coleman recalls a phone call he got from Ryan's brother-in-law, Don Shigagawa, who was also the principal of the junior high school Coleman's daughter Ashlyn attended. Shigagawa said he was having a special drug awareness school assembly and asked Coleman to ask Nolan to be the guest speaker.

"He's your brother-in-law, you should ask him," Coleman said.

"But I think he'll do it more for you than he will for me," replied Shigagawa.

When Coleman worked up the nerve to ask Ryan, he agreed—with one stipulation.

"Only if Ashlyn stands on stage with me," he said.

"So there they were, just the two of them," says Coleman. "Ashlyn held the microphone, fielded questions, and relayed them to Nolan, who answered them. Not only did that make my daughter's day, but it made the day for everyone else involved as well."

According to Don Sanders, Ryan's longtime business partner, "Nolan is the kindest, most pleasant, most gentle person you'd ever want to meet—until he gets on the baseball field. Then everybody's his enemy. He doesn't have all the degrees that everybody's talking about, but I could not name you one person I've ever met that has more common sense, better judgment, and better instincts."

Astros pitcher Jim Deshaies (1985–91) agrees that when Ryan played he had the rare ability to compartmentalize the opposite sides of his nature.

"Tommy Browning and I were high school opponents and college teammates," recalls Deshaies. "Tom was pitching for the Reds in 1985, and Nolan had pitched the night before. Tom didn't know Nolan. Later he said to me, 'What's the deal with Nolan? He walks around out there like he's the king.'

"'Well, he is,' I told him. 'He has a body language when he's on the mound that says, I'm in charge of this game, and this is my event, and it's mine to win or lose.'

"But I also said that off the field you don't get any of that. He's as folksy and as good-natured as can be. But on the mound, Nolan is absolutely the king.

"Everybody has that ability to differentiate to a certain extent. But with some guys there's an intensity, a focus when they go to the mound that can turn off all the outside stuff. And Nolan had that ability in spades. When he took the mound he was basically saying, 'I don't have to be a nice guy. I'm just Nolan Ryan the Express, and here it is, boys. You're going to eat some fastballs tonight.'"

It's impossible to know for certain if Ryan's Texas roots and upbringing are the reason for his persona. But those who know him best believe there could be something to it.

"Texas was a Republic, and if you give the people of Texas their choice today, they'd probably vote to go back to being a Republic," says fellow Texan Gene Coleman. "It was forged out of honor and history, hard times, stubbornness, and so forth—and that's Ryan.

"Nolan's teammates always called him 'Big Tex,' and when you think of 'Big Tex' you think of John Wayne, Stephen Austin, Sam Houston—those guys who were bigger than life."

Born in Bonham, Texas, but raised in Oakland, California, former Astro Joe Morgan seconds the notion that Lone Star Staters are inherently different.

"You look at Roger [Clemens] and Nolan, they had real big legs and that's where strength in their pitching came from," he says. "Josh Beckett is from Texas, but isn't as strong as they are. He is a different type of a pitcher, but obviously there is something in the water that breeds those types of guys. I don't know if it is their upbringing riding horses or whatever, but there is something there."

Says Andy Pettitte, who grew up in Deer Park, a suburb of Houston: "Us Texans have a little bit different mentality than some other people."

"Horse hockey," or a similar version thereof, says longtime manager Jim Leyland.

"There's no [bleeping] Texas Mystique," insists Leyland. "Texas is a big [bleeping] state with a lot of [bleeping] baseball being played there. That's all there is."

Hall of Fame sportswriter Tracy Ringolsby has known Ryan since the late 1970s. The Wyoming native has seen a lot of cowboys and doesn't think Ryan's characteristics are uniquely Texan.

"I met a lot of guys from Texas, and Nolan's character is a personality trait," he says. "When he pitched he had to have a certain amount of toughness, but he didn't have to be that way in real life. I don't think his baseball demeanor was his true demeanor, because you would have seen it more often if it was.

"I think that the 'Ryan Mystique' was just focus. It was his ability to focus on the challenge at hand. It's why he's been successful at everything he's done. He has the ability to channel his energy and focus into whatever he has to do to be successful."

• • •

On April 8, 1984, Houston's All-Star second baseman Dickie Thon was hit in the head by a pitch from Mike Torrez of the Mets. The impact broke the orbital section of his left eye, forever altering Thon's career. He tried returning the following season but suffered from blurred vision, headaches, and nausea.

In the off-season, when Thon enrolled for classes at a college in Alvin, Ryan tried to get him a job at the campus. During Thon's comeback attempt in 1985, Nolan pitched him extra batting practice and was as supportive as a teammate could be.

"Dickie wasn't into the workouts, because all he could see was the blurred vision and couldn't see the light at the end of the tunnel," recalls Gene Coleman. "And so Nolan would make him these bets—that if Dickie was able to accomplish such and such by such and such a date, Nolan would give him something or do something. Same thing with Glenn Davis—he made some bets with Glenn to try to get him to do certain things."

Because of Ryan's competitive nature, what can get lost is his compassionate and nurturing side. Because of his reputation as such an intense, no-nonsense competitor, even new teammates were wary of Ryan.

"You felt someone with the intimidation level Nolan had, it would carry over to his personal life," says Don Baylor, who joined the Angels in 1977. "I wasn't even sure if I could go up and talk to him, but he was more open than I expected. Second baseman Jerry Remy was a good friend of his, and I became a part of that group. We just kind of hung out together and did things. So I respected him in a way I hadn't done with a teammate in a long time.

"You wanted to play with him and behind him, and you were going to defend him. Even if he knocked somebody down, you were not going to let anybody get near him. I remember one time after I got hit, Nolan asked me, 'Who do you want me to get?' I said, 'Don't worry about it. I'll get somebody on the double-play or something. You pitch your game.'"

Rod Carew was another player who found out upon joining the Angels that there was more than a single dimension to Ryan.

"I used to wonder about Nolan, because after he'd punch you out he would always get the ball back and kind of strut around the mound," says Carew. "And I'd think, *I wonder what this guy is like? Is he cocky, or what?* But when I got to know him I realized he's the ultimate professional and one of the nicest people I've ever met in the game."

"The moments I had with Nolan on the field were absolutely special," says Reggie Jackson. "They were prized moments that belong to me and probably Mays and Aaron, and those guys that he ratcheted up against. If Nolan Ryan talks about the challenge of facing Reggie Jackson, that is a tremendous compliment. This guy is the hardest thrower in the history of baseball, but off the field he is a Southern gentleman and a wonderful guy.

"Nolan Ryan is a special person in my life. I love him and I love his family. When we get together, they are special times. We spent a day together one winter in Austin. I just completely enjoyed his presence, and it was a wonderful time in my life to be around him."

Whitey Herzog managed the Texas Rangers in 1973. When the Angels were in town, Herzog arrived at the clubhouse and found a package with his name on it. Inside was a large framed photo of Herzog and Ryan with a personal inscription from Nolan.

"I consider Nolan one of the best people I've ever known in baseball," says Herzog. "I knew him from the time he was 18. I was on his ass a little bit in Instructional League and made him work a little bit harder. A couple times when he'd doze off, I'd say, 'Nolan! Wake up!' or something like that. But he and I were always close.

"When I coached with the Angels, his wife, a lovely person, had dinner for me once in a while 'cause my wife was back home with the kids, who were in school, and they couldn't join me until June.

"So our friendship is very, very good, and the night when he sent that picture, I was touched. I got it hanging in my den. It's just beautiful. He wrote, 'To Whitey—Thanks for all the help along the way.'

"That's one of the nicest things I ever got."

"He has all those good qualities, like opening the door for a woman, always kind and good to his mother, and very nice manners," says Ruth Ryan. "He is more of a Southern gentleman–type and polite, but when you are out there in the field it is totally different. Out there you have to stand your ground and be aggressive and have all those kinds of qualities. I don't think it's like he tried to be like that. I think that was just Nolan's personality. He doesn't ever try to be like somebody. He doesn't act the part. He is who he is and what he is.

"He doesn't treat the owner of the California Angels or Houston Astros any differently than he would treat kids that shine shoes. There is no difference to him. If you have good character and are a good person, he will like you; if there is someone that is mean or has a character he doesn't like, he won't give you the time of day. He won't be mean, but he probably won't be friendly.

"He is good at reading between the lines and very good at deciphering things. He rarely offers information on himself, choosing to let the other person talk while he listens. He lets people prove their true colors, good or bad. He'll tell you that people tell a lot about themselves and their character by the things they say."

Nolan and Ruth Ryan were brought up in the Methodist Church, and Ruth says they never forgot the lessons they learned as youngsters. They say grace at every meal and are charitable to friends and family, and try to be patient with fans and people who make demands on their time.

"I think everything we do and say, and how we act around other people, has to do with God and our religious upbringing," says Ruth. "'The Golden Rule' is a part of who we are."

"I always thought just because I was blessed with the ability to throw a baseball and have some neat things happen to me, that it didn't really entitle me to think that I was any better than anybody else and act any differently," adds Ryan. "Even though those things happened to me I am still who I am, that was just my attitude."

• • •

In Ryan's autobiography, he devoted all of two sentences to the 1984 season. Three trips to the DL limited him to 184 innings, and he finished 12–11, with a 3.04 ERA and 197 strikeouts.

For the Astros as a whole there wasn't much to write about, either. Their 80–82 record excited no one, least of all the fans who showed up at home games in steadily declining numbers. Infielder Phil Garner put it best when he called the Astros "a bunch of nice guys with very little edge."

The malaise emanating from the top of the organization had reached the field. Without a spark from somewhere, the Astros were destined to keep struggling.

6

Stamina: 1985

To improve is to change;
to be perfect is to change often.

—WINSTON CHURCHILL

To celebrate the arrival of 1985, the Ryans invited conditioning coach Gene Coleman and his family to spend the holiday with them at the Gonzales ranch. The plan was to go out to dinner on New Year's Eve, then watch the Cotton Bowl the next day.

"Nolan likes these little hole-in-the-wall, out-of-the-way places," says Coleman. "He'd never been to this place called the White Leghorn Inn that his ranch foreman recommended. It was in Westhoff, 10 miles out of Gonzales, which is 10 miles out of nowhere.

"We get there and this place was a dump. It basically had a jukebox, a pool table, and the main dining room. When we walk in, there's a couple old cowboys sitting at the bar drinking Longnecks, and one of them looks up at us and says to his buddy, 'That thar's Nolan Ryan!'

"'Naw it ain't,' says his buddy. 'Nolan Ryan wouldn't eat at a dump like this!'

"We sit down and the waitress comes over. She's wearing blue jeans and a T-shirt. She puts down the silverware and napkins, and Reese Ryan, who was nine at the time, says, 'Look, Mom, they've got napkins that look just like paper towels!'

"The food wasn't very good either, and after we finish, the waitress comes over with the bill and Nolan says, 'Ma'am, could we see your dessert menu?'

"'Our what?'

"'Your dessert menu. You got some good homemade pies and cakes?'

"She says, 'We got Mars bars, Snickers, and Baby Ruths.' So we went to the local Dairy Queen, had a Blizzard, and went home and watched Johnny Carson.

"The next morning we got up early and rode around the pasture in my Bronco II to look at his deer. We were all piled inside, and I think I picked up every nail and rock Nolan had in that pasture, because I had one flat after another ever since then.

"Later that season we were in Montreal, and Nolan took my daughter out to dinner for her 12th birthday. 'Nolan,' she said, 'why on earth did you take us to that place for New Year's?' And he said, 'Because you'll never forget it.'"

• • •

By 1985 crowds had grown so sparse at the Astrodome that Ruth Ryan felt a sense of dread whenever she attended games. An oil crisis, the struggling economy, and uninspired baseball kept crowds down at the Dome; attendance was as low as 2,600 for some games. The Astros' total of 1,184,314 was 10th out of the 12 teams in the National League that year.

"The Astrodome always seemed a little hollow," recalls Ruth. "It was sort of outdated and beyond its prime and just wasn't a fun place to watch a ballgame. It was dreary and there wasn't much excitement in the air at all. That was hard."

The Astros got off to a slow start and never were really in contention all season. But Ryan's 8–6 first half impressed Padres manager Dick Williams enough to invite him to join the NL All-Star squad in Minnesota. Ryan threw three innings of shutout ball in the Midsummer Classic, but most notable were his 0-2 count "bow ties" to Rickey Henderson and Dave Winfield. The brush back of Winfield was an obvious reminder that Ryan hadn't forgotten their 1980 altercation, when Winfield charged the mound and almost decapitated him. This time the big man just shook his head, but after the game Yankees manager Billy Martin irately complained that Ryan had thrown at his ballplayers for no apparent reason.

"I'm not out there to hurt anyone," Ryan responded, "but for me to be the best pitcher I can be, I have to be a power pitcher. That's the way I've pitched my entire career. I'm not the nicest guy in the world when I walk on the field."

"Nolan had a funny way of letting a few get away when Winfield came up," says Terry Puhl. "Those two didn't like each other."

At 38, Ryan still threw in the mid-90s, and his wicked assortment of pitches made every opponent's at-bat an adventure. A leader by example, teammates looked up to Ryan for his humility and work ethic.

Second baseman Phil Garner joined the Astros in 1981. "Scrap Iron" would play seven stellar seasons for the Astros and become one of Ryan's good friends and a hunting buddy. In the early 1990s, Garner would manage against him. Like most veterans who played with Ryan, Garner understood there was much more to his game than wins and losses.

"You strut your stuff when you have guys like Ryan that are just the best on the planet," says Garner. "When you have a great player like him on your team, you know he's great and everybody else knows he's great and you pump your chest out because he makes you feel like you're as good as him. We weren't, of course, but Ryan made us feel that way, and that's why you're usually a little better when you have those kinds of people around.

"Nolan threw a 15-inning game against Boston, and who has done that in modern-day baseball? There were games he threw 200 pitches. Who does that? He came back from severe injuries and was even more effective. Who does that? I don't think you look just at his won-lost record and identify Nolan Ryan. You look at the total picture of the man.

"And longevity does matter in this game. It is a significant part of being great, because if you stick around for 25 years, you're doing something right for those last 15 years. Most guys are only going to play 10 to 15 years, so you're doing something pretty remarkable. And the way he threw was even more remarkable."

"Not just longevity, but successful longevity," adds sportswriter Tracy Ringolsby. "That's a special mark of excellence in the game, to be able to pitch that length of time. If he pitched 20 years, that's 15 wins a year. That's a lot of success and a lot of durability. And he did it as someone who threw a lot of pitches in a lot of innings. It wasn't anything soft and easy, the way he pitched. There was a lot of grunting and groaning. It was always fun to be in Cleveland or someplace that was nearly empty and hear his grunts echoing off the stadium."

In 1985, the circle change Ryan started experimenting with four years earlier was finally perfected. Now, with command of his three pitches, Ryan was a better control pitcher in Houston than he had been with the Angels. His velocity may have dipped slightly, but he was hitting his spots better.

"Nolan was never as wild as they gave him credit for being," says Joe Morgan. "He always wanted to make a perfect pitch or whatever, but he was not wild, and that was something that surprised me the most.

"He had been in the American League and I had been in the National League, and I had seen stories that he was a little wild, and then when we became teammates and I watched him pitch from second base, he was never wild. He might miss his spot a little bit here and there, and every once in a while he might be high. I think if he got a little more of the plate he would never have ever walked anybody, because he was not wild."

What impressed Morgan most was the way Ryan controlled games in the late innings.

"Nolan was unique in that he didn't go into the sixth inning and start looking for help. When he got to Houston I read he had won like 103 out of 106 games when he went to the ninth inning with a lead. I thought it was a misprint. Just compare that to guys you see today who go to the fifth inning and start looking for help from the bullpen. Like Bob Gibson and Sandy Koufax, he got better as the game went along. Guys like that, once they see the goal line, you weren't going to beat them."

Another factor in Ryan's longevity was pitching indoors for half the season. At the Astrodome, Ryan didn't have to contend with weather delays. Warm-up throws made in bad weather will wear any pitcher down, especially one in his late thirties.

Playing close to home was also an asset. When Ryan had a day off he stayed home, slept in his own bed, and relaxed around the ranch. Plus, he had a strong support group on the Astros; players such as Craig Reynolds, Alan Ashby, and Terry Puhl would become lifelong friends.

But the primary reason Ryan remained effective into his late thirties was his trust in and partnership with Gene Coleman, and the latter's implementation of the latest technology on Ryan's behalf. Coleman was the first, for instance, to consistently use a speed gun and chart its results. In 1985, realizing Ryan had lost a few miles per hour on his heater, Coleman used old videotape of Ryan pitching to measure his stride. Comparing the old footage to current video, he saw that Ryan's stride had grown longer, which forced him to open up quicker and lose velocity and control.

To rectify the problem, Coleman calculated the exact spot where Ryan's front foot should land on the mound after every pitch, and marked the distance with tape on the weight room floor. On days Ryan pitched, Coleman had him stand on the tape, close his eyes, and throw, then open his eyes and see where he landed.

"Nolan would do this five or six times," says Coleman. "When he felt comfortable he was stepping in the right direction and distance, he'd take it out to the mound."

By documenting each pitch and speed, Coleman says, Ryan knew not only the velocity and number of pitches he'd thrown but also the types of pitches and counts that got him into trouble.

"I said to Nolan, 'Do you realize Doc Gooden throws about 80 percent first-pitch curveballs, and our hitters put maybe one into play?'

"'I don't throw first-pitch curveballs,' he said.

"'Why's that?'

"'They're hitting about .300 off of me on first-pitch curveballs.'

"So I went back and looked at the charts and he was right. They were 3-for-10. But I also knew he threw 50 first-pitch curveballs and only 30 of them were strikes. Hitters were only putting three into play and taking the rest of them. So if the guys that were actually swinging at first-pitch curves are hitting .300, the other 17 guys aren't even swinging at it. I found if you present Nolan that kind of information and he makes the changes, he may begin to throw more first-pitch curveballs."

Coleman's ability to get into Ryan's head helped keep the pitcher healthy and effective enough to average about 30 starts per year for Houston. Credit goes to Ryan for being open-minded enough to appreciate the knowledge Coleman possessed, and then going out and applying it.

• • •

In 1985 Ryan pitched his 200th complete game and became only the fifth pitcher in history to win 100 games in each league.

On July 11, Ryan was only seven strikeouts away from becoming the first pitcher to cross the 4,000 threshold. Baseball commissioner Peter Ueberroth was among the 20,000 fans chanting "Nolan! Nolan! Nolan!" on every pitch to the red-hot New York Mets. In the sixth inning, with the count 0-2, Ryan got former Astro Danny Heep to swing and miss at a curveball in the dirt, and number 4,000 was in the books.

As catcher Mark Bailey trotted to the mound to shake Ryan's hand, his teammates on the field and players in both the Astros and Mets dugouts applauded. Ryan tipped his cap several times. The ovation subsided when he threw a pitch to the next batter, Howard Johnson, but flared up again when Ryan struck out Rafael Santana and pitcher Sid Fernandez to run his total to 4,002.

"It's possible that Steve Carlton will pass the 4,000 mark," said Ryan, whose fastest pitch was clocked at 97 mph. "But I don't think any of the other veteran pitchers will do it. There are just so many factors involved. You're talking about years of consistency and being healthy enough to pitch enough innings."

Carlton, Roger Clemens, and Randy Johnson would eventually join him on the 4,000-strikeout mountaintop. But Ryan always prided himself on being the first one there.

At the end of the season the Astros as a whole finally began showing signs of life. En route to another .300 season, veteran outfielder Jose Cruz racked up his 2,000th career hit, and first baseman Glenn Davis knocked out 20 home runs and had 64 RBIs. Kevin Bass belted 16 homers, Bill Doran 14, and Mark Bailey added 10, for a team total of 121 round-trippers, the most since 1973. In the bullpen, Charlie Kerfield showed promise as a setup man, and closer Dave Smith notched 27 saves.

The brightest star was pitcher Mike Scott, whose split-fingered fastball wreaked havoc on the opposition. Scott won 18 games that season, and along with Ryan, Niekro, and Knepper, the Astros finally had the makings of a formidable staff.

Ryan finished the year 10–12, with an ERA of 3.80 and 209 strikeouts. Most notable were his 35 starts and 232 innings. At 38, he had stayed relatively injury free, too.

Although the team was just 83–79, in 1985 pieces were falling into place that would make the next season one of the most exciting in the 25-year history of the Houston Astros.

7

Orange Fire: 1986

"In the 1986 playoffs we had a player by the name of Billy Hatcher," recalls Nolan Ryan. "One game the Mets had got him out his first two at-bats. After the second time he came and sat by me and said, 'Nolan, that guy started me with a fastball away every time in order to get ahead of me, and he's going to do it again—only this time I'm going to hit him off the wall.'

"Next time up, he hit a double in the alley off the first pitch away.

"Here was a guy that just didn't go up there and swing at pitches. He knew the patterns that were established and made adjustments. That's the kind of mind-set good hitters have, and that's why as a pitcher you want to know who the guys that make adjustments are and those that are just hackers."

Ryan knew some hitters were smarter than others, and that to remain effective he needed to constantly study each of them to discern any weaknesses.

"I would go out and watch the opposing team take batting practice," he says, "because they will tell you what pitches they hit well and what pitches they don't. I would've loved to stand right behind the cage, but you couldn't do that when the other team was hitting. So I'd sit on the bench and listen and watch."

Ryan got to work as soon as he arrived at the ballpark. His teammates might relax, play cards, or engage in playful banter, but Ryan believed that as long as he was at the park he should be doing something constructive. Whether studying hitters or lifting weights, he tried to use his time wisely.

His workmanlike attitude, according to eldest son Reid, came from a determination to take nothing for granted that was handed down from his parents, who were reared in the Great Depression and worked hard all their lives.

"The Ryans are a very serious family," says Reid. "My parents look at their parents, who sacrificed for their kids, and sometimes they feel guilty about enjoying life. I think that is one of the reasons my dad played so long. He understood clearly what his parents went through and how tough it was for them to support their family. His philosophy has always been, 'When the sun comes up, you go to work, and when it goes down you keep working. And every opportunity that you have, be thankful that you have it.'

"That's what drove my dad. Because of his upbringing, he never settled. Every day he thought he could improve himself."

"I was the last of six kids, and my dad had two jobs to support his family and put his kids through college," adds Nolan. "I saw him get up at 1:00 AM every night, and he and I did that [paper] route from the time that I was in first grade until I graduated from high school.

"So I knew what work and what dedication was, that was instilled in me through my father, and I have never forgotten that. I never looked at money as an entitlement. I appreciate every dollar I earn and I'll try to earn every dollar I can, because that's part of my background."

That drive to succeed set him apart and was a reason for Ryan's intense concentration and maximum effort whenever he pitched.

"What you have to do is learn to focus and then maintain your focus, and you can't get distracted," he says. "That's why I was an aggressive pitcher—because I had to get in that state of mind of being effective.

"Am I competitive today? No. I am completely burnt out on it and have no interest in competing in anything. I had to do it for a living, and it took a lot of effort and preparation for me to get into that state of mind to be aggressive and competitive, and that's just not something I want to do anymore.

"But when I played, you just developed that ability. You pitch enough and you start learning about yourself, what you can and can't do. It was something I had to work on constantly. When you evaluate a game, whether good or bad, what happened in that game and how you handled situations and how it affected you and impacted the game—you had to think about those things.

"Same way with a batter. And that's why I like to tell the Billy Hatcher story. When a hitter goes to the plate, he needs to lock in what he has to do and what he is looking for, and review his observation of the pitcher. Guys that don't do that, they just go up there and react to pitches, and those are the guys you could get to easily."

• • •

For many fans, the Astros were barely an afterthought going into 1986. Aside from the addition of bench coach Yogi Berra and the aforementioned Hatcher, the team was unchanged from the year before. Some in the media predicted they would lose 100 games.

But beneath the surface, things were stirring. Former Reds GM Dick Wagner had already replaced GM Al Rosen, and manager Bob Lillis had been fired in favor of Hal Lanier. A protégé of Whitey Herzog, Lanier knew the game and was a firm believer in speed, defense, and pitching, and he fit the current Astros team to a T. But according to Terry Puhl, Lanier could be abrasive, in contrast to the passive but likable Lillis.

Lanier began the season with starters Ryan, Mike Scott, and Bob Knepper, and quickly added rookie Jim Deshaies to the mix. The chemistry worked, and Houston shocked everyone by winning eight of their first 11 games, zooming into first place and staying there for 137 days.

Ryan himself did not get off to such a hot start; pain in his elbow limited his innings. Even worse, he had a new in-house nemesis in Dick Wagner, who'd become team president the year before.

Wagner had joined the Astros with a long but checkered résumé. During 15 years as a front office executive with the Reds, his marketing skills helped set a series of attendance records. As assistant to GM Bob Howsam, Wagner was responsible for building the Big Red Machine that won four pennants in the 1970s, and world championships in 1975 and '76.

But after becoming president and general manager of the team in '78, Wagner's opposition to free agency allowed many of the Reds' top players of that decade—including Pete Rose, George Foster, Tom Seaver, and even manager Sparky Anderson—to leave for greener pastures. In 1981, the Reds failed to make the playoffs after putting together baseball's best record in the strike-interrupted season. After Wagner traded Foster, Ken Griffey Sr., and Ray Knight that off-season, Cincinnati had the worst record in '82—the year Marge Schott, a limited partner in Reds ownership, famously hired an airplane to pull a banner over Riverfront Stadium urging the team to fire Wagner.

Wagner was not popular during his tenure in Houston, to say the least.

"He was a jerk, probably more so than [John] McMullen," according to minority shareholder Don Sanders.

Ryan thought he was acting like one on May 31 when Wagner put him on the 21-day DL without even bothering to check with the team physician beforehand. Ryan was 3–6 then, with 59 strikeouts.

It was the first time in his career that anyone other than the manager had removed him from the field. Ryan questioned the decision but went along for the good of the team.

Ryan checked with Dr. Frank Jobe in Los Angeles about the elbow. When Jobe said he needed Tommy John surgery, Ryan thought his career might be over. At 39, he felt there wasn't enough time for him to have the operation and go through the extensive rehab. So he decided to hang in there as best he could.

When he returned June 24 to face Cincinnati, the pain persisted but he made it through five innings and got the win.

The All-Star break gave Ryan a much-needed respite at his ranch. He invited teammates Mike Scott, Bill Doran, and Jim Deshaies and their families to join him. Everyone enjoyed swimming in the river, playing basketball and ping-pong, and just hanging out, though there were a couple scary incidents involving the host. During a spirited game of hoops, Ryan twisted his ankle.

"Pitching coach Les Moss was with us," recalls Deshaies, "and we fabricated a story about Nolan stepping in a hole while he was out walking the fence line. I think he missed a start."

It could have been much worse when Ryan gave a skeet-shooting lesson to Deshaies' wife, Laurie. "She hadn't shot very much and kept missing," said Deshaies, "and after Nolan showed her how to do it, she hit one of the clay pigeons and started yelling, 'I got it! I got it!' And as she yelled she spun around and put the barrel of the gun right in Nolan's chest. She could have shot him, but Nolan reached over real slowly and picked up the barrel and pushed it over to the side."

Ryan had a good month in July but rarely pitched a complete game; he was 3–1 with 55 strikeouts, when Wagner once again put him on DL for 14 days.

Wagner's rationale was that he wanted to conserve Ryan so he would be fresher down the stretch, but Ryan didn't buy it. He knew resting the elbow wouldn't help. He appealed to Wagner to keep him on the roster, but the GM wouldn't budge.

"Nolan didn't like to take no for an answer," recalls Gene Coleman. "If you could convince him otherwise he might listen, but to just arbitrarily put him on the DL and say, 'Hey, this is the way it's going to be,' he wasn't into that. Nolan's idea was, 'Let's talk this over a little bit,' but with Wagner it was never like that."

In his 1990 autobiography, Ryan wrote: "I was disappointed that Dick didn't have more regard for my judgment and experience. I felt he was treating me like some young player, and I felt that I deserved to be given more respect."

Ryan stewed on the sideline with his team in the thick of a pennant race. When he returned on August 12, Houston was still leading the West by four games.

Ryan dominated the Dodgers that day, allowing just two hits in six innings and bringing his record to 8–7. He remained strong the remainder of the month, though he rarely got past the sixth inning.

Tommy Lasorda's claim that the Astros were only "renting first place" was debunked when Houston dominated the second half of the season, going 49–25. During the September stretch drive Ryan pitched some of the best baseball of his career. Allowing just eight earned runs the entire month, he struck out 40 in 33 innings and allowed only 13 hits. Perhaps most notably, he only walked 13 batters.

"The biggest change I saw in Nolan in the late '80s was he stopped walking people," says Alan Ashby. "Through 1984 he had never started a game in which he hadn't walked a man, but by '85 he put it together and walks were no longer a big issue. By '86 the days of walking five-plus hitters were over, and he became the best I have seen of Nolan Ryan."

The Astros ran away with the division, clinching it in glorious fashion.

Jim Deshaies recalls the three games in the Dome against Los Angeles and San Francisco the week Houston clinched the division that exemplified its exemplary pitching staff.

"In the first game I threw a two-hitter, striking out the first eight batters," he said. "The next night, Nolan comes out and pitches eight innings of one-hit baseball and strikes out 14. After the game I'm shaving, talking to Alan Ashby. I say, 'Alan, you would think Nolan would let me have the limelight. Here I am, a rookie, I have this big game, and he kind of one-ups me the very next day.'

"Ashby says, 'You know, I think Scottie [Mike Scott] is gonna show you both up.'

"So the next day Scottie goes out and throws a no-hitter to clinch the division. We went two-hitter, two-hitter, no-hitter to clinch the division."

One of the stars of the bullpen that season was reliever Charlie Kerfeld. At 6'6" and 225 pounds, Kerfeld was a gentle giant, one of those lovable irreverent types that bring life and spontaneity to the clubhouse, and the kind of whacked-out character for whom Ryan developed an affinity.

One of Kerfeld's quirks was wearing the same ragged T-shirt featuring The Jetsons underneath his jersey for every game, because the Jetsons' dog was named Astro.

In the bullpen, Kerfeld, Dave Smith, and Larry Anderson occasionally donned Conehead masks. Sometimes Kerfeld arrived at the park in Rambo fatigues or wearing pink high-top tennis shoes. In 1987, when he learned teammate Jim Deshaies had signed for $110,000, he insisted on getting $110.037.37, on the grounds that his uniform number was 37. Kerfeld also had 37 boxes of orange Jell-O tacked on to his contract.

That same season, Ryan and Terry Puhl were in the Shea Stadium clubhouse prior to the second game of a doubleheader when the TV flashed on Kerfeld in the bullpen feasting on a plate of BBQ ribs. Evidently, former Met Rusty Staub, a noted chef, had some ribs on hand, and Kerfeld had gotten hold of a rack. John McMullen was in his suite in the press box at the time and wasn't at all pleased to see his ace reliever scarfing down ribs during the game. He immediately called manager Hal Lanier and ordered him to fine Kerfeld.

For all his eccentricities, Kerfeld could pitch, and in 1986 he had a career year, posting an 11–2 record and a 2.59 ERA as the setup man for closer Dave Smith. His unexpected performance was a key reason for the Astros' success that season. Kerfeld led the National League in won-lost percentage and finished fourth in Rookie of the Year balloting.

When the Astros clinched the Western Division, Kerfeld downed champagne and beer like a sailor just home from six months at sea. In a clip posted on YouTube, Kerfeld can be seen with a big grin on his face, nonchalantly tossing full cans of beer into the stands.

In the clubhouse later during a live interview, Kerfeld can be seen guzzling beers with the delight of a frat boy. When Ryan was being interviewed by a TV crew, Kerfeld made his way over and gleefully poured a beer over the head of the all-time strikeout leader. Ryan took his own champagne bottle, shook it, and gave Kerfeld a dose of his own medicine.

"Nolan always had an affinity for Charlie Kerfeld, who was kind of the anti-Nolan," recalls Jim Deshaies. "He got a kick out of those kinds of guys. He liked the characters, because he never could be one. He had to take care of his business. But he liked the colorful guys, the misfits, and the crazies. I remember watching that little dynamic with great delight."

Several players had career seasons in '86. Glenn Davis hit 31 home runs and drove in 101 runs; Kevin Bass hit .311; and Bill Doran and Billy Hatcher also performed well. But the Astros' real strength was pitching. With 18 wins, 306 strikeouts, and a 2.22 ERA, Mike Scott became the first Houston pitcher to win the Cy Young Award. Bob Knepper (17–12) and Jim Deshaies (12–5) were solid, and Ryan—12–8, 3.34 ERA, 194 strikeouts—helped anchor a staff whose 1,160 strikeouts were the fourth-highest in baseball history. With Kerfeld and Smith in the pen, the Astros had very few holes.

• • •

The 1986 Astros finished 10 games ahead of the Dodgers, and the New York Mets won their division by 21.5 games. With Dwight Gooden, Ron Darling, Ray Knight, Gary Carter, and Darryl Strawberry, the Mets made for a formidable foe in the NLCS.

There was no love lost between the teams. All year the Mets accused Scott and Ryan of scuffing baseballs, and New York had beaten Ryan three times.

It was Scott vs. Gooden in the marquee opener in the Dome. Anyone not expecting a pitchers' duel either hadn't been paying attention or spent the entire season buying beer and hot dogs. Glenn Davis hit a solo shot in the second inning that ended up being the game's only run; Houston won 1–0, as Scott pitched a five-hitter and struck out 14.

In Game 2, Ryan, pitching with a sore elbow, retired 10 straight before the Mets broke through for two runs in the fourth inning on a Gary Carter RBI double and Darryl Strawberry's sacrifice fly. Ryan was lifted in the fifth after an RBI single by Wally Backman and a two-run triple by Keith Hernandez.

Bob Ojeda held Houston to just one run and the Mets won 5–1 to even the series at one game apiece.

"The New York Mets finally found a pitch they could hit last night," said Bruce Jenkins of the *San Francisco Chronicle*. "In defiance of logic, legend, and the Houston Astros, that pitch was Nolan Ryan's fastball."

"We were a fastball-hitting team," said Wally Backman, "and Ryan was a fastball pitcher."

"I feel real disappointed right now," said Ryan. "I thought I had pretty good stuff, but I let it get away from me. After Mike won last night, we wanted to go to New York winning two in a row. It's not over. This just means we're going to have to go in there and win. It will just be a little tougher."

Lenny Dykstra's two-run homer in the bottom of the ninth off Dave Smith won Game 3 for the Mets 6–5. Bob Knepper had pitched flawlessly, allowing four hits through five innings, but in the sixth the Mets scored on a fielding error by Craig Reynolds. With two men on, Darryl Strawberry, whose career batting average against Knepper was a mere .100, blasted a three-run homer to tie it.

Scott was brilliant in Game 4, limiting the Mets to just three hits in the Astros' 3–1 victory.

Game 5 was postponed because of rain, and Lanier took advantage of the extra day by moving Ryan into Deshaies' spot. With the series tied at two games each, the stage was set for a Gooden-Ryan showdown—or, as one sportswriter billed it, "The new Nolan Ryan vs. the old Nolan Ryan."

The old Ryan struck out eight of the first 12 batters he faced. His only mistake came in the fifth, when on a 3-2 count Strawberry turned on a low fastball and hit a line drive that just made it over the right-field wall. The homer knotted the game 1–1, and with the exception of a Keith Hernandez base hit in the seventh, Ryan held the Mets hitless until he was lifted after the ninth.

He had limited the Mets to just two hits and a walk, a performance all the more remarkable because Ryan pitched half the game with a severe injury. In the Astros' fifth, he was at first when Bill Doran hit a ball to second for a fielder's choice. Ryan went into second base standing up, and upon hitting the bag felt a sharp pain in his foot. As the game progressed the pain worsened. Only afterward was it determined that he had pitched the last four innings with a fractured heel.

A botched call by first-base umpire Fred Brocklander in the second didn't help the Astros' cause. With Kevin Bass on third and Jose Cruz on first, Craig Reynolds appeared to clearly beat out a double-play ball thanks to a slow pivot by Mets shortstop Rafael Santana. Bass would have scored the game's first run, but Brocklander said Reynolds' foot was above the bag and not on it when Santana's relay arrived to Keith Hernandez, and he called him out.

"I saw the replay," said Brocklander. "I go with my call. It was a bang-bang play. As close of a tie as you'll get."

"If he said he saw the replay," responded Reynolds, "all I can say is that he missed it."

Said Astros manager Hal Lanier, "If it goes our way, we win in nine."

But it didn't, and the Mets ended up winning 2–1 in 12 innings, thanks to Gary Carter's RBI single.

The loss was crushing for Ryan and the Astros.

"I gave us an opportunity to win," Ryan said, "and we didn't take advantage of it. Sometimes it doesn't work out in your favor."

"Nolan had one of those games where he was totally dominant, and with the exception of Strawberry's homer, he was incredible," said Alan Ashby.

"He sprained his ankle badly, yet continued to pitch nine innings of one-run baseball," adds Jim Deshaies, unaware at that time that the injury was in Ryan's heel. "That's where some guys are kind of otherworldly, in their ability to block out pain and still compete."

That night, according to Ruth Ryan, Nolan was tight-lipped and silent. "That game and the defeat to Philadelphia in the 1980 playoffs were his most disappointing losses," says Ruth. "Those were very rough on him."

In his autobiography, Ryan said: "I wanted to win that ballgame as much as any other one I've ever pitched. Working in a game like that with my team's back against the wall, I get even more withdrawn, more honed in on my pitching, than I normally do."

The series shifted back to Houston, with the Astros needing to win the final two games to avoid elimination. The Mets wanted to win Game 6 at all costs to avoid facing red-hot Mike Scott in a winner-take-all Game 7.

For eight innings, the Astros' Bob Knepper was brilliant. He took a two-hitter and 3–0 lead into the ninth inning before the Mets rallied for three runs to force extra innings.

In the 14th inning, Wally Backman singled to right. Bass' throw to the plate sailed over Ashby's head, and Strawberry scored. Down 4–3, the Astros tied it in their half of the inning, when Billy Hatcher hit one of the most memorable homers in franchise history, high and deep off the left-field foul pole.

In the 16th, the Mets broke it open with three runs off battered Houston reliever Aurelio Lopez to take a 7–4 lead. The game seemingly out of hand, Astros fans started heading for the exits.

But behind the clutch hitting of Doran and Glenn Davis, Houston rallied for two more runs that inning to cut the deficit to 7–6. Astros runners were on first and second when the longest game in postseason history finally ended, as Kevin Bass struck out against Jesse Orosco.

"When we got Kevin Bass to strike out to end the game, it was like my brain stopped," said Mets third baseman Ray Knight, whose big hit had broken the tie during the three-run rally in the 16th. "I was afraid he would get a hit and we'd be playing all night. I was numb. It took a second to sink in that we won the series. I'm emotionally drained. My legs are still shaking."

"We went into the postseason, the Mets beat us, and they were the best team that year," says Ashby. "But our pitching staff was amazing. We had Nolan and Mike back to back, and Mike Knepper had a nice season. We had a legitimate shot to win that thing, but it got away from us at the end."

Historians have called Game 6 of the 1986 NLCS one of the greatest ever played. The Mets won the NLCS with a powder-puff .189 team batting average, and then went on to take the World Series against Boston with an assist from Red Sox first baseman Bill Buckner, whose infamous botch of an easy ground ball enabled the Mets to squeak by in Game 6 and then win Game 7.

Around December of that year, Ryan's elbow stopped hurting. To him it proved he had been right not to have the Tommy John surgery seven months earlier. But Wagner remained unconvinced, and the GM was determined to keep Ryan on a short leash in the coming season.

That didn't bode well for anyone.

8

Alpha Dog: 1987

> I remember when the Astros dropped this 100-pitch count on Nolan. He was fit to be tied and ready to fight, because he believed he was being taken out of games he felt he could have finished. He had pitched games with the Angels where he'd thrown over 200 pitches, and he thought he was still capable of doing that and should be allowed to. But ultimately I think the pitch count wound up helping him a bit. I think he got stronger and stronger in his later years.
>
> —ALAN ASHBY

As the 1987 season commenced, Nolan Ryan's refusal to get his elbow operated on only strengthened Dick Wagner's intention to lessen the pitcher's workload.

A pain-free and effective April didn't change Wagner's mind. Despite a month that included two 135-pitch games, a 2.45 ERA, and 36 strikeouts in 25⅔ innings, Wagner ordered Hal Lanier to put Ryan on a 115-pitch limit. The last time Ryan had a pitch count was when he was with New York, but then Rube Walker had not strictly and arbitrarily enforced his limit of 150 pitches, which is what Wagner intended to do now.

Ryan believed it was a pitcher's job to finish what he started. That's what pitchers traditionally did until the late 1970s, when marquee relievers like Goose Gossage came into their own and, as salaries escalated with free agency, owners felt obligated to use their high-salaried relievers as well as protect their starters by limiting their pitches.

Ryan felt pitch counts lowered the bar and limited his ability to build endurance. He also knew his teammates looked to him to be the stopper and eat up innings. Because of the pitch count, a basic element of his game was suddenly pulled from under him.

"Nolan didn't like it," says Ruth Ryan. "He felt pitchers should not be limited when they were still throwing well and were in good enough shape. Even now he doesn't think it all that important. He doesn't think you need to take a pitcher out just because he has thrown a hundred pitches. Everybody is different, and some guys need to come out before that. He wanted it to be an individual thing, and he did not want to be limited. He felt that a pitcher should have a say-so about it."

At a meeting about the pitch count, Wagner told Ryan: "Last season, every time you pitched a game over 130 pitches, you had trouble in your next start."

To back up his argument, Wagner had gone to the trouble of making up a chart showing Ryan's results after 130-pitch games. But show-and-tell didn't interest Ryan, and he paid his boss' handiwork no mind.

"The circumstances were different in '86," he told Wagner. "I was pitching every fourth day and had an arm problem. The longer I pitched, the more I aggravated it. This is totally different."

"The numbers don't lie," reiterated Wagner. "After 130 pitches you have not been effective."

Case closed.

"What bothered Nolan wasn't the pitch count as much as the way it was proposed to him," says Gene Coleman. "If he had been asked first, his reaction might have been different. But arbitrarily handing down the sentence was a blow to Nolan's pride. He wanted to be in control of his destiny and didn't want some doctor or GM who never stepped on the mound to say, 'You can't be throwing so much.'"

Ryan was generally slow to anger, but according to Don Sanders, Wagner's pitch count sent him "into orbit."

"With the great ones, they're usually just slow to anger. If they're angry they rarely show it," says teammate Phil Garner, who played for five seasons with Ryan. "And then they have this great desire to be number one, to be better than anyone else. They're alpha dogs—they've got to lead the pack. And that's the way Nolan was. He just had to lead the pack when it came to all those things.

"We cannot overlook genetics with these guys who are that good. They're just better than everybody else, number one, they're physically gifted; and number two, they're mentally gifted. What I mean is they have a unique demeanor and persona. I rarely saw guys like Nolan get mad. I was around Rollie Fingers, Catfish Hunter, Robin Yount, Craig Biggio, and Jeff Bagwell, and they're unique in that they have a temperament that is very stable and even-keeled. Willie Stargell was the same way."

But Wagner's edict stood, and Ryan was consistently forced to leave games earlier than he would have liked. In the late 1980s, Ryan averaged 16.2 pitches per inning, so usually by the sixth inning he had met his quota and was pulled. As the season progressed his stats took on a Jekyll-and-Hyde quality. At the All-Star break his record was 4–10, while his ERA was an exemplary 3.17. By season's end, his numbers were so out of whack that historians are still trying to figure them out.

"More often than not, I was forced to leave the game after reaching my pitch limit," says Ryan. "Then the other team would tie up the score, or I wouldn't get a decision. Or, we'd be trailing by a run or two, and I'd come out of the game. Our team would sometimes tie it, and I wouldn't get a decision. Or, I'd leave trailing by a run or two, and we wouldn't score and I'd get the loss."

"If he was pitching and the ballclub was not scoring, it could get ugly in the dugout sometimes," says Alan Ashby. "It got tense 'cause he was calling out the hitters on a regular basis. But it just seemed the harder he squeezed the more it was around our necks.

"Nolan was loaded with Texas dry wit and humor, but he was born with intensity. A lot of people said, 'Hey, look, Nolan is just a .500 pitcher,' but it wasn't through a lack of intensity. The guy wanted to win more than anything, and that impressed me most over the years I played with him. He had great stuff, was a good guy and teammate and the whole bit—but, boy, he wanted to win!"

And, as always, Ryan protected his teammates. Garner recalls a game against the Dodgers where Ryan's code of protecting his hitters and his controlled aggression came together.

"The Dodgers were just beating us like crazy," recalls Garner. "Tommy Lasorda's laughing at us. I'm playing third and I can hear him in the dugout, telling jokes. So Steve Sax hits a home run, and now Tommy's really hooting and hollering. I walk to the mound to our pitcher Frank LaCorte, and say, 'Frank, do you hear what's going on in their dugout?'

"He says, 'Yeah, do you want me to hit somebody?'

"Yeah, hit the next guy in the butt. We got to send them a message.'

"So Frank hits Kenny Landreaux in the hip. Kenny drops his bat and he's walking toward the mound and puts his hands up like, *Why me?* And LaCorte charges him. He fires down his glove, and now we got a fight.

"When the fight hits the paper the next day, the Dodgers' Pedro Guerrero comes out with a paragraph that fills half the side of the paper, and every other word is bleeped out. 'I'll kill the mother&*$%! If the mother&*$% hits me, I kill the mother&*$%! Ain't nobody hit me like that! I'm gonna kill 'em!'

"Well, as fortune would have it the Dodgers were scheduled to come back to the Dome the next week, and Nolan's pitching. The first time Guererro's up Nolan hit him right above the ear hole with a 99-mph fastball dead-square-center on the helmet. It was the best hit I ever saw in my life. The ball doesn't shoot up but bounces right straight back to the infield. And it doesn't knock Pedro on the ground. He just drops to his knees and sits there for a second, then goes down to first base and stays on the bag.

"It was interesting, because Pedro didn't go 'kill the mother&*$%!' And he didn't charge the mound. Pedro stayed in the game, and his next at-bat Nolan got two strikes on him and threw him a nasty curveball and Pedro hit a bullet right back through the middle of the box.

"I don't know if Nolan hit him intentionally or not. Nolan would never say. He was very professional about that."

Another teammate who can vouch for Ryan's dual nature is part-time utility infielder and pinch hitter extraordinaire Harry Spilman.

The Georgia native met Ryan when he joined the Astros in 1981. Both came from the country and had small-town sensibilities, and when

After signing a four-year, $4 million contract with the Houston Astros after the 1979 season, Ryan joined a staff that included knuckleballer Joe Niekro. Seated between the two pitchers is Don Sanders, a minority owner of the team and Ryan's future business partner. (Don Sanders)

Ryan threw the fifth no-hitter of his career, against the Los Angeles Dodgers in the Astrodome, on September 26, 1981. (Houston Astros)

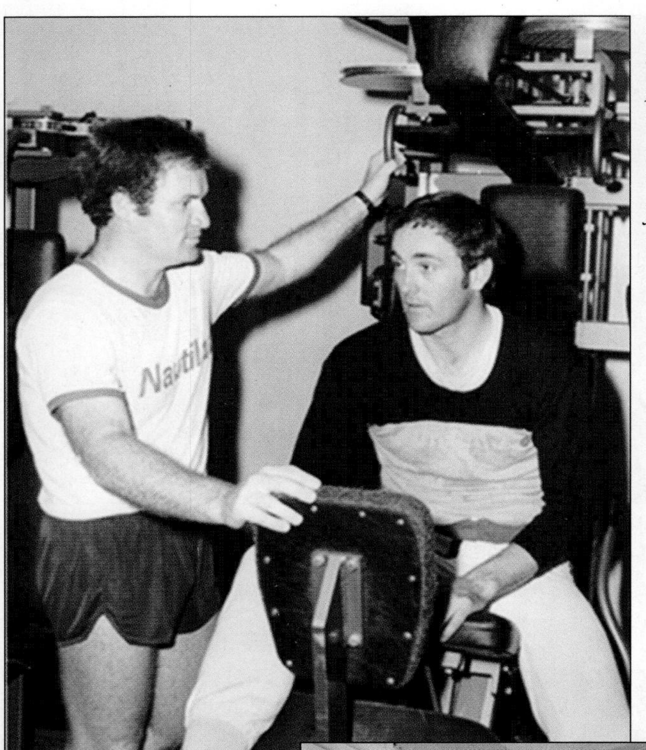

One of the secrets to Ryan's success and longevity was his personalized fitness regimen, revolutionary for a pitcher at the time, aided by long-time conditioning coach and friend Gene Coleman. (Gene Coleman)

A cattleman at heart, Ryan began raising registered beef while with the Astros. He also made as much time as he could for his family, including great-nephew and namesake, Ryan. (Mary Lou Williams)

Ryan moved on to the Texas Rangers following the 1988 season. On August 22, 1989, he struck out familiar foe Rickey Henderson and became the first pitcher to ever record 5,000 career strikeouts. (AP Images)

Ryan's unprecedented seventh no-hitter came against the Toronto Blue Jays on May 1, 1991. It is a mark no other pitcher is likely to ever reach. (AP Images)

The partnership between Texas pitching coach Tom House and Ryan resulted in an unprecedented run of success. The pair fine-tuned the pitcher's workouts and mechanics and kept Ryan productive well into his forties. (Texas Rangers)

One of the most memorable moments of Ryan's career: putting Chicago's Robin Ventura in a headlock after the White Sox third baseman had charged the mound during a game in 1993. (AP Images)

Following his retirement in 1993, Ryan launched several business enterprises, including ownership of the Round Rock Express, a minor league team run by his son, Reid, pictured here with Nolan's grandson, Jackson. (AP Images)

Ryan's induction into the National Baseball Hall of Fame came in 1999, the first year of his eligibility. In recent years, some baseball historians have attempted to minimize some of Ryan's accomplishments, but he remains one of only two pitchers in the Hall with more career strikeouts than innings pitched (the other is Sandy Koufax). (AP Images)

In February of 2008, Ryan was hired as president of the Texas Rangers, and in 2009, he was part of a group that took ownership of the franchise. Under his stewardship, the team reached back-to-back World Series in 2010 and 2011, the first trips to the Fall Classic in Rangers history. (AP Images)

The six Ryan children gather for a photo: (left to right) Jean, Judy, Robert, Nolan, Lynda, and Mary Lou. (Mary Lou Williams)

Today, Ryan is the happy patriarch of a sprawling family that includes three children and seven grandchildren. (Kelly Gavin)

Spilman wanted a home in the Alvin area, Ryan sectioned off a 12-acre parcel of his property for Spilman and his wife, Kim. They built a modest house and lived there for several years; the two families spent countless hours together. Harry often assisted Ryan with ranch chores, and Kim worked as an executive assistant at Ryan's office.

"I used to help him work cattle," recalls Spilman. "I didn't know a lot about it, but I knew Nolan had a keen eye for what he was looking for. Just like he'd look out on the field and size up players, he had an eye for cattle, too."

But Spilman's biggest contribution was catching for Ryan in the off-season.

"It was like he had a built-in catcher, and it worked out good for both of us," says Spilman. "I don't think people realize how much he threw in the off-season. Some days we'd be out there up to an hour, just throwing. He would start out slow in January and build up, and by the time it was time to go to spring training he was just about ready to pitch in games."

Spilman shared some unique experiences with Ryan, like the time they did a wildlife survey on a ranch Ryan bought in Three Rivers, in south Texas.

"Nolan rented a helicopter, and when the guy got there the helicopter was on the back of a trailer and he couldn't get the damned thing cranked up. I was wary about getting on it in the first place, but the guy finally got it cranked up and Nolan said to me in that deadpan way of his, 'Why don't you go for a test ride before we both get on it?'"

Spilman named his first son Ryan in honor of the man he considers the most easygoing, nicest person he's ever been around.

Except on the days Ryan pitched.

"In the 1970s and '80s there was always some mingling during BP and before the game, but on the days Nolan pitched he didn't have any friends on the opposing team," Spilman says. "After I went to the Giants in '86, you couldn't tell we were good friends."

Spilman and Ryan often kidded about what would happen if they ever faced one another. "I'm gonna take you deep," Spilman told him. "You'd better be ready," Ryan responded, "because it's coming down the express lane!"

In their first game on opposing sides, Spilman hit a home run off Ryan. The next time he faced Spilman, Ryan struck him out.

"A few years later," recalls Spilman, "somebody published a list of every strikeout he had, and the hitters. My name wasn't on it. Nolan made sure a corrected list was published."

Spilman retired as a player in 1989. He joined Ryan's Round Rock Express in 2005 as a coach, and currently is a minor league instructor for the Rangers.

• • •

At the end of August the Astros were in second place, 4.5 games behind San Francisco. But in September they went 9–18, wiping out any chance they had of making the playoffs. The defending Western Division champs finished in third place, 14 games behind the Giants.

Ryan had 51 strikeouts in 37⅔ innings in August. He tossed his best game of the season on September 9 against San Francisco, a six-hitter with 16 strikeouts in eight innings. One of his fastballs was clocked at 96 mph. The magnanimous Wagner responded by raising Ryan's pitch count to 125.

Despite leading the league with 270 strikeouts—his highest total in eight seasons—and walking only 87 batters—his lowest number in years—Ryan finished the year 8–16 with a 2.76 ERA, and didn't complete a single game all season.

"Maybe Dick Wagner would like to take credit for extending my career," he wrote in his autobiography. "But somehow I think I could have completed a lot of games without hurting myself. I mean, I was a 40-year-old strikeout king with a fastball that could still get in the high 90s. I had broken a big league record by averaging 11.48 strikeouts per nine innings."

Ryan was named the 1987 "Consort Control Pitcher of the Year." The more prestigious Cy Young Award went to reliever Steve Bedrosian of Philadelphia. Ryan was voted fifth by the writers.

Though justly proud of winning his second ERA title and, his pitch count notwithstanding, leading the league in strikeouts, Houston's alpha dog was weary and wary of the high-handedness of McMullen and Wagner. With Ryan's contract up after the 1988 season, there was no telling what the Dynamic Duo would spring on him next.

9

Houston, We Have a Problem: 1988

> John McMullen was a person who was very difficult to like. If everything was screwed up and in turmoil, he was happiest. You meet people like this. They just don't want to be happy and they just can't be happy. If everyone was sitting around having a good time and John walked in, everything just changed. John could go in the clubhouse or wherever, and a kind of a pall just came over everybody.
>
> John had some good qualities. He made things happen; he could make decisions quickly and move on. From that standpoint I had a lot of respect for him in his business arena. But as far as being a people person, he just wasn't that. He just really created a negative atmosphere.
>
> —DON SANDERS

Dick Wagner was relieved of his duties after the 1987 season and replaced by his assistant, Bill Wood, Houston's former minor league director.

The ongoing drama concerning Nolan Ryan and Wagner's pitch count certainly contributed to his dismissal, but in fact Wagner's time had come. The man who once fired Sparky Anderson as manager of the Cincinnati Reds because he wanted to "mix up the coaching staff" went to work with AL president Bobby Brown in the commissioner's office.

Surprisingly, Wagner and Ryan parted on friendly terms, and the GM extended Nolan's $1.1 million contract another season before he left.

In a tough Western Division race the 1988 Astros started strong. As late as the middle of August they were just a game and a half out of the lead, but then another weak September wiped out any chance to catch the Dodgers. The 82–80 Astros finished in fifth place, 12.5 games behind L.A.

First baseman Glenn Davis led the team with 30 home runs and 99 RBIs, but except for Terry Puhl (.303 in 113 games) no other Houston batter hit over .300. On the pitching side, Mike Scott, Bob Knepper, and Jim Deshaies all notched double-figure victories.

The 41-year-old Ryan started 33 games and had an ERA of 3.52. His 230 innings—his most in three years—was ample proof that the conditioning regimen he and Gene Coleman had perfected was still working. Unhampered by a pitch count, his 228 strikeouts and 9.3 per nine innings again led the league.

One pleasant surprise that occurred at midseason was the emergence of a scrappy young catcher from Seton Hall. Craig Biggio would go on to play 20 exemplary seasons with the Astros, and he credits Ryan, in part, for his impressive start.

"I came out of 'A' ball and got invited to the big league camp and made an impression on Nolan [because] I could block his breaking ball," Biggio said. "He was a supporter early on and a big reason I got to the big leagues as quickly as I did."

On September 14, Biggio caught Ryan's 100th win in the National League, a 13-strikeout performance against Cincinnati. In a game later in the season, there was another event that sticks in Biggio's memory just as indelibly.

"Buddy Bell was playing third, I was catching," says Biggio. "The inning before, Nolan made the last out and had run to first on a ground ball. Back then, when a pitcher returned to the mound you'd let him throw his warm-up tosses, and then run to the mound and ask, 'Hey, you okay? Need a breather?'

"I got halfway out when Bell started screaming at me, 'Get back there you little [bleep]! He's in better shape than all of us!'

"I stopped in my tracks and looked at third. I thought to myself, *That's Buddy Bell!* Then I looked at the pitcher and thought, *That's Nolan Ryan!* Who am I going listen to?

"There was no winning that battle. So I just put my head between my legs and walked back. What Buddy said was true. Nolan was in better shape than all of us."

On September 19, Ryan threw two strong innings against Los Angeles at the Dome before being lifted because of a leg injury. Danny Darwin replaced him in the top of the third, and the Dodgers went on to win 1–0.

When the season ended two weeks later, Ryan was 12–11 and still on the DL.

Two days after that, Ryan was traveling north in his truck on Hwy 35, heading to a meeting at the Dome with new Astros GM Bill Wood.

He had been down this stretch of road a thousand times. He knew every signpost and farm from Alvin to Houston, the 26 miles of asphalt as familiar as the stitching on his Rawlings glove. It was fall, the weather was cool, and Randy Travis' low-timbre rumbling from the truck's speakers matched Ryan's mood.

If you wonder how long I'll be faithful
I'll be happy to tell you again
I'm gonna love you
Forever and ever
Forever and ever, amen

Despite the run-ins he'd had with McMullen over the years, Ryan still liked being an Astro. He probably could have made more money pitching somewhere else, and maybe won more games, but that wouldn't have made up for living at home the last nine years and seeing his three children grow up.

But things had changed so much since he first got to Houston. The Astros had morphed from a family-oriented club into something more controlling and corporate. What he disliked most was McMullen's edict barring kids from the clubhouse; the Dome had been a second home to Reese and Reid Ryan, but in the last few years, unless it was on Sunday, they weren't welcome there anymore. But Ryan hadn't thought too much about it—being able to live and work at home for a million dollars a year made up for a lot.

As he neared the Astrodome, Travis' baritone gave way to Steve Wariner and his new hit single, "Lynda." Ryan thought about his old GM, Al Rosen. A former MVP with Cleveland, Rosen had understood the rigors of a ballplayer's life, but he had since moved on to San Francisco.

The club's fifth-place finish hadn't made anybody happy, but Ryan figured he had earned his keep. He had got out from under the hated pitch count and again led the league in strikeouts, had a decent ERA, and at 41, could still throw in the mid-90s.

The plan was to play a couple more years, get his 300th win, and then retire with Houston.

But as he turned off the engine and got out of the truck, an uneasy feeling came over him. Bill Wood was a company man, hired to do McMullen's bidding. Sure, he'd done some good things as farm director, like signing Bill Doran and Glenn Davis. And he had performed well as Wagner's assistant. Third baseman Ken Caminiti was his boy, and so was the new good-looking catcher, Craig Biggio.

But Wood's corporate demeanor made Ryan uncomfortable, and the pitcher was wary on his way up to Wood's office. As it turned out, he was wary with good reason.

Wood got right to the point: "Nolan, we want to offer you a contract for 1989, and we'd like you to consider taking a 20 percent cut from your present level. You had a remarkable career, you've accomplished a lot, but at 12–11 ..."

Ryan felt like a Dave Winfield roundhouse right had just hit him in the noggin.

The rest of Wood's speech was a blur. Later Ryan remembered something about incentives and returning to form, but it was the disrespect that came through loud and clear.

"I finished strong and everybody knows it," Ryan countered. "There's no doubt I can still pitch effectively. I've always been honest and fair, and if I ever get into a situation where I don't think I'm worth what I'm making, I'll let you know."

But Wood didn't back off an inch. He was sending a message from McMullen: *Nolan, you're not going anywhere, so you'll take what we give you. You're 41 and at the tail end of a long career. You don't want to move, so here's our offer. It's the best you're going to get, so just sign and be grateful.*

By the time Ryan got back to his truck he was already considering his options.

Somewhere south on Hwy 35, George Strait crooned, "Am I Blue." Ryan rolled the window down, gulped a mouthful of fresh air, and pondered his future. Reid was in high school, Reese was starting junior high, and Wendy was in grade school. Then there was Ruth. She had built a nice home here, and pulling up stakes now wouldn't be fair. Plus, his mother was still in Alvin; she needed him around, and the kids loved her.

It was worth one last shot. Only this time he would go over Wood's head and talk to the big boss himself.

"Nolan never made it public," recalls Gene Coleman, "but he went in to talk to Dr. McMullen. He said, 'Look, you know I've been here nine years and I'm making the same money, plus incentives.'

"Nolan never got a raise the entire time he was in Houston. He made the same salary, $1.1 million. Mike Scott was making $3.3 million, Bob Knepper and Joe Niekro were making over $2 million, and Jim Deshaies was making a million. Nolan was the lowest-paid pitcher we had. He was *Nolan Ryan*, and yet he was the lowest-paid pitcher, and he was bringing fans in.

"He told McMullen, 'All I want is the same amount, plus incentives. If I don't make my incentives, you don't have to pay me.'

"And they said, 'No. You have to take a 20 percent pay cut, because, you know, you were 12–11.'

"It ended when Nolan was told, 'Why don't you go out and test the free agent market, and then come back and talk to us.'"

Ryan's first call was to his friend and business partner Don Sanders.

"I'm not going to re-sign with the Astros," he told Sanders. "I just can't stay here."

His second call was to his agent, Dick Moss.

"You're going to be amazed what we can do," Moss told Ryan. The agent's phone was barely back on the cradle before he started filling out the forms for free agency.

But Ryan was torn. He didn't really want to leave Houston. He had chosen the Astros to be close to his family. His own roots were here, and they ran deep.

• • •

Nolan was born in Refugio, near the Gulf Coast, in 1947. At the time his family lived in nearby Woodsboro, where his dad was a refinery supervisor for Humble Oil. Nolan's birth certificate read "born Refugio, January 31," because that's where the closest hospital was.

Nolan's future high school basketball coach, Aubrey Horner, was a youngster in Woodsboro when Ryan was born. "I was at his house, because my mother and I were over there helping to take care of the children," recalls Horner. "Mom was real good friends with Mrs. Ryan. I was four or five years older than Nolan's brother Robert, and I knew all the girls.

"My mother went over to stay with them until Mr. Ryan went over to pick up Mrs. Ryan and bring Nolan home. I was sitting there playing with his sisters, they had their crib and everything fixed. When they came in the front door with Nolan, he looked completely normal. His right arm wasn't bigger than his left arm."

Six months later, Mr. Ryan was transferred to the Scanlon Oil company near Alvin. Mrs. Ryan liked it because there were oak trees everywhere and the place's small-town feeling.

"Alvin was kind of like the show *Happy Days*," recalls George Pugh. "We had the Dairy Land, where everybody would congregate and listen to music. At the American Legion Hall they had dances on the weekend. Those were the two main things we did.

"There was also a drive-in and an indoor theater. To keep away the mosquitoes at the drive-in, you'd have to put those little incense-burning things in there. And it was so hot you had to keep the windows down.

"It was a small community and we all went to church. And if you were doing something you shouldn't have been doing, someone would see you and your parents would find out about it.

The Ryans rented three different houses before purchasing a modest beige house on Dezso Drive, across from Mustang Bayou. According to George Pugh, Nolan was always throwing things—"rocks, footballs, and baseballs." His primary targets with the rocks were the turtles and snakes residing on the banks of Mustang Bayou.

Young Nolan was a bit rebellious and didn't have lofty ambitions. Horner remembers that he wanted to play ball at a university someplace, marry Ruth, live in Alvin, and become a veterinarian. Horner says Nolan was good but not great in Little League, had an obsession with cattle, and, like most boys in Alvin, he cruised the local Dairy Land for girls.

But Ryan's Texas roots go much deeper than Alvin.

In 1835 Nolan's great-great-great-great-grandfather, Isaac Milton Ryan, had 13 children, nine slaves, and a farm in Mississippi. His brother, John Jacob, lived nearby; John Jacob's son Isaac worked in the cattle and timber trades. Whether it was an act of nerve, a lust for adventure, or a suggestion of family friend Jim Bowie, no one knows, but one day Isaac joined a fighting unit formed by a friend of Sam Houston to help Texas gain its independence from Mexico. The unit was called the New Orleans Grays.

When the Grays crossed the Sabine into Texas, appreciative settlers presented them with a homemade flag that read, FIRST COMPANY OF TEXAS VOLUNTEERS FROM NEW ORLEANS. Beneath the logo were an eagle and the words, GOD AND LIBERTY.

After liberating the town of Bexar from the Mexicans, Isaac and his company reassembled in an abandoned mission called the Alamo. Determined to quash the rebellion, the following February, Mexican president Santa Ana led an army of 1,500 men to Bexar to oust the rebels.

Isaac was listed on the Alamo's muster rolls as a private and infantry rifleman. Commander Col. William B. Travis ordered his unit to guard the north wall, the garrison's most precarious position.

For 12 days the wall held. When the Mexican Army made its final assault with 2,000 troops on March 6, Isaac was most likely among the first to die. The records state only that he "Fell with Travis, on the north wall where a battery of eight-pound cannons was located."

As the Mexicans searched the carnage for survivors, the scorched banner of the New Orleans Grays was lifted from the ruins and presented to Santa Ana as a war trophy. The banner confirmed his fear that the uprising was not just a local fight and rather involved the United States.

Unbeknownst to the dictator, Isaac and his fellow Texans had acted independently. Nevertheless, Santa Ana had the flag shipped back to the Mexican capital, where it rests to this day in the national museum.

Nolan's great-great-grandfather, John Ira, and his brother built churches in Mississippi. Although they had cousins fighting for the Confederacy, there is no record that they themselves saw action. With the end of the war, the South they'd known had forever changed, and the brothers and eight-year-old William Franklin—Nolan's future great-grandfather—searched elsewhere for opportunity.

In the summer of 1865, they headed for the Texas frontier. Within a year the brothers had settled in the southern part of Angelina County on a 400-acre tract of land they called "Old Ryan Field." At the dedication of Isaac's new home, a revival meeting was held and a committee was formed to select a location for a new church and school.

By August of 1866 the church was ready. It wasn't much, a simple log house with a dirt floor and a stick chimney for heating.

Some Ryans eventually settled on a ranch near Kenedy, in Karnes County. That's where Nolan Ryan Sr. grew up.

"We have a picture of Dad when he was a little boy, sitting on the running board of an old car," says Nolan's sister, Mary Lou Williams. "It was the first car they ever had, and my dad and grandfather took a buggy and two mules and traded them for that car in Kenedy, Texas.

"They were really a close-knit family and always were. My dad worked with my grandfather on the farm. He started out at college, but always worked and supported my grandmother and his three sisters and my family. That's just what my dad did. And Nolan doesn't have that kind of a life, but that's just what he does."

• • •

"Nolan wanted to stay, but he really had no choice," says Gene Coleman. "McMullen's attitude was intolerable. So Nolan goes out and the first offer he gets is from Japan for almost $6 million. Then the Angels offered him $3 million and the Yankees $4 million, and so forth. And Nolan went back to the Astros and said, 'Okay, here's the range.'

"And the Astros said, 'Really? Well, let's talk.'

"And Nolan said, 'No, I'm not going to talk to you. I wouldn't sign here for $10 million! It's the principle of the thing. The way you treated me over these negotiations, why should I come back now?'"

"They thought that Nolan was at the end of his career, and if he wants to stay here he will sign for anything," says Ruth Ryan. "I don't think they thought about him leaving the Astros, and I think that was purely John McMullen. I liked him, but he was such a brash man. Nolan thought, *If they don't have confidence in me or think that much of me, I might as well go somewhere else.*"

Says Coleman, "McMullen said, 'Well, Nolan's disloyal. We gave him a million dollars and he went to the highest bidder.'

"What he didn't say is that they'd asked him to take pay cut."

Ryan had played nine seasons in Houston, one year longer than he did in Anaheim. He had found his groove in Houston; his mechanics improved, as did his control. He and Gene Coleman had done some revolutionary things with their conditioning programs. But it was time to go.

A few days after Thanksgiving, Ryan was in Alvin taking care of his mother, who'd been injured in an auto accident. Wood called and asked Nolan to come to Houston for a meeting. Ryan politely declined, saying he needed to look after his mom.

He later found out the Astros had scheduled a press conference that day. The plan was for Wood to tell him they were not going to offer him arbitration, which meant he could take their best offer or leave it. That meant that if he didn't sign by January 22, he couldn't negotiate with the Astros again until May 22. By not showing up at the meeting, Ryan had unknowingly avoided a very public power play.

Around this time, Texas Rangers GM Tom Grieve called Moss to see what the Astros were up to. Grieve figured there was no way they'd let Ryan go, and that McMullen was just doing some creative negotiating.

When Moss told Grieve there were "no guarantees," the Rangers GM realized something was indeed up and he broached the possibility of Ryan coming to Arlington.

When Ryan heard about this, everything changed. If the Rangers were serious, it meant he had a viable chance to remain in the state of Texas.

Grieve asked John Young, the Rangers' National League scout, for a report on Ryan. When Young called him one of the top five pitchers in the NL, Grieve was sold.

"I was feeling very confident," Grieve recalls. "I knew the kind of guy Nolan was and the influence he would have on our team and our fans. I had a scout we trusted, and without his recommendation I don't think we go after him. We were just not a franchise that could pay top dollar for that kind of person unless he was effective. When I informed owner Eddie Chiles and president Mike Stone that Ryan might be available, Chiles didn't hesitate: 'Sign him. I don't care what it takes.'"

At the winter meetings in Atlanta a month later, several other teams chased Ryan, including the Astros. When Houston didn't increase their offer enough, they were phased out.

"I don't think the city ever forgave McMullen for losing Nolan," recalls Don Sanders. "There was just article after article and comment after comment about it afterward, and it went on for years. Normally, something like that happens, and two weeks later everybody's moved on. Even today, there are still comments about how McMullen and Houston lost Nolan Ryan."

"I thought it was a real shame that Nolan wasn't coming back, and I didn't figure that he had many years remaining," says Alan Ashby. "But logic doesn't work with a guy like Nolan. He already had defied all the odds with five no-hitters at that point, and the strikeout record. But then it was like, 'Okay, you don't think I'm good enough? I'm going to go ahead to Texas and step this up another notch.' And he does exactly that at an age where it shouldn't be feasible."

To Terry Puhl, Bill Wood was a good man who made a bad mistake.

"Bill thought that the Houston Astros shouldn't be paying Nolan Ryan that kind of money," he says. "And he and McMullen convinced each other they were right, not realizing they were dealing with a baseball icon. They thought players were all on the same level, and they are not and never will be. We ended up replacing Nolan with Jim Clancy, a very nice guy, but...

"We all knew Nolan wanted to stay. But he had an element of professionalism about him that said, 'Okay, if I have to go somewhere else to play, I'll have to go.' He never badmouthed anybody. He just realized it was time to go.

"But he was definitely missed. You take a Nolan Ryan off the team, it's like a gaping hole you'll never fix. Management would say, 'Oh, yeah, we fixed it with Jim Clancy,' but it wasn't even in the same stratosphere."

It took Houston nine years to reach the playoffs again.

What Ryan would accomplish with the Texas Rangers would have a lot of people shaking their heads in disbelief—and maybe McMullen and Wood kicking each other's behinds.

PART VI

The Perfect Storm: The Texas Rangers: 1989–93

1

Talkin' Country: 1989

> Part of the fun for Nolan was changing clubs and leagues. I don't think he could have played 27 years just with one club. To him, new teammates and new families made things interesting.
>
> —REID RYAN

Bobby Valentine sighed as he added his empty coffee cup to the mounting stack of soda cans and room service trays on the nearby table. For the last three days, the Atlanta Hotel suite had been Ground Zero for Texas at the winter meetings. As manager of the Texas Rangers, Valentine knew the Yankees, Giants, and Angels were interested in Nolan Ryan, and that Texas didn't have the money to outbid them. But he also knew the Rangers had a couple big things going for them. First and foremost, they played in Texas; secondly, Valentine and Ryan had been friends since 1972, when Valentine joined the Angels in the blockbuster trade with the Dodgers that also sent Frank Robinson to the West Coast.

They'd met for the first time at the California State Fair in Pomona. Valentine was leaving the booth where customers knocked milk bottles down with a softball; the guy in charge had to finally run him off because he'd won too many prizes. Valentine walked away with two huge teddy bears, one on each shoulder, when a pretty girl came toward him and smiled.

Valentine thought, *Wow! A pretty girl is smiling at me because I'm carrying teddy bears!* "Hi, how are you?" he said. "Would you like a teddy bear?"

"No, I don't really want a teddy bear," she said with a smile, "but I want to welcome you to the California Angels. I'm Ruth Ryan, and this is Nolan."

As Valentine recalls, "Nolan was walking a little behind her, but I didn't really notice him, as you can imagine."

Valentine and Ryan became close friends. Originally a shortstop, Bobby moved to center field just in time for Ryan's first no-hitter. Less than a week later, at the Big A against Oakland, Valentine caught his right leg in the chain-link fence leaping for a ball off the bat of Dick Green. His ankle snapped so badly it gave chills to those attending to him.

The Angels tried bringing him back, and during his comeback in 1975 Valentine thought he was going to make the team. But right before the season started, he was sent down to play for the Charleston Charlies in West Virginia. Valentine wondered if he was being punished for some reason, because Charleston was the only Triple A team at the time that still took buses.

In any case, two months later Valentine went to Salt Lake City from Charleston, and then got called back to the big leagues.

His first week back, the Angels were in Detroit. After one game Valentine joined Bruce Bochte, Nolan, and Dave Chalk at Lindell AC, a notorious sports bar within walking distance of the ballpark.

"We were having a couple beers," recalls Valentine, "when I got up to go to the bathroom. Jerry Adair, who was at the bar, swung around and stuck out his leg like he didn't want me to pass."

Adair was the Angels infield coach, and it was his critical evaluation that had sent Valentine to Charleston.

"He started to go into how I had made his summer miserable, because he had to answer questions from the press about why I wasn't with the team," recalls Valentine. "I said, 'Maybe we can discuss this after I go to the bathroom, but I really have to go.'

"Adair stood up and grabbed me by my shirt. I lost my temper and punched him in the face, knocking him over the little banister that separated the bar from the seating area. I jumped over the banister and was in the process of finishing the job when a bouncer threw me out the side door into the parking lot.

"There happened to be a sportswriter and an umpire at the bar with Adair, and I figured for sure my career was over. As I lay on the pavement, I envisioned my future passing in front of me. I knew if this got out to the world, I'd be the bad guy who fought with the coach and should be banned from baseball.

"Nolan came out, and after settling me down he talked me into walking back to the hotel. He assured me that he'd handle everything that happened inside the bar."

Two weeks later, Valentine was traded to the San Diego Padres.

"Later," recalls Valentine, "Nolan called me and said he talked to the umpire and the sportswriter, who assured him no one would ever know what happened in that bar. Nolan took care of business, took care of his teammates. If it weren't for him putting a lid on that, I wouldn't have played another two years. I wouldn't have coached, and probably would never have had the chance at managing. I owed all that to Nolie."

Fourteen years later, Valentine was about to return the favor.

"The Rangers were leaning a little on me on account of my relationship with Nolan and on the fact that he was 'Big Tex,'" says Valentine. "Our owner, Mike Stone, said repeatedly that Nolan Ryan was a 'Texas treasure' and that the Rangers, as the only Texas major league franchise negotiating, were obligated to keep him in Texas.

"When the negotiating began, we asked Nolan and his agent, Dick Moss, if we could come back last with our offer, and they agreed. So in between our first meeting and our last, I kind of circled back to find Ruthie, who was in the adjoining suite. 'Other than money,' I said, 'what were the Ryans looking for from a team?'

"One of the things she and Nolan wanted was that their kids be allowed in the clubhouse. I assured her that not only would the kids be allowed in the clubhouse, but that the Rangers would do whatever necessary to give Nolan all the time he needed to be with his family.

"It seems to me we agreed to a contract without money even being mentioned."

Another big concern for Ryan was his conditioning program. Valentine said Rangers pitching coach Tom House knew what he was doing and would serve him well. All Ryan knew about House was that he was a California guy and a bit of a maverick. When Valentine told him House had a PhD in sports psychology and had worked with Gene Coleman in the minors, Ryan was intrigued. The primary reason he was still pitching at his age was his workout regimen; Coleman had added several years to his career, and Ryan wondered if House could do the same.

By now Houston and San Francisco were out of the Ryan derby. That left the Yankees, Rangers, and Angels in the hunt. Originally, Ryan leaned toward a second stint with the Halos. Owner Gene Autry wanted him badly, and according to Ruth, Jackie Autry, Gene's wife, was on the phone constantly pleading the Angels' case.

"Jackie kept telling him, 'Nolan, you could take us to the World Series!' And she said they would top any offer he got from the Yankees or anybody else."

Ruth, of course, was angling for Texas. It would keep the family closer to home and make life less stressful.

"I told Nolan I would love it if we stayed in Texas, and that the fans there knew him and would accept any contribution he could make to the Rangers," she recalls. "Besides, at this point I just can't up and leave home again."

Ruth and the family trumped the Autrys' deep pockets. "You're right," Nolan told her. "Let's stay in Texas."

Grieve recalls the moment Ryan officially became a Texas Ranger.

"Bobby and I were out jogging at about 7:00 in the morning, and when we got back up to my room there was a message from Mike Stone saying, 'I'm in Dick Moss' suite with Nolan. Get over here as soon as you can. I think we've got a chance to sign him.'

"So Bobby and I went over there and we literally put the contract in front of Nolan and Moss. They told us what he wanted and we signed it. My guess is the figure was Nolan's number, and that he knew it was a solid number for him and one we could digest, too."

Feeling their oats, Grieve and Stone pushed the envelope.

"How about an option?" Grieve asked.

"I don't know if I want to play another year," Ryan told him.

"Well, let's just put it in there in case you do," responded Grieve.

"We made it two or three hundred thousand more than the first year, and he pitches five years," recalls Grieve. "Bobby and I left the room to change our clothes for the press conference, and as we closed the door, we both looked at each other, jumped up, and did a high-five out in the hallway. We felt like fans. We couldn't believe that Nolan Ryan was going to be a Texas Ranger. It was an incredible day for us, and it turned out to be an incredible day for our fans, too."

Ryan may have planned to retire as an Astro, but now he was faced with the chore of uprooting his family, changing leagues, adapting to a new strike zone, and explaining to his friend Gene Autry his reasons for choosing the Rangers over the Angels.

Ryan was aware that pitching in Arlington's heat and humidity, compared to the air-conditioned comfort of the Astrodome, would be a challenge for any pitcher, much less one in his forties. And without Gene Coleman around to help, Ryan wondered how he'd handle it.

• • •

In Arlington, fans and press bombarded the Rangers with requests for tickets, interviews, credentials, T-shirts, hats, and anything remotely connected with Nolan Ryan. Season ticket sales doubled before he even threw his first pitch.

Having Ryan on board gave the Rangers instant credibility and their first legitimate superstar in the team's 18-year history. Since the team's arrival in Texas in 1972, it had languished in mediocrity, but now with Ryan and hitters such as Rafael Palmeiro, Julio Franco, and Ruben Sierra, the Rangers had a strong nucleus upon which to build.

"We took Bobby Witt, Kevin Brown, Kenny Rogers—a bunch of kids that were 4–30 in the minor leagues—and put 'em right in the big leagues with Charlie Hough and Nolan Ryan, and we won," says Tom House. "In a sense, it was a perfect storm for a whole bunch of us. We had the right mix of young kids and salty veterans that were all on the same page."

When House got the word Ryan was on board, he took out his charts and computer and went right to work. It was the biggest challenge and greatest opportunity of his coaching career. He had been champing at the bit to find someone with whom to share his cutting-edge conditioning concepts, and he knew how much Ryan had benefited from his own mentor, Gene Coleman, in Houston.

But there were some nagging questions. House had been an adequate pitcher during his own playing career, to put it charitably, while Ryan was a true giant. Would the discrepancy color their relationship? House was a former California hippie, Ryan a Texas cattleman. Would Ryan look at him with respect or disdain?

Any doubt about Ryan's commitment was erased on his first day of spring training. After a brief warm-up, Ryan threw batting practice for 45 minutes; as if that wasn't enough, after practice he spent an hour running the bleacher steps, followed by another hour in the weight room.

Jeff Torborg, Ryan's old mentor and battery mate with the Angels, was managing the White Sox when they played the Rangers in a Grapefruit League game.

"You'll think I'm making this up," says Torborg, "but at Port Charlotte there was a long staircase that went up the side of the clubhouse. I watched Nolan run that staircase the entire game—and you know how long spring training games get, 'cause you're using all kinds of different pitchers and people. I stood there in the dugout watching him that whole game, and he was so willing to work. Jeez, what a worker!"

Ryan and House got along famously. There were no pre-conceived biases, and, best of all, Ryan was open to House's outside-the-box ideas.

During the first few weeks of spring training House focused primarily on conditioning, and left Ryan's mechanics alone. But his inquisitive mind soon got the best of him. Aware Ryan had lost a little zip in his fastball, House wondered if the drop-off was simply due to age, or if there was something in his delivery that nobody, including Nolan himself, had noticed.

One of the prime tools in House's coaching arsenal was a new computer program called a Motion Analysis System. It enabled him to see if a pitcher was getting the maximum out of every aspect of his mechanics. After running images of Ryan's delivery through the program and translating it into 3-D stick graphics, House detected a subtle tilt in Ryan's head that caused his entire body to lean left and his arm to drop. By opening up too fast, he was losing maximum momentum toward the plate. Although it seemed almost trivial, House knew any dip in Nolan's arm could have ramifications.

During warm-ups the next day, House told Ryan that'd he'd put his motion through a computer analysis and determined that the pitcher's delivery was off by a couple millimeters.

Ryan stared at him and asked, "You did what?"

House started to repeat what he'd said, and Ryan put down his glove and took him aside.

"Look, Tom, I appreciate what you're doing, but when we talk pitching can you not talk computer?"

"'Not talk computer?' What do you mean?"

"Talk country."

"Talk country?"

"Yeah, let's talk country now. You can talk computer all you want with your other guys. Let's keep it simple! Can we do that?"

In plain English, House told Ryan that he was not getting maximum leg extension and velocity on his pitches because his huge leg kick was causing his head to tilt left, forcing his spine angle to shift. House suggested that when he lifted his front leg, Ryan should try sandwiching his body. This would force his back to remain straight, stabilizing his spine angle and preventing his head and body from leaning.

Every inch of inappropriate head movement, House explained, was costing him two inches of release point. By stabilizing his head, they could get him closer to home plate and put less stress on his arm.

"Not only should you recover faster," House said, "but we should be able bring back a couple miles per hour to all your pitches."

Ryan nodded and said nothing. The next day as House watched him warming up, he saw the change. Ryan felt the difference, and a smile danced between them as their eyes met.

"Straightening my head certainly was a correction I was able to make and benefit from," says Ryan. "Not only did it help me become more directional and consistent, but it also helped me with the breaking ball and being able to locate my fastball."

As Ryan would soon find out, those extra couple miles per hour that House gave him would change things drastically... for the opposition.

One of Ryan's gifts is his ability to break down thoughts, actions, and motions to the basics.

"Nolan, as with all elite individuals, gets it quicker and see things a little bit different than John Q. Average," House says. "They see the world a little bit different: the person they are, the person they want to be, and the person that people see. Their triangle is a little bit skewed, on the plus side. They don't see failure or successes like you or I do. They have a little bit different read and the ability to back it up.

"To get through to him I had to simplify. He didn't want complex. 'Just make it simple, make it country,' he'd tell me over and over."

During three major transition points in his career, Ryan gravitated to individuals who made significant changes in his style. In Anaheim, it was pitching coach Tom Morgan, who revamped his delivery. In Houston, it was conditioning coach Dr. Gene Coleman, who altered his routines to correlate with the aging process. And in Arlington, it was House, who overhauled everything.

"He is a sponge wanting more information," says Ruth Ryan of her husband. "He knew how intelligent those three guys were, and he knew that what they did and said were helping him. He also knows that he has to take people's advice, assimilate it, and take out what applies to him and then try to use it. He had great confidence in those three people, because he saw the benefits of it."

• • •

Ryan's Texas Rangers debut was in Arlington on April 6, 1989. When the first Detroit batter went down on strikes, four homemade placards adorned with the letter "K" simultaneously appeared throughout the park. Such signs would become fixtures at the ballpark for the next five years.

Ryan allowed four runs and struck out eight in five innings; he got a no-decision in a game Texas won. He fared better in his next start in Milwaukee, taking a no-hitter into the eighth inning and racking up 15 strikeouts along the way. Two starts later, he took a no-hitter into the ninth in Toronto before a two-out triple by Nelson Liriano broke it up. Two more low-hit games followed, and by the end of June the oldest pitcher in baseball was leading the majors in strikeouts, and his record was an astonishing 9–3.

John Blake, Rangers vice president of public relations, recalls those as groundbreaking days for a team that had never been in the national spotlight before.

"The Rangers were never really any kind of national baseball story, and then in April '89, Nolan [brought one no-hitter into the eighth inning and another] into the ninth inning and is on the cover of *Sports Illustrated*," Blake said. "That was huge for us at the time and we needed it, because it really brought credibility to the franchise."

Using techniques derived in part from Coleman, Ryan ran in the pool, lifted, threw, sprinted, flexed, and stretched five hours a day, six days a week. Prior to Ryan, marathon workouts in baseball were unheard of. The lifestyle of most pitchers hadn't changed since the days of Babe Ruth: a few laps and a couple beers after the game, and maybe dinner with a dame to cap it off.

When Ryan was in the weight room, House was alongside him. They worked together to come up with fresh, cutting-edge protocols that accounted for Ryan's advancing age.

"It became less stretching and more flexing," recalls House. "We did way more aerobic activity. We did a lot more running in the pool, where there was less wear and tear on the joints. Because he likes his meats, desserts, and beer, we started monitoring nutrition a little bit. I told him if we're going to eat those things then we got to be smart about how to do it, and to his credit he listened and actually applied it. He took new information and made it work within his lifestyle."

House reconfigured the weight room at Arlington Stadium to make it as efficient and accessible for Ryan as possible. Since workouts began at 6:30 AM, House gave Nolan his own set of keys so that if he arrived early, he could open the clubhouse door, turn on the music, and get right to work. Players' spouses and kids could join them to make morning workouts a family ritual.

Ryan felt out of sync whenever he missed a workout, so House went to great lengths to ensure that facilities were always available. In Cleveland, Ryan pitched a Saturday night game that ran long because of a rain delay, and didn't get back to the hotel until 1:00 in the morning. The Rangers had an arrangement with a downtown health club to let Ryan work out at 6:00 AM on a Sunday.

Said House, "I'm thinking, *It's 6:00 in the morning, we played a game last night, and I'm going down to meet Nolan Ryan to lift weights. What's wrong with this picture?* Well, nothing's wrong with it. Now that I've gotten to know Nolan, I know that's just the way he is. I realize that's why he's still throwing as hard as he is at his age. Unbelievable. He does what it takes to prepare himself, no matter what it takes."

Ryan has nothing but praise for House and his groundbreaking programs.

"Because Tom had unconventional approaches to pitching, he had a reputation for being a little off-center," Ryan says. "The typical pitching coach of our era developed his theories and philosophies through his own experiences as a pitcher and by watching those who were successful. Up until now there wasn't a lot of science behind it. Tom tried to understand the mechanics of throwing a baseball scientifically. His goals were to find the most efficient ways to maximize a pitcher's potential and stay away from injury.

"Steroids never came up. That thought never crossed my mind, and to my knowledge it never crossed Tom's mind. I grew up in the period of the drug culture, but drugs were something that never interested me at all. As far as I remember, steroids were never even discussed privately. I was into making sure my routine allowed me to bounce back."

Years later, Ryan would bemoan the stain that steroids and performance-enhancing drugs have left on the national pastime.

"I saw it [steroids] in my career and it's a shame, because they are rewriting the record books," he said. "Those records that were established were the benchmarks. Steroids distort those records and diminish what the game once stood for and what we've been doing for over a hundred years. I think that baseball and the players organization are weak in that area, and by ignoring steroids for so long, they have harmed the true integrity of the game. I'm not real optimistic that we will see any great changes, but time will tell."

The constant challenge for House was to create programs that would maintain Ryan with as little wear and tear as possible. Through trial and error, Ryan decided his heaviest weight routine should be the day after he pitched. That way he would have three or four days to recover until his next start.

A good example of their give-and-take relationship concerned squats, an exercise Ryan had always considered a core component of his program. House deduced that a lot of Ryan's leg problems were a result of his squat workouts, but Ryan said he wasn't giving up squats and challenged House to find a way to resolve the issue.

"He didn't mind being assertive with something he knew he needed to have," House says. "He might say, 'No, I'm gonna hang on to this. I'm not changing.' So as a coach it forced me to create a way to get around the problem, and it made me get better. In this case we found out a way for him to do a squat-like motion with a little bit less stress on his Achilles, knees, and lower back."

"I think his open-mindedness and desire for information, as well as his desire to get better as a pitching coach, was what made him so unique," says Ryan.

Some of the routines they came up with were derived from House's experience in Japan. "He went over there and got a lot of interesting ideas," says Ryan, "and we would try and incorporate them into our workout scheme. If we felt we were getting benefits from it we would integrate them into our regular workout program. If not, we didn't.

"A good example of that was the towel drill and working on your delivery on flat ground. I thought that was a good drill, because it put less stress on my motion. So after we played long toss, that's how we finished up."

Years later, Ryan noted House's contributions and their friendship in his Hall of Fame acceptance speech at Cooperstown.

Their special association was in part forged by necessity. At 42, Ryan was twice as old as many of his teammates. With House, who was roughly the same age, Ryan had someone to relate to and bond with. Between the weight room and the field, House spent so much time with Ryan that he became privy to a side of him usually reserved for family and close friends. House became aware that the discipline and work ethic Ryan displayed in the weight room was a direct expression of his high standards. Ryan simply refused to perform without preparing to give his absolute best. Never was that more evident than on the days he pitched.

"On game day, Ryan would carry on a conversation but it was very peripheral," says House. "I didn't see the killer instinct until the national anthem, and then it was as if he was in a different world. On the mound there was no wasted emotion—he was all tunnel vision, surgical. In competition there was very little waste of anything. He'd say, 'I'm going to pitch a season one quality pitch at a time. I can't do anything about the last pitch or anything about two pitches from now. The only thing I have any capability of managing is the next pitch. So this next pitch is going to get 100 percent.'"

The 1989 season saw Ryan's best start in years. He took a no-hitter into the eighth inning three times in his first 15 starts, and by the All-Star break he had pitched two one-hitters. He led the majors in strikeouts and had 10 wins. In July, he became the oldest pitcher ever to win an All-Star Game, throwing two innings of scoreless ball in front of a familiar and enthusiastic crowd in Anaheim.

Pitcher Mike Gubicza of the Kansas City Royals was in the AL bullpen with Ryan. Gubicza was hesitant to approach him, but finally did so and was pleasantly surprised.

"I found him more than accommodating," he says. "I asked how he was able to keep his velocity on his fastball at that stage of his career, and he emphasized the importance of a strong lower body. Not only can that maintain your career and fastball, but also your command from the fifth through the ninth inning.

"He also told me that the one thing that really helped his endurance was, after running foul poles, always ending with five 60-yard sprints. I incorporated this into my own routine, and it probably added several years to my career."

Like everyone else, Gubicza couldn't help but be impressed by the seemingly effortless delivery and firmness of Ryan's fastball.

"The whole bullpen was mesmerized," Gubicza says. "When he finally went into the game, Chuck Finley, myself, all those guys—seasoned big league pitchers—we all went up to the bullpen gate and peered out at him like little kids. I'm watching that leg kick and him hiding the ball and then *vooom*! I'm thinking, *Man, if I could only duplicate that.*"

Gubicza followed Ryan in the contest, and after the game in the clubhouse "I shook his hand and said, 'Congratulations, Nolan, you did well. I really appreciate the insight and the time to talk to you.'"

Ryan gave Gubicza a quizzical look and said, "What do you mean? This is what I love."

House had helped Ryan regain several miles per hour to his fastball, and his mechanics had never been tighter. He also had his on-field strategy locked in.

"Nolan would literally program his games before he took the field," says House. "He'd meet with the defense and go over hitters and how he wanted people to be lined up behind him. Then he'd tell the catcher, 'Do not let me deviate from this plan.'"

House remembers a game in which Ryan did deviate from his plan, and it cost him a chance at another no-hitter:

"We were playing Detroit on August 10, and Dave Bergman was up. Nolan said to his catcher, Chad Kreuter, 'Look, he will continue to foul my fastball off, but he's a breaking ball hitter, so do not let me shake to a breaking ball on Bergman.'

"I then heard him say, 'Chad, what did I just tell you?'

"Kreuter said, 'Don't let you shake to a breaking ball on Bergman.'

"So he's got a no-hitter in the ninth inning, and Bergman fouls five or six fastballs off and it's a 1-2 count. The sign goes down and Nolan shakes off to a breaking ball. Then Kreuter puts fastball down again. But again Nolan shakes off to a breaking ball. I'm going, 'Aw, shit! Nolan's going against what he told Kreuter he wanted to do!'

"Finally, Nolan wins. He throws the breaking ball, and Bergman gets a base hit just over the shortstop's head. Now, Nolan was angry, but not that he gave up the base hit. He was angry that he overrode Kreuter. So what does he do after the game? He runs up to him and says, 'Chad, I apologize.' Nolan Ryan just lost a no-hitter to Dave Bergman in the ninth inning, but he goes to Kreuter and said, 'Chad, I apologize, you were right, I was wrong.'

"I asked Kreuter afterward, 'How many times did he shake you off?'

"'Three times,' he said. I said, 'Why didn't you stick with it?'

"He said, 'That's Nolan-[bleeping]-Ryan. What am I going to do? I'm a rookie!'

"Nolan lost his focus that night, but he didn't get angry at anyone but himself. He had the hair on his ass to walk up to Kreuter, who was a friend, and say, 'Chad, it was my fault, I'm sorry. Don't feel bad if the press second-guesses you. You had nothing to do with that. That was my call.'

"Do you see why a plan for Nolan helps? He lost his focus—but he didn't blame anybody else."

By August, another long-awaited milestone—Ryan's 5,000th strike-out—was imminent. He was only six away facing the Oakland A's on August 22 in front of a crowd of 42,869 that included a large contingent of Ryan's family and friends from Alvin.

Driving to the ballpark that night, Ryan was so nervous he missed the freeway exit to the stadium and had to turn around. But in the locker room the nerves disappeared; Ryan even told House "It's either going to be [Rickey] Henderson or [Jose] Canseco for my 5,000th K."

"As we got closer to the strikeout milestone, every ball got thrown out," House recalls. "Rickey Henderson was 998, Ron Hassey 999. We went through a lot of baseballs that night, because every strikeout leading up to 5,000 had to be thrown out."

In the fifth inning, Ryan was just one strikeout away when Henderson returned to the plate. Chad Kreuter, handpicked by Ryan for his ability to block his curveball, was behind the dish.

"The strange thing about that at-bat," recalls Kreuter, "is that when Rickey came to the plate, he said to me, 'If Rickey strikes out, Rickey wants to take the ball out to Nolan.' I kind of looked at him with an expression like, *What the hell are you saying*? When he repeated it, I told him, 'If Rickey strikes out, Rickey can go sit down on the bench!'"

With flashbulbs exploding throughout the stadium, Henderson worked the count full. Then Ryan uncorked his 73rd pitch of the game, a 96-mph heater that burned past a swinging Henderson. Kreuter recalls the pitch having a late cut to it, but it was definitely a strike.

Before the game, Kreuter had asked Ryan, "What do you want to do when you break the record?"

"I want to continue on as if it didn't happen," responded Ryan.

"I said, 'We're not going to be able to do that, 'cause everybody's gonna stand and we're gonna have to stop the game.' And he said, 'Well, let's just make it as low-key as possible.'"

After the strikeout, the catcher ran out to the mound, shook Ryan's hand, and showed him the ball. "All Nolan said was, 'Toss it in and get me a new one,'" Kreuter recalls. "Ryan wanted to stay focused on trying to get a win and not let that detract from what the Rangers were trying to do as a team. He was always thinking team first and not wanting the attention centered on him."

Before the game Kreuter also talked with the infielders, and it was agreed they would all go out to the mound when the strikeout record was broken, congratulate Ryan, and then get on with the game. But it wasn't that simple. As the other Rangers joined Ryan on the mound, the stands exploded with a standing ovation that lasted 25 minutes. President George Bush offered his congratulations via a prerecorded video played on the center-field scoreboard.

Ryan's response was to twice doff his cap. Then he went back to work. He finished the night with 13 strikeouts. Unfortunately, the Rangers lost 2–0.

"If you haven't been struck out by Nolan Ryan, you're nobody," Henderson boasted to the press. "After the game, he told me, 'It had to be somebody, but I'm sorry it had to be you.'

"It really is an honor. Roger Clemens throws hard, but Nolan has more success with what he does. Nobody in baseball can do what he's doing."

Personally, Ryan was just glad it was over with. "The day off yesterday gave me a lot more time for things to build up, I was nervous at the start, but then I settled down," he said. "I didn't want to walk Rickey Henderson, so I went with the fastball. If somebody asked me before the game what pitch I would throw, it would have been a fastball."

According to PR man John Blake, Ryan's 5,000th K kicked the Rangers' publicity campaign into another gear.

"We made a big deal about the 5,000 strikeouts and turned that into a national story," he says. "We got the national media to come down, and then it all snowballed from there. Attendance goes up and eventually the new stadium gets built because of us getting Nolan."

The milestone raised the excitement swirling around Ryan to an even higher level. He had to hire a full-time secretary just to handle his fan mail. But for all the noise and accolades, Ryan and House didn't deviate from what got them there. The day after the Oakland game, it was business as usual at the gym.

• • •

As '89 came to an end, it was obvious that the best thing about the Rangers' season had been the reemergence of Nolan Ryan. He performed brilliantly, and with a week left in the season he was 15–10 and within 12 strikeouts of 300, a milestone he'd not passed since 1977. Although the mark held little personal significance, he realized it might be meaningful to the Rangers organization.

Ryan was shagging balls in the Arlington outfield one afternoon when House told him he could pass on the final road trip if he wanted. With the team in fourth place, manager Bobby Valentine felt there was no use risking his arm with another outing.

Ryan told House that he'd go west with the team, take his turn in the rotation, get his strikeouts, and then head home for the winter.

"He went to Anaheim, pitched five innings, got his 13 punchouts, and called it a day," House recalls. "What's amazing is he had called how it would happen in the outfield a week earlier. He needed 12 Ks and got them, then packed his bags and went home. That's the kind of stuff he did. After that season I was sure he could strike out people at will."

As pitch counts and old records were eclipsed, House could only wonder what was next. How long could Ryan and the Perfect Storm keep going?

2

Lining It Up: 1990

> Playing in the big leagues is a dream. Preparing to play in the big leagues is a nightmare.
>
> —NOLAN RYAN

> Age is an issue of mind over matter. If you don't mind, it doesn't matter.
>
> —MARK TWAIN

Nolan Ryan originally signed for just one season with the Rangers, but given the success and popularity he achieved in 1989, there was never a doubt he would be welcomed back.

The new ownership conglomeration, headed by George W. Bush, eagerly signed him for his option year, and Tom House got to thinking even more creatively about ways to elongate Ryan's career.

House maintains that a key component of Ryan's continued success was the unqualified trust he established with the Rangers. A good example of it was the fact that in the entire time Ryan played for Texas, he was never required to undergo a single physical examination. When Ryan arrived in Arlington in 1989, concerns about his elbow had passed, and he figured there was no sense looking for trouble by subjecting himself to all kinds of tests.

"Tom, I'm like a used car," he told House. "What you see is what you get. If they did a physical and MRIs on me, they wouldn't touch me. But I'll go to post. If they don't believe it, then I'm not playing anymore."

That was good enough for Rangers management. "With Ryan's age and stature, there had to be trust on both sides," says House, "and that's what [Bobby] Valentine and [Tom] Grieve gave him. There were no MRIs of his shoulder, nor would they look at the elbow."

House had never seen anyone so adept at knowing what ailed him as Ryan.

"I have a big mouth and was always chirping." House says. "When we first started warming up in the bullpen, he'd say, 'Tom, shut up until I get it lined up.'

"'All right, I'll shut up,' I told him. But then curiosity got to me and I asked, 'What the hell does "line it up" mean?'

"He said, 'I don't know, but when I've lined it up, I can kind of see my body from the inside, and I know what hurts and doesn't hurt and what's stiff and isn't stiff. Once I get all these pieces put together, then you can talk to me. But leave me alone til I line it up.'"

Intrigued, House started asking around. A neurologist told him that "lining it up" was basically a motor-learning pattern for the very gifted.

"We learn by hearing, seeing, and feeling," says House. "But the very gifted can actually see their bodies from the inside. Their kinesthetic awareness and understanding of where their body is in space, and how they move, is what makes these guys special. Nolan was my first experience with a kinesthetic genius. Once I learned that, I would leave him alone until he said, 'Okay, let's go to work.'"

Ryan needed to be thoroughly lathered up and loose before stepping to the mound. It had always been standard practice for pitchers to use the mound to loosen up before the game, but Ryan found his pregame workout pitches were taking a toll. In his twenties and thirties it had been no problem for him to toss 60 to 80 pitches on the sideline to get sufficiently warm; as he entered his forties, he couldn't maintain that pace and still recover properly between starts.

To solve the problem, House began a series of protocols designed to simulate Ryan's pregame rituals without overthrowing. Using exercises in part derived from what House learned in Japan and also from Gene

Coleman, Ryan started running step-behinds, crossovers, throwing on flat ground, using towel drills, and throwing footballs. Seeing baseball's all-time strikeout king tossing spirals may have seemed unorthodox to traditionalists, but throwing a football not only duplicated the motion of throwing a baseball, it placed less stress on Ryan's arm.

All this enabled him to knock off up to 30 pitches from his pregame warm-up. By the time he finished and went to the bullpen mound, just another handful of pitches would do it. The logic was simple: the fewer pitches thrown on game day, the less stress on the arm and quicker the recovery.

Other pitchers soon began taking a keen interest in Ryan's workouts and began integrating his procedures into their own routines. What Ryan and House did was pioneering, and today many of the top arms in baseball owe much of their success to their groundbreaking concepts.

Recalls House, "I'd say, 'Nolan, what do you think about this?' He'd say, 'Well, I can't tell you what I think, but I'll tell you how I feel.' That's how the exchange went. Yin and yang, you know, computer hippie and Texas cowboy. And that collaboration was not only good for Nolan and me, but also good for baseball, because a lot of the stuff trickled down through the system with Roger Clemens, Jamie Moyer, and Randy Johnson. Nolan touched all those guys, or the protocols have touched all of them."

"When I came here, I certainly didn't feel like I knew all there was about pitching and mechanics," says Ryan. "The pitching coaches I had before didn't understand the concept of pitching on flat ground versus off the mound, and how much less stress it put on your arm. When you get into your forties, timing and coordination are part of the things that the aging process affects, so I had to dedicate more time to those two things.

"In addition to throwing the football, Tom increased my long toss and we threw more off flat ground than off the mound. With the football, I said, 'I'll try it and see,' and once I saw that it was successful, I continued throwing it for the five years I was here."

None of which is to say that Ryan was Superman. Like any athlete in his forties, he suffered aches and pains and injuries from the stress on his body. After going 4–0 in April of his second season with the Rangers (and striking out 16 against the White Sox on the April 26), Ryan went on the 15-day DL on May 18 thanks to back spasms caused by a fractured vertebrae.

His second scheduled start coming off the DL was at Oakland on June 11.

That morning he got a phone call at the Oakland Airport Hilton from a former Angels batboy attending Sonoma State University in Northern California. The friend wanted to know if he and Ryan could meet for lunch during the home stand, as they usually did whenever Ryan was in town. Figuring the Rangers had arrived the day before, the caller waited unitl 9:00 AM to phone, and was surprised when a groggy-sounding Ryan answered. In fact, the Rangers had arrived only hours earlier.

"I woke you up, didn't I?" asked the friend apologetically.

"That's all right, I was gonna get up anyway."

"You're not throwing tonight, are you?"

"Yeah…"

"Oh, boy, I'm sorry. I hope it won't throw you off."

"Don't worry about it," Ryan assured him. "I'll be okay."

Ryan said he would leave a couple tickets for his friend that night, and told him to call the next morning to make arrangements for lunch.

Even though Ryan had said he was okay, his friend worried all day long that he had disrupted his routine, and as a result, Ryan would have a poor outing that night.

Back in Texas, something told Ruth Ryan that she ought to be there for Nolan's game. At the last minute, she hustled Wendy and Reese to the airport (Reid stayed home to play a baseball game of his own) and they got on a plane and headed west.

The defending world champion Oakland A's were a formidable club, and facing them in their ballpark with a bad back made Ryan's job even tougher. Because he was still recovering from injury, Bobby Valentine insisted on a pitch count of 60 to 65, and Ryan readily agreed. Rangers starting catcher Mike Stanley was recovering from a shoulder injury, so backup catcher John Russell was behind the plate. Although it would be the first time Russell had worked with Ryan, the catcher wasn't worried. When he was with Philadelphia, he had caught veteran hurlers Steve Carlton, John Denny, and Jerry Koosman. He knew what Ryan expected of him: a regular tempo, steady flow, and to let him call the pitches.

But once he got a load of Ryan's pregame warm-up, what Russell expected was disaster.

"I thought he'd last about one-third of an inning," Russell recalls. "The ball wasn't coming off his arm very good and there were a lot of misfires. You could tell he was protecting his back a little bit. Coming down from the bullpen I'm thinking, *This is going to be a rough night!*"

Though he was not sharp out of the gate, Ryan used an assortment of pitches to get through the first three innings unscathed. In the fourth, he got upset with umpire Don Denkinger for blowing a call, and after a brief shouting match was warned by the ump to quit showing him up. The next batter, Willie Randolph, hit a shot to deep left-center that was slowed down by the night air enough for left fielder Pete Incaviglia to make the catch at the wall.

By the fifth inning, recalls Russell, "Ryan had flipped the switch and his stuff was becoming more exceptional with every pitch." Home runs by Russell and Julio Franco had the Rangers ahead 5–0, but in the sixth Ryan's back tightened up so badly he considered coming out of the game. He had exceeded his pitch count by then, but Valentine wasn't about to take him out with a no-hitter going.

In the Rangers dugout between innings, Ryan's teammates gave him a wide berth in keeping with the long-standing belief that talking about a no-hitter while one was in progress was a jinx. Even the trainers wouldn't go near him on the bench, and so Ryan went to Reese, sitting in the dugout, and asked him to rub his back.

"I realized you weren't supposed to talk to the guy pitching a no-hitter, but when he talks to you first you don't have much of a choice," says Reese. "So I just went along like it was any other game and started rubbing his back. I didn't bring up the fact that he was pitching a no-hitter, and neither did he."

The sight of Reese and his dad that night has stayed with Bobby Valentine ever since. "The thing I still get chills about wasn't the last out," says Valentine. "The scene I'll remember is Nolan on the bench with his son rubbing his back and patting him on the leg, giving him a pep talk. No one else could bear to talk to him. That was a wonderful sight."

Ryan got through the seventh, and Oakland manager Tony La Russa tried shaking things up by having Carney Lansford pinch-hit with one out in the eighth.

"Whew—nice game to pinch-hit!" Lansford said to Russell when he arrived at the plate. Three fastballs on the outside corner later—all "just unhittable," according to Russell—Lansford sat down. The next Oakland batter followed him back to the bench.

In the Oakland ninth, leadoff pinch hitter Ken Phelps struck out. Speedster Rickey Henderson was next. Russell figured if Henderson got a hit, it would likely be a broken-bat or infield single. "I called fastball, but Ryan kept shaking me off," Russell says. "I knew he wanted to throw a curve, but I was worried Rickey might chop or bloop the ball. He threw it anyway, and Rickey's heart was in it but his butt wasn't. He kind of bailed and couldn't get out of the box."

The Rangers shortstop that night was Jeff Huson. The rookie had made an indelible impression on Ryan back in spring training. In an intrasquad game on his first day with the club, he tagged Ryan for two base hits and walked twice.

"I'm going up for my fifth at-bat, and Nolan's got his brim pulled down over his eyes like he always does," recalls Huson. "I've not officially shaken hands with this legend, and he looks at me and says, 'Boy, how many hits do you have off me today?' This is a simulated game where there are no fans, nothing going on, and I said, 'Zero.' And he goes, 'Good answer.'

"I managed to get a broken-bat single over the second baseman's head, and when I got to first base Ryan tipped his cap. In the locker room afterward I had him sign the bat, and from that point on we really clicked."

Now, with one out in the ninth, the fastest runner in the game hit the ball toward Huson.

"Rickey kind of checked his swing and I got a good read on it," Huson recalls. "I charge and make the throw, and as soon as I let it go I knew I've got him. When Raffy [Palmeiro] catches it at first, I can see our whole dugout jumping up and yelling. I ended up by the mound as the ball went around the horn and came back to me. I'm about two feet away from Nolan when I toss him back the ball, and he goes, 'Nice play, Huey.' I go, 'Thanks, Tex.'

"I hadn't been nervous until then. He's going to get his sixth no-hitter, and nobody had ever done that before, and I was thinking, *Wow, this is unbelievable! I'm a part of history!* But it wasn't until he said, 'Nice play, Huey,' that it really sunk in."

Ryan's first two pitches to Willie Randolph were fastballs down and away.

"He was missing the plate by a foot and the pitches weren't thrown very hard," recalls Russell. "All I could think was, *Oh, my god, he lost it on the last hitter!*"

Ryan paced around the mound and was telling himself something. Then he threw a nice fastball to Randolph, who popped it up to right fielder Ruben Sierra in foul ground for the final out.

"The thing was over, and I'm running out to Nolan," Russell said. "He wanted to shake hands but I'm like, no! And I jumped up in his arms. He said, 'Nice job.' Then the wave of teammates hit us.

"Talking to him afterward, I think what touched him most was the support of the team, and how excited we were for him and how special it was for us to be a part of it."

Sticking with his regular postgame routine, Ryan conducted interviews on his stationary bike. "What makes this one so meaningful was that it came so late in my career and so much time had elapsed between my fifth and sixth," he said, peddling away.

Ryan struck out 14 and walked only two Oakland batters. At 43, he was the oldest pitcher in history to throw a no-hitter and the only one to have tossed one in three different decades.

"It was amazing the focus that Ryan showed that night," says Russell. "In that era, some of the guys, as the game went on, got stronger. We used to say they could smell the win. It was their game and they weren't going to do anything to change that. You could just see it in Nolan that night. As the game went on he got sharper, stronger, and the focus and intensity he got in his eyes grew with every pitch."

The no-hitter was Ryan's fifth win of the year and the 295th of his career.

By the time Ryan left the clubhouse, every restaurant in the area had closed. With nowhere else to go, he and the family went to their room at the Airport Hilton and ordered pizza.

Former Angels GM Buzzie Bavasi probably had the most memorable reaction. The man who years earlier had let Ryan leave the Angels sent Ryan a telegram that read: "Nolan, some time ago I made it public that I made a mistake. You don't have to rub it in."

Ryan's historic sixth no-hitter instantly elevated him from baseball superstar to national icon. Hospital nurseries filled up with newborns named Ryan, and offers for product endorsements and television commercials piled up. Ryan was now a full-blown celebrity, a burden the laconic Texan never sought but bore with stoic acceptance, because of his sense of obligation to the fans that supported and counted on him.

He did his best not to be distracted by the uproar. Two days after the no-hitter, Ryan flew down to Los Angeles to meet with Dr. Lewis Yocum about his aching back. Yocum diagnosed a stress fracture and prescribed exercises and medication. By July 20, Ryan was 10–4, with 299 total wins. He didn't miss another start all year.

About two months later the Rangers were in Anaheim. The onetime Angels batboy who'd unintentionally awakened Ryan the morning of the no-hitter was in town to work in the visiting clubhouse. Ryan was sitting on the sofa when they saw each other, and even before greeting him Ryan demanded to know, "Where were you the next day? Weren't we supposed to get together?" The friend explained that he tried several times to get through but the switchboard operator refused to connect him to Ryan's room.

"Yeah," said Ryan with a sigh. "That was a real mess that day."

• • •

Ryan was never overly concerned about numbers. When Ryan was with the Astros, *Los Angeles Times* columnist Jim Murray asked him about going for 5,000 strikeouts. "How many do I have now?" Ryan asked with obvious embarrassment. "I'm not really sure exactly what it is—4,000 or so. I'm not a record book fanatic. I'm not big for setting goals."

"The only record Nolan really wanted to achieve was winning 300 games," says Ruth Ryan. "When you are pitching a no-hitter or striking out guys in a game, you're not thinking about records. It just happens. Yes, he wanted to pitch long enough to win 300 games, because as he got closer to it he felt it's kind of like icing on the cake."

To Ryan, 300 wins meant professional validation. Three hundred wins was a towering, unmistakable testament to durability, consistency, and longevity. It proved to his critics he was a power pitcher to be taken seriously. Plus, as Don Sutton made clear six years earlier, 300 wins was a certain ticket to the Hall of Fame.

Ryan's first try for 300 was in Arlington on July 25, against the Yankees. The atmosphere was like that of a playoff game. Media from all over the world were on hand, and with the constant hounding Ryan was feeling the pressure. His back was still troubling him, and, unable to find his groove, the Yanks scored seven runs off him in eight innings. The Rangers won 9–7 in extra innings, but Ryan was not involved in the decision.

"That wasn't the way I planned it, but I didn't get it done in Arlington, so I'll be glad to get it done in Milwaukee," Ryan said after the game.

In the intervening six days, the scrutiny from the press and fans intensified to the point that Ryan couldn't leave his hotel room. By the time he took the mound in the concrete mausoleum known as Milwaukee County Stadium on July 31, it had been 11 days since Ryan's last win, and he just wanted the "quest" over with. Ruth was on hand for the occasion, and Reese and Reid came along as batboys for the Rangers.

Ryan's business partner Don Sanders also flew up with family and friends in Sanders' private plane.

"We had lunch with him," recalls Sanders. "Everybody sat around and Nolan told war stories and he was pretty relaxed. Ruth later said that was the best thing that could have happened, because before that he just sat in the room and watched the clock tick. We kind of kept his mind off the game, and I think he appreciated it."

Ryan had a decent warm-up, and as he, House, and Reese walked from the bullpen to the dugout, flashbulbs exploded all over the stadium packed with 51,000-plus fans.

There was plenty of excitement at Arlington Stadium, too. The Rangers televised the game on the big Diamond Vision screen and opened the gates to local fans, charging them just $3 for parking. In between innings of the game, pop-fly catching contests and a speed gun in the bullpen for kids to test their arm kept the 7,828 fans entertained. And every time a ball was fouled off in Milwaukee, a free baseball was awarded to the fans in Arlington.

Milwaukee was scoreless for two innings and then went ahead 1–0. From then on Ryan pocketed the curve and kept the Brew Crew at bay with his fastball. The Rangers put together a rally in the fifth and were leading 5–1 in the eighth when second baseman Julio Franco botched two double-play balls, allowing the Brewers to score twice and cut their deficit to 5–3. Ryan had thrown 146 pitches, with eight strikeouts, and Bobby Valentine was faced with a difficult decision. If he removed Ryan now and the Brewers went on to win, Ryan would undergo another agonizing week of scrutiny until his next start. But Ryan was spent, so Valentine gave the ball to Brad Arnsberg to nail down the save.

In the Rangers' ninth, Franco atoned for his two errors with a grand slam to cap a six-run inning, and Arnsberg pitched the last four outs for the save.

Texas won 11–3, and Ryan became the 20th pitcher in history to win 300 games.

"I'm relieved it's over with," Ryan said afterward. "The last 15 days, emotionally, have been the toughest 15 days I've gone through. I really wanted to get it done. I didn't want this to be an ongoing deal. For me, 300 wins means relief."

It also meant a marketing bonanza. Madison Avenue and sponsors lined up to have Ryan hawk their wares. BIC Razors offered men 43 years old and older a free trial pack of metal shavers. Ryan also became a pitchman for Wrangler jeans and Advil, his face adorning billboards nationwide.

Ruth recalls the time the family was out for a drive and passed an office supply company's 30-foot billboard with a 15-foot-high picture of Nolan's face. "What is that?" shrieked 13-year-old Wendy from the back seat. "Why, that's ol' handsome dad," Nolan said with a smile.

Inundated with lucrative deals and offers, Ryan was becoming an industry—and a very wealthy man. He purchased two banks and poured money into his burgeoning ranches and Beefmaster cattle. But he didn't let his popularity or status change his values or lifestyle.

The two stellar seasons Ryan put together in 1989 and 1990—and the additional fans he drew to the Rangers—also sent a strong message to Dallas and the surrounding area that the NFL's Cowboys weren't the only game in town anymore. Coincidentally, just as Ryan and the Rangers were becoming a force in Arlington, a new ownership group led by George W. Bush and Rusty Rose was taking charge of the franchise. Bush borrowed $500,000 in 1989 to buy a small stake in the team, and then convinced the other owners to make him general managing partner and have his co-partner Rose take over the financial side. Bush drew a salary of $200,000 and immediately began lobbying for a new ballpark to replace crumbling Arlington Stadium, a modestly refurbished minor league park, with a new state-of-the-art facility.

Not long after, Bush started being mentioned as a potential candidate in the 1990 campaign for governor of Texas. But political insiders dismissed the talk on the grounds that Bush's résumé was too light on real-world experience. Bush's performance with the Rangers—with a big boost from Ryan on the field—changed that perception.

"The Bush-Rose group came in right after the success Nolan had in '89 and '90," says John Blake, who was in charge of the Rangers PR department at the time. "Nolan brought credibility and showed that the Rangers could bring more national attention to the city, and that had a lot to do with the new ownership group being able to cut a deal with Arlington to build a new stadium.

"We got a referendum passed in 1991 for the bonds, and Nolan was very involved in that. It brought a Texas hero to Arlington, and that kind of precipitated what followed afterward.

"Unfortunately for us, his success didn't bring in a lot more money, because at Arlington Stadium we had 20,000 $4 seats, and that's basically what we were filling up. That in itself showed the ownership group we needed a new stadium so we could make money as opposed to just selling out.

"I will always contend that because they signed the deal to build it in October 1990, and passed the bonds in January of 1991, that Nolan had a big role in getting us to that point. Without those two years, would we have gotten a new stadium in Arlington? I don't know, because that franchise wasn't exactly going anywhere. But in 1989 and 1990, when he had 301 and 232 Ks, respectively, he brought to Dallas the credibility necessary to finance a new ballpark."

Securing financing for a new ballpark was no mean feat. The new stadium deal gave Bush credibility, and in 1994 he was elected governor of the Lone Star State, the springboard to his election in 2000 as president of the United States.

The Rangers finished third in the AL West in 1990, 20 games behind Oakland. Ryan was 13–9, with a league-leading 232 strikeouts (averaging 10.2 per nine innings) and a 3.44 ERA. The Rangers eagerly exercised a $3.3 million contract option on Ryan for another season, with an option for another one after that. General manager Tom Grieve called the action "just a formality."

3

Ryanmania: 1991

> Nolan's key was his optimism. And he never lost it, because he knew he was the most prepared, and he had passion for the game. I tell these kids, "If you don't have passion, don't play." If it seems like work, it isn't worth it. At the end of the day, that's what kept him going.
>
> —TOM HOUSE

The voice on the phone was official and crisp: "Please stay on the line for the President of the United States."

As Nolan Ryan's personal secretary, Kim Spilman was used to dealing with phone calls from powerful folks, but this one really got her attention. Baghdad was in flames, bombarded every night to soften it up for a ground invasion. America was at war. *Why would President Bush be calling the office now?* she wondered.

After putting the president through, Spilman beat it back to Ryan's office to see his reaction. Ryan had known George H.W. Bush since the late 1960s when Herbert Walker, the president's uncle, was a minority owner of the Mets and George H.W. was U.S. Ambassador to the United Nations. Bush also lived in Houston, and since he was an Astros fan, he and Ryan had crossed paths often over the years. And now the president's son, George W. Bush, was president of the Rangers.

The reason for the call was that the White House was planning a shindig in the East Room for the Queen and Crown Prince of Denmark, and President Bush wanted to personally invite Nolan and Ruth to the event.

Ryan told the president he was scheduled to speak at a cattlemen's civic group in Cotulla that same day, and since keeping his commitments was important to him, it was doubtful they could make it to Washington, D.C.

Spilman wasn't buying it. She knew that Ryan had already been invited to White House events twice before, declining both times because of scheduling conflicts.

"Look, if you call the people in Cotulla and said you were invited to the White House, I'm sure they would understand," Kim told her boss. "They would just schedule it for another night."

Ryan uncomfortably regarded his calendar.

"You do it," he said finally.

Ruth was in a quandary. The White House reception was a formal event, and there was nothing in her closet appropriate for such an occasion. She made a thorough search of area department stores, but couldn't find anything that seemed right. Finally, a friend suggested Loehmann's, a discount chain that had some formal-type dresses with the tags ripped off. There Ruth spotted a nice black gown with beads around the neckline. There were no dressing rooms, so she paid the $125 and had her mom do alterations on the sleeves.

A White House limo met the Ryans at the D.C. airport. After an extensive security check at the White House gate, they were escorted to a large suite in the southeast corner of the second floor. Several pieces of antique furniture linked to the Lincoln White House were in the room, the centerpiece a large, ornate bed bought by Mary Lincoln on one of her extravagant spending sprees. It's doubtful the Lincolns actually slept in the "Lincoln Bedroom," although other presidents did in subsequent years. Actually, that was the room where Lincoln's cabinet met during the Civil War. Honest Abe's greatest speeches were drafted there, including parts of the Gettysburg Address, a handwritten copy of which was displayed in a glass case in the corner of the room.

The Ryans were unpacking when a familiar "Yoo-hoo!" trilled in the hallway. Barbara Bush and her dog, Millie, welcomed Nolan and Ruth warmly. A few moments later the president joined the group with his dog, Ranger. President Bush then led everyone, including the dogs, on an extensive tour of the grounds.

Dinner guests that night included General Colin Powell, CNN president Tom Johnson, Katie Couric, actress Melanie Griffith, and her husband, *Miami Vice* heartthrob Don Johnson. Ruth and Nolan would be seated at separate tables, and at hers would be fellow Texans Walter Cronkite (who'd briefly attended the University of Texas, at any rate) and Secretary of State James Baker, so she would feel right at home.

At the reception the guests were introduced separately, followed by a reception line for the president, Mrs. Bush, and the Danish Royals. During the introductions, a reporter asked Ruth about her dress. She was aghast. In a sea of $8,000 designer dresses and A-list celebrities, why did the reporter have to choose her? And how would she explain that she had purchased the dress at a discount store for $125?

Fortunately, she didn't have to, because just then Griffith and Johnson entered the room. The gorgeous actress wore a spectacular designer gown that amply showed off her equally spectacular physical attributes, and everything and everyone else in the room was forgotten.

In Alvin, a big night on the town was two-stepping it at the local dance hall or a family outing at Joe's BBQ. Ribs weren't on the White House menu, but lobster medallions and crown roast of lamb were. Dessert was raspberry soufflé, followed by a classical violin concerto.

After dinner, the Ryans joined Griffith, Johnson, and some Bush family members in an upstairs parlor to chat. Around midnight, the president rounded up some Rangers and Astros jackets for his guests to wear and led them and the dogs on another jaunt around the driveway.

Back in the Lincoln Bedroom, Nolan and Ruth were too excited to sleep. It had been a memorable night, and a vivid reminder of just how far the Ryans had traveled since their first studio flat in Queens in 1968.

• • •

On April 2, the Rangers scheduled an exhibition game at the University of Texas at Austin. On the mound for the Longhorns was 18-year-old freshman Reid Ryan. Scheduled to pitch for the Rangers was his 44-year-old father.

The event received plenty of national hype, but in the Ryan family there was concern. Dad didn't want Reid to be embarrassed, and Reid didn't want his dad to be injured or set back. Ruth's worry was that the university was using Reid for promotional purposes to generate revenue for the college.

But Reid was nobody's puppet. The future president of the Houston Astros was hip to the situation and rolled with it. He looked out for his pop and even warned Nolan that the UT pitcher's mound was full of craters. The Rangers immediately dispatched their grounds crew to Austin to make sure the mound met major league specifications.

The last thing Nolan wanted was to see his son manhandled and humiliated by big league hitters. But the object of his concern acted like a kid in a candy store; a natural with the media, Reid's constant jokes and buoyant attitude helped settle his folks' shaky nerves.

Ruth had the honor of throwing out the first pitch, and once the game began she relaxed and enjoyed the Ryan family's "Field of Dreams" playing out in front of her.

For two innings Reid held his own; he allowed four runs, but a couple Rangers hits were bloopers. Dad went five innings, giving up three runs on five hits, walking three, and striking out seven. The five collegians who got hits off the old man made certain the balls were removed and later autographed by him.

Nolan's fastball was clocked at 92 mph in the first inning; Reid's fastest pitch was 84. The Rangers won the game 12–5.

"It was a strange night," Ryan told reporters afterward. "My intensity level wasn't there. It showed. I was distracted watching him."

"This is one of the funnest things I've ever done," Reid told reporters before joining his teammates for a night on the town. "It's been the best couple days of my life."

During their playing days, Reid (who would later pitch in A ball) and brother Reese used humor and tact to deflect the rude and jeering catcalls from the opposing dugout or some yokel in the stands. In high school, Reid made his folks proud the time he shot down some opposing players who tried to rattle him by yelling insults about his famous dad.

"Yeah, Nolan Ryan's my dad," he told the big mouths from his position on third base. "He's been in the big leagues 27 years. Is that the worst thing you can say about him? And, by the way, just what do y'all dads do?"

Reid eventually transferred from UT to Texas Christian University. Upon his graduation in 1994, the Texas Rangers drafted Reid in the 17th round. He had talent but hadn't inherited his dad's fastball, so making the majors was no sure thing.

Reid had a decision to make—take a chance at pro ball or take the more prudent course and go directly into the working world.

Recalls family friend George Pugh, "Nolan told Reid something I later told my own boys: 'You get small windows of opportunities in life you'll never get a chance to take advantage of again. Always take advantage of those opportunities, because after that window closes you don't want to go around always wondering how things would have turned out if you'd have done something different.'

"Reid said, 'I don't want anyone thinking I'm going to be another Nolan Ryan, but I'm going to at least give it a shot to make sure I don't regret something later.'"

Reid never made it to the majors, but says his minor league playing experience helped immensely in his later career as an executive in baseball.

• • •

Ryan went into the 1991 season determined to help get the Rangers to the playoffs. The club's potent offense included rookie slugger Juan Gonzalez, who would become the 18th player to have a 100 RBI season before his 22nd birthday; first baseman Rafael Palmiero (.322, 26 homers); outfielder Ruben Sierra (.307, 116 RBIs); Julio Franco (league-leading .341); and third baseman Steve Buechele (.267, 18 homers).

Combined with a young pitching staff that included Kevin Brown, Jose Guzman, Kenny Rogers, and Jeff Russell, the Rangers were projected to be strong contenders for the AL West title.

Rogers, who would go on to win more than 200 games over a distinguished 20-year career, played with Ryan for five of those years, and had a hard time keeping up with the 44-year-old workhorse.

"I tried to work out with him but I couldn't handle it for very long," Rogers says. "Not everyone could duplicate his work ethic, but if you watched him on the mound you could see things you could copy, such as how he controlled the game, kept composed, and how he went about things.

"Even when he was throwing 95, it was still one of the best fastballs in the game because it had that extra gear hitters just don't time real well," adds Rogers. "Some of his 5,000 strikeouts were right down the middle of the plate, but the hitters didn't catch up to them because they had that gear, like a Mo Rivera fastball, that you just can't time. You just lose it for a period of time and you can't catch up to it."

Ryan got off to a decent start in April, going 2–2, with 37 strikeouts in 29⅔ innings. He still had a healthy fastball, but the aches and pains that nettled him the previous season persisted. The morning of May 1 was typical. Ryan awoke with a backache, a tender heel, and a split callous on the middle finger of his pitching hand. He didn't feel like pitching, but it was Arlington Appreciation Night, the Toronto Blue Jays were in town, and Ryan hated disappointing anyone. With a roster of young stars like Roberto Alomar, Joe Carter, and John Olerud, the Jays were in second place in the East, a half game behind Boston. The Rangers were in third, three back of West-leading Oakland.

Ryan took some painkillers before heading to the park and called Ruth in Alvin and told her he just hoped to get through the game. At the ballpark his back was so bad that during the pregame meeting he strapped on a heating pad. "I don't know about you, but I feel old today," he told Tom House. "My back hurts, my finger hurts, my ankle hurts—everything hurts."

Trainer Bill Ziegler went to work on him, and while Ryan was getting his rubdown, ESPN flashed to Oakland, where Rickey Henderson had just stolen his 939th stolen base to break Lou Brock's record.

"They showed Rickey holding the base over his head, boasting to the world like, *I'm the greatest,*" recalls Ziegler. "I'll never forget the expression Nolan had. He just kind of rolled his eyes like, Whatever.

"I always wondered if Rickey's display gave Nolan a little extra motivation that night."

House recalls Ryan's pregame bullpen session as one of the worst he'd ever seen.

"Nolan was bouncing his curveball, huffing and puffing on his fastball. He had no location, and his changeup was non-existent. I'm thinking, *Whoops, this is not real good.* After he was done, we had a little conversation, and he walked up to the clubhouse to change his shirt. I'm thinking, *Oh, man, Nolan just quit.* So I hustle to find Bobby [Valentine] and tell him we better get somebody going because I don't think Nolan's going to post—and if he does, it's gonna be a quick one."

"Tommy came into the dugout and looked as if he saw a ghost," recalls Valentine. "I said, 'What's going on?' And he was kind of speechless. Right about then, Nolan came back down from the clubhouse. He had missed the national anthem and was toweling his head and putting his hat on. He waited for the rest of the team to hit the field, and before leaving the dugout said to me in that Texas drawl, 'Get someone ready.'

"I didn't know what he was talking about, but as he went out to the mound, House said, 'I think it's over, Bob. Nolan couldn't reach home plate in the bullpen.'

"I had a real bad feeling in my stomach after that. I was thinking I was going to have to be there when Nolan walked off the mound for the last time. While he was warming up and bouncing balls during his final warm-up, I called down to the bullpen to get someone ready, just in case."

Then Ryan proceeded to blow everyone away. After striking out one in the first, he struck out the side in the second.

"He struck out three batters on 13 pitches," says House. "His fastball was averaging 97 mph, and I'm going, *Holy crap, what's going on here?*

"When Nolan got back in the dugout, he said, 'Tom, I don't know, but this is one of those darn days.'

"Then he addressed the bench: 'Boys, get me one! That's all I'm gonna need today.'"

"That night, for whatever reason, Nolan wanted to establish his curveball," says catcher Mike Stanley. "That was going to be a weapon he needed to use. As it turned out, his curve became ineffective and it was his fastball that was the lethal weapon. Once the curve petered out, he switched to his ace. He just adapted to the situation, as only Ryan could do."

The only thing close to a hit that night was a sixth-inning blooper by Manny Lee that center fielder Gary Pettis grabbed off his shoe tops.

"I thought for sure it was gonna drop in there, but somehow Gary got there," Stanley recalls. "That was really the only time I thought there was any doubt about Nolan's dominance. Once I saw Pettis grab it, I felt pretty good about Nolan being able to lock in to shut it down."

Ryan walked just two and at one point retired 18 straight Jays. There were two hard-hit balls by Mark Whiten—a deep fly ball to center in the fifth and a line drive to right in the eighth—but that was it.

In the Rangers' third, Pettis made it home on a throwing error. Ruben Sierra's two-run blast later in the inning made it 3–0.

As word spread about what was unfolding at the ballpark, people eager to witness history headed there in droves. Mickey Herskowitz of the *Houston Post* likened it to the famous closing scene in the 1989 movie *Field of Dreams*, with a stream of car headlights going back for miles flowing toward the stadium.

Tracy Ringolsby of the *Dallas Daily News* had attended stock shows and rodeos with Ryan. Ringolsby was present for Ryan's 300th win and his 5,000th strikeout, and was even in New York in 1977 the night Ryan threw 218 pitches. But he wasn't at the ballpark this time.

"I was out of town," says Ringolsby. "I flew in on the morning of May 1 and planned to go out to the stadium that night. But my wife said, 'No, we need to go someplace for dinner.'

"Turns out she was having a surprise birthday party for me. We were in the back room at this Mexican restaurant with a group when the owner came in and said, 'Nolan's got a no-hitter through six innings out in Arlington Stadium! It's on TV in the bar.' So we all moved to the bar and I started drinking margaritas. It was much easier to drink than to just be at a bar stone-cold sober.

"That's the closest I've been to one of Nolan's no-hitters."

Mike Stanley's mind-set entering the ninth was to stay out of Ryan's way and play tight defense. If Ryan bounced a curve or changeup on a third strike, the catcher wanted to make sure he'd block it and tag the guy or throw him out at first base.

"He had a great game plan going," says Stanley, "so it wasn't about me calling the game or which pitch to call, because I knew ultimately Nolan was going to make that decision."

When the ninth inning began, Ryan had struck out 15 Jays. Devon White and Glenallen Hill had three Ks apiece, and every other batter in the lineup had gone down at least once on strikes.

An inning earlier, ESPN had switched its live coverage to Arlington, and as a nationwide audience looked on Ryan got Manny Lee and White on sharp grounders to second baseman Julio Franco. Now all that stood between Ryan and his seventh no-hitter was future Hall of Famer Roberto Alomar.

Ruth, who was back in Alvin, asked neighbor Jim Stinson if she could watch it on his satellite dish. Instead, Stinson offered to fly Ruth to the game in his private plane, and she gratefully accepted.

As Alomar approached the plate, Ruth recalled that Roberto's dad, Sandy, had been Nolan's teammate on the Angels. Roberto was just a toddler then and always asked Nolan for pitching tips. But the batter standing at the plate now was no toddler.

Alomar swung through Ryan's first fastball, then fouled off the second. Ryan's third fastball was low. After another foul ball, Ryan wasted a curve.

The crowd had gotten louder with every pitch, and Alomar and Ryan did all they could to concentrate. Ryan tossed back two balls from the home-plate umpire before settling on one he liked, and then fired another fastball that Alomar fouled away.

"The final pitch, Nolan wanted to go right after Alomar," recalls Stanley. "He threw him a fastball and Robby swung right through it. I got the picture in my game room, and off to the side the little scoreboard says 93 mph.

"Nolan punched his fist in the air and gave a big grin. I ran up to him, kind of gave him a hug, and then got mobbed. Everybody was jumping up and down, throwing their gloves up and yelling. I couldn't hear anything with the crowd noise."

"We were clueless," said an awed Joe Carter in the Toronto clubhouse.

"Nolan was in a zone where normal people don't go," said Tom House.

"You could see it in his eyes," said Stanley. "You could hear him talking to himself. You could see he really sensed the moment and knew what to do with it. And that, to me, was the exciting part. Watching Nolan and his mannerisms and the way he went after it."

Of Ryan's 122 pitches that night, 83 were strikes, and 63 of them were fastballs. His fastest pitch was a 97-mph heater to Carter in the fourth.

"This is my most overpowering night," Ryan told reporters. "Everything kicked in for me there in the first inning, and it just got better as the game went on. I had the best command of all three pitches."

Ryan was especially pleased to finally throw a no-hitter in front of the home crowd. To celebrate, Valentine cracked open the bottle of champagne he'd been saving for when the Rangers got to the World Series. Ryan waited until he got off his exercise bike before taking a sip or two.

"I had held on to the game ball and put it in my pocket," Stanley recalls. "Later on, I saw [Ryan] on the bike and gave it to him. He didn't say much, something like, 'Thanks, I appreciate your help behind the plate.' Not that it was old hat, but for Nolan it was his seventh time doing it. In my mind it was an unbelievable feat, but he was just laid back like it was no big deal. It was just a special moment in my life."

When he got off the bike, Ryan did an interview for the local TV affiliate. "I'm glad I got to do it in front of the home crowd, and especially since it was 'Arlington Night' at the ballpark," he said.

Trainer Bill Ziegler couldn't believe what he'd heard.

"I'm like, who even knows it's 'Arlington Night'?" says Ziegler. "I was always amazed just how aware he was of everything around him."

When Ryan and House walked out of the clubhouse together several hours later, House was still trying to figure out what had happened. How could Ryan have gone from such a terrible warm-up to throw one of his greatest games ever?

"Nolan, help me out again," he said. "You threw 21—pardon the expression—horseshit pitches before you walked in the clubhouse. I mean, what—"

"It wasn't getting any better in the bullpen, it had to be better on the mound," Ryan said. "I did everything I could possibly do to prepare for today's game. I figure if I hadn't wanted to work, I shouldn't have hired out."

"Those are the kinds of things people don't understand about Nolan," says House. "He's the most prepared superstar I've ever been around. I knew a little bit about Michael Jordan, I knew Larry Bird, I knew a little more about Joe Montana and Dan Marino. I see what Kobe Bryant does. And all those people who are wonderful athletes and hugely successful,

I've never seen anybody work harder at their craft on and off the field than Nolan Ryan did."

Ryan's seventh no-hitter sent shock waves throughout baseball and beyond. In the months ahead, Ryanmania was off the charts. Fans filled parks wherever he pitched in anticipation of another no-hitter or to just say they had seen one of the game's all-time greats.

Autograph seekers mobbed Ryan everywhere he went. He tried to accommodate them by scheduling certain times at the ballpark—both at home and away—to sign, but it was never enough.

"Everywhere we'd go, Nolan had kind of the Henry Aaron–Barry Bonds thing," says House. "He couldn't travel on the bus. He'd have to take cabs, use different names in the hotels, but invariably they found him. And he'd always say, 'I'll sign for 10 minutes, so get in line. If anybody gets out of line, I'm stopping.'

"And he'd dutifully sign for 10 minutes and then leave. He never said no, but he always put limits. He managed his stardom or fame really well."

Before joining the Rangers, Ryan figured he didn't have the personality to be a front man in a commercial or advertising campaign. But he learned how to play the part over the years, and by 1991 he was the prime pitchman for Southwest Airlines and Advil. He also was spokesman for a soft drink company and an oil company, and a baseball card company marketed a set that featured just him.

"It just kind of evolved over the years," Ryan said of the commercials. "I've had many requests and finally took the attitude, 'If you're going to do them, enjoy it and do them well.' It's still not my favorite thing, but I've become more comfortable with it."

"He's the Jimmy Stewart of players," said agent Matt Merola. "No one has higher credibility. He embodies everything everyone loves. I mean, if you want Brooks Brothers, you go to Central Casting. If you want someone you can believe in, Nolan is it."

At 7:30 the morning after the no-hitter—just four and a half hours after he went to bed—Ryan was lifting weights in a room beneath Arlington Stadium. But at age 44, wear and tear was inevitable. Ryan had two stints on the DL in 1991 that cut into his number of starts. His 173 innings and 27 starts were below his average, and the fewest since his 1981 strike-shortened season in Houston.

Still, he went 9–2 after June 6. On July 7, he retired 18 straight California Angels and took a no-hitter into the eighth before his old nemesis Dave Winfield singled.

Ryan's best month was September, when he went 3–0, with 36 Ks in 32 innings. He finished the season 12–6, with 203 strikeouts and a very respectable 2.91 ERA.

The Rangers finished third, 10 games back of the eventual World Series champion Minnesota Twins. But batting champ Julio Franco's league-leading .341 average and Juan Gonzalez's 27 homers and 102 RBIs weren't remembered as much as how Ryan destroyed conventional logic and continued to dominate AL hitters at age 44.

Ryan had now played 25 seasons and made more than $17 million. A substantial part of his earnings went to purchase three tracts of ranchland in central and west Texas. In the off-seasons he looked forward to shifting gears and swapping his baseball knits for denim and disappearing into the cattle culture, far from the pressures of baseball and the incessant demands on his time.

"Baseball did not define him," says Reid Ryan. "To him it was just a job, and although he enjoyed playing, his first love and passion was the cattle business. When the season ended, he always went back to ranching and the family and to the things he really enjoyed. That way, when baseball season came around again, he was always fresh and ready to go."

"I think that anybody that needs to recharge their batteries and relax their brain needs an outlet," agrees Ruth. "Psychologically and emotionally, he loved the ranches, because he could relax there. When the season ended he didn't go off and play in a charity golf tournament or go on vacations or hang with his buddies. He wanted to spend that time with us, but he also wanted to do something outdoors, something that he enjoyed, and he deserved that.

"When he came home, people in Alvin who knew him as a kid would want to talk to him about the season or his latest exploit. It seemed the whole town was abuzz, and they would want him to speak at a banquet or have 'Nolan Ryan Day.' But he didn't necessarily like talking about those things. Even though people meant well, he would get tired of it, because he had spent the whole year answering questions to the media and other people. But he was patient in regards to that, and he never forgot about the people that cared about him all along.

"Ranching was always something he loved. A man has to have his identity, and Nolan always thought, *What will I be when I am not in baseball?*

"It turns out the ranching life was really good for him."

The old expression "All hat, no cattle" definitely does not apply.

"I oversee the purchasing of all cattle, do the selection for the breeding, the billing comes through me, and I work with the employees in the pen, whether it be branding or cleaning," says Ryan. "It's hard work and not nearly as romantic as it appears.

"If it wasn't for the baseball I wouldn't have been able to afford to get into the cattle business. Baseball enabled me to be able to do that."

3

Pass It On: 1992

> Nolan called me one time during the winter. He said, "I just want you to know that I made up my mind I'm going to retire, and you'll probably read about it in the paper." He then gave me a list of about 20 reasons why he was going to quit.
>
> About two days go by, and he gives me another call. "I just want you to know I'm not gonna retire. We're gonna sign for another year and it's gonna be announced, and I just want you to know it."
>
> I said, "Okay, that's good. But what about all those reasons you gave me for retiring?"
>
> "The Rangers gave me 4.4 million reasons not to," he said.
>
> —GENE COLEMAN

By the time the 1992 season started, Nolan Ryan had become a cottage industry, his face on billboards, books, and magazines; his name attached to burgers, jeans, and boots. Prices for his baseball cards were soaring, and lines were 10-deep whenever he signed autographs. For a rural kid with small-town sensibilities, the affection was a bit much, and while he didn't mind the money that fame brought, he could have done without all the attention.

Some of it was negative. "Why is Ryan sticking around so long?" grumbled critics. "He's no longer effective. He doesn't need the money. What more does he have to prove?" The fact was that since he joined the Rangers in 1989, each subsequent year he had pitched fewer innings and spent more time on the DL. At 45, his body was no longer standing up to the rigors of a 162-game season.

What his critics overlooked was that Ryan was still helping to anchor the young Rangers staff, chewing up innings and raising the bar for those around him, not to mention bringing fans and revenue to the park in every city he visited.

He was a role model and an international icon, and advertising and TV revenue jumped whenever he pitched. He was good for the game, and the consensus was that he was worth every penny Rangers president George W. Bush was paying him.

Once one of Ryan's earliest critics, columnist Jim Murray of the *Los Angeles Times* had changed his tune about the pitcher, no longer carping about Ryan's numbers and wasted potential. Now Murray was writing things like:

> Ryan should go to the Hall of Fame. The arm should go to the Louvre.
>
> Ryan is a John Paul Jones pitcher. When you think he has had enough, he has just begun to throw.
>
> When Nolan Ryan stops pitching—if he ever does—his arm should hang in the Smithsonian. Right alongside Lindbergh's airplane and Lee's sword and other great artifacts of our nation's history…

In honor of his 26th season in baseball, Ryan was given the ball on opening day in Seattle. The outing wasn't exactly museum-quality; he lasted just 4⅓ innings, giving up five hits and three runs (only one earned) before being lifted on account of sore legs. He was immediately placed on the 15-day disabled list, giving critics ammunition to claim that Father Time had finally caught up to him.

Ryan, who knew his body better than anyone, disagreed.

"I think the people's attitude is because of my age, anytime something happens, I think people look for that to be the injury that finishes me off," he said. "And I look at it from the standpoint that it's more of a nagging, nuisance-type thing."

Ryan didn't pitch again until April 30, against Chicago, and then lasted only 2⅓ innings and was tagged for seven earned runs. He would go 11 starts, only once pitching beyond the seventh inning, before winning his first game, on June 28 against Detroit.

On July 4, 40,000 fans were present in Arlington when Ryan pitched his first gem of the season. He went the distance, three-hitting the Yankees in a 4–1 win. His 13 strikeouts on 135 pitches proved that if he remained healthy, he could still be effective.

Five days later, with the Rangers in third place, 6.5 games behind the division-leading Oakland A's, manager Bobby Valentine was fired. Club president George W. Bush named Toby Harrah, a former All-Star infielder and a Rangers fan favorite, as interim manager. Tom House was retained as pitching coach.

Ryan was sad to see Valentine go. Their friendship went back to when both were with California and Valentine was a rising star.

"Bobby was an overachiever," says Ryan. "His days at the Angels were frustrating, because he came there expecting to play shortstop and they put him in the outfield. When he broke his leg and it didn't heal properly, it basically shortened his career, which was very frustrating, because he was a very talented athlete.

"As a manager, I felt like he knew his players and the game as well as anybody I ever played for. He would certainly take risks to manufacture runs. I enjoyed playing for him."

With the Rangers treading water, the task of keeping fans coming to the park fell to Ryan. By now his popularity was such that he was besieged everywhere he went. There was no such thing as a simple trip to the mall, because as soon as he was spotted the autograph hounds started baying. Going to the airport was worst of all. That's where Hoggy Price came in.

During Ryan's tenure with Texas, Richard "Hoggy" Price ran the umpires' clubhouse at Arlington Stadium. He also happened to be a part-time Delta Airlines baggage guy with connections. Nolan liked the way Hoggy rubbed game balls, as well as his down-to-earth demeanor and irreverence. But according to Tom House, one of Hoggy's biggest assets was his access to airports.

"There was a time during Ryanmania when everywhere Nolan went, Hoggy went too, because he had no one else to facilitate all this crap," House said. "Hoggy was key with a lot of stuff that had to do with transportation. And as Nolan got bigger, he needed someone he knew as a go-to guy that could facilitate getting through security. Now everybody has private jets, but the team was still flying commercial with Delta when Nolan joined, so having Hoggy around just made things a whole lot easier."

Not every member of the Rangers appreciated Ryan's situation and the necessity of making things easier for him, says House.

"The Rangers had a pitcher named Kevin Brown who, for whatever reason, was offended by the special treatment Ryan was receiving. He didn't realize that the perks Hoggy and others in the organization provided for Ryan made it easier for Ryan to function, and, therefore, be a more productive and valuable teammate."

Brown went so far as to openly complain about Ryan's perks at a team meeting.

"I never heard Nolan Ryan badmouth anyone," recalls House, who was at the meeting. "But Nolan got up and said to Brown, 'You're a hard man to like!' and left the room.

"Kevin Brown was jealous of the money Nolan was making and the perks. The irony is that a couple years later Brown penned a $105 million deal with the Dodgers, structured with exactly the same perks Nolan had toward the end of his career."

While Ryan went 4–0 in July, the Rangers continued to founder. On August 6, the team was 55–56, 11.5 games behind first-place Oakland, which happened to be in town that week.

A recent addition to the A's outfield was former American League batting and base-stealing champion Willie Wilson, who had been feuding with Ryan since the mid-1970s. The talented but troubled Wilson had once spent almost three months in jail for dealing cocaine.

Things came to a head on August 6. Ryan cursed Wilson in the top of the second after the Oakland outfielder showed him up with a big swing and a miss. When they faced each other again in the seventh inning, relates Tom House, "Wilson hit a triple and Ryan backed up third, and when the play finished he was walking back to the mound when Wilson started screaming, 'You old goat! You ought to hang it up! You shouldn't even be on the field!'"

When Ryan got back to the dugout, he checked the lineup card and informed Toby Harrah that despite his pitch count, he intended to go back out to the mound for the next inning. "I'm gonna pitch to Wilson," he said, "and I don't give a damn what happens, Toby! I'm throwing through the eighth inning! You hear what I'm saying?"

When Ryan sat down, Harrah turned to House and asked, "What was that about?"

"I think," replied the pitching coach, "Willie Wilson's in trouble."

Next time Wilson came up, Ryan drilled him behind the knee with a fastball on a 1-1 count.

As Wilson limped off the field, home-plate umpire Richie Garcia told Ryan to call it a night. It was "Cushion Night" at the ballpark, and when Ryan got the thumb the fans reacted by tossing their cushions onto the field. Amidst the shower of foam, Garcia took Ryan aside and said almost apologetically, "You know I had to throw you out because you hit him."

"Well, if I was gonna hit him on purpose, I would have hit him in his eye," Ryan responded tersely.

"Now, Nolan, you can't tell somebody you're gonna hit a guy in the head," Garcia said more sternly.

"I didn't say if I was gonna hit him in his head," corrected Ryan. "I said I'd hit him in his eye."

After a 20-minute delay caused by the cushion shower, the Rangers ended up losing 2–0. Afterward, the weary Garcia proclaimed, "I'm not going home after throwing that man out of the game. I'm staying in this locker room until every damn Texan goes to bed!"

In their respective clubhouses, Ryan and Wilson gave their version of events to the media.

"Willie has some problems if he thinks he can scream obscenities at people and not have them say something back," Ryan said, conveniently not mentioning his dressing down of Wilson in the second inning.

Wilson's reply: "You can't do anything against him or he gets mad. I respect Nolan, but I lost respect for him for doing that. Me and Nolan are two different things. I'm a guy who's gone to jail, I'm the bad guy, the eight-ball. He's the legend. But he can [throw at you] and hurt you, and nobody can do anything to him."

More than a few players complained of a bigger strike zone when Ryan pitched, and some accused him of scuffing the ball, a trick former Astros teammate Mike Scott allegedly used. During one game against Seattle with Ryan on the mound, Mariners players collected foul or tossed-out balls and lined them up along the back of the dugout to be inspected later by the umpires.

Seeing this, Ryan promptly drilled two Seattle batters in the back.

"Those baseballs disappeared faster than a Randy Johnson fastball," said Tom House. "The lesson was that if you were going after Ryan, you would pay."

Andy Van Slyke, a tough, no-nonsense outfielder for Pittsburgh and St. Louis, faced Ryan several times over his 13-year career. The three-time All-Star says Ryan got plenty of breaks.

"Of all the pitchers I ever faced in my 13 years in the big leagues, Nolan had the biggest strike zone," claims Van Slyke. "Umpires just would bow to his command. With the 5,000 strikeouts, seven no-hitters, and the stare, he had a mystique and he could intimidate the umpires, and as his career was coming to a close it was something he took advantage of.

"I don't think he did it consciously. It's sort of like Clint Eastwood, who never knew he was tough and sexy until someone told him he was. And when Nolan was at the end of his career, he was kind of like Clint Eastwood."

Hoggy Price recalls a game Ryan pitched with fellow Texan Durwood Merrill calling balls and strikes. Before the game, Price said, "I told Nolan, 'Why don't you call over to the umpires' room about 6:05 when the umpires get in and talk to Durwood?' So he calls over there and I answer and tell Durwood it's for him.

"'Aw, Richie, who is it?' he says.

"'Just a call, Durwood,' I said. I downplayed it 'cause I didn't want the other umpires to know who was calling.

"Durwood gets on the phone. I could just imagine what Nolan's telling him, 'cause Durwood's going, 'Yeah, yeah...oh, you know it...yeah... oh, yeah...aww, okay...all right!'

"When he hung up it was like his chest was filled with helium. When he left to go to the field his mind was so messed up he didn't even have his chest protector on.

"Durwood says, 'That was Tex. Us two Texans are gonna ride off into the sunset together tonight.'

"Well, I think Durwood had like a 26" plate that night, and Nolan took a no-hitter into the seventh inning. When Durwood came back into the umpires' room afterward, he said, 'Aw, Richie, we almost got it!'

"Evidently, Nolan worked him good."

"Everywhere we went was a sellout," recalls Bobby Valentine. "Often I'd let him finish an inning and he'd be on the bench when I removed him, but sometimes when he ran out of gas [on the mound] he would give a little sign to tell us he was tiring and to come and get him. So I'd go out to the mound, signal to the relief pitcher, and as [Ryan] walked off he would tip his hat and people would give him a standing ovation.

"This was unfortunate, because I was left waiting for the reliever, and the fans would boo and throw stuff at me. You'd think I was the biggest villain that ever lived for taking this guy out of the game. Finally, I tried to make a pact with him. I said, 'Hey Nolan, how about the next time I go out we both wait for the reliever and then after I give him the ball we walk off the mound together? That way I don't have to take this abuse for doing what I think is my job. How's that sound?'

"He agreed that was a good plan, that there was no reason for me to be booed and get hit with crap thrown from the stands. But we never walked off together. He'd always conveniently forget, and when I got to the mound he'd walk off alone and I'd proceed to get pummeled."

There was no official pitch count for Ryan in Texas. For the most part, he deferred to Valentine's judgment, but when the game was on the line or his competitive juices got the best of him, things got dicey. House found this out during a game in early '89 when Ryan's pitch count approached 100 and Valentine sent his pitching coach to the mound.

"Tom, I'm doing horseshit, but it's way better than what you got warming up in that bullpen, so get the hell off my mound!" Ryan told him.

Back in the dugout, House told Valentine, "Don't go out there, Bob. It's ugly."

An inning later, Valentine did venture out himself to yank Ryan. He was the manager, after all.

"Bobby," said the pitcher, "one of us is leaving the mound—and it ain't gonna be me!"

Valentine shrugged and walked sheepishly back to the dugout.

During Bobby Valentine's tenure in Texas, he and Ryan kept on good terms, and they're friends today. There was an occasion in the spring of 1991, though, when their mutual loyalty was tested. It involved a situation with outfielder Pete Incaviglia, a team favorite with impressive power but also a propensity to strike out. Debating whether to cut Incaviglia, Valentine approached several veterans on the team for their input.

"It was my first experience as a manager where the press just killed me," recalls Valentine, who ended up cutting Incaviglia. "Randy Galloway of the *Dallas Morning News* butchered me in the paper for acting as executioner. Like I was the only one who wanted Incaviglia out, and all his teammates were so supportive of him, and so on.

"But I had asked Nolan and some of his teammates about it, and they agreed with me. But when Galloway went around and asked them, players supposedly said I didn't confer with them. The truth was there were four of them I had conferred with, including Nolan, and I understood they didn't want to get their hands dirty, bloody. And I was never going to give Nolan up. I understood that he had to be a good teammate. But..."

According to House, even Ryan's pregame preparation had an element of mystique:

"After his last warm-up pitch, Nolan would stroll toward home plate, make eye contact with the umpire, and then look over at the Rangers bench and squint. He'd then walk over to the on-deck circle and try to make eye contact with the upcoming hitter.

"The veterans looked anywhere but in his eyes, but the youngsters, the first-time guys walking up to the plate, stared right back, and it was all over right there.

"He'd look at them and give 'em what I called 'chicken lips.' And when you saw the chicken lips with Nolan, it was giddy-up time."

Ryan says everything he did on the mound was strictly business.

"They always felt that when I walked out in front of home plate before the game, I was purposely trying to intimidate the opposition. But I'd just go down there and check the ground and make sure it hadn't been watered down too much. That way, in case somebody bunted or there was a topper, I knew what I was getting into going into fielding the ball."

It was a well-known fact around the league that a huge Ryan pet peeve was a rookie bunting against him.

Gene Coleman remembers playing the Reds just after they called up a youngster from the minor leagues. Nolan was pitching, and Cincinnati infielder Buddy Bell and some of the other players told the kid, "Just drag bunt, 'cause this old man can't field his position."

"Sure enough," says Coleman, "the kid lays a bunt down, but it goes foul. And Nolan walks in toward the catcher, gets the ball, and looks the kid in his eye—just kind of stares at him with that John Wayne look he had. The next pitch separated the kid from his helmet. And the Astros, they look over in the opposing dugout and they're just dying laughing, 'cause they'd set the kid up. They knew you don't bunt off of Nolan."

"If the opposing hitters took all that to mean I was sending them a message, I didn't have a problem with it," Ryan says. "I sure wasn't gonna tell 'em any different. And if somebody tried to drag bunt on me and they weren't successful, the next pitch was usually inside just to send 'em a message that maybe they ought to re-think that."

That's not to say Ryan had lost his sense of humor—ask Bill Ziegler, the team trainer for four of the five years Ryan was in Texas.

In 1992, WBAP radio in Dallas had a popular host named Hal Jay, who did the "Rangers Report" and was close to several Rangers, including Ryan and Ziegler.

One afternoon, Ryan asked "Zig" if he could use the phone in his office to call into Hal's live broadcast. When put on the air, Ryan said he had breaking news about pitcher Bobby Witt, who had just injured his arm and gone on the DL. Hal and his listeners were all ears.

According to Ryan, it was Ziegler's girlfriend, "Bertha Hogg," who was responsible for Witt's injury. What followed was a long and hilarious monologue about Bertha and her twin sister, "Beulah," peanut-eating regulars at Rangers home games. Ryan relayed how the jealous Ziegler almost yanked Witt's arm out of its socket when he saw the pitcher helping himself to Bertha's goobers.

"It's all over a woman, isn't it Nolan?" asked Hal, playing the straight man.

"They get you every time, don't they?" answered Ryan.

After Hal thanked Ryan for calling, Ziegler—still teary-eyed from laughing so hard—got on the line and said, "Hal, that's it. We're not using my phone anymore!"

Ryan hadn't called just to show off his story-telling skills. "I thought Zig could use a laugh," he explained to Ziegler's assistant, Danny Wheat. He was referring to the fact that Ziegler's mother had just died.

"He wanted to get my mind off things," Ziegler says. "That's the way Nolan is. He would find different ways to make you feel good. He was as loyal as they come."

For his birthday one year, Ryan handed Ziegler a wad of Kleenex. "Inside was a knife he had made special for me with NOLAN RYAN engraved on the blade," says Ziegler. "I still got it. It's in my safe deposit box in the bank."

Ziegler says what impressed him most about Ryan was the pitcher's loyalty and humility.

"Nolan made himself one of the guys. Everyone felt comfortable around him, because he made you feel that way. He didn't demand anything, and there were so many guys who had done a lot less than him that had pretty large egos."

Currently a trainer on the professional rodeo circuit, Ziegler was also impressed by Ryan's resiliency and high threshold for pain.

"People just didn't realize it wasn't easy for him to put that much trauma on his body, throwing so hard for so long," Ziegler said. "But he never complained. He pitched with things that put other pitchers on the disabled list. In rodeo they'd say he 'cowboy'd up.' Nolan cowboy'd up a lot. He was tough."

When Ryan suited up he demanded the best of himself and expected the same from his teammates. Anyone who didn't live up to his expectations or failed in his responsibilities was going to hear about it.

"I'm not going to name names, but once we had a couple outfielders that were kind of in their own zone," recalls House. "On four or five different occasions Nolan would make his pitch, the ball was hit right where the defense was supposed to be, but the defense wasn't there.

"There wasn't a confrontation in the dugout, but out of the corner of my eye I saw Ryan tap the pair responsible on the head, and they disappeared up the tunnel. And then Nolan came walking back out and sat down, and a minute later came the two offenders, heads down, looking like school kids coming out of the principal's office.

"I was told later that basically Nolan read them the riot act, and it went basically along these lines: 'Next time you do that, I'm gonna rip your friggin' head off! Do you understand what I'm saying? Last time I'm going to warn you.'

"Very seldom did it happen twice."

Ryan sought every edge in competition, and showed little sympathy for anyone who stood 60 feet, six inches in front of him. But if you happened to be a struggling young pitcher with unlimited potential, he didn't hesitate to display a kinder, nurturing side.

Twenty-eight-year-old Randy Johnson of the Mariners was a mess when the Rangers rolled into Seattle on August 7, 1992. A typical performance for him was the one he had given on June 10 in Arlington: four innings, 92 pitches, five earned runs, six walks, and two hit batters. To Nolan Ryan, the spectacle of a talented young pitcher getting trounced like that was appalling. Johnson was like him—a power pitcher with uncommon gifts—and it irked Ryan to see someone with that kind of ability self-destruct.

By the time the Rangers arrived in Seattle, things had gotten even worse for Johnson. He was 7–12 and led the league in walks, wild pitches, and hit batsmen.

After 26 years in the game, Ryan could readily detect a pitcher's weaknesses and flaws, and he saw several in Johnson. In addition to being very emotional, he'd been landing wrong after each pitch, which jarred his body and caused all sorts of problems. Watching Johnson get pounded yet again, Ryan said to House, "Enough is enough. When a guy with a 98-mph fastball beats himself up every five days, it's time to make a change."

The following day, Johnson was walking near the Rangers dugout for a bullpen session when House pulled him aside.

"Nolan and me have seen you pitch long enough to realize there are some mechanical things that haven't been cleared up yet," House told him. "We'd like to give you a little input."

Johnson was shocked.

"At the time, all I knew about power pitching was, give me the ball and I'll throw it really hard," recalls Johnson. "But after three seasons under my belt with not much success, I was willing to listen to anybody."

Especially if that anybody was Nolan Ryan. Their initial meeting took place in the tunnel between clubhouses. Ryan showed Johnson how his hard landing was disrupting his delivery and explained how excessive emotion affected his concentration.

"Nolan said I was opening up too quickly," recalls Johnson. "By landing on the heel of my foot instead of the ball, it would spin and my knee and body would follow, throwing all my momentum toward third base. He and Tom basically straightened me out, enabling me to correct my arm angle, make me consistent, and have all my momentum going toward home plate."

Putting what he learned from Ryan and House into practice, Johnson recorded 34 strikeouts in his next three starts, then 45 Ks in three consecutive starts a month later—the second-highest total in baseball history after Ryan's 47 in 1974.

On September 27 in Arlington, teacher and pupil finally squared off.

"It was one of my biggest games up to that time," recalls Johnson. "I struck out 18 on 160 pitches in eight innings. What was really neat, though, was after Nolan came out of the game in the seventh, he didn't go upstairs but continued to watch me from the dugout."

The intervention of Ryan and House, says Johnson, "is something I will never forget. I was surprised someone playing in a different organization would actually take me aside and try and help me. It's not very often the opposing pitcher and pitching coach will take a player from another team and actually mentor them."

Leading up to 1992, Johnson never knew what would happen when he pitched. He might strike out 10 and walk 12. As good as his pitching coaches were up to then, for some reason they were never able to impart the information needed to turn his mechanics around. That all changed when he connected with Ryan and House.

"Without a doubt, Nolan and Tom had the biggest impact on me in such a short period of time," Johnson declares. "It was the big turning point of my career. From that point on, I became more of a consistent pitcher."

And a more intimidating one, according to Coleman, who got to know the "Big Unit" when Johnson played in Houston.

"Nolan told him, 'Randy, big as you are, you should be intimidating. When you go out there and they get a hit off you or you make a bad pitch and you show all that emotion, those guys in the other dugout are saying, 'Hey, we got him now!'" Coleman said. "'You're just building up their confidence when you show emotion. You don't ever want to show a chink in your armor.' And so you look at Randy and he covers his face with his glove, because Nolan told him. That's where that came from. It's from part of that week he spent with Nolan. Roger [Clemens] got that too, and Andy Pettitte got it from Roger."

Ryan calls helping Johnson just part of the process of "passing on" to the next generation.

"Through watching, discussions, or instruction, I had benefited from being around certain pitchers," he says, "and if I can help further someone's career, I want to do that. So if somebody ever calls me or wants me to talk or watch 'em, I'm open to that."

His friends say Ryan's greatest attribute is his respect for others. He calls it "treating people the way you want to be treated."

"I think people know when someone is sincere, and I think people understand that I try to be straightforward and sincere with them," says Ryan. "It's the same working with players and pitchers. If somebody wants to learn something from me and is willing to listen and work on it, I'm very supportive of that. But if they're just wasting everybody's time, we need to move on, and they need to go about their business and do something else, and I need to get back to whatever's important to me."

Ruth Ryan marvels at her husband's ability to listen and learn. She thinks it's rooted in the dyslexia that forced Nolan to process and absorb things differently from a young age.

"Some people are auditory learners, and because Nolan had dyslexia he had to listen," she says. "That is how he learned. He struggled with reading and writing, but he could listen and retain anything, and still does. That has been a huge asset. He is good at reading between the lines and very good at deciphering things. He rarely offers information on himself, choosing to let the other person talk while he listens. He lets people prove their true colors, good or bad. He'll tell you that people tell a lot about themselves and their character by the things they say."

Boston's Roger Clemens burst onto the scene in 1984, and resembled Ryan when it came to on-field attitude and pitch velocity. In 1986 he broke Ryan's record for strikeouts in a game (20). Clemens' 24-year career as one of the most dominant pitchers in major league history included 354 wins, a 3.12 ERA, and 4,672 strikeouts—third-most all time.

Accusations of performance-enhancing drug use would later tarnish his legacy, but in 1992 "The Rocket" was presumably clean and mowing down the competition at a record pace. As the two premier power pitchers in the game, the September 7 contest in Arlington featuring Ryan and Clemens was highly publicized. Ryan pitched a strong 8⅓ innings, allowing two earned runs on six hits. Clemens also went eight frames, allowing just three hits and no runs. Boston won 3–0, but that had no effect on Clemens' enduring respect for Ryan.

As a youngster growing up in the Houston area, Clemens frequently visited the Astrodome to study Ryan's mechanics. It wasn't hero worship that drew Clemens to Ryan but something more practical: he wanted to know how Ryan generated his speed and where that fearsome energy came from.

"When I was 15, watching Nolan do his warm-ups or get a *Sports Illustrated* shot to study his mechanics was useful," Clemens said. "We didn't have the video and all the crazy stuff we have now, so I had to find other methods to study him."

Clemens discovered that it wasn't just arm speed that made Ryan throw hard, but rather his legs, how he stayed closed throughout his motion, and how he pulled his glove through his left side to get a consistent leg lift.

Once he started making a name for himself in Boston, Clemens and Ryan would occasionally meet. After exchanging pleasantries, Ryan would tell the youngster, "I'm watching you and I like the way you're going about it," or, "Hey, you got a good curveball, you should use it a little bit."

"When you're in your early twenties and you have somebody like Nolan mention that, it carries a ton of weight," says Clemens. "It's no different than when I met Yogi Berra for the first time. He said, 'You know, I watched you many times, and you could have pitched in our era.' Those are compliments from the best of the best."

What Ryan contributed in regards to conditioning was no less than revolutionary, says Clemens.

"When I first got to the big leagues, the day before you pitched you weren't supposed to do anything but eat your favorite meal," he said. "Nolan changed all that for a lot of people. When he first lifted weights he was banging 'em out on those old Nautilus machines and the baseball people didn't encourage him. Nowadays players have taken those workouts and really tweaked them and taken them to a new level.

"But he's the reason we can all get in there now. He had a wonderful work ethic back when nobody was supposed to really have one. He had a routine that he believed in and trusted, and in the long run it made us all better.

"He passed the baton on, and I took it and ran with it. I tried to pass some good will to Roy Halladay, Chris Carpenter, Roy Oswalt, or anybody I could pass it on to.

"The way we looked at it, the way you beat yourself up behind the scenes, conditioning-wise, you were up for any challenge on the field mentally. Being in tune with everything, the game becomes easier. When it came to conditioning, the day we pitched was our day off."

Ryan and Clemens have remained friends to this day, and Clemens is always on hand for any Ryan-sponsored event for young pitchers, such as the Elite Camp in Houston.

"I've gotten to know him through a number of events and have been impressed with how caring he is to my family and how kind he is to me," says Clemens. "Getting to know his boys has been special, and Ruth has been great to [my wife] Deb and my family. We've watched each other's families grow up and we own parts of the Round Rock and Corpus Christi teams together."

To be linked with the Ryan Express is a great compliment, says Clemens.

"There is a difference between being a power thrower and a power pitcher, and we took pride in being both," he says. "Nolan began his career as a power thrower, but by the time he reached Houston he had successfully made the turn.

"We didn't want the hitter to feel comfortable. I knew the hitter was trying to feel comfortable and I didn't want him to feel comfortable, and I'm sure that Nolan felt the same way."

• • •

August 1992 was hard on Ryan and the Rangers. He went 0–5 with 37 strikeouts in just 32 innings. There wasn't a single day when something didn't hurt, and at one point the overall discomfort got so bad he considered retiring. The Rangers had him on an unofficial pitch count and he rarely went past seven innings, which accounted for some of the disparity in his won-lost record.

But Ryan's intense daily workout regimen never varied. In visiting cities, he and House usually left the hotel by 6:30 AM, going to a local pool where Ryan, wearing a harness, ran in the water for 45 minutes. Then he'd eat a low-carb breakfast and head to the ballpark to begin a weight training routine that lasted several hours. Only then did the trainers go to work on his myriad ailments.

Rejoining House on the field, Ryan did his stretching routine, followed by a football toss and a short bullpen session. Then he'd sprint for a half-hour and return to the trainer's room.

According to House, the workouts served a dual purpose. In addition to keeping him fit, it was the only time during the day that Ryan could be with his family and was not bombarded by the media or fans.

"Superstars have no time of their own," says House. "I saw it with Henry Aaron and I saw it with Nolan. We found out when we worked out between 6:00 and 7:00 in the morning that not too many people are up at those hours. So that became his and my time and eventually our family time. The Rangers allowed Ruth and the kids to come in and lift with Nolan and me, and I could bring my wife and children in. It was serious work, but what a relaxing environment that was to prepare, compete, and repair.

"That morning work was probably the highlight of my coaching career. It was fun to work hard, and I felt we were doing something different than anybody else, and it was, I think, prolonging the career of a legend. It was also relaxing to him and made him happy.

"Because he loved what he was doing, he didn't have any mental burnout. I can't say what he did with the other teams, but with us we were always tweaking and varying programs. Mental burnout is neuro stagnation, which is the net result of monotonous overtraining—always doing the same thing the same way. We had routines but not rituals. Ryan had a smorgasbord to choose from that got all the work accomplished with different approaches. We made sure it didn't become boring for him."

Reese Ryan agrees the time spent with his dad in the gym was special.

"He felt like if he was going to be at the stadium that he was going to be doing something to get better," says Reese. "There were a lot of guys who came to the park at 2:00 in the afternoon to play cards, eat, and BS. But Nolan felt, 'If I'm going to be at the ballpark, I'm going to be getting better.'

"I have to believe he would have gone on pitching forever if his body would let him. He never got tired of the game or got to where he lost that desire to play. He just got to the point where his body would not allow him to compete to that level, and he didn't want to be there if he wasn't the best pitcher in the rotation."

It might come as a surprise that the music Ryan played in the weight room wasn't all country and western.

"Would you ever think Nolan Ryan—Texas legend, John Wayne personified—liked Elton John and the Pointer Sisters?" says House incredulously. "In fact, Nolan went to the guys in charge of the music when they were introducing players, like 'Hells Bells' with Trevor Hoffman, and it was either Elton John or the Pointer Sisters for Nolan."

By August 31 it was "Hells Bells" for the Rangers. With the team languishing in fourth place, 15.5 games out, outfielder Ruben Sierra and pitchers Jeff Russell and Bobby Witt were traded to Oakland for Jose Canseco. Texas finished 77–85, 19 games back of Oakland. It was obvious that more changes were coming. Clearly, Toby Harrah would not be coming back.

Ryan struggled to a 5–9 record, with a 3.72 ERA and 157 strikeouts. While his competitive fire burned hot as ever, how much longer Ryan's body would allow him to continue pitching remained a question. Critics said he should have already been put out to pasture, but admirers hoped they'd get a chance to see him pitch for at least one more season.

While the baseball world debated his future, Ryan hunkered down at the ranch with his Beefmasters, horses, and family, took some Advil, and debated the issue with himself.

5

A Fighting Farewell: 1993

Father Time is undefeated.

—CHARLES BARKLEY

There was a pall in the Ryan living room as everyone got seated for the annual preseason meeting. Nolan's career had always been a family affair, with Ruth, Wendy, Reid, and Reese having an equal vote on whether he'd play another season.

Ryan had seriously considered retiring in 1992. Constant pain and trips to the DL made him realize that the marathon workouts he endured to stay in shape were no guarantee against injuries.

There were other factors to consider. The team's new manager, Kevin Kennedy, was well respected, but Ryan had no personal connection to him. As all managers do, Kennedy wanted his own pitching coach, which meant farewell to Tom House. His replacement, former Dodgers ace Claude Osteen, had credentials but was nowhere near the cutting-age technician and innovator House was. Ryan would sorely miss House, not just on the field and in the weight room but as a friend, confidant, and mentor.

"I really enjoyed my relationship with Tom, and I didn't have that many close friends on the team," says Ryan. "Also, I was physically starting to develop little nagging injuries. I always had to rehab, and that gets old.

I also knew the team wasn't going to be that competitive, so it was time for me to move on and do other things I wanted to do."

When Ryan told his family he was leaning toward retirement, no one offered much of an argument.

"We had always talked and he had always asked, are we going to come back for next year?" says Reese. "But this time it was different. All I remember saying was, 'I'll miss seeing you pitch.'"

Ruth's emotions were mixed. Her entire adult life had revolved around baseball, and now she wondered how she would use her time. But her worries paled in comparison to those of her husband. What would he do with his competitive fire? The allure of competition was the primary force that kept him in the game. The money was also a factor, of course, but the desire to outlast an opponent and beat him was Ryan's true calling. What would he do to fill the void? He had the three ranches, the two banks, and a variety of other projects, but would all of that—or any of it—be enough to satisfy his competitive appetite?

At the Baseball Writers Dinner in Arlington on February 9, Ryan announced publicly what his family already knew: the 1993 season would be his last one in uniform.

"I'd rather be premature in leaving baseball than stay too long and have to retire in an awkward situation," Ryan told the assembled press. "I wanted to make sure the question of retirement wouldn't be a distraction or have it hanging over the team.

"I wanted to go to spring training without having to deceive anyone. I wanted fans to have the opportunity to watch me pitch again, and I wanted to let them know I was going to retire. There's also the physical part of it. It became more difficult for me to find workout time and I seemed to have become more vulnerable to injury. At my age, it takes longer to recover."

When news hit that the upcoming season would be Ryan's last, ballparks and teams across America prepared to say good-bye. Special presentations and awards would be waiting for him wherever he went. He would do his best to makes his scheduled starts and not let anybody down, but with so many ailments that would prove difficult.

The farewell tour began auspiciously against Boston on April 9. Ryan allowed four hits and one unearned run in six innings, and Texas won 3–1. But his next start against Baltimore chilled any hope that it would be an idyllic farewell. In the fourth inning Ryan came down hard on his landing foot and tore the cartilage in his right knee, requiring surgery and a six-week stint on the DL.

His next start, on May 7 in Kansas City, was almost a carbon copy of the previous one. Ryan lasted four innings before a strained left hip put him back on the shelf for another nine weeks. It wasn't until July 19 that he got his second win, a five-inning, three-hit, six-strikeout performance against Milwaukee.

For the rest of the season Kevin Kennedy had Ryan on a pitch count, and he never went beyond the seventh inning. But the fact that at 46 he was still pitching at all was a statement in itself, and despite the rough first half, fans still came out in droves to see him one last time.

Ryanmania reached its zenith as his impending retirement grew closer. Standing ovations accompanied him every time he stepped on the diamond. Autograph fever also reached its apex; Ryan tried to comply but the demand was overwhelming. Even opposing players requested his signature, and the amount of memorabilia waiting for him to sign in each visiting city was staggering. In an effort to control the onslaught, Ryan designated one day per series as "Signing Day." Items were collected and Ryan put in the time to make sure everything got signed.

Ryan's former teammate Jim Deshaies was with Minnesota at the height of Ryanmania, and recalls that some of his teammates were put off by all the attention Ryan got—up to a point.

"They had a sign on the Rangers visitors clubhouse saying, Nolan Ryan will only sign autographs on the third day of the series, and our players would get upset about it. 'Who does he think he is?' they'd ask.

"But some of these same guys would send over jerseys, balls, bats, and hats, and demand that Nolan sign them."

"Why did Nolan Ryan sign, sign, sign, and sign some more?" Tom House asked. "Everybody thinks, *Ahh, he's just trying to make money*. But what would happen if he *didn't* sign a whole lot? What would be the value of his signature? Would any low-end fan be able to afford his signature? He makes a concerted effort to sign as much as he can to keep the price down."

"I did have some trouble with the memorabilia people that hung out," says Ryan. "I could tell by what pens they used that it wasn't some guy just wanting my autograph, but a dealer. But overall I didn't have a problem signing. Fans were supportive of me and kids are going to look up to somebody, and the way I looked at it was that if you're in a position to be an influence, why wouldn't you want to be a positive one?"

Between marathon workouts and signing sessions, Ryan pitched. He made three starts in July and was 2–3 entering August, with a 5.58 ERA and 27 Ks. When Chicago rolled into Arlington on August 2, the Rangers were in a pennant race—in third place, 6.5 games behind the White Sox. Few would have guessed that by the time the series ended, Ryan's profile would rise higher than ever.

• • •

Of all of Nolan Ryan's achievements, few garnered more attention than the 20-second skirmish between Ryan and veteran third baseman Robin Ventura. The fight has come to symbolize his Texas toughness, and it made Ryan a symbol of middle-age defiance.

Much has been made about the "Ventura Fight" but most don't realize its roots started three years earlier in Florida.

In the 1990s, Chicago's Craig Grebeck was one of baseball's smallest everyday players. Just 5'7", he compensated for his lack of stature with the attitude of Goliath.

During a spring training game against the Rangers in 1990, Grebeck hit a home run on the first pitch and pumped his fists triumphantly as he jogged around the bases. Sitting on the Rangers bench, Ryan stared at the Lilliputian and made a mental note.

A few months later the Rangers were at Comiskey Park. Ryan was on the mound, and Grebeck hit a home run off him. As he had in Florida, Grebeck whooped it up rounding the bases.

When Ryan got back to the bench, he asked House, "Who is that boy?"

House told him Grebeck's name.

"How old is he?" asked Ryan next. "He looks like he's about 12."

"He's pretty young," said House.

"Well, I'm gonna put some age on the little squirt. He's swinging like he isn't afraid of me."

"Sure enough," recalls House, "next time up [in the teams' next meeting], plunk! Nolan hits him right in the friggin' back. Grebeck was 0-for the rest of the year off him."

Thus began three seasons of constant strife between the Texas Rangers and Chicago White Sox.

"It didn't help," says House, "that Chicago hitting coach Walt Hriniak taught his hitters to cover the outside third of the plate. He even had his hitters dive toward the plate in order to cover the outside corner.

"That was encroaching on Ryan's turf. His fastball spent so much time on the outside half it could have taken up residence there. 'Half the plate's yours, half is mine,' was Ryan's thinking. 'You don't know what half I want. But if you're going to take away half of the plate that I want, you're gonna pay.'

"He hit a bunch of White Sox. They had a philosophy that didn't quite fit in with Nolan's philosophy, and we had three or four fights with them, because Nolan would pitch into hitters that were diving."

Robin Ventura disagrees. It wasn't batting stances that caused the friction, he says, but a good old-fashioned bean-ball war.

"Hriniak didn't have anything to do with it," Ventura claims. "At the time in baseball the zone was low and away, and that was where pitchers were getting you out. We weren't the only team doing it. It was the kind of pitch that was getting called, so you just had to be able to go out and get it."

In any case, altercations between the two teams accelerated:

> August 17, 1990: Ryan hit Grebeck again in his first at-bat on the first pitch. Three innings later the Sox retaliated by hitting Rangers third baseman Steve Buechele.
>
> September 6, 1991: Ryan hit Ventura in the back at Arlington.
>
> August 2, 1993: Two days before the Ventura fight, Roger Pavlik of the Rangers hit Ron Karkovice. Chicago retaliated by hitting Dean Palmer twice and Mario Diaz once.

"We had a lot of going back and forth that season," says Ventura. "Guys were getting hit regularly, and it was just one of those things where something was going to eventually happen."

The night before the fight, on August 3, the White Sox manhandled the Rangers 11–6. Ryan was slated to start the following day against Alex Fernandez.

In the first inning, Ventura tagged Ryan for an RBI single. In the Rangers' half of the second, Fernandez hit Rangers leadoff batter Juan Gonzalez on a 2-2 pitch. When Ventura came up again in the third frame, Ryan's first pitch plunked him on the back.

"If you look at the replays, the ball wasn't really that far inside," says House. "It was just barely off the plate and it went off Ventura's back. Robin was starting toward first base when he abruptly turns and charges the mound instead. And the closer he got to Nolan, the bigger he looked. If you watch it in stop action, you can see Ryan's eyes were like a deer's in a headlight.

"So everybody was surprised by what Nolan did next: *Bam! Bam! Bam!* Three punches right on Ventura's noggin!"

Rangers catcher Pudge Rodriguez had undergone facial surgery for a fractured cheekbone 40 hours earlier and was wearing a big bandage. As the man closest to the action, he had an excellent perspective.

"Nolan Ryan didn't try to hit him," says Rodriguez. "He just tried to pitch in like everybody else, and it just got away. It was a very intense game. Robin Ventura had hit Ryan hard in the first inning, and [Ryan] was trying to keep him off the plate.

"Ventura charged to the mound but he didn't do a good job, and Nolan Ryan grabbed him and hit him pretty good. I was trying to hold [Ventura] off, but they were two big guys. I tried to cover myself because I have a scar on my face, and so I just grabbed [Ventura] from the back but that didn't do much."

Rangers shortstop Jeff Huson watched it unfold from the bench.

"All I could think about when it was happening was, *What's Robin thinking?*" Huson recalls. "You don't charge the highest authority—that's just the way it is. I was shocked when he went out there. I remember Nolan saying that early in his career Dave Winfield had charged the mound and he didn't do anything about it, and later he vowed that if anybody ever charged the mound again he was going to take the offensive."

To this day, Ventura maintains it was no big deal and that his reaction was pure instinct.

"Everybody on both teams knew [Ryan] was hitting guys, and the mentality on our club was when he hits us, we're gonna hit one of them. So whoever got hit, I'm sure he would have went. He had hit Grebeck on purpose and he had hit me on purpose. It was going to happen no matter what. It just happened that Ryan was well known. Had it been anyone else, it would have all been forgotten.

"Nobody said 'You had to go, charge the mound,' and we didn't talk about it beforehand. There was so much friction going on between us that eventually whoever got hit was probably going to charge anyway."

Ryan's recollection of the incident echoes House's.

"There was a buildup between the Rangers and the White Sox, and what Tom said was accurate about them diving into the ball," he said. "But Grebeck, their little center fielder, had had a lot of success off me and he was diving into the fastball, so I hit him one time. Not with the intent of hitting him—I was trying to get him off the plate and back him off, and I hit him.

"Earlier in the year I had a fight with Chicago over them hitting one of our guys, but certainly there hadn't been any issues between Robin Ventura and myself. In that particular game, his first time up I left a fastball out over the plate and Ventura hit a line drive to left field, so I felt like I had to get him off the plate. Next time I came in on him and hit him right behind the shoulder blade, but it wasn't on purpose."

Regarding the rumored bounty supposedly put on him by the Sox, Ryan says, "I heard there was some kind of a vendetta, but do I know that for a fact or not? I don't know that for certain. As far as I know, Robin just reacted."

When Ventura charged toward the mound, he slowed down just enough to run into a Ryan headlock. Nolan got in four quick right hands on the top of Ventura's head. His fifth and final punch got Ventura square in the face.

Both benches emptied, and the main combatants disappeared under the surge of humanity. Ventura eventually emerged unscathed, but Ryan remained trapped beneath the pile and was nearly unconscious when help came from an unexpected quarter.

"All I remember is that I couldn't breathe," says Ryan. "I thought I was going to black out and die, when all of a sudden I see two big arms tossing bodies off of me. It was [Chicago's] Bo Jackson. He had come to my rescue, and I'm awful glad he did, because I was about to pass out. I called him that night and thanked him."

As two of the game's biggest stars, Jackson and Ryan were natural rivals. Their friendly feud began in 1989, when Bo was with the Royals.

"I had 3-2 on him," recalls Ryan. "I knew if I threw him a curve he'd probably chase it, but instead I threw him a fastball up to see if I could get it by him. As soon as it left my hand I knew I was in trouble, 'cause I knew it was gonna be down. When he hit it, I had to turn to see where it went because I knew he really got it. It turns out he hit it two-thirds up the way in straight-away center field in old Arlington Stadium."

"I was watching Bo as he went around," adds House, "and boy, it was impressive. Two superstars in the moment, and as Bo is jogging around first base, Nolan makes eye contact and Bo makes a gesture like, *I gotcha!* and Nolan gives him a look like, What the hell is he talking about?

"Well, the next time Bo's up, first pitch is a curveball, and Bo was like spaghetti-legged. Nolan struck him out six more times after that. I think he faced Bo 20 times, and struck him out 12 times."

The day after Jackson's tape-measure home run, when Ryan came out for stretching at 4:30, nobody was on the field.

"I'm thinking, *I may have the time wrong,* when all of a sudden I hear way off in the distance, 'Hey, Nolan!'" he recalled. "I look out and the whole team is sitting in the bleachers where the ball landed, and they're waving at me. They were making sure I wasn't going to forget it."

In a 1990 home game against Kansas City, Jackson led off the second inning with a one-hopper back to the mound that caught Ryan square in the mouth.

"Nolan was more embarrassed than hurt," recalls trainer Bill Ziegler. "He was bleeding like a stuck pig. So in between innings the Rangers team doctor, Dr. Mycoskie, stitched him up. He pitched the rest of the game with black stitches coming out of his lip and blood all over the place."

Kansas City's George Brett later said, "Nolan's scary under normal conditions, but facing him when he was all bloody was another level of intimidation altogether."

The Jackson-Ryan rivalry was rooted in mutual respect, so it wasn't so surprising that Bo came to his rescue on August 4.

Ruth Ryan was awfully glad he did.

"After Ventura rushed the mound, everyone in the park, including my kids, went wild," recalls Ruth, who was seated in the family section. "When Nolan didn't come out of the pile, I got concerned. With his bad back, sore ribs, and other ailments, he could easily have suffered a career-ending injury."

When Nolan finally did emerge, he was visibly winded and his jersey was unbuttoned. Otherwise, he seemed to be intact. But a few moments later there was more pushing and shoving and the fight resumed. This time, Ryan and Ventura remained on the fringes, but some other players really got into it. Rangers coach Mickey Hatcher had a bloody gash above his eye, and Chicago manager Gene Lamont was taking on all comers. Several White Sox players taunted Ryan and he considered rejoining the fray, but the umpires restrained him.

When it was finally over, Ryan remained in the game and Ventura and Lamont were ejected.

Of all people, Craig Grebeck, whose gesture somewhat precipitated the tension three years earlier, came off the bench to pinch-run for Ventura. Ryan promptly picked him off first.

In a show of stubborn focus, Ryan pitched four more innings. When he left at the end of the seventh, he had struck out five and given up three hits, with one earned run.

Texas won the game 5–2, but the score was really irrelevant.

"It was a split-second thing," Ryan told reporters after the game about his brawl with Ventura. "All you can do is react. You don't have time to figure out your options."

Lamont believed his player getting hit wasn't an accident, and admitted his getting tossed was an act of protest after Ryan was allowed to remain in the game.

"I think our guys felt Nolan hit guys on purpose and that was probably part of the reason Robin charged the mound, and they didn't like it," says Lamont. "I'm also positive there wasn't a vendetta. If there was one, it was without me knowing about it, and if that was the case our players would have been out there a lot quicker than they were."

Leaving the park, Ryan figured he'd heard the end of it, but at the postgame dinner at a nearby restaurant, Reid Ryan and his friends couldn't stop rehashing the action. Brother Reese had videotaped the game, and when the family returned home, he entertained all comers by replaying the brawl over and over.

When Reese asked his dad, who was in the kitchen sorting the mail, if he wanted to view the fight, he responded with a firm no.

He was in a distinct minority. Broadcast networks were showing the fight continuously, and the late-night talk shows picked it up. The next morning the melee was front-page news.

"Remember the Alamo!" George W. Bush proclaimed in the *Dallas Daily News*. "I saw Nolan square away like a bull and thought, *This guy [Ventura] has lost his senses*. It was a fantastic moment for the Rangers and elevated [Ryan's] legend."

Chicago's Jack McDowell insisted Ryan was culpable and was pleased that Ventura charged him. "Ryan had been throwing at batters forever, and no one ever had the guts to do anything about it," the Sox pitcher complained. "Someone had to do it. [Ryan] pulled that stuff wherever he goes."

Fans across America were polarized. Ryan was their perpetual good guy in the white hat, and some didn't know what to make of their hero throwing punches in the middle of the infield.

Arguments raged at dinner tables across America about whether Ryan did the right thing. *The Dallas Morning News* said it was bad for baseball. FIGHT GIVES GAME A BIG BLACK EYE, argued its headline.

When ESPN's Peter Gammons insisted that Ryan hit Ventura on purpose, the pitcher had heard enough.

"If Robin had stopped before he got to the mound, I wouldn't have attacked him," Ryan explained to ESPN. "But when he came out and grabbed me, I had to react to the situation."

Ryan thought the incident would eventually fade, but as time has passed interest in that dustup has never subsided. The Ventura fight has become a part of American folklore, an integral part of Ryan's legacy. Photographs of the fight are as common as postage stamps, clips of it are shown every season, and the clip has been viewed more than half a million times on YouTube.

For almost two decades the two key combatants never crossed paths. Closure finally came in 2012, when Ventura was named manager of the White Sox. Early that season, Ryan and Ventura discreetly met in the Rangers Ballpark in Arlington tunnel. Ryan congratulated Robin on getting the manager's job; Ventura gave Ryan kudos for his recent successes in Texas.

"I have nothing but respect for Robin and wished him the best," said Ryan.

A man of his word, as team president Ryan issued a standing order that footage from the fight—previously shown before Rangers games—not be played on the scoreboard.

Ventura, who was suspended two games over the incident, harbors no grudges.

"I don't sit around thinking, *Oh, my gosh, I should have done different,* or whatever. I do get tired of talking about it, though. Mostly it's press from Texas saying we want to talk to you about it."

Ventura has always been known for his class and affability, and is highly respected in baseball circles. Here's hoping people remember him for something other than being the guy who got in a brawl with Nolan Ryan.

• • •

Ryan went 3–0 that August, and although his strikeout ratio was low, he helped keep the Rangers in second place and in contention with Chicago for the Western Division crown.

Entering September, the Rangers were 5.5 games out of first and Ryan was 5–3 for the season. He seemed to have gotten over the hump physically, and his last trip to Anaheim promised to be memorable. He was scheduled to throw the series opener on Friday, September 17.

The Anaheim faithful were ready for him.

From the length of the line, you might have thought the Rolling Stones or the pope was in town. It wound five rows deep around the front of Anaheim's Doubletree Hotel before curling into the street. But the people weren't there to experience rock 'n' roll nirvana or receive a papal blessing. They had cards, balls, gloves, plastic helmets, and photos to hand over to the balding, middle-aged gentleman rancher-ballplayer from Texas who 15 years earlier played for the California Angels. When spoken to, Ryan would answer graciously and with a smile as he signed his name over and over again.

The autograph session was a totally impromptu affair, not the brainstorm of a publicist. Whether Ryan saw it as his responsibility or civic duty, only he knew. Maybe it was just the simple pleasure he got from making people happy. When his ride pulled up in front of the hotel to take him to the ballpark, Ryan informed the driver he would need another half hour before he was ready to leave.

When he finally did get to the stadium, he dressed and met with some sportswriters. When the police informed him that there had been a death threat, Ryan shrugged it off and went outside where hundreds more fans awaited a chance to get his autograph.

A few hours later, there was a stirring in the crowd when he made his way to the bullpen for his pregame warm-up. On his return to the dugout, some 60,000 fans stood and cheered. The ovation went on for five minutes, and followed him the entire way back to the bench. He modestly doffed his hat and then took a seat in the Rangers dugout and prepared to take the Anaheim Stadium mound for the last time.

When Ryan struck out leadoff batter Luis Polonia to record the Angels' first out, the stands erupted again.

He tossed seven strong innings, striking out five, and allowed four hits and one unearned run. In the fifth, Ryan whiffed leadoff hitter Greg Myers for the 5,714th strikeout of his career. When Ryan departed, the game was tied 1–1; in the eighth, the Angels scored a run off Rangers reliever Craig Lefferts to make it 2–1, and that was the final score.

Nobody knew it at the time, but Ryan's seven innings at the Big A would be his last hurrah. He had been feeling tenderness in his right elbow all season, but with just a few weeks remaining he figured he could get through the season.

With probably three starts left after the upcoming series in Seattle, he would finish his career properly in front of the home crowd in Arlington.

In the late 1980s, while he was with Houston, Ryan had visited Dr. Frank Jobe in Los Angeles to inquire about pain in his elbow, and was told he likely needed Tommy John surgery. Ryan considered it, but decided that taking a year off at his age and then a long rehab process wasn't worth it.

"I'm gonna throw as hard as I can for as long as I can, and if it blows out, it blows out and I walk away," he said. "That way, I've done everything that I can do. If it interferes with any of my ranching activity, I'll get it fixed, and if it doesn't interfere—well, leave it alone."

What was billed as Nolan Ryan's "Seattle Farewell" at the Kingdome on September 22 had been anything but memorable. Three first-inning walks, followed by a grand slam by Dann Howitt, wasn't what folks expected. Even more disconcerting than the 5–0 score was Ryan's pained expression after the last fastball to Mariners first baseman Dave Magadan.

Close observers had noticed a similar grimace during warm-ups. Now, as trainer Danny Wheat rushed out to the mound, the fans held their collective breath. After a brief exchange with Wheat, Ryan walked off the mound, his right arm dangling loosely at his side. Suddenly, the crowd exploded with a prolonged ovation. Without looking up or stopping, Ryan doffed his cap and entered the dugout. He marched directly to the trainer's room and stoically waited for a doctor.

He didn't need X-rays to know what was wrong; the pop and then the burning sensation after his last pitch said it all. As the trainers worked on him, he asked someone to tell Ruth he was okay. Equipment manager Zack Minasian double-timed it to the stands.

In the Seattle dugout, ace left-hander Randy Johnson put down his pitching charts and started up the ramp to the Rangers clubhouse.

"I knew what was going on, because our team doctors were going over and looking at him," Johnson recalls. "So I just kind of tagged along, if you will, just went over there to see how he was doing and send my regards."

In the stands, Minasian knelt in front of Ruth Ryan's row and waved her over.

"He wanted me to tell you he's gonna be okay," he said quietly.

"How bad?" she asked.

"We don't know, they'll need to do the X-rays first," Minasian said.

The examination revealed that the ulnar collateral ligament that keeps the elbow attached to the muscle had been severed. For a 46-year-old power pitcher, it was the worst possible news.

After the game, an impromptu press conference was held next to the clubhouse. In addition to the media, present were team officials, doctors, trainers, two managers, and Ruth Ryan.

Flashbulbs exploded when Ryan entered the room. The ice bag on his arm seemed to entirely cover his damp Texas Rangers T-shirt. Typically, he didn't mince words or try to sugarcoat what happened.

"It popped like a rubber band," he said in a voice as flat as Texas. "The doctor's pretty sure and I'm pretty sure. There's no way I'll ever throw again."

For Ruth, to have it happen so suddenly was difficult to accept.

"I shed a few tears at the press conference," Ruth says, "but then we went out to have a quiet dinner after the game. He didn't really want to be visiting with people or anything like that. We ate dinner together and talked and that was that. I think Nolan was relieved. He wasn't happy about how it ended, but it was like a weight had been lifted off of his shoulders."

For those who knew him best, Ryan's end in Seattle came as no big surprise.

He finally ran out of bullets, thought Gene Coleman upon hearing the news.

In Brenham, Texas, former Mets scout Red Murff couldn't help but wax nostalgic. Three decades earlier he had discovered Ryan on a high school sandlot. It had been Murff's tenacity that forced the Mets to sign Ryan, an act that would change so many lives, his included. Putting down the paper, Murff peered into the blue Texas morning and sighed. *Even as a kid he had it! That kid Nolie always had it!*

In San Diego, Tom House wondered if things might've turned out differently had he been with Ryan in Seattle.

Don Sanders hadn't made the trip. Had he known Seattle would be the site of Ryan's last game, he would have found a way to be there. He was at home in Houston when he got the news. His thoughts were similar to Coleman's.

He went out with his boots on…

Ryan headed back to Texas believing the game, and the associated media circus, was behind him.

Not quite.

Reese Ryan was at home at the time.

"When I got back after baseball practice, there were about 30 satellite trucks pulled up in the yard," he recalls. "I said, 'Hey, you guys are gonna have to leave.' They said, 'Well, you know we're waiting on your dad.'

"Then I called Nolan. 'There are 30 satellite trucks sitting in our front yard. What do you want me to do?'

"'Well, tell 'em I'll be there in a little bit,' he said.

"So I told the press guys where to park their trucks, and we set up a press conference on the tennis court. We got all the lawn furniture and had everyone sit down. I told them they'd get 30 minutes.

"It worked out well. When my folks got home, Nolan walked straight over to the tennis court, sat down, and talked to the press."

"The kids were happy to see us," recalls Ruth. "They had written 'Welcome Home, Dad' on two retirement lawn chairs and put them in the entry way.

"They were just happy to have him home."

• • •

Ryan's big league career began on a muggy September in Flushing Meadows in 1966. It ended 27 years later on plastic grass in the great indoors in Seattle.

What he accomplished in between will be analyzed, celebrated, and scrutinized for as long as players tie up their spikes and fans buy hot dogs.

He played longer than any player in history, and through it all handled himself with class, dignity, and a Texas-sized sense of humor.

He revolutionized the game with his work ethic and conditioning routines. He set dozens of records no one will ever touch.

He earned the respect of his peers, fans, and the press. He set an example for both kids and adults to live by.

He remained faithful to his wife and made sure his kids experienced the ride with him.

He didn't take things for granted and remained authentic to the end. He did not buy into the hype, good and bad, or take to heart what critics and hero-worshippers said about him.

When the lights were their absolute brightest, he remained loyal to his friends, teammates, and family.

He was humble, tough, kind, and stubborn. He believed in God, and he was mortal.

"I know who I am," Ryan once said. "I'm a country kid from Texas with the ability to throw a ball and the dedication to keep myself in shape. I'm just a man."

PART VII

The View from the Top: 1994–

1

A Brief Respite

Nolan Ryan found retirement difficult.

After pitching 27 seasons in the big leagues, adjusting to life without the high that comes from competing at the highest level, along with the company of the clubhouse, wasn't easy. Especially the latter.

"The number one thing I missed is being on a team," says Ryan. "You can't replace that feeling. I missed the adrenalin rush of competing, but being on a team and the camaraderie of my teammates is what I missed most."

According to Ruth Ryan, the first couple years were the toughest.

"He went right into other jobs, but he admitted nothing could take the place of playing," she says. "Nothing else he did gave him the adrenalin or the emotional high of being in competition, so it was more of an adjustment than he thought it would be.

"I tried to get him to play golf one day, and we were out playing and he got aggravated. I got real mad and said, 'I am not playing golf with you acting like that! It's just a game, and we are supposed to be having fun!' And then I walked off.

"He said, 'Well, I'm not used to not being good at it.'

"He was used to being the best, and was frustrated with the feeling of being something less. He has never acted like that since. We play with our kids and family and have a good time with it. But he had to realize he can't have that meanness and competitive fire that he had in baseball."

Tom House says the comedown is natural, that the thrill of competition is a positive homeostasis that's addictive to the brain's blood chemistry.

"It's a life-or-death thing," House maintains. "It's fight, flee, or freeze, and it's satisfying, because you get resolution every day. It's called the terminal adolescence, and it's why ex-athletes don't do really well in the short term. They can't find anything that gives them that same high or low or that same resolution in the real world.

"Eventually they all make the adjustment, but there's something about competition and preparing for competition that becomes addictive. It's biological and in their lifeblood, and it has to be a passion, because the highs and lows of putting it out there for people to see, to boo or cheer, is life on the edge."

Following his retirement Ryan signed a service contract with the Rangers as a special assistant to the president. His duties included tutoring young pitchers and advising the front office on baseball matters. He also helped raise his grandkids, bought and sold two banks, opened a seafood restaurant near Three Rivers, expanded his cattle operation, marketed natural beef, and worked for Texas Parks and Wildlife Commission under Texas governor George W. Bush.

In 1999 he was elected to the National Baseball Hall of Fame in Cooperstown, New York, with 98 percent of the vote. During his induction speech, he made a point of thanking the mentors and coaches who helped him during his career, singling out Jimmie Reese, Tom Morgan, Jeff Torborg, Gene Coleman, and House.

"He had written down seven or eight points and people he had wanted to mention, and that was it," recalls Ruth of the speech. "I told him later he amazed me because I knew him as a kid, and his personality back then was rather shy and unassuming. Over the years I saw a transformation from a person that didn't ever want to speak in public into a wonderful speaker who never had one note in his hand."

That same year, Ryan, his sons, Reid and Reese, and longtime friend Don Sanders formed Ryan-Sanders Baseball. Their goal: to construct a state-of-the-art facility near Austin and bring professional baseball back to the area.

Land was purchased in Round Rock, north of Austin, and Dell Diamond was built. Prior to its inaugural season in 2000, the group purchased the Jackson Generals of the Southern League, with the intention of moving the team to Round Rock. They renamed them the Round Rock Express and they were an immediate success. The family-oriented franchise became one of the crown jewels of the minor leagues.

Crowds flocked to Dell Diamond. The Express broke the Texas League single-season attendance record in its first year, grabbing the league championship along the way. Over the next four seasons, attendance continued to increase, and the Express appeared in the playoffs three more times.

On Easter Sunday in 2000, Ruth and Nolan were walking around Dell Diamond when he complained of shortness of breath, chest pain, and fatigue. Ryan's grandfather and mother suffered from heart disease, and his older brother had already suffered a heart attack, so there was plenty of cause for concern.

Physicians at Round Rock Hospital diagnosed an irregular EKG and recommended that Nolan be transferred to Austin Heart Hospital for further testing and diagnosis. Doctors there said he had a blockage to his left main artery and needed immediate surgery. It turned out that the problem was not a blockage but a spasm of the coronary artery; Nolan has a condition called Prinzmetal's angina, which can be alleviated with drugs and proper care and caution. The bypass operation left Ryan's heart in a compromised state and changed his body chemistry; he now takes certain medications and has his heart monitored closely.

This kind of occurrence might understandably have caused serious anger and resentment, but Ryan never complained publicly. Advised that he had grounds for a lawsuit against the physicians, Nolan and Ruth chose not to pursue legal action. There have been several heart scares since then, but they proved to be recurrences of his angina, and overall Ryan is in good health.

• • •

The on-field successes at Round Rock had Ryan-Sanders Baseball eager for more. In 2003, the group purchased land in Corpus Christi and built another state-of-the-art facility. In 2004, it acquired the Triple-A Edmonton Trappers of the PCL and announced its intention to move the club to Round Rock. This paved the way for the Double A franchise to relocate to the Gulf Coast of Texas, where they were renamed the Corpus Christi Hooks. Both teams would serve as feeders for the Houston Astros.

Whataburger Field in Corpus Christi was immediately hailed as one of the minor league's best facilities. The Ryan-Sanders team now had two quality franchises and a reputation as a competent group that knew how to operate.

In 2005, the Houston Astros finally made it to the World Series for the first time in team history; several players on the roster were alumni from Round Rock and Corpus Christi. In recognition of his contributions, the Astros asked Ryan to throw out the first pitch for Game 3.

When his service contract with the Rangers expired in 2003, Ryan took on similar administrative work with Houston. His new five-year commitment included participating in player development, pitching instruction during spring training, and evaluating talent.

Back in Arlington, meanwhile, Tom Hicks, the new owner of the Texas Rangers, was in trouble. A series of business blunders, including bloated contracts to pitcher Chan Ho Park ($65 million) and slugger Alex Rodriguez ($252 million), had brought the team to the verge of bankruptcy.

Hicks, who would have just three winning seasons in 11 years, desperately needed help. He turned to Ryan, whose contract with Houston expired in 2008, and asked if he would consider going to work for him as team president. Ryan was intrigued. It was a once in a lifetime opportunity to get back into the major leagues at a decision-making level.

To those closest to him, the idea that Ryan would even consider the Rangers position seemed out of left field. At 61, he had already accomplished more than 10 men. And with innumerable responsibilities already on his plate, plus a heart condition, why on earth would he want to take on more?

"I was shocked when Rangers vice president Jim Sundberg kept calling him to discuss the possibility of him running the Rangers," recalls Ruth

Ryan. "When Nolan first told me about it, I just shrugged it off. When he mentioned it a second time, I said, 'You are really serious about this.'

"He said, 'I am seriously considering it, Ruth, but I am not going to do it if you don't want me to, or if you have any doubts about me taking this job. I won't do it and I will say no. So, tell me right now whether you would. I want your full support. Otherwise, I won't take it.'

"I thought for a minute and said, 'You know, as long as you are not traveling with the team, it would be fine with me.'

"At the time, I didn't think about how all encompassing it would be and how he would be controlling all these different aspects of the team. Not just the players, but the front office and attendance, everything. But as soon as he took the job, he was so happy to be back in baseball that I realized he really missed it more than I thought."

When she heard about Ryan's new job, his sister, Mary Lou Williams, called him and said, "What are you doing? You have a ranch, a bank, and two baseball teams. Why do you need another job?"

"This is what I've always wanted to do," he told her, "so this is really important to me."

"He was never afraid to take something on," says Mary Lou.

• • •

As he did in all his endeavors, Ryan jumped in with both feet. When Tom House called to congratulate him on his new position, he couldn't help but smile as Ryan said he was "up to my rear in alligators" and asked if he could call on House to help "figure out where the holes in our pitching staff are."

When House asked Ryan why he had accepted the responsibility of running a major league franchise, he wasn't surprised by the answer.

"I would like to make a positive difference in baseball on the field and off the field before I retire," Ryan said.

Ryan's departure from Houston left locals shaking their heads. Once again the Astros had lost their favorite son to their American League rivals to the west. Many in Houston questioned why management had not offered Ryan a similar role with their club, but it was too late.

"I think Nolan felt like he was just a toy in Houston," says sportswriter Tracy Ringolsby. "I don't think he felt he was really able to impact things. And he's not a guy that just does things to hang around.

"When he was in Anaheim, Buzzie Bavasi would get ticked off because Nolan worked cattle all winter. 'He could lose his fingers with that cattle!' Buzzie complained.

"Nolan's response was, 'I'm not going to ask somebody to do something I won't do.'"

On February 8, Ryan addressed the press at Arlington Stadium on his new role.

"I don't come in with any preconceived ideas of what I want to do or what needs to be done," he said. "I think it'll be a learning process for me. I'm going to try to get my arms around our organization so I'll have a better understanding of who we are and what we do and what I can do to help us be better."

2

The Making of an Owner

> He's honest and a humble man, and he treats everybody like family. You know where you stand with Nolan, all the time. He's never full of BS, and that's the quality about him that I love.
>
> —RON WASHINGTON

Nolan Ryan's dress shoes slipped slightly when he stepped onto the dewy grass for the first time at the spring training home of the Rangers in Surprise, Arizona. The sun was just peeking over the horizon, and gazing out at the conglomeration of colors, Ryan felt invigorated. His decisions would forever alter the future of the franchise; an entire organization would be counting on him to steer a drifting ship.

As he made his way to the empty dugout, Rangers players in bright blue practice jerseys began trickling out of the clubhouse. Only a few acknowledged Ryan, but as their new boss he had a responsibility to each and every one of them. He also had a responsibility to owner Tom Hicks to produce a winner, and to be successful, he would be dependent on his young GM, Jon Daniels, and second-year manager Ron Washington.

Washington had had his problems. In 2007, he and first baseman Mark Teixeira butted heads, and the rising star had been dealt to

Atlanta. Things had also been tense between Washington and catcher Gerald Laird.

Daniels was a different story. Hired in October of 2005, at 28 he was the youngest general manager in baseball history. The Rangers had a disappointing third-place finish that season. A year later the team finished dead last, 19 games behind the Angels. Under the circumstances, Ryan might have done what many other new club presidents do when they come on board—clean house.

There wouldn't have been many complaints if he fired an unproven manager and a wet-behind-the-ears GM with no track record and replaced them with more seasoned baseball men. But Ryan had always judged people by their character, and there was something about both Washington and Daniels he respected.

He also knew the team was in rebuilding mode. Daniels had moved away from the notion of signing big-name free agents, an approach that had gotten them into their current malaise, and was now attempting to build the team from within.

As more Rangers flooded the field, Ryan's experienced eye surmised that the team had some genuine talent. If youngsters and prospects including Nellie Cruz, Josh Hamilton, C.J. Wilson, Elvis Andrus, and Chris Davis ever achieved their potential...

Soon the ballpark became alive with the sounds of batting practice, and Ryan headed back to his office. He had some serious decisions to make and met with his GM.

Jon Daniels recalls those crucial first few weeks after Ryan joined the club.

"A year and a half before Nolan came on board, we had put a plan in place to rebuild the organization from the ground up in scouting and development, and Nolan believed in the same philosophy," Daniels said. "Despite a lot of media calls to make changes and accelerate the process, Nolan understood that wasn't possible. My assumption is he takes a similar tack with his other businesses. He doesn't look for the shortcut or the quick fix. He believes in investing in good people and investing in the infrastructure, and building from the ground up.

"So, when he first got here he listened to the good baseball people and they said, 'Hey, it's premature to make any sweeping changes—this is not the right move. Let's sit back and wait a little while.' And he listened. Nolan trusted them, and ultimately he made the right decisions.

"We were trying to bring in good baseball people, and who better are you going to find than Nolan? You look at all the ex-athletes who tried to do this but haven't succeeded—Matt Millen, Isiah Thomas, Michael Jordan, and other guys that tried to jump into those leadership roles—and it didn't work out.

"But Nolan's a good baseball person first, and he's able to put his ego aside and apply his knowledge and communicate it in such a way that the players of a completely different generation are able to absorb it and use it. And he's also able to talk to coaches and let them ultimately do the work so that he doesn't necessarily have to have his thumbprint on everything."

The 2008 Texas Rangers finished in second place, 21 games behind the Angels; in attendance they ranked 25th out of 30 major league teams. The following year there was marked improvement. The Teixeira trade had brought in a bundle of prospects, including shortstop Elvis Andrus, pitchers Neftali Feliz and Matt Harrison, and catcher Jarrod Saltalamacchia. In 2009, the Rangers again finished in second place, but 10 games behind the Angels.

Things were starting to shift. In 2010, *Baseball America* said the Rangers had the best minor league prospects in the majors. While Daniels concentrated on revamping the roster, Ryan concentrated on his area of expertise: pitching. One of his better moves was bringing in respected pitching coach Mike Maddux from Milwaukee in 2009. Ryan and Maddux had worked together at Round Rock, and he knew Maddux's capabilities. Ryan also brought in Round Rock manager Jackie Moore as bench coach that year, and then ordered the entire organization to re-think their ideas about pitch counts, something that had irked him since his playing days in Houston.

"In an effort to improve stamina, arm strength, and go deeper into games, pitchers—particularly young ones—need their arms to be challenged to throw more, not less," he says. "So I made it clear throughout the organization that pitchers needed to push beyond what was normally accepted."

He also emphasized improved player conditioning and heavier workloads. In 2010, on their way to the franchise's first pennant, a rejuvenated Rangers pitching staff threw more innings with more success than at any time in the team's recent history. In 2011, Rangers pitchers broke the team record for most shutouts.

"My first couple of years here, our starting pitchers could go only five innings," says Ron Washington, who began managing the Rangers in 2007. "When Nolan came in, he talked about conditioning our pitchers' bodies and minds. He never mentioned pitch counts, just going deep in the ballgame.

"His mind-set was to get pitchers not looking over their shoulder after five innings, and to work their way through situations where maybe in the past we went out there and yanked 'em. We still watch pitch counts, but it's not something that we talk about."

Pete Rose likes that approach.

"Nolan was another one of them guys like the old-time pitchers—Gibson, Carlton, Seaver," says Charlie Hustle. "They didn't even want to look down in that friggin' bullpen. They didn't want anybody to come in and close that game for 'em. They didn't want anybody coming out there and saying, 'Jesus, Bob, you got 115 pitches! You have to come out!'

"Gibson would tell the manager, '[Bleep] you! I have 115 pitches? I got five days to rest before I come out here again!'

"I agree with the pitch count for this reason only: you have a guy whose coming back from surgery, say, and you want to limit him to 75 pitches or something. But for a guy who's in the rotation, every inning is important."

For all the changes, 2010 began on a sour note. In early March, a reporter discovered that Washington had tested positive for cocaine use the previous season. At the time, Ryan wondered about the consequences of keeping a manager with a history of drug use, but after making discreet inquiries he learned that the players unanimously backed Washington. There would be no firing and no resignation. Ryan decided the best course of action was to let Major League Baseball step in, evaluate Washington, and put him in its rehabilitation program.

"We felt we owed him the same treatment we offered all our employees in a situation like this," Ryan later said, "and that was to give them assistance."

Ryan told the media that descended on Surprise that the Rangers believed in second chances; that Washington had apologized and promised to stay clean; and that all was forgotten and forgiven.

Ryan didn't want his manager's fate dictated by MLB or the press, and Washington has never forgotten his support. The skipper recalls being surprised when he got the summons to see Ryan that March.

"I got called up in the office and there was Nolan sitting behind his desk," says Washington. "He mentioned a reporter had gotten the story but said, 'We were going to stick with you the first time, and we were going to stick with you now. But the thing I need to know is, do you think you will be able to handle the media blitz?'

"I said, 'Of course I can handle the media. As long as I know I have the support of you guys, I'm good.'

"That second meeting was an opportunity for the Texas Rangers to bail on Ron Washington, but Nolan remained steadfast. And that's why he's a class act, and that's why the Texas Rangers organization is where it's going right now—because of the steadiness of his hand and Jon Daniels' and everyone else that has anything to do with decisions that are made in the organization.

"Nolan could have ended my career as a baseball person, but he didn't. He took the criticism for hanging with me and I will always cherish and remember that. The only thing I can say is, hey, he loved me."

Washington's situation was actually the least of Ryan's problems. On May 24, Hicks filed for bankruptcy. A complicated legal process followed that involved bad loans, parking lots, Arlington Stadium land, and lawsuits. Hicks, it was determined, had defaulted on $525 million worth of loan payments, and by July he was borrowing money from MLB in order to keep his club from going under.

Hicks started making plans to sell the team and began scouting prospective buyers. A consortium headed by Pittsburgh lawyer Chuck Greenberg, team president Nolan Ryan, and oilmen Ray Davis and Bob Simpson emerged as front-runners. They agreed the land surrounding the ballpark would be sold to the group in a separate deal. The sale price would be $575 million and cover all loans, including monies owed Alex Rodriguez, Michael Young, and pitcher Kevin Millwood.

The deal was almost completed when one of Hicks' principal lenders, Monarch Alternative Capital, said they opposed the package on the grounds the final proceeds would not fully repay Hicks' defaulted notes. The Monarch group had purchased a portion of Hicks' debt after Hicks defaulted, and argued he'd passed up a better deal from Houston businessman Jim Crane. The difference was close to $300 million, and the extra cash, Monarch claimed, would have resolved issues involving land sale and other creditors to whom Hicks owed money.

A long legal battle ensued, and MLB decided the best way to resolve it was by placing the Rangers into public auction. Hicks was stripped of any responsibility in the auction process, and MLB threatened to seize control of the club if the sale wasn't completed within a designated time frame.

The auction was set for August 4 in Ft. Worth, and the courthouse was filled with press and curious onlookers. Only one other MLB-approved group would be participating, a consortium headed by Jim Crane and Mark Cuban, the flamboyant owner of the NBA's Dallas Mavericks.

Ryan-Greenberg had the opening bid, and three additional bids followed. Just after midnight on August 5, with the bid at $593 million, the Crane-Cuban group folded. Ryan-Greenberg won with an offer of $385 million plus the assumption of $208 million in team liabilities.

"It was an emotional roller coaster," a smiling Ryan said amidst a flurry of handshakes and praise. "You go to court one day and it didn't go your way, but you go back another day and it would. It's a relief."

Ryan-Greenberg had to pay $100 million more than their original offer. A week later, MLB and the other 29 team owners approved the sale.

• • •

Meanwhile, the 2010 Rangers were doing everything right on the field. Daniels' formula was producing spectacular results. The club won the division by nine games and faced a tough Tampa Bay club in the ALDS. The Rangers surprised everyone by defeating the Rays in five games and advancing to play the tough New York Yankees in the Rangers' first ALCS appearance.

Texas was ahead in the series 3–2 on October 22. Ryan was with his family in the owners' box for Game 6 at Arlington Stadium. His team was ahead 6–1 when Ryan's 10-year-old grandson, Jackson, jumped over his aisle to witness the final out beside his grandparents.

When Neftali Feliz got Alex Rodriguez to strike out and send Texas to the World Series, Jackson's grandpa reached over and embraced him and his grandma in one glorious family hug as fireworks exploded overhead.

In an especially poignant touch, at the postgame ceremony Ryan received the William Harridge Trophy awarded to the AL champion from MLB representative Jackie Autry, widow of Gene Autry, Ryan's all-time favorite owner.

Against San Francisco in the World Series, the Rangers ran into a buzz saw of starting pitching and lost in five games. It was a tough way for a glorious season to end, but there was no doubt that in the three years since Ryan's arrival, the team had gone from doormat to a member of baseball's elite.

Two and a half million fans had rolled through Arlington Stadium in 2010, the Rangers brand had expanded across the state, and the team's name was synonymous with winning.

Things got even better in 2011, but not before a few bumps in the road during the off-season. The signing of free-agent third baseman Adrian Beltre caused a bit of a stir; veteran Michael Young had been a fixture at the hot corner for several years, and Beltre's arrival threatened his position. When Washington asked Young to change positions, it was a bitter proposition for the proud veteran. He had always done everything the Rangers asked of him, and Young hinted that he would just as soon be traded.

With spring training just weeks away, Ryan decided he'd better step in. He went directly to Young's house, and within an hour everything was settled. The veteran stayed.

"One of Nolan's greatest strengths is that he simplifies the art of communication," says Young. "His philosophy is straightforward: I give you the truth, you give me the truth back, and we can get to the bottom of things really quickly.

"I learned from Nolan that communication should never be difficult. Let someone know how you feel, speak openly and honestly, respect where the other person is coming from, and be open-minded. Nolan has those things down to a T.

"At no point in our conversations did I feel he wasn't genuinely listening to what I had to say. It's something I really appreciated, and it's a relationship I'd love to see continue to grow."

The Rangers got off to another strong start and were rolling along in first place when, on July 7, Ryan was faced with another challenge no team president ever wants to face.

In the second inning, 39-year-old firefighter Shannon Stone reached out to catch a foul ball tossed into the stands at Arlington Stadium by Rangers center fielder Josh Hamilton. The ball fell short, and Stone tumbled over the railing headfirst to the concrete floor 20 feet below. Stone died of cardiac arrest caused by massive trauma to the head en route to the hospital.

The most unfortunate witness to the tragedy was Stone's six-year-old son, Cooper, whose repeated screams of "Daddy!" echoed through the ballpark.

Equipment man Hoggy Price had never seen his boss so distraught.

"Every employee's emotions were affected," says Price, "and none more than Nolan's. He was hurting. During the press conference he spoke from his heart as a father and a grandfather would. It not only calmed the fans but it calmed the baseball world and the families of everybody involved."

Ryan reached out to Stone's widow and asked how she would best want her husband honored by the ballclub. They decided on a statue in front of the stadium.

"I thought it was appropriate," Ryan said. "I think we want to have a memorial for Shannon Stone, and I want the fans to see it and remember Shannon and Cooper and that they represent what I think we're about, and that's making memories for our fans and family."

The team won the division by 10 games, swept through the playoffs against Tampa Bay and Detroit, and in their second straight World Series faced the scrappy St Louis Cardinals.

The Rangers lost in seven games. They probably should have won in six.

Twice in the penultimate game, the Rangers were just one strike away from the championship and let it get away. A ball hit over the head of right fielder Nelson Cruz in the ninth and a clutch hit by the Cards' Lance Berkman gave St. Louis second life, and the Rangers lost 10–9 in the 11th inning.

For Ryan, the devastating defeat was reminiscent of his agonizing losses in the 1980 and 1986 playoffs. Witnesses said his head was hanging down as he walked the long hallway deep inside Busch Stadium moments after losing. He was wearing a long black overcoat and looked like he was going to a funeral.

When the Rangers lost Game 7 the next day 6–2, they had to face the off-season knowing they were the only team in baseball history to get so close to a world championship in consecutive years and see them both slip away.

• • •

The Rangers managed to regroup in 2012. In February, they took a $111 million gamble by signing pitcher Yu Darvish of the Hokkaido Nippon Ham Fighters from Japan's Pacific League.

Asked at the Rangers Fan Fest what he had been doing over the off-season, Ryan quipped, "Just signing Japanese pitchers."

The Darvish acquisition proved fortuitous. Once he got acclimated to American baseball, the right-hander emerged as one of the elite pitchers in the league and the ace of the Rangers staff.

According to Darvish, one of the reasons he signed with the Rangers was the leeway Ryan gave pitchers to throw as long as they could.

"I remember his name ever since I was a kid," said Darvish. "The first time I heard it was when I saw the book he wrote [*Nolan Ryan's Pitcher's Bible*], which was published here but also in Japan. I never read the book, because I wasn't able to understand it. But the fact that he was able to publish a book like that, I automatically thought he was a great pitcher.

"No one influenced me to come to the States—it was my own decision—but I was aware that Mr. Ryan was the owner, and I knew that could be a real good influence on me, especially when it came to the pitch count. Since Nolan threw so many pitches in a game compared to the other teams, I figured the Rangers might be a little more understanding about my feelings toward the pitch count.

"In Japanese baseball they don't really care about pitch counts. If you are a starter, they expect you to finish the game you start. I think Nolan Ryan understands that kind of philosophy, so that has been a real good influence. When I was struggling for a period in 2012, I asked Mr. Ryan what he did to prepare himself and we talked about it. I tried to emulate and imitate what he did."

Darvish helped the Rangers significantly in 2012, going 16–9 with 221 strikeouts. Nevertheless, after being in first place the entire season, the team folded in the final week and lost the division to Oakland. The Rangers had to settle for one of the two wild card spots, but failed to advance after losing to Baltimore in a one-game playoff.

In the spring of 2013, majority owners Bob Simpson and Ray Davis promoted GM Jon Daniels and COO Rick George and named them co-presidents of the club. Ryan was stripped of his president title and made CEO. He had no immediate public comment, fueling media speculation that he was unhappy and would jump ship.

Ryan stalwart Randy Galloway of the *Fort Worth Telegram* blasted Simpson, Davis, and Daniels for their treatment of a Texas legend. Why, wondered Galloway and other reporters, would ownership strip Ryan of his authority after all he'd done for the Texas franchise?

Some speculated that as the Rangers' success story grew, so had the ambition of Daniels, who felt he had proven himself worthy of the responsibility most GM's share: full autonomy on baseball decisions. Though it had never been his intention to run the ballclub on a daily basis, Ryan did want input on non-roster positions. The hiring of pitching coach Mike Maddux and bench coach Jackie Moore are prime examples.

"Nolan always had input when asked on the roster," wrote Evan Grant in the *Dallas Daily News*. "He certainly had a big hand in developing the pitching philosophy three and four years ago, but in terms of making actual personnel decisions on players, he really left all of that to Jon Daniels."

Facing a public relations disaster, Simpson and Davis flew Ryan to Ft. Worth in their private jet and let him know he still had final say. Ryan remained as CEO.

On the field, things went well for the Rangers until the final month of the 2013 season. The pitching staff was stellar and posted a lower team ERA than the previous season. Darvish led the way, going 13–9 with a league-leading 277 strikeouts and a 2.83 ERA. Closer Joe Nathan anchored the bullpen, saving 43 games.

Unfortunately, the young, inexperienced Rangers hitters didn't hold up their end when it counted. Gone were AL MVP Josh Hamilton, catcher Mike Napoli, and the club's all-time hit leader, Michael Young. Then, slugger Nelson Cruz was suspended for the last two months of the season for PED use. Cruz's bat was missed most during the September stretch drive, when the team dropped seven straight games. During that swoon the Rangers lost the top spot they'd occupied for most of the season to Oakland, and it looked like it would take a miracle for them to even nab the second wild card spot.

Darned if they didn't pull it off, winning their last seven games to clinch a tie with Tampa Bay for the second wild card. But in the tiebreaker, rookie left-hander Martin Perez gave up three runs early, and the Rangers made several costly base running blunders. David Price was overpowering for the Rays, and the Rangers lost 5–2 and failed to make the playoffs for the first time in four seasons. In the silver lining department, the Rangers again reached the 3 million mark in attendance.

Not long afterward, bench coach Jackie Moore and farm director Tim Purpura—both Ryan appointees—were let go by Daniels, as was first-base coach Dave Anderson. According to various sources, Ryan and Daniels had a heated discussion about the dismissals.

"You look for reasons and I haven't found any, other than me being a Nolan guy," Moore told ESPN Dallas/Ft. Worth.

"We're ultimately proud of winning 91 games and all that, but we're not where we want to be," said Daniels. "It's not on either Dave or Jackie. It's on us as an organization."

On October 17, a press conference was hastily called to announce that Nolan Ryan was leaving the Texas Rangers.

"You don't just wake up one day and make a decision of this magnitude," Ryan said. "It was something I'd been thinking about off and on for a while now. I felt like it was probably time for me to move on. It just felt like what I needed to do."

Ownership denied any responsibility for Ryan's decision.

"From a corporation standpoint, Nolan's authority didn't change at all," Davis insisted. "On all major decisions on baseball, Nolan made all final decisions."

Ryan didn't dispute that, at least publicly.

"I don't look at it from that perspective," he told the assembled media. "I just look at it from where and what I want to do going forward, and that's what really drove my decision."

That Ryan pointedly referred to his departure as a resignation, while Davis called it a retirement, spoke volumes about the gulf between the two men.

"I don't know what a year from now might bring," Ryan said. "This may be the final chapter of my baseball career."

The following Sunday, he returned to an empty ballpark, packed up his personal belongings, and made his final exit with no publicity or fanfare.

The man who had twice helped save the franchise from the doldrums departed alone, leaving behind a statue of himself in the center-field concourse and a Texas-sized legacy no one will ever come close to equaling.

Ryan had found himself on the wrong side of a power struggle. He felt his opinions and ideas on the baseball end were no longer embraced and that he was being been pushed aside.

"There was a segment of people I didn't enjoy dealing with," Ryan later told journalist Tracy Ringolsby. "We were on opposite pages, and they had an agenda. It was not an easy decision. But it was the right one. I was frustrated."

How the Rangers will fare without Ryan is unknown at this point, but they are indisputably in better shape than when he arrived in 2008. From the field to the executive offices to the concession stands and beyond, Ryan's imprint is all over the franchise.

Throughout his tenure as president Ryan was particularly popular with his pitchers. With his wealth of knowledge, they actively searched him out, including Matt Harrison, CJ Wilson, and left-hander Derek Holland. Nicknamed the "Dutch Oven," Holland has been around since Ryan's arrival in '08. Since then the 28-year-old has established himself as the team's number two starter and has become popular with fans for his humorous antics and wacky impersonations of Harry Caray and Arnold Schwarzenegger.

His success on the mound, says Holland, is due in large part to the man he says was "kind of like a father to me."

"Nolan's door was wide open and I walked right in," says Holland. "He's helped me with both the mental aspect of the game, and letting me see how I can be me and still be out there and do my job.

"He knew how to interact with us, stayed humble, and understood what we needed to do and told us how to do it. To see his work ethic and how he carried himself on the field gave me ideas of how to conduct myself. He's helped me out tremendously and had done a great job.

"He was a mentor and a friend. He helped me on and off the field. I'm devastated to hear the news that he's retiring. I'm going to miss him."

3

Legacy

As a pitcher, I would put Ryan number one as the greatest right-handed arm I've ever seen.

—WHITEY HERZOG

To many, Nolan Ryan's legacy as a player is as fixed as the brass lettering on his Hall of Fame plaque; his records speak for themselves. Ryan broke scores of them during his career, and while his won-lost percentage can be interpreted in different ways, there's no argument about his longevity and the impact he had on the game. In the history of baseball, only 19th century star Cap Anson, a first baseman, played as long as Ryan's 27 years.

When it comes to Ryan's legacy among modern players, the judgment of New York Yankee Derek Jeter is typical.

"I didn't have the opportunity to play against him. I only know him from seeing highlights and things that I've heard," he said. "But longevity is the biggest key. To be successful for that long is something most of us strive for and something you don't see in baseball too often."

Detroit ace Justin Verlander probably comes closest nowadays to Ryan in terms of speed and potential to throw no-hitters (he has two of them to date).

"He's still my idol," says Verlander. "That's why I always asked guys like Kenny Rogers and Pudge Rodriguez, 'How did Ryan pitch that long, and what was his work ethic like?' You can be born with natural talent and throw hard, but something was going on where he was able to mix his God-given talent with his work habits. Even today, his work ethic is something that is known extremely well within the baseball community. I think he shaped work ethic for pitchers, big time, particularly lower-half core. So in that capacity, he lives on."

When Mariano Rivera was growing up in Panama, his passion was soccer. It wasn't until the early 1990s, when he entered pro baseball, that Rivera became aware of Ryan.

"I learned from Nolan Ryan how to attack the game and what baseball should be like for pitchers," says Rivera. "He did what he did because he was a maniac working. He had that work ethic and it was an example to us, because he started all that stuff with conditioning.

"I saw the results, how successful he was, and that was an eye-opener. I also saw how he related to the game and respected it. When you see power pitchers like Roger Clemens and Randy Johnson, they reflect on Mr. Nolan Ryan. He was the power pitcher, the guy who worked hard and never cut corners. He was always straightforward, the one with the best work ethic you could find in pitchers.

"He worked hard and it carried over to his business. I think baseball deserves that. I think baseball has been good for us, and baseball needs people like that."

"Nolan said the first thing that set him apart was genetics, because they set your upper limit," says Gene Coleman. "Number two was work ethic. There are a lot of people who maybe have the genetics to be a gold-medal winner, but they're bronze-medal winners or they don't make the team because they don't work. The third thing, he said, was mechanics. Nolan had perfect mechanics, which he worked on and took great pride in. He wanted to show the world he was 'Nolan Ryan, pitcher,' not 'Nolan Ryan, a freak who could simply throw hard.'"

"Pitching is a lot like golf," says Reid Ryan, "in that you're never there. It's not like weight lifting, where you lift 300 pounds and now you've arrived. You never master pitching, and I think that's something that always drove him.

"Deep down inside, he was a competitor. All the kids in his family were highly competitive. The girls were valedictorians, and his brother was a great football player in high school and college. The competitive nature in somebody—and especially in pitching—is to go right at 'em, and that's the kind of philosophy his family shared.

"I'd say the camaraderie of his teammates, the competitive nature of the game, being the best pitcher he could be, and trying to hone his craft were some of the elements that drove him."

Ruth Ryan maintains that one of her husband's strengths was that he never looked at getting old as a deterrent.

"Age was never an issue to him," she said. "When he joined the Rangers in 1989 he was 42, and he knew he would have to work harder than anyone to remain competitive. He couldn't slack off and rest during the off-season, and during the season he'd have to have real dedication and do the workouts the day after he pitched, the next day, and so forth.

"It was what he had to do, and it's how he looked at things. It was never, 'I am setting an example to the world,' or 'Look at me, this is working.' It was more, 'I have to do this workout or I won't be able to pitch this year.'

"It was about being practical, and ever since I've known him, he is Mr. Practical."

Money was certainly a factor for Ryan, but according to Tom House, it was never the prime motivator.

"Nolan is a very proud person, and I believe it was all about competition. I honestly feel he enjoyed it," he says. "All the crap he went through, all that stuff went away when he walked between the lines. He was born to compete. I don't know any of the superstars out there at the moment, but I bet if you ask Michael Jordan what he misses the most, it's the competition. If you ask Larry Bird or Joe Montana, it would be competition. The second thing, I'd bet, would be the camaraderie of the clubhouse."

But House emphasizes that for Ryan, everything else was runner-up to his family.

"The unconditional support from his wife and children about baseball was crucial. For him to bring his family with him to the weight room and on the bench, and for all of them to stay in Texas, meant everything. The

Texas Rangers were a really, really family-oriented team, and that allowed Nolan to remain his competitive best. It really was a perfect storm."

It would be impossible to overstate the importance of Ruth Ryan to her husband's career and success. Twice she saved his career by talking him out of quitting. He called her up to three times a day. Ryan has a large capacity for loyalty, empathy, love, and friendship, and it requires reciprocation. In Ruth, he found someone to appreciate his attributes and give back fully.

"Nolan signed with the Texas Rangers not because of me, Bobby [Valentine], or Tom Grieve," House says. "It was because Tom, Bobby, and the Rangers organization told him, 'Your family can travel with you, they can come to the ballparks, and your kids can be batboys. Your family can do whatever you want with them.' And that allowed baseball, as his kids were getting to their teenage years, to be a family project and not just a Nolan Ryan project.

"And the driver behind all that was Ruth."

Ryan himself says his longevity was rooted in the value system formed in his youth.

"You choose what your values are and how you are going to live your life, and I was very fortunate that I had two loving, caring parents I looked up to, and they had an impact on how I lived my life," he said. "I chose to try to be as good a player for as long as I could be and dedicated myself to it. I was also fortunate that I stayed away from any career ending–type injury, and that my family enjoyed the lifestyle and being associated with baseball. Genetics also played a role, in that the aging process probably didn't affect me as early in my career as it did some other people, and that I was committed to being in as good condition physically as possible. All those things were factors that came into play in my longevity."

Ryan obsessed little over his records; if pinned down, he probably wouldn't even remember most of them. Of his major accomplishments, one he does cherish is his seven no-hitters, because they were a team effort.

"You don't go out with the attitude that you were going to try and accomplish a no-hitter," he says. "I threw only one in Little League and one in high school, and that was it. It wasn't like I was a no-hitter style of pitcher, so they really never crossed my mind.

"I was a strikeout pitcher and my hero was Sandy Koufax, so when I got into a position to possibly break his no-hitter record, it was very exciting to be in a position to surpass somebody I looked up to."

Ryan is surprised his single-season record of 383 strikeouts has lasted more than 30 years, but one can understand why. Although the strikeout-to-innings ratios are increasing in today's game, pitchers don't get the complete games they used to. They are also on five-day rotations and not compiling enough innings. Ryan felt if anyone had a chance to break the mark it would be Randy Johnson, who came closest with 372 in 2001.

• • •

Along with the respect Ryan earned came a measure of envy.

"People talk about how the greats in the game make other players better, but in baseball I don't know if that exists very much," says former Astro Jim Deshaies. "It's more of a mano a mano, hitter vs. pitcher thing.

"Everyone brings different skills to the table. I was a left-hander that didn't throw particularly hard, so what could I really learn from Nolan other than the work ethic, the approach, how to be serious, how to be a professional?

"There was a lot of envy. But that's just the nature of the game. When you watch a guy throw 98 mph, you go, *Man, I wish I could do that.*"

Of course there are critics, including some in the press who consider Ryan a great pitcher but not one of the greatest.

Jayson Stark, a respected columnist at ESPN, made waves in 2007 when he wrote in his book, *The Stark Truth,* that Ryan should not have been chosen over Steve Carlton, Tom Seaver, Grover Cleveland Alexander, and Jim Palmer on baseball's All-Century Team.

Stark acknowledged that Ryan was a great pitcher but pointed out that of the 22 pitchers in the 300-win club, he ranks last in winning percentage (.526) and has the worst walk rate (4.67 per nine innings); he also claimed that while Ryan's teams weren't powerhouses, they weren't as lousy as some make them out to be. Ryan's winning percentage, Stark noted, was only .027 percent higher than the other pitchers on his teams (.499).

The fact that Ryan never won the Cy Young Award, added Stark, speaks volumes about his overall performance.

Sabermetrics sage Bill James advises the Boston Red Sox and has three World Series rings on his fingers. His revolutionary analyses have changed the way the game and its players are evaluated. When it comes to Ryan, James has been less than enthusiastic. In his heralded 2004 book, *The New Bill James Historical Abstract,* he ranked Ryan 24th on the all-time list and called him one of the "most unusual pitchers"—but not the greatest—"of all time."

To James, Ryan was more interested in overpowering hitters than pitching to contact, and too often he threw "un-hittable pitches, one after another, even to weak hitters, even when he was behind in the count."

"The ease-up-and-let-the-fielders-do-their-work software had never been installed on his machine," added James. "From the beginning of his career to the end, a Nolan Ryan game featured strikeouts, walks, and very few hits. His flaws are so numerous that they loom like an elm tree over all discussions of Nolan Ryan; but sportswriters choose not to acknowledge his faults because it makes for dry reading and doesn't live up to the lofty plateaus that propelled Ryan out of the class of ordinary players."

In truth, Ryan's career path shows a pitcher who was adaptable and who, as the years passed, became smarter, more finessed, and learned to pitch to contact.

For example, in Ryan's fourth no-hitter, in 1975, his fastball was ineffective early, so he went to his curve as his out pitch. He ended the game with a third-strike changeup to Bobby Grich—hardly the pitch to use if Ryan was intent on blowing the ball by people.

In Ryan's fifth no-hitter, in 1981, Steve Garvey—hardly a slouch as a contact hitter—was due up fourth in the top of the ninth. Ryan didn't want to take any chances with him and was determined to finish with the third batter, Dusty Baker, a notoriously bad curveball hitter. After retiring the first two Dodgers, Ryan went after Baker, got two quick strikes, and then served up a curveball in the zone with the goal of making him hit a ground ball to the left side—which was exactly what happened.

When Ryan faced Pete Rose when Rose was gunning for the all-time NL hit record in 1981, Ryan threw to contact in Pete's first at-bat.

"I was trying to get a ground ball out of him," recalls Ryan. "I tried to throw a fastball away on the next one, and he hit a soft line drive over shortstop for a base hit to tie Stan Musial's record."

In a 1990 interview with the *Los Angeles Times*, Ryan revealed the mind-set he had on the mound late in his career.

"There's a timing mechanism to good hitting, and I don't care how hard you throw, there's a certain percentage of hitters on every team who are selective enough to be able to wait for one pitch they can handle," he said. "Or, they get ahead of the count and sit on the fastball. I still throw the fastball 65 to 70 percent of the time. It's still my bread-and-butter pitch and the pitch that makes my other pitches more effective—but my other pitches have the same effect on the fastball."

He was not the same pitcher in 1992 that he was in 1968. At different stages of his career he had to adapt to the aging process, and find new methods and pitches to make up for the slight drop in velocity. That also meant throwing to contact.

Incredibly, Bill James goes so far as to say that Ryan didn't deserve the second-highest Hall of Fame vote in baseball history. The better question is, how was it that someone who pitched at the top of his game for 27 years, had 5,714 strikeouts, 324 wins, and seven no-hitters was completely left off of six writers' Hall of Fame ballots?

But perhaps most dubious was James' claim that to appease Ryan and his following, sportswriters would say that he was good enough to attract 10,000 extra fans a night. That number, James maintains, was overblown, and at most Ryan drew an extra 500 fans per night.

Apparently, James wasn't present at Arlington or on the road on nights Ryan pitched during his tenure with Texas. Attendance jumped so much during that period (1989–1993) that it enabled the ownership group to make plans for a new ballpark. When Ryan appeared, fans came in droves; during 1989, in Ryan's first year at Arlington, Rangers attendance jumped from 1,581,901 in 1988 to 2,043,993. It was the first time in club history that the team drew more than 2 million fans. By 1993, Ryan's last year, the Rangers drew just over 2.2 million.

"There's no doubt that Ryan's five-year presence in Arlington was a significant factor in the Rangers being able to get public funding for Ameriquest Field in Arlington," says Tom Grieve, the Rangers GM at the time. "The thing about Nolan is the credibility he brought to our franchise. With Nolan Ryan in a Rangers uniform, the Texas Rangers had arrived as a respected major league franchise. That boosted our exposure around Texas and across the country. People were interested in watching the Rangers play even on nights when Nolan wasn't pitching, because Nolan Ryan was a part of our franchise."

How does Ryan respond to his critics? He usually ignores them, although there have been times when his feelings have surfaced.

"Lots of it [criticism] comes from people who don't like you," Ryan told Frank Luska of the *Dallas Morning News* in 1992. "They stir you up to get a reaction, or they're young people who don't know any better. A lot of it is sheer ignorance."

Accusations that Ryan was a mere .500 pitcher—as well as excessive praise from his supporters—will probably be around as long as there are three bases and a pitcher's mound. Opinions are biased in both directions.

Whether Ryan pitched to contact doesn't really matter. What is important is that his stats are secondary when reviewing his total impact on the game.

Ryan's numbers don't define the most important part of his legacy. Thousands of parents didn't name their kids after him because he pitched no-hitters and struck out thousands of batters or did or didn't pitch to contact. They wanted their kids to emulate his character. Records and players come and go, but a person's character and the standards he lived by continue on.

Babe Ruth isn't as beloved for his 714 home runs as much as for his gargantuan spirit and loveable and generous demeanor. Jackie Robinson isn't remembered as much for stealing bases as for his courage. The same goes for Hank Aaron and Lou Gehrig, whose dignity and grace under pressure outshines their respective 755 home runs and 2,130 consecutive games played. Cal Ripken Jr. is remembered for his humility, generosity, and grace as much as for his work ethic and durability. Roberto Clemente is revered for his integrity and pride as much as his rifle arm.

Nolan Ryan was and is a living example of how to lead a good and productive life; that is perhaps his greatest legacy.

• • •

Ryan's playing career was significant and unprecedented. No player in history has played so long at the top of his game; few have so influenced their own generation, as well as succeeding ones, by their work ethic and integrity.

But Ryan didn't play the game of baseball to be a revolutionary or a role model. He played because he enjoyed the competition, he wanted his team to win, and he wanted to make a good living and support his family. He followed his intuition and his heart, and things seemed to work out wherever he went. Perhaps that's why there seems to be a sense of destiny about his career.

As Reid Ryan explains, "You look at my dad's career, he really went through three different eras. He went from daytime World Series, wool uniforms, and playing against Hank Aaron and Willie Mays in the 1960s to the early '90s—steroids, the Bash Brothers, and ESPN.

"If you broke them down, his years with the Mets were exciting, because they won a World Series and it was the end of an era in baseball. But I think the years with the Angels were probably the most enjoyable for him and my mom, because of the way the organization was run by Gene Autry and how Southern California was at that time. I don't think he could have asked for a better situation to blossom into a pitcher.

"Going to the Astros was coming home. They had some good teams during that time, and his mother and all his friends and family got to see him, so that was a special time.

"The last five years of his career were really more about him, us three kids, and my mom. It was a time all of us were old enough to really savor every game. For five years, every game was kind of like it was his last game, because at his age you never knew.

"But all the years were enjoyable. And his career, in a lot of ways, was kind of like life, with its different phases and ups and downs. Every time he changed teams, it was almost like it was a different phase of his life, and it was meant to be."

As for Ryan's future, it's easy to imagine him staying put at one of his four Texas ranches, enjoying his grandkids, and contemplating the horizon from his front porch.

"If it hadn't been for the Rangers, I think he'd probably want to be the world's greatest cattleman right now," says Gene Coleman. "He loves Texas history and collects all those first editions—Walter Prescott Webb, J. Frank Dobie, and so forth.

"His daughter, Wendy, and her husband, Andrew, live on a ranch in Amarillo that's just under a million acres. Andrew's grandfather was a partner of legendary cattleman Charles Goodnight, and part of Palo Duro Canyon is on the ranch. They have a hundred-year-old house that's all stone. Nolan goes out there, and what he loves to do most is talk Texas history."

If he tires of tending to his land, might Ryan run for political office one day? The possibility can't be discounted out of hand. More than once over the years, Ryan has been mentioned as a possible candidate for governor or agricultural commissioner in the state of Texas. Politicians gravitated to Ryan throughout his career because of his integrity and conservative sensibilities. Richard Nixon was a staunch fan with whom Ryan frequently corresponded, and presidents George H. W. and George W. Bush are close personal friends; the latter was often Ryan's guest in the owners' box during Ryan's tenure as Rangers president.

Whether Ryan has left the game of baseball for good is anyone's guess. The lure of the game and the yearning for another challenge might conceivably bring him back.

And even if he has finally ridden off into the baseball sunset, it's hard to picture Ryan taking to a rocking chair for the rest of his days.

Unless, of course, somebody bets him he can't do it.

Sources

Books

Ed. Pingel, D. Kent and Jennifer Briggs. *Nolan Ryan: The Authorized Pictorial History*. Fort Worth: The Summit Group, 1991.

Fehrenbach, TR. *Lone Star*. New York: Tess Press, 2000.

Fehrenbach, TR. *Seven Keys to Texas*. El Paso: Texas Western Press, 1983.

Goldman, Robert. *Once They Were Angels: A History of the Team*. Champaign: Sports Publishing, 2006.

Golenbock, Peter. *Amazin. The Miraculous History of New York's Most Beloved Baseball Team*. New York: St. Martin's Press, 2002.

James, Bill. *The New Bill James Historical Baseball Abstract*. New York: Free Press, 2001.

Libby, Bill. *Nolan Ryan: Fireballer*. New York: Putman, 1975.

Murff, Red with Mike Capps. *The Scout*. Dallas: Word Publishing, 1996.

Newhan, Ross. *The Anaheim Angels: A Complete History*. New York: Hyperion Books, 2000.

Ryan, Nolan and Harvey Frommer. *Throwing Heat*. New York: Avon Books, 1990.

Ryan, Nolan and Jerry Jenkins. *Miracle Man*. Dallas: Word Publishing, 1992.

Ryan, Nolan and Mickey Herskowitz. *Nolan Ryan From Alvin to Cooperstown*. Lenexa: Addax Publishing Group, 1999.

Ryan, Nolan and Tom House. *Nolan Ryan's Pitcher's Bible: The Ultimate Guide to Power, Precision, and Long-term Performance*. New York: Simon & Schuster, 1991.

Ryan, Nolan with Bill Libby. *The Other Game*. Waco: Word Books, 1977.

Ryan, Nolan with Mickey Herskowitz. *Kings of the Hill: An Irreverent Look at the Men on the Mound*. New York: HarperCollins, 1992.

Ryan, Nolan with T.R. Sullivan and Mickey Herskowitz. *Nolan Ryan: The Road to Cooperstown*. Lenexa: Addax Publishing, 1999.

Ryan, Ruth. *Covering Home*. Dallas: Word Publishing, 1995.

Stark, Jayson. *The Stark Truth*. Chicago: Triumph Books, 2007.

Trujillo, Nick. *The Meaning of Nolan Ryan*. College Station: Texas A&M University Press, 1994.

Periodicals/Newspapers

Dallas Daily News
Ft. Worth Telegram
Houston Chronicle
Life magazine
Los Angeles Times
The New York Times
New York Daily News
Sports Illustrated
The Sporting News

Online Resources

Ancestery.com
Baseball Almanac
Baseball Reference
ESPN/Dallas
ESPN MLB
Mets Mesmerized Online
The Newberg Report
Two Guys Talking Mets Baseball
Yahoo MLB

Music

Clement, Jack. "Let's All Help the Cowboy Sing the Blues" from *Dreaming My Dreams*; performed by Waylon Jennings. RCA, 1975.

McDill, Bob and Allen Reynolds. "Gypsy Woman" from *Dreaming My Dreams*; performed by Waylon Jennings. RCA, 1975.

Nelson, Willie and Waylon Jennings. "Good Hearted Woman" from *Wanted: The Outlaws* (anthology); performed by Willie Nelson and Waylon Jennings. RCA 1976.

Overstreet, Paul and Dan Schlitz. "Forever and Ever Amen" from *Always and Forever*; performed by Randy Travis. Warner Bros.,1987.

Reynolds, Allen. "Dreaming My Dreams" from *Dreaming My Dreams*; performed by Waylon Jennings. RCA, 1975.

Spicer, Amilia k. "Shine" from *Wow and Flutter*; performed by Amilia k Spicer. Free Range Records.

Stutz, Carl and Edith Lindeman. "Red Handed Stranger" from *Red Headed Stranger*; performed by Willie Nelsen. Columbia, 1975.

Acknowledgments

Special thanks to Ruth and Nolan Ryan for your friendship and support. Your generous hospitality, contributions, edits, and everything else you did for this book—and for me over these past 40 years—has helped me (and so many others) in more ways than you can know or I can express. This book was written in part to honor that friendship.

Thanks also to Reid, Wendy, and Reese Ryan for your ongoing support and friendship, as well as your hospitality and interviews at Round Rock.

This book never could have reached its potential had it not been for the editing skills of Pete Ehrmann. Pete's unique gifts at putting together a sentence never cease to amaze. Your quick turnarounds, professionalism, and expertise is much appreciated.

The commitment of Tom Bast at Triumph Books to get Ryan's story out in print is the reason this book is available on a national level.

Adam Motin, managing editor at Triumph Books, was determined to make this book a priority project. His final edit is presented on these pages.

Tom House's insights helped bring Nolan's seasons in Texas into much clearer focus. No one understood Ryan's tenure in Arlington better than Tom.

For nine seasons in Houston, Dr. Gene Coleman worked beside Ryan, experimenting with new routines that helped combat the aging process. Doc's insights were key to the Astros sections of the book.

Tim Mead, vice president of communications with the Los Angeles Angels: your guidance and support of my work through the years is greatly appreciated.

Eric Kay, the Angels manager of communications: your press passes and steady support throughout the entire process helped considerably.

Sherry Clawson, executive assistant at Round Rock: thanks for your support and for being there in a pinch.

Jon Madian: your storytelling skills, guidance, and patience helped to make this book a reality. You helped guide the project from start to finish. Your diligence and support is appreciated.

Bill Wallen of Redding, California: you exhibit some of the best of Ryan's attributes, including loyalty, toughness, perseverance, and a good sense of humor. Thanks for staying the course.

David Black: your professionalism and loyalty is highly valued.

Tom Duino: your feedback and support along the entire five-year journey is appreciated.

James Doss: your edits, optimism, and photo discs helped significantly.

Rick Goldman: your outstanding edits of the early days gave the book a strong foundation and helped get the deal done.

Amilia k Spicer: your realization that Nolan's life and career was and is a love story helped give the book a much clearer focus.

Marshall Terrill: your guidance when key decisions needed to be made was huge.

Rick Clemens: your loyalty, friendship, and help in getting the book writing started is appreciated.

William Gifford: thanks for your optimism and support through the process.

Kevin Kendall: your boundless faith, edits, and friendship will not be forgotten.

Mary Lou Williams: your family photographs and help on the book really made a difference.

And finally, thanks to all the of the book's participants for their contributions:

Part I

James Watson, Aubrey Horner, George Pugh, Mike Capps

Part III

Whitey Herzog, Jerry Koosman, Mary Lou Ryan (Williams)

Part IV

Jeff Torborg, Art Kusnyer, Tom Egan, Bobby Winkles, Lee Stanton, Rudy Meoli, Clyde Wright, Jerry Remy, Rod Carew, Bobby Grich, Don Baylor, Ross Newhan, Ed Farmer, Jim Palmer, George Brett, Ken Singleton, Ron Guidry, Reggie Jackson, Rick Smith, Bob Anderson, Dr. Jules Rasinski, Mike Port, Buzzie Bavasi, Tracy Ringolsby, John Moynihan

Part V

Dr. Gene Coleman, Enos Cabell, Joe Morgan, Pete Rose, Alan Ashby, Art Howe, Reggie Smith, Stretch Suba, Jim Deshaies, Terry Puhl, Dennis Liborio, Brad Mills, Craig Biggio, Harry Spilman, Don Sanders, T.R. Fehrenbach

Part VI

Bobby Valentine, Tom House, Jeff Huson, Kenny Rogers, Mike Stanley, John Russell, Ivan Rodriguez, Chad Kreuter, Andy Van Slyke, Mark Gubicza, Roger Clemens, Andy Pettitte, Gene Lamont, Jim Leyland, Robin Ventura, Randy Johnson, Zack Minasian, Tom Grieve, Hoggy Price, John Blake, Bill Ziegler

Part VII

Ron Washington, Michael Young, Yu Darvish, Derek Holland, Jon Daniels, Derek Jeter, Mariano Rivera, Justin Verlander

Friends/Consultants

Jesse Hoffs, Randy Pennington, Charlie Baker, Nate Eisenman, Brad Sturz, Bob Case, William Beck, Dean Chance, Steve Vucinich, John Klima, Scott Garner, Jeff Neumann, Noah Amstadter, Mitch Rogatz,

John Blake, Rich Rice, Courtney Krug, Chris Peixto, Amy Bean, Debbie Bowman, Cinda Fitzpatrick, Eileen Colgin, Chuck Richter at Angelswin.com, Hector H. Vazquez, Brian "Bubba" Harkins, Vince Willet, T.J. Jara, Geoff Bennett, Dave Shaw, Lou Sauritch, Rob Basom, Martin Marin, Rodney Gaston, Adam Russell, Brian Corralejo, Conejo Angels, Jerry Frizell, Joey Cooperman, Bill Madden, Jonathon Eig, and Rob Wilson

Betty, Marcus, Riley, Mitch, and Cassy Wallen

Kevin, Amy, Kadin, Greg, Mike, and Sally Kendall

Ken and Katie Pope

Fern, Liz, and Ray Lang

Jack and Jackie Goldman